GUN DIGEST BOOK OF
AUTOLOADING PISTOLS

By Dean A. Grennell

DBI BOOKS, INC., NORTHFIELD, ILLINOIS

ABOUT OUR COVERS

F.I.E., of Hialeah, Florida continues to be one of the most active importers/manufacturers in the firearms industry. Our front cover features F.I.E.'s TZ-75, a beautifully made 9mm, semiauto double action pistol. The magazine capacity of the TZ-75 is a remarkable 15 rounds. To the right of the TZ-75 is F.I.E.'s Titan, 12-shot, 380 ACP semiauto.

Our back cover also features F.I.E. products. On the left is F.I.E.'s Mini-99, an abridged version of the KG-99 on the right. The semiauto Mini-99 weighs in at 40¾ ounces, features a 20-round magazine and is chambered for the 9mm Luger. The KG-99 weighs in at 45 ounces, is also chambered for the 9mm Luger and features a 36-round magazine. The KG- and Mini-99 are both blow-back operated. **Photos by John Hanusin.**

Produced by
Charger Productions

Publisher
SHELDON FACTOR

Editorial Director
JACK LEWIS

Production Director
SONYA KAISER

Art Director
KRISTEN BUNN

Associate Artists
DANA SILZLE
JOHN VITALE
CYNTHIA FORREST

Photo Services
C'EST DAGUERRE LABS

Production Coordinator
BETTY BURRIS

Copy Editor
CHRIS WILSON-SKINKER

Contributing Editors
JOHN BREATHED
ROGER COMBS
TOM FERGUSON
CLAUD HAMILTON
CHUCK KARWAN
HARLAN RUST

ISBN 0-910676-59-3   Library of Congress Catalog Card Number 83-072348

CONTENTS

ACKNOWLEDGMENTS 5

1. THE LONG QUEST FOR FIREPOWER 6
   The urgent need for weapons superior to those of the enemy
   has stimulated progress in weaponry from rocks to rockets!

2. OPERATING PRINCIPLES OF AUTOLOADING PISTOLS 32
   Many approaches have been tried for making self-loaders work
   and this discusses some salient — and a few unlikely — examples.

3. RIMFIRE AUTOS 54
   Comparatively easy on noise and recoil, less expensive to fire,
   these often deliver outstanding accuracy as an added bonus.

4. COMPACT AUTOS 76
   Neither the most powerful nor the most accurate, their quality
   of being available when needed is perhaps their greatest virtue.

   POCKET PISTOLS 94
   Originally so called because they were carried in pockets — not
   because they went "pocketa-pocketa," the concept has become slightly
   obsolescent, as discussed here.

5. MILITARY & POLICE AUTOS 104
   Many pistols fit this group, but the choice of ammunition is sharply limited.

   9mm vs. .45 ACP 108
   Will the U.S. stay with the .45 ACP or switch to the 9mm? Here are
   notes on that and related subjects.

   SMITH & WESSON 9mms 112
   Off the Ransom Rest, these may be the most accurate service arms around.

   AIR FORCE CUSTOM COMBAT .45 AUTO 120
   Air Force personnel produce a custom combat auto at virtually no
   cost to the taxpayer!

6. THE BIG AND FANCY AUTOS 126
   As autos go, these are the counterparts of the Rolls-Royces and
   Ferraris; no Cadillacs need apply!

7. THE IVY'D HALLS OF LFI 130
   Schoolday memoirs of a student at Massad Ayoob's Lethal Force Institute.

8. ACCESSORIES FOR AUTOS/AUTO MAGAZINES/IMPROVING
   THE BREED/CLASSIC AUTOS 136
   In which we speak of many things pertaining to auto pistols.

9. AMMO FOR AUTOS, INCLUDING WILDCATS 142
   A pistol isn't much use, if you don't have the proper fodder for it!

10. SIGHTS FOR AUTOS 150
    No one ever said it was supposed to be simple — and it isn't!

11. AUTOLOADING PISTOL HOLSTERS 154
No matter the size or intended use, there is a holster for every pistol.

12. RELOADING FOR THE AUTO PISTOL 162
Those empty cases can be turned back into perfectly good cartridges, at a
respectable saving in cost out of pocket!

LOADS TO MAKE THE LUGER WORK 174

13. BULLETMAKING FOR AUTO PISTOLS 180
You can buy your bullets, as many do, or you can build your own, at a
gratifying conservation in cash flow, and have fun doing it!

14. COLLECTING TRENDS IN AUTO PISTOLS 194
Viewed as eminently collectible, certain autos command special interest and
tips are included on others destined to increase in value over the coming years.

15. CAVEAT EMPTOR, AND ALL THAT... 208
If prime collector items are in expensively short supply, someone will try to
generate a supply to meet the demand — clandestinely!

16. THE CELLINI M.B.R.R. 218
Vito Cellini doesn't care a fig for Newton.

17. SMALL AUTOS VS. SNUBNOSE REVOLVERS 226
In which Hamilton essays a comparative evaluation of the two basic designs
and makes his final choice.

18. ACCURACY CAPABILITIES OF THE AUTO PISTOL 232
Autos can group surprisingly well — provided you can control the human factor!

19. ROUTINE CARE AND MAINTENANCE OF AUTO PISTOLS 242
Proper procedure commences before you fire the first shot from a new gun!

20. FACTS, FIGURES AND ASSORTED HANDY DOPE 250
Getting the facts you need from calculator or scratch paper.

21. HANDLING DOUBLE-ACTION AUTOS 256
How to make the most effective use of this increasingly popular feature.

CATALOG SECTION 270
Assorted self-loaders and applicable statistics.

DIRECTORY OF MANUFACTURERS 286

ACKNOWLEDGMENTS

Welcome to the book at hand, commonly termed "BAP," for short. Although it carries my name on the cover, its final aspect represents the work of a great many helpful others, hence the motive for this page. In the previous book — PARD III — I listed a number of people within the firearms industry as especially helpful and, only after it was too late to correct it, realized I'd forgotten to mention Bill Ruger; a painfully glaring omission which I propose to rectify here, albeit belatedly and blushingly.

I believe most of the contributing editors appear among the book's illustrations, with the exception of John Breathed, whose Chapter 15 I regard as one of BAP's major showpieces. There should be a photo of him nearby, covetously clutching a choice hunk of hardware out of Oberndorf on the Neckar. If the sample of Breathed's prose whets your appetite for more of the same, about $18.95 should procure a postpaid copy of *System Mauser* from Handgun Press, 5832 S. Green St., Chicago, IL 60621.

Hamilton and Karwan are veteran contributors to such works and I'm pleased to be able to include a pair of items from Tom Ferguson in BAP, along with Roger Combs' treatise on holsters and the like. If you find, as I do, that Fergusonian prose tends to be addictive, he does a column for *Gun World* every month, as does Chuck Karwan.

Apart from that, my cordial and heartfelt thanks go to Sonya Kaiser, Kristen Bunn, Betty Burris and Chris Wilson-Skinker.

John Breathed

Longtime friend and employer Jack Lewis was of inestimable assistance in getting BAP kicked out of the chute, as was the book's publisher, Sheldon Factor.

As so many times in the past, my wife Jean rates special mention for putting up with me during the sometimes trying process of getting a book dragged kicking and screaming from the old IBM typewriter. I've included a credit to C'est DAGuerre Labs for photo services, which is to say that Jean rates still more thanks in that area if for no other reason than not complaining over-bitterly on the fixer stains around the kitchen sink.

Last but not least, much gratitude to you, the gun-loving, book-buying public, without whose support, none of this would be possible. May your tribe proliferate prodigiously!

With cordial best regards,

Dean A. Grennell

CHAPTER 1

THE LONG QUEST FOR

FIREPOWER

The Urgent Need For Weapons Superior To Those Of The Enemy Has Stimulated Progress In Weaponry From Rocks To Rockets!

THE HUMAN RACE has been around for quite a number of years and it appears to be doing fairly well at the moment. I'll pause briefly if you want to knock wood on that comment. It was not always this easy.

Having developed as an omnivorous species in a world all too thickly populated by carnivores — some of which were considerably larger — weaponry played a vital role in development, not to mention survival of the species.

There were problems in teeming abundance. For one, it was a day to day, lifelong struggle to keep from getting converted into groceries by a roving sabertooth, wolf, bear or perhaps an unlikely species hardly known to zoologists of the present. At the same time, you had to keep yourself in groceries, along with other members of the family, tribe or whatever. It was, well, a jungle back then.

At the earliest outset, there was little more than what we might term personal weapons; the swung foot, clubbed fist, shearing teeth, clutching fingers or gouging claw/fingernail. They must have worked to some extent because here we are. Our ancestors made the grade obviously, and yes, we should be grateful for that.

Homo sapiens, as a species that's us, of course — had a few good things going, particularly after the race got into the habit of going about on their hind legs so as to free the front ones for performing useful tasks. The opposed thumb — shared by a few of the other primates — was a decided asset. It, more than anything else, turned us into a race of tool makers and tool users and that made a vast lot of difference.

We can only theorize that, in some conflict beyond the first pale dawn of history, a sore-beset combatant, scrabbling about, happened to clutch a handy hunk of rock and swung it against his/her opponent's skull with gratifying effect. We can picture the winner regaining breath and gazing at the slightly smeared rock with a profoundly speculative expression. Perhaps a thought ran across the mental screens to the gist that, "The hand that cradles a rock rules the world." A slightly garbled version of that aphorism is still current, having lost a little in translation.

Thus then the percussion weapon made its debut and it may have been a stick of wood instead of a rock. It was an effective extension of the personal weapon and it didn't hurt when you hit someone with it the way it did if you used

"The hand that cradles a rock..."

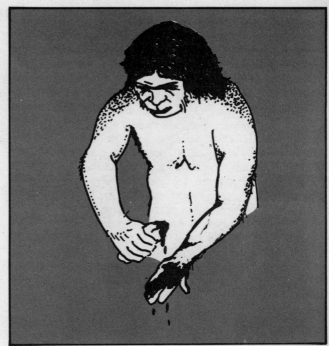

your fist. Centrifugal force wasn't even understood dimly, but its effects were apparent and the smarter dawn-people used it gratefully.

On and on it went. Someone figured out how to lash a rock to the end of a stick and someone else discovered that sharp-edged rocks worked the best. Thus came the first primitive ax came into use, similar to the one Alley Oop used to carry in the comic strips.

Someone may have found a hunk of flint or obsidian with both a useful edge and a sharp point on one end and began to appreciate the useful virtues of the first knife. We can theorize that, initially, such things were sought in likely patches of talus and scree. Talus, as it was once explained to me, is a rock larger than your head while scree is a rock that's smaller.

Whether it was a sudden discovery or a long and gradual evolution, we can't say but an interest developed in improving the knives that occurred naturally and it was found that, if you held the end of an antler against the edge of rock and pushed just so, a chip flew off and you could more or less shape the things to taste.

With some tough vines or strips of rawhide, it was possible to secure a suitable rock to the end of a stick, thereby fashioning the primal prototype of the sort of ax Alley Oop toted in the comic strip.

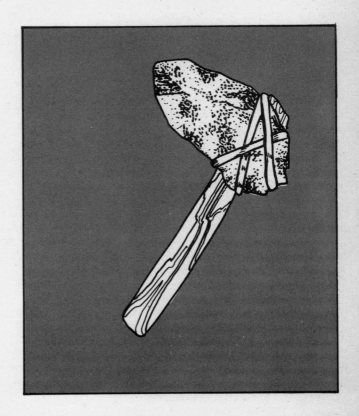

The process worked better with flint than with most other natural forms of stone and reached stages of development and skill that we of modern times would find difficult to match. Safety glasses being unknown, many a primitive flint knapper must have lost the sight of one or both eyes from flying chips.

Flint, shaped to a long, double-edged point, could be lashed to the end of a stick, much in the manner of making a stone ax and its formidable capabilities were noted. For about the first time, a good hand with a spear could deal with prey or foe while staying out of their immediate reach and that was quite a gain. Then came the discovery that you could throw the spear to excellent effect and that well may have been the first occurrence of the projectile weapon. Perhaps they'd taken to hurling rocks earlier, or at least to dropping them down the sides of cliffs at would-be intruders. The details are dim and it was before my time.

What I find highly impressive is that the bow and arrow concept was discovered, invented or, at least, it came along and, having manifest advantages, it was developed to a surprisingly high state of the art. Even with the benefits of modern technology, it's not easy to build an efficient bow and a good set of arrows. Even the more promising woods need to be split and seasoned carefully. A bow made of green wood leaves a lot to be desired. The bow string is subject to severe stress and much prone to break, usually at the most embarrassing possible moment. When you run out of the arrows, the bow is little more than a poor club.

Nevertheless, the bow and arrows appeared and must have represented a quantum leap in comparison to what had been available earlier. Along the way over various parts of the world, they worked up throwing sticks to make the spear far deadlier than when hurled by the unaided arm. Try making one of those from scratch without blueprints, some time!

Other races, other weapons: The throwing stick or boomerang is truly formidable when well made and hurled by skilled hands. The really effective ones do not return to the thrower and the ones that do are little more than toys. Take two lengths of cord joined by a small pouch and you have the sling used so tellingly by David to get Goliath off his case. Join three cords at one end and fasten a small rock to the free ends and you have a bolas, still in use in remote places.

Hollow out a reed or split a straight stick, channel it down the centers and lash it back together and you have a blowgun that can be used to hurl small darts by the pressure built up in the human lungs. Again, these present more challenge to make and use effectively than most people really need, but it can be done and it has been done.

Fire had been harnessed and put to any number of good uses, long ere that. Various utensils were moulded from damp clay and allowed to harden usefully, often in the heat

of the fire and it was discovered that if you heated them to a sufficiently high temperature, they stayed hard, even if in contact with moisture. The trade of the potter came into being and it was noted the fire burned hotter when gusts of wind hit it. Some time after that, forced draft was applied to the flame for the sake of doing a really nice job of firing the pots.

Given a fire burning at a temperature higher than it would under normal combustion, it's generally believed to have led to the discovery that certain minerals yielded metals when heated sufficiently. Copper is nearly the only metal, apart from the precious ones, occurring in natural state and early man was quick to explore the potential of such funny rocks that could be hammered into shape. Tin came to be known and it was found that copper mixed with tin formed a metal somewhat more useful than either by itself. With that, we had the first dim dawn of the bronze age and the gradual twilight of the stone age. It was another quantum leap for *H. sap,* the tool maker and user.

Access to metal opened a broad vista of projects that couldn't be handled by materials such as wood, stone or ceramics. Weapons to that time were almost exclusive of the sort that could be carried and used by a single individual. Given metal, it became possible to develop and use team weapons capable of concentrating the muscle power of several men and/or horses, or that of but one man spread over an interval.

Without whittling things to an unduly fine point, team weapons included such engines of war as can be lumped under the broad and loose designation of catapults. Most such devices had their precise and specialized term such as mangonel, biffa, or onager. The last derives from the name applied to the wild ass of the dry plains of central Asia, a Latin word stemming from the Greek *onos agrios,* mean-

An early variety of the catapult; rather a small one. Windlass was used to draw the string back against the torque of a pair of twisted strands. It could be used to shoot quite a variety of projectiles, as noted.

ing ass of the fields. The flipping pivot arm of the military version was, presumably, reminiscent of the frisky kick of its equine namesake.

Several approaches were employed to store a large amount of energy for abrupt release. In some, such as the biffa, the short end of the pivot arm held a box containing some number of tons of rocks or similar heavy material and a large sling was attached to the end of the long arm. A windlass arrangement raised the weight and brought the sling pouch into place. Other approaches depended upon the torquing of massive strands of rope or the drawing of a monster bow.

In their heyday, what we're terming the catapult was used to hurl some rather improbable projectiles. Fortified castles were contemporaneous with it and the besieging forces brought up their catapults or built them on the spot. If an emissary from the castle sallied forth with a truce offer that was deemed unacceptable, the hapless soul might be bound hand and foot, loaded into the pouch and lofted back by air as a decisive way of saying, "No, thanks." Dead horses, plague victims and assorted camp garbage, among other unsavory materials, were regarded as good catapult fodder of opportunity, in case you regard chemical/biological warfare as something of recent origin.

Such engines of war were the progenitors of modern artillery and incendiary mixtures such as Greek fire sometimes were used in ship-to-ship or land-to-ship combat, since fire at sea was a deadly threat to the wooden ships of the era.

At the other end of the scale, getting back to one-man weaponry, metal hardware enabled design and development of the crossbow — likewise known by many specialized terms — so it could incorporate a bow with a pull so heavy as to defy the most powerful human ever born. It was simply a matter of designing in a system of levers or a windlass arrangement for cocking. It cut down the rate of fire proportionally but a well designed/built/served crossbow did not lag all that far behind a lot of modern firearms in terms of delivered foot-pounds of energy (fpe), although it surely did in rate of fire.

All of these weapon systems, in the final nitty-gritty, depended upon muscle power and, while their delivery could be concentrated into noteworthy doses, their rate of operation was unacceptably slow, in about direct proportion to their vigor. Readying a really capable crossbow for its next shot probably occupied the better part of a minute and, during that time, the crossbowman was agonizingly vulnerable to any hostile foe such as a mounted lancer. In the present state of the art, it might be possible to fashion a rapid-fire crossbow, perhaps one capable of full-auto shooting at a good cyclic rate, but the motive is lacking because we've found other approaches that work better.

The fabled English longbow seems to have appeared about the Thirteenth Century. Earlier bows were about a yard in length. Much of the employment of such bows was from horseback and that was about the practical maximum for such use. The English longbow was about five feet and it was usually shot by troops on foot. A good bowman with

While we've not as yet seen fit to develop a full-auto crossbow, some state-of-the-art refinement has been done on the conventional bow. It's called the compound bow, operating by means of an incredibly complex set of pulleys, cams, levers and whatnot. As the string is drawn, it builds to a maximum draw-weight, then goes "over the hump," so the arrow can be held fully drawn, under vastly lighter muscular effort.

Here's a closer look at one of the wee widgets that makes the compound bow work, in case you'd like to see if you can dope out the basic principles of it.

Candidly, it baffles me all to heck and gone. But it's intriguing to speculate what effect it might have had upon history if such things had been developed sooner.

a proper quiver could nock an arrow, come to full draw, aim and loose, then repeat the operations, all within an impressively brief span of time, achieving good accuracy at a considerable distance. A massed phalanx of longbowmen could put a fearsome number of arrows aloft and could maintain the withering cloud for as long as the supply of arrows lasted.

That was perhaps the first instance of rapid shooting and the English used it to excellent effect. As with all other forms of weaponry to that point, the bow was muscle-powered. Some of the catapults and engines of that design used teams of horses to get the apparatus cocked and ready for the next shot but it was still muscle-power and thus somewhat limited as to maximum effect.

The next major stage in weapons development was the harnessing of chemical energy in the form of early examples of gunpowder. Incendiary compounds such as Greek fire had been employed — chiefly in naval warfare or in seige engines — for a long time. It is believed that the Chinese first discovered the properties of saltpeter —

potassium nitrate or KNO_3 to give it the chemical designation — when mixed with sulfur and/or charcoal, probably at some point prior to 1000 A.D. A remarkably civilized people in that era, they seem to have used their primitive powder principally for fireworks rather than exploring its potential for driving projectiles.

The useful property of potassium nitrate is that its molecule contains one atom of potassium (K), one of nitrogen (N) and three of oxygen (O). When a moderate amount of heat is applied, two of the oxygen atoms separate to form a molecule of free oxygen — O_2 — thus making it available to support the combustion of an atom of sulfur into sulfur dioxide, or one of carbon into carbon dioxide.

The reaction generates gaseous by-products along with a considerable amount of heat and portions of solid residue. Thus, in burning, gunpowder develops a pressure that is vastly greater than normal atmospheric pressure and, if applied to the base of a projectile, it moves it up the barrel and out the muzzle with considerable alacrity.

If a good grade of gunpowder is burned in a container

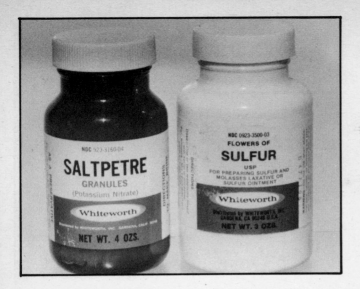

Above and right, the three basic ingredients that — when properly blended and compounded — had a most profound impact upon history over the past six centuries or so. They are the components of black gunpowder, the compounding of which took more deering-do than most would regard as prudent. What I'm saying is that you should not essay to make your own gunpowder...

The little derringer below is a modern replica of the sort of sleeve-weaponry once favored by riverboat gamblers and allied shady gentry. It works with percussion caps and, when both the hammers are cocked, a continuous pull of the trigger trips first one hammer, then the other.

Here are a couple of cannon on exhibit in the courtyard of Kungsholm, in Sweden. I'd estimate they date from somewhere around 1655, give or take the odd century. A matched pair, the lower photo shows details of the fanciful treatment of the muzzles. Such barrels were usually cast from moulds and that must've been a project!

sufficiently strong to contain it, the resulting pressure is on the order of 85,000 pounds per square inch (psi). That is termed its bomb pressure or closed bomb pressure and it's about 5782 times as great as the normal atmospheric pressure of 14.7 psi. Put another way, the theoretical maximum pressure obtainable with black gunpowder is 5782 atmospheres. In normal use, the gunpowder burns over the space of a brief interval and the projectile commences to move, making additional volume available for the powder gas to occupy and the resulting peak pressure is far below the figure just quoted.

The word about gunpowder traveled rather slowly by way of India and Arabia, finally coming to the attention of an English monk, Friar Roger Bacon *(circa* 1214-1294), and he included a description of the formula and manufacturing process in a general encyclopedia of useful knowledge he wrote about 1267.

Bacon's original formula specified forty-two percent of saltpeter and twenty-nine percent each of sulfur and charcoal. Those proportions were followed quite closely for many years and were eventually refined by trial and error to a mixture of 75-15-10 in the order given. As chemistry

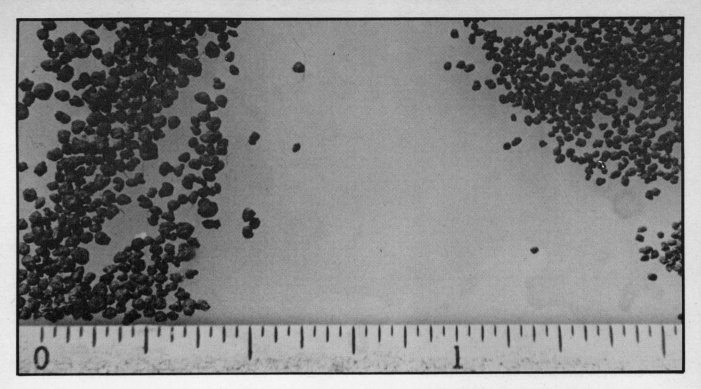

Modern black gunpowder is graded according to granule size. That's Fg on the left, FFg on the right, shown against a scale graduated in 1/16-inch increments. Making the granules smaller increased the available area of the total surfaces, thereby increasing burning speed as combustion takes place on the surface of the granule.

became a more precise science, it was worked out that the ideal proportions were 74.64 saltpeter, 13.51 charcoal and 11.85 sulfur.

Even given the correct recipe, early powder was rather feeble in performance. Until about 1425, it was made by grinding up charcoal, saltpeter and sulfur as finely as possible and then stirring them together thoroughly. The resulting compound was an extremely fine dust called *serpentine* powder. The operation of dry-grinding and mixing gun powder was extremely dangerous, and it still is.

The process of *corning* gun powder — forming it into grains — was developed early in the Fifteenth Century. That consisted of moistening the dry ingredients as they were being pulverized and mixed, then pressing the doughy mixture into cakes that were dried. The cakes were broken into pieces of the desired size and graded by means of sieves into particles of fairly uniform size. With a few refinements, such as glazing the granules with finely powdered graphite, that is essentially the process as employed to the present. It should be emphasized that the operation of manufacturing black gunpowder, despite its apparent simplicity, is extremely dangerous — even when performed by highly trained personnel with all of the necessary safety arrangements observed scrupulously. When attempted by intrepid amateurs, powdermaking is a reliable downhill shortcut to disaster. That is by way of noting that, if you try your hand at making powder and blow both legs off, don't come running to me. You've been warned.

As a usual rule, the *Encyclopedia Brittanica* is the absolute pinnacle of strait-laced propriety, but their 1956

Pyrodex is the latterday replacement for black powder being somewhat cleaner burning, although slightly more difficult to ignite. Can at right is P grade, for use in pistols, about equivalent to the FFFg black.

edition, under the heading of Gunpowder, carried a brief discussion of the binding agents that were tested for comparative efficiency for moistening the ingredients. They seem to have tried virtually everything with varying degrees of success, including urine, wine and the urine of wine drinkers. It was noted the last performed about the best of anything. That scrap of esoteric lore seems to have been

13

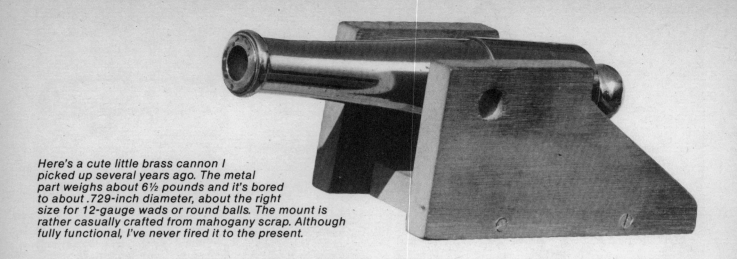

Here's a cute little brass cannon I picked up several years ago. The metal part weighs about 6½ pounds and it's bored to about .729-inch diameter, about the right size for 12-gauge wads or round balls. The mount is rather casually crafted from mahogany scrap. Although fully functional, I've never fired it to the present.

omitted in later editions and may not have been present in earlier ones. I note it as a possibly amusing example of the dedication expended upon research and refinement of the powdermaking operation.

Early in the Fourteenth Century a German monk, one Berthold Schwarz, picked up the torch — cautiously, one assumes — and went on to explore the potentialities of black gunpowder as a propellant and disruptant. Gunpowder was being used in cannon at least as early as 1346, according to an entry in a set of *World Book* encyclopedias copyrighted in 1967, in which it is noted, "Schwarz is said to have invented a firearm which exploded shells by the action of gunpowder."

For a long time after that, igniting the charge of powder to fire the shot was a major problem. The first approach was to provide a small opening called the touch hole near

Pencil points to the touch hole atop the breech of the canon illustrated above. Bored through into the chamber, a small amount of fine-grained powder is placed on/in the touch hole and ignited to fire it.

the breech end of the barrel. A small amount of fast-burning powder was poked down into the hole and bit was allowed to heap up at the top. To fire the gun, a torch was applied to light the priming charge. Later, slow matches were developed by soaking a length of cord in a concentrated water solution of saltpeter and allowing it to dry. That tended to keep the cord or slow match smoldering so it didn't go out just when you needed it. The same general approach continued in use for artillery until at least as recently as the American Civil War.

For guns small enough to be carried and used by an individual, they provided a device — also called a serpentine — that held the length of ignited slow match in readiness. When the lever at the other end was pressed, it pivoted the end of the match down to ignite the powder in the touch hole. The resulting system was known as the *match lock.*

About that time it was noted that a shower of sparks could be produced if a roughened steel wheel were spun against a piece of pyrites and a firearms ignition system was designed to make use of that. A small clockwork motor was wound to put the spring under tension and, when the trigger was pulled, the wheel spun to deliver a shower of sparks to the pan containing the priming powder. When ignited, the fire flashed down through the touch hole to set off the main charge in the barrel. This was termed the *wheel lock.* Its great virtue lay in the fact that the gun, once prepared, could be fired on a moment's notice without the need to strike a spark and get the slow match going. Occasionally, the priming charge failed to communicate the fire to the main charge, giving rise to the phrase, "a flash in the pan."

Striking flint and steel against each other and directing the resulting sparks toward a small quantity of tinder had been used as a popular technique for starting fires for a long time. The next stage in the development of firearms used a striker that held a small piece of flint. When cocked and triggered, it swept under spring pressure to strike a flange of steel called the *frizzen* pivoting that forward to expose the priming powder in the covered pan. Guns of that design

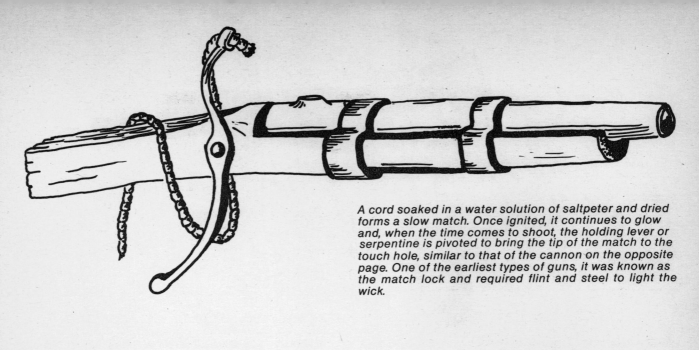

A cord soaked in a water solution of saltpeter and dried forms a slow match. Once ignited, it continues to glow and, when the time comes to shoot, the holding lever or serpentine is pivoted to bring the tip of the match to the touch hole, similar to that of the cannon on the opposite page. One of the earliest types of guns, it was known as the match lock and required flint and steel to light the wick.

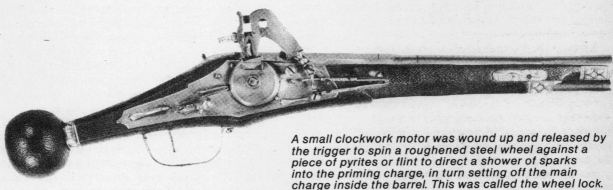

A small clockwork motor was wound up and released by the trigger to spin a roughened steel wheel against a piece of pyrites or flint to direct a shower of sparks into the priming charge, in turn setting off the main charge inside the barrel. This was called the wheel lock.

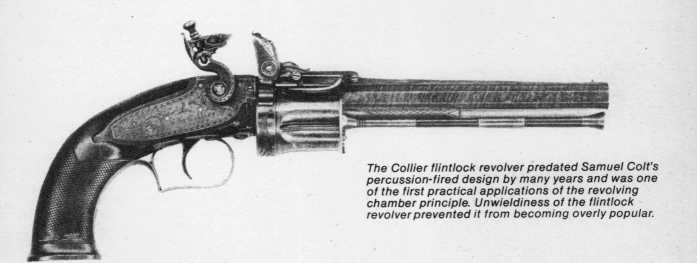

The Collier flintlock revolver predated Samuel Colt's percussion-fired design by many years and was one of the first practical applications of the revolving chamber principle. Unwieldiness of the flintlock revolver prevented it from becoming overly popular.

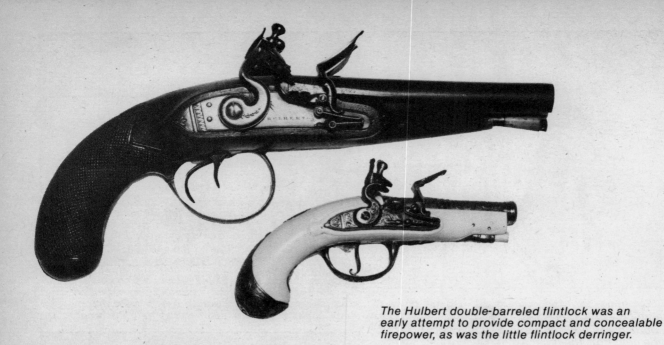

The Hulbert double-barreled flintlock was an early attempt to provide compact and concealable firepower, as was the little flintlock derringer.

were termed *flint locks* and the system was in widespread use up through the American Revolutionary War.

About 1807, a Scottish clergyman, the Rev. Alexander Forsyth, patented the application of fulminate of mercury for the discharge of firearms. Forsyth did not invent the percussion cap; his design made use of loose mercuric fulminate, but his concept was to blaze the way for the research that produced the percussion cap, about 1816. Fulminate of mercury, as well as the fulminates of certain other metals, has the property of exploding under sharp impact. It was a fairly simple matter to put up the fulminate in the base of a small copper cup, sealed from the elements

with a layer of foil. In use, the open end of the cap was placed over the tapered end of a nipple threaded into the breech of the barrel. When the upper end of the cap was struck by the falling hammer, the fulminate exploded, driving hot gas and incandescent particles down through the hollow center of the nipple to ignite the charge.

The *percussion* system, was a vast improvement over the flint since it eliminated the variable amount of time between pulling the trigger and the actual firing of the charge. At the same time, it was considerably more impervious to rain and moisture.

There remained an urgent need for subsequent shots

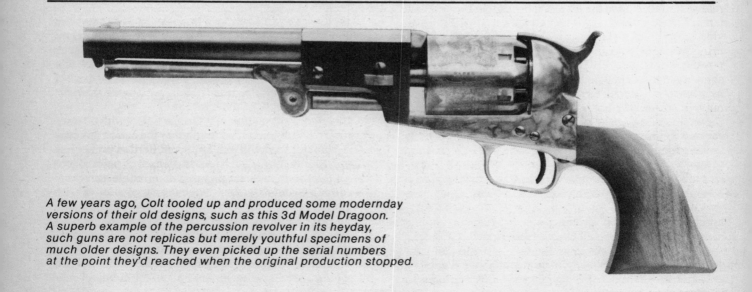

A few years ago, Colt tooled up and produced some modernday versions of their old designs, such as this 3d Model Dragoon. A superb example of the percussion revolver in its heyday, such guns are not replicas but merely youthful specimens of much older designs. They even picked up the serial numbers at the point they'd reached when the original production stopped.

Here you have a (rather crudely) cross-sectioned head of a Boxer-primed cartridge. For obvious reasons, cutting was done on a spent primer. You can see the dent from the firing pin in the cup, just over the point of the internal anvil. The wafer of priming compound was thus set off by percussion.

Cross-section of a .22 rimfire case head, showing the hollow rim that holds the priming compound all around the circumference of the head. Note the slightly thicker area of the case wall near the head.

The Berdan-primed case can be identified readily by the fact it has two flash holes instead of the single, centrally located flash hole of the Boxer system.

available with minimal delay. It is possible that they had double-barreled flintlocks, but the system was not well adapted for multiple firing. With the advent of the percussion system, double-barreled rifles and shotguns, as well as pistols, became practical and fairly popular. At the same time, repeating firearms were designed and built that employed a revolving cylinder to put a given number of loaded chambers in line with the single barrel of the gun. This system proved extremely popular for handguns and was used in rifles to some extent although there seems to have been few revolving shotguns.

A variant of the revolver was the pepperbox, with a cluster of barrels, each being brought into firing position as the hammer was cocked or the trigger pulled.

It remained for the fixed cartridge to be developed to really capitalize upon the potential benefits of the new systems. The percussion revolver and its conceptual kin provided a number of shots — typically, six — available for firing with great rapidity and then you had to get out the powder flask, the sack of balls and the tin of caps and spend some amount of time getting things in readiness for your next burst. If you took on seven antagonists, or missed one out of a sextet, you had a problem; a *bad* problem.

Several cartridge systems were introduced, meeting varying amounts of acceptance or apathy. Among the earliest forms was the *rimfire* cartridge, with its priming compound — still fulminate of mercury at that time — carried in a hollow space around the rim of the cartridge head. When struck by the tip of the hammer, the priming mix was crushed and set off, igniting the charge of powder. The approach had several advantages and it remains in wide use to the present for small cartridges such as the .22 short, long or long rifle. It was once used for cartridges of considerable size but the *center-fire* primer offered advantages as to strength of the case head for larger rounds and came to be adopted all but universally.

There were and still are two basic designs of center-fire primers. The Berdan system utilizes an anvil that's integral to the case head, with two small flash holes opposite each other and slightly off-center. The Boxer primer, on the other hand, carries its own small anvil in the open front of the primer cup and has a somewhat larger single flash hole, located in the center of the case head.

The significance of that is that a fired case with a Boxer primer is easy and simple to deprime by the action of a centrally located decapping pin. The spent Berdan primer has to be pried from its pocket by some manner of pointed tool and patiently applied leverage. It is possible to reload Berdan-primed cases, but at the expense of a lot of time and bother.

The Boxer priming system is employed almost universally for center-fire cartridges in this country while ammunition of that type nearly always uses the Berdan primer in other parts of the world. Curiously enough, the Berdan primer was developed by an American, the Boxer primer by a Briton.

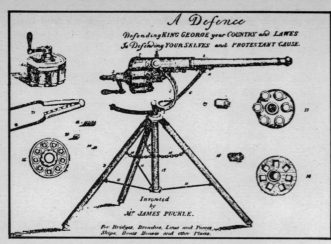

Mr. James Puckle's "Defence" dates from 1718 and, as a novel black-humor touch, the design included the use of round bullets for Christians, square ones to employ against Turks. It seems likely Puckle's brainchild never got beyond the blueprint stage.

Even with the appearance of fairly modern cartridges, the rapid-firing gun that could hold its pace over an extensive number of shots had to await the arrival of smokeless powder or nitro powder to use a more accurately descriptive term. It was mentioned earlier that some amount of solid residue is left in the burning of black gunpowder and the accumulation of such residues posed a severe problem in multifiring guns.

It's not that efforts were not made to produce rapid-firers early. At least as long ago as 1718 an Englishman named James Puckle took out an English patent on a fearsome device he called the Puckle Defence which, as he put it, "discharges so often and so many bullets, and be so quickly loaden, as renders it next to impossible to carry any ship by boarding."

The Billinghurst Requa had a flat row of barrels and chamber assemblies for quick loading. A cap lock set off a train of powder to ignite charges in sequence.

As well as can be determined by examining the patent drawing, the Puckle gun had a single barrel with a six-shot breech turned by means of an integral crank and ignited with a slow match. The entire breech assembly was replaced with a fresh one after firing and it was mounted on a tripod, complete with a primitive arrangement for elevating and traversing.

As an added touch of black humor, Puckle designed his gun to fire round balls at Christians and cubical projectiles at Turks. The exact rationale behind that is not readily apparent. There seems to be no record that the gun of the warlike Mr. Puckle was ever used in combat against foes of

The Montigny Mitrailleuse, from about 1851, had a barrel similar to that of a small cannon, bored with thirty-seven holes. Loaded with charge racks such as the one in use here, it was fired selectively, but did not prove overly effective due to lack of maneuverability.

any creed whatsoever. Indeed, there is considerable doubt that it ever passed a function test.

An early multifirer that functioned with reasonable efficiency was the Billinghurst Requa Battery Gun. That appeared about the time of the Civil War and, as with most such designs of the era, it was wheel-mounted in the manner of an artillery piece. It had a flat layer of twenty-four barrels and it was fed by clips of cartridges, each with a hole in its base. The cartridges were inserted into the barrels and a fresh priming train of black powder was poured to cover the touch holes at the base of each. The entire batch was set off by a single percussion cap on a nipple, by means of a fairly conventional hammer and trigger.

The Billinghurst had no provision for selective fire. It was purely a matter of turn loose of all two dozen or keep quiet and, when fired, the bullets endangered not much over two feet of space in a horizontal line although it was probably possible to get in a small amount of traversing during the interlude it took the powder train to get from one end of the rack of barrels to the other. The Billinghurst was demonstrated in front of the New York Stock Exchange at

The Gatling gun, patented in 1862 and later years, saw service at least as recently as 1910. It was produced in many calibers and design variations, as noted.

the onset of the Civil War toward the objective of winning capital for its development and production. It was not a roaring success. Only a few were made and, so far as is known, one was actually employed at Charleston, South Carolina.

The Montigny Mitrailleuse predates the Billinghurst slightly, having been developed in Belgium during the period from 1851 to 1869. It resembled a small artillery piece in appearance, with its barrel bored with thirty-seven parallel holes in a hexagonal pattern. It was loaded by

A contemporary of the Gatling was the Palmcrantz, seen here in the Swedish Royal Army Museum. Like the Gatling, it was hand-cranked for operation.

means of a breech plate carrying the cartridges and fired by turning a crank to release the corresponding firing pins to set off each cartridge in turn. It is reported that, properly served, the Mitrailleuse could deliver about ten clips per minute or 370 shots.

Adopted in 1869 by the French government, the Mitrailleuse saw action in the Franco-Prussian War, but to little or no good purpose. In the same conflict, the Germans used a few Gatlings, likewise to little effect. It was not so

much that either gun was ineffectual but, rather that the troops and their commanders had no idea as to how to employ them strategically.

Dr. Richard Jordan Gatling (1818-1903) patented the gun that bears his name in 1862. It saw no more than limited use in the Civil War, partially because models of that time used percussion-capped steel chargers rather than modern cartridges. Immediately after the war, the Gatling was adapted to use conventional cartridges — either rimfire or center-fire — and the Colt Company commenced manufacturing them. With various improvements, the Gatling continued in production until about 1910.

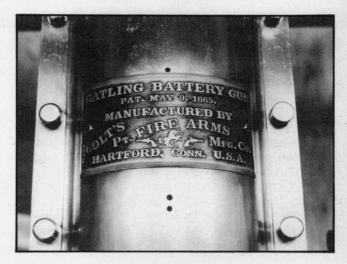

The name plate affixed to a Gatling in the Swedish Royal Army Museum shows a patent date of 1865.

The Gatling gun was a manually operated repeater, not a machine gun. As its crank was turned, the cluster of barrels rotated about a common center and, in the course of turning a complete circle, the spent case was extracted, a

Here's the overall view of that Swedish Gatling. For a long time, designers regarded rapid-fire guns as merely a specialized form of artillery and did not incorporate the maneuverability to make them effective.

fresh round was chambered, the striker was cocked and, as it came into position, it was fired again. I seem to recall having seen photos of small Gatlings — probably chambered for the .45-70 Government cartridge — on mounts secured to the backs of camels for desert warfare. I can only imagine it must have been a remarkably interesting experience to gattle-forth a burst while astride a camel, considering the probable effect upon the beast's composure!

Electric motors and the current with which to make them hum were not all that common and readily available in the salad days of the Gatling and it appears that no one thought to replace the hand crank with applied power. The clockwork motor was well bedded in the state of the art at the time and it's faintly puzzling that no one thought to fit a Gatling with some manner of oversized phonograph motor that could be cranked up in advance to make the gadget blurt busily in time of dire need.

In point of fact, the Gatling's basic principle became the heart of the modern Vulcan high-speed gun, capable of a sustained cyclic rate of fire on the order of thousands of rounds per minute.

There were other contemporaries of the Gatling, less commonly recalled today. The Hotchkiss revolving cannon was similar in concept, although larger; usually ship-mounted and capable of discharging sixty to eighty shots per minute. It was hand-cranked, as was the Gardner machine gun, a gravity-fed, cartridge-firing quick-firer bearing a close general resemblance to several modern machine guns, except for the operating crank on the RH side of its receiver. Some of the Gardners had as many as five barrels and sets of feed mechanisms. It was about the first example of such a gun with any pretense of portability and could be used off a sturdy tripod mount, with no need for the wheeled carriage. In the single-barreled version, the packing weight of the Gardner was only about two hundred pounds and it could be served tellingly by a crew of three or four.

Along the way, there was the McLean repeating cannon and, with it, the Palmcrantz Nordenfeldt machine gun. The latter has always sounded to me like the sort of gun a Walter Mitty might dream of firing, pocketa-pocketa. Like so many of its peers of that time, it was gravity-fed and multi-barreled, with anywhere from two to six barrels parallel in horizontal arrangement. They were all loaded by operation of a loading lever and fired in volleys. It could chug forth several hundred rounds per minute and it was quite popular as a shipboard defense against small torpedo boats which were a worrisome vexation to naval commanders of the era.

Gunpowder — either the saltpeter-based or nitrocel-

A shipboard installation of the Palmcrantz-Nordenfeldt machine gun: still hand-cranked, but probably a handy rig for discouraging boarders. Note the complete absence of any type of shielding for the grim-looking gunner.

Another just-plain Palmcrantz, likewise from the Swedish Royal Army Museum: six guns together.

lulose-type — was the driving force in the guns just discussed. It has been a front-runner for the past several centuries but that's not to assume it never had any competition. Several approaches for launching projectiles have been explored. In a visit to the Royal Swedish Army Museum, in late 1974, I encountered a remarkably ingenious mechanism called the Fleetwood — presumably in honor of its inventor/designer.

In the years of my early boyhood, a standard fixture in grocery stores was the hand-cranked coffee grinder. Usually, these had a fairly massive flywheel with the crank jutting out, parallel to the axle for the wheel. The Fleetwood went a step further and carried one such large flywheel and crank on each side of its breech mechanism, with a good-sized barrel jutting toward the enemy.

It appears to have been designed for shipboard mounting and there are a pair of cranks to regulate elevation and movement in azimuth — left/right — directions. Presumably a husky Swede would apply himself to each crank while a third took care of the aiming. On a full cycle of the two flywheels, a piston was withdrawn and then driven back to compress the air while a round lead ball of about 10mm diameter was fed into the breech and shot at the appropriate cycle point.

Compressed air has by no means been neglected in the search for effective ways to launch projectiles. In the Spanish-American War, the Rough Riders tried out an ingenious system for hurling projectiles containing the then-new and still rather hysterical explosive called dynamite. If you tried to drive a shell filled with dynamite by the direct explosion of a black powder driving charge, the brusqueness of acceleration was quite apt to set off the bursting charge about midway down the bore, to the severe distraction of the gunners and all others nearby.

Above and below are two views of the hand-cranked compressed air gun on display at the Swedish Royal Army Museum. The tag reads, "Kulspruta fm/ Fleetwood 1846 Kaliber 10mm Sverige." Kulspruta appears to be the Swedish term for rapid-fire weapons in general and the mounting suggests this one was emplaced aboard ship. Projectiles appear to have been chambered automatically so as to deliver one aimed shot at each complete turn of the flywheels.

The dynamite cannon used by the Rough Riders in the Spanish-American War of 1898 used a charge of powder to compress the air for launching the dynamite-bearing projectile.

The dynamite cruiser U.S.S. Vesuvius packed a trio of three compressed air cannon, each of fifteen-inch bore diameter, powered by compressors driven by the ship's engines. The muzzles of the battery can be seen here a short distance abaft the prow. Presumably aimed in azimuth by steering the ship, in the manner of most fighter aircraft, elevation must have been controlled by moving the gun and/or by regulating the air pressure. Probably the zenith of air artillery development, there is no record the guns were used in combat.

The Rough Riders' air-cannon — if I understand the principle rightly — used a charge of gunpowder to drive a piston to compress a considerable quantity of air and that was fed to the breech area behind the shell carrying the dynamite to launch it without unwanted adventures.

A contemporary system was designed into a warship, the *U.S.S. Vesuvius.* Its keel was laid in 1887 and it was completed at a total cost of $350,000 — a respectable amount of money at that time. With a length of 252.3 feet, a mean draft of 10.6 feet and a beam of 26.5 feet, its displacement was 929 tons and its engines, rated at 3795 horsepower, gave it a top speed of 21.4 knots. It was built around a battery of three pneumatic cannon, each fifteen inches in bore diameter and fixed to the ship's construction so as to be aimed by the ship's heading in the manner of the fighter aircraft of WWI and later conflicts. Elevation may have been subject to adjustment and/or regulated by the air-pressure at the time of shooting.

Another enigmatic gem from the Swedish Royal Army Museum, this sled-mounted muzzleloading cannon has not one but three side-by-side bores visible in muzzle.

The Lewis gun made the scene in plenty of time for use in WWI. A true machine gun, it was gas-operated, usually chambered for the .303 British cartridge and 'fed from the flat drum magazine atop the breech. Gun shown here is courtesy of J. Curtis Earl.

Like the Rough Riders' field piece, the guns of the Vesuvius were designed to hurl dynamite-filled projectiles but it appears she never managed to realize her destiny and $350,000 gurgled down the drain in futile vain. It is rather a pity, since it must have been one of the few recorded instances in which the War Department was willing to go along with a new idea. It may have reinforced their usual reluctance about such things.

Other avenues of projectile propulsion have been explored with little or nothing by way of encouraging results. They've tried driving them by steam pressure, by centrifugal force and they've gone so far as to construct a sort of in-line electric motor to accelerate ferrous projectiles by ongoing magnetic attraction in much the way the armature of a motor is made to spin.

"There are two ways to shoot a blowgun," an associate once observed. "You can blow from the back end or you can suck from the front and then get out of the way, *real fast!*"

Nitrocellulose powder is king of the mountain among today's propellants, not so much because it's terribly great but solely because nothing else fails anywhere nearly as well. If you release compressed air, its pressure begins to drop the instant the projectile starts to move. When powder is ignited, it takes a small interval to reach peak pressure and the heat of its combustion adds considerably to the useful effect.

The firearms discussed to this point could not fire of their own volition, once triggered, requiring some amount of outside manipulation to keep the cycle going. The man who seems to have ushered the world into the machine gun era — for better or worse, as may be debated, and has been — seems to have been an American by name of Hiram Maxim. Even Maxim had to have the bee implanted in his bonnet.

It was in 1883 that Maxim was displaying his electrical inventions at an exposition in Europe when another American — name not readily retrievable — advised him that if he really wanted to roll up a bundle, the thing he should do was to make it quicker and simpler for the Europeans to do away with each other.

The suggestion dropped into fertile topsoil. Maxim returned to London, set up an experimental laboratory and took two years to design and patent a recoil-operated

and Spandaus spat into each other's muzzles, fraying their respective crewmen quite seriously, with few aware of the bitter irony that both had been spawned on the same drawing board.

The Maxim had been well and truly blooded some years earlier. Dually mounted and termed a "Double Maxim," they emitted their lethal staccato brays here and there in the Boer War and in other minor conflicts recalled less vividly.

Maxim harnessed the force of recoil to operate his machine gun but there were other forces suitable for tapping, including the downbore gas pressure. That approach was explored by an American inventor, one John Moses Browning, who visited the Colt works in the early 1890s with a machine gun design that was operated by gas taken from a port near the muzzle. When fired, the jet of high-pressure gas struck a cuplike part fastened to the end of a lever, driving it downward and rearward to transmit the force back through an actuating rod to work the action through the rest of the cycle of extracting the spent cartridge case, cham-

Sir Hiram Maxim usually gets credit for invention of the first true machine gun capable of automatic fire by using the force of recoil to operate the feed mechanism. Thus, at some point in the era from 1883 to 1889 firepower took the final step to its present form.

machine gun; the first true example of the breed according to most reference sources.

Given additional development and refinement, Maxim persuaded the British government to adopt the Maxim automatic machine gun in 1889. It was manufactured in Britain by the Vickers works until after the end of WWI and in Germany at the Spandau arsenal, as well as in numerous other places. When WWI flared up, Vickers

bering a fresh round and firing it, assuming pressure upon the trigger had not been relaxed.

Colt introduced Browning's design in 1895 as the Colt Browning automatic gun and it was adopted before the outbreak of the Spanish-American War by both the Army and Navy.

Unlike the Maxim, which cooled its single barrel by a water-filled jacket surrounding it, the Colt Browning was

Here is one of the Model 1895 Colt-Browning machine guns that operated by tapping combustion gas from a small port in the bottom of the barrel about six inches back from the muzzle. The gun is from the private collection of J. Curtis Earl, a machine gun dealer operating from 5512 North Sixth Street, Phoenix, AZ 85012. Earl can supply a large illustrated brochure for $5 to those interested in this type of weaponry.

air-cooled by means of integral fins not unlike those around the cylinders of most motorcycle engines. The Colt Browning had a relatively low rate of fire, about four hundred rounds per minute and its usual employment was off a tripod mount. Since the mount put it rather close to the ground — for obvious strategic reasons, mindful the foe might be retaliating in fire — the shuttling lever up front could occasionally kick dirt back into the gunner's face and that in turn led to an informal christening of the Colt Browning as "the old potato-digger."

Various other forces connected with firing the cartridge were explored and discarded along the way. One attempted to utilize the kickback of the primer into a small recess around the firing pin. Others scouted the possibilities of a ring or series of rings at the muzzle and axial to the bore. One time or another, they seem to have tried out nearly everything short of perpetual motion and I'm not entirely certain that can be ruled out.

Browning went on to consider the recoil-operated approach and designed some notably effective gun systems around it in the years just prior to entry of the U.S., into WWI. The designs were sufficiently advanced to remain in widespread use through WWII and my own personal experience with such things. While the primary topic of the book at hand is not machine guns, they represent the primal progenitors of the autoloading pistol and, as such, possibly merit a bit of further discussion if the reader is willing to endure the tangent---?

There is a vast and steadfastly-held conviction on the part of the general public that if you can just put forth enough bullets, one or more of them are certain to hit the intended mark via the grim rigor of mathematical probability. Not to raise your hostile hackles, friend, but that "ain't necessary so." It is that there are up to an infinity of vectors

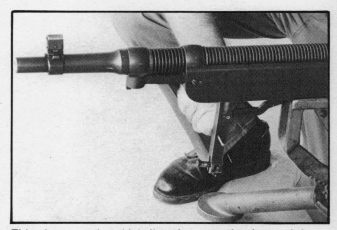

This shows my hand hauling the operating lever of the Colt-Browning to the limit of its travel, suggesting the reason for nicknaming it the "Old Potato-Digger."

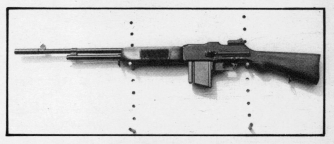

A WWI Browning Automatic Rifle or BAR, likewise from the J. Curtis Earl collection, shows gas tube and port beneath the barrel; caliber was the .30/06.

that can score misses, and will do so, while the number of vectors representing hits is manifestly finite.

Permit me to illustrate and clarify that, hmm? At one point in my military career, I was one of the instructors on a machine gun training facility at Harlingen Aerial Gunnery School (HAGS) near the town of the same name in the southern tip of Texas. Each student was firing a flexible, air-cooled Browning, caliber .30 and there were perhaps thirty students and the same number of guns on the line. Each student fired a two-hundred-round belt of cartridges on their little chain-link belts and the students had been given the command to latch the first round of the belt into battery, followed by the command to commence firing. The first few desultory bursts had been loosed when a rangy Texas coyote burst from behind a clump of sagebrush and galloped at flank speed down the line of targets.

That had to approach or perhaps surpass the ultimate varminter's daydream. I tend to doubt that any military body has ever achieved the degree of discipline that would have kept every single one of those trainees studiously engaged in firing at their assigned target, meanwhile icily ignoring the highballing *Canis latrans.* As you'd rightly suppose, every muzzle of every gun on the line locked onto the hapless critter and every trigger finger clamped down as if in the extremity of *rigor mortis.*

A vast gout of pale dust spumed upward where the coyote had been and, long before it had a chance to subside, the coyote flashed out of the left edge of the cloud. Manifestly unscratched, he had slammed the throttle to the firewall, cut in the afterburner, the supercharger, and was flogging sheeg out of the hands in the boiler room.

There was a prodigious gobble of white noise at unguessable decibels as every gunner on the line threw a hasty bead and cut loose again, followed by another plume of white dust, a further re-emergence of the berserkly-frightened prairie wolf and...well, play it again from the top; several times; *e da capo.*

I am going to have to ask you to accept my unsupported word of honor that, in the course of firing nearly 6000

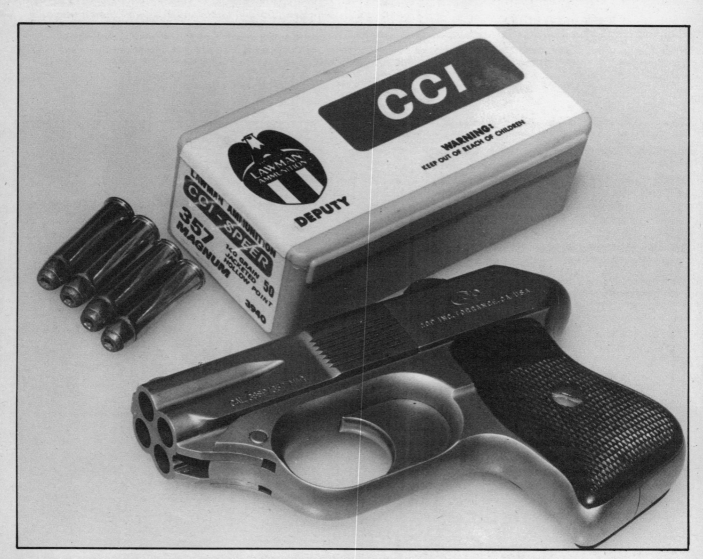

A modern adaptation of an early principle to provide follow-up shots is the COP — for compact off-duty pistol — with its four barrels chambered for the .357 magnum cartridge. A rotating striker sets off each shot in turn.

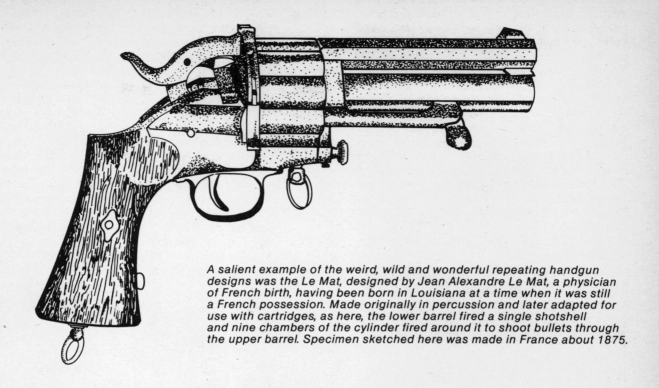

A salient example of the weird, wild and wonderful repeating handgun designs was the Le Mat, designed by Jean Alexandre Le Mat, a physician of French birth, having been born in Louisiana at a time when it was still a French possession. Made originally in percussion and later adapted for use with cartridges, as here, the lower barrel fired a single shotshell and nine chambers of the cylinder fired around it to shoot bullets through the upper barrel. Specimen sketched here was made in France about 1875.

A really mystifying what's-it from the Swedish Royal Army Museum has a crank-opened breech but little or no further clue as to its modus operandi. There was no helpful identity tag on this. Your guess's as good as mine as to what it is, how it worked — if it worked!

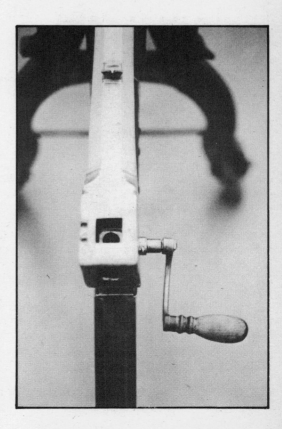

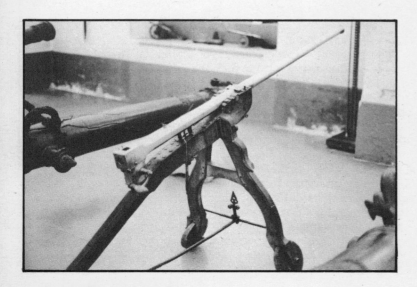

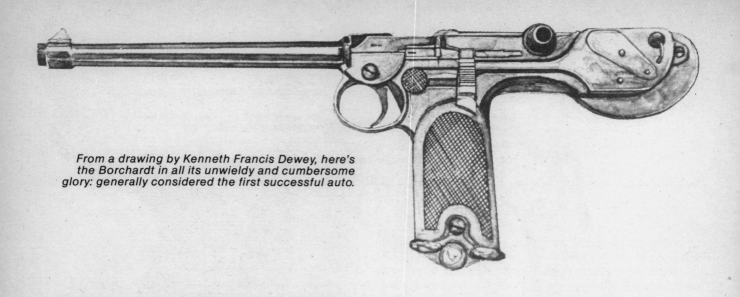

From a drawing by Kenneth Francis Dewey, here's the Borchardt in all its unwieldy and cumbersome glory: generally considered the first successful auto.

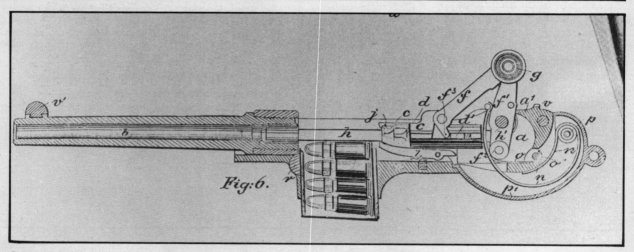

Some details of the Borchardt's toggle-lock action, from the patent drawing.

rounds of .30/06 ammunition at a distance of hardly more than two hundred yards, not so much as one hurtling bullet ever impinged upon coyotely flesh. I found the experience quite educational. During the course of the episode, I lost practically all of the faith I'd ever held in the efficacy of full-auto fire. Others may covet and lust after the pocketa-pocketa guns but not yours ever so humble and truly. I've fired them and admit they have their uses, but their utility is limited and you can color me jaded.

As we have seen, machine guns had fairly well won their niche in the scheme of things prior to the final decade of the Nineteenth Century when the first successful autoloading pistol made its appearance. Most sources give credit for that to Hugo Borchardt. Born in Germany, he emigrated to the United States at the age of 16, working in this country as a design engineer for a number of years. In the early Eighties, he returned to Europe and, on September 9,

1893, took out a patent on his design for an autoloading pistol which was made for a brief time by Loewe before that firm merged to form the Deutsche Waffen und Munitionsfabrik (DWM).

The Borchardt used the toggle-block locking system later incorporated into the Parabellum or, as it's more frequently termed, the Luger pistol. Like most of the current designs, its magazine was contained in a recess within the grip portion. Production of the Borchardt was suspended in 1899 as the first versions of the Luger went into production. Apart from its primacy in the scheme of things, the Borchardt had few other virtues.

Another auto pistol from Germany, the Bergmann, appeared in 1894 and, having nothing much to emulate, its design varied considerably from any auto pistol to that point or most since then. The magazine was positioned ahead of the trigger guard and several approaches were

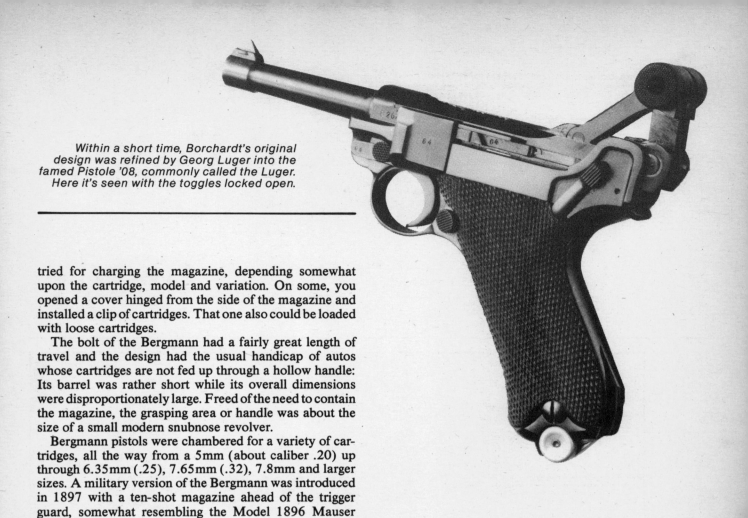

Within a short time, Borchardt's original design was refined by Georg Luger into the famed Pistole '08, commonly called the Luger. Here it's seen with the toggles locked open.

tried for charging the magazine, depending somewhat upon the cartridge, model and variation. On some, you opened a cover hinged from the side of the magazine and installed a clip of cartridges. That one also could be loaded with loose cartridges.

The bolt of the Bergmann had a fairly great length of travel and the design had the usual handicap of autos whose cartridges are not fed up through a hollow handle: Its barrel was rather short while its overall dimensions were disproportionately large. Freed of the need to contain the magazine, the grasping area or handle was about the size of a small modern snubnose revolver.

Bergmann pistols were chambered for a variety of cartridges, all the way from a 5mm (about caliber .20) up through 6.35mm (.25), 7.65mm (.32), 7.8mm and larger sizes. A military version of the Bergmann was introduced in 1897 with a ten-shot magazine ahead of the trigger guard, somewhat resembling the Model 1896 Mauser pistol.

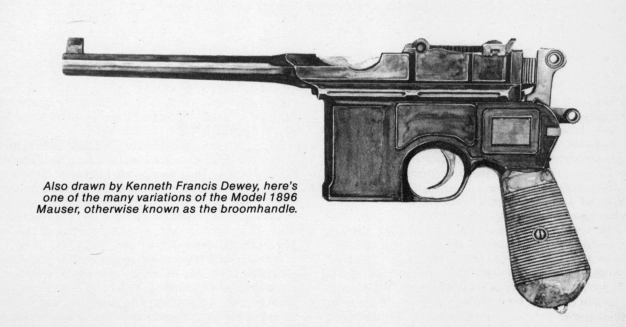

Also drawn by Kenneth Francis Dewey, here's one of the many variations of the Model 1896 Mauser, otherwise known as the broomhandle.

John M. Browning designed the Model 1902 Colt for the caliber .38 rimless smokeless cartridge. This is the sporting model, priced at $18.50, then.

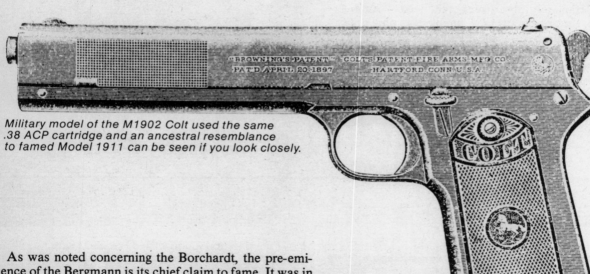

Military model of the M1902 Colt used the same .38 ACP cartridge and an ancestral resemblance to famed Model 1911 can be seen if you look closely.

As was noted concerning the Borchardt, the pre-eminence of the Bergmann is its chief claim to fame. It was in 1896 that Paul Mauser took out a patent for the auto pistol known by several names such as Military Model Mauser, Model 1896, broomhandle or spikenose. Germans refer to it as the *kuhfusspistole* or cowfoot pistol. Differing from the Borchardt and Bergmann, the Model 1896 Mauser remains in some modest amount of current use although it has not been produced in appreciable quantities since the end of WWII.

Along the way, the Model 1896 Mauser pistol played some decisive parts in shaping the world we know today, for better or for worse. Fairly early in the Boer War, a young British subaltern with his saber arm out of commission from a wound, drew his trusty broomhandle and used it to shoot his way out of a closing circle of foes. His name was Winston Churchill; yes, *that* Winston Churchill.

A variant of the Model 1896 Mauser has a twenty-round detachable magazine and a fire-selector lever enabl-

ing it to be switched from autoloading to full-auto or, in the German designation, a schnellfeuer (speed-fire) version. The book, *Automatic Arms,* by Captain Melvin M. Johnson USMCR and Charles T. Haven, on page 35, notes, "It was with two of these that King Alexander of Yugoslavia was assassinated at Marseille. Several people in the near-

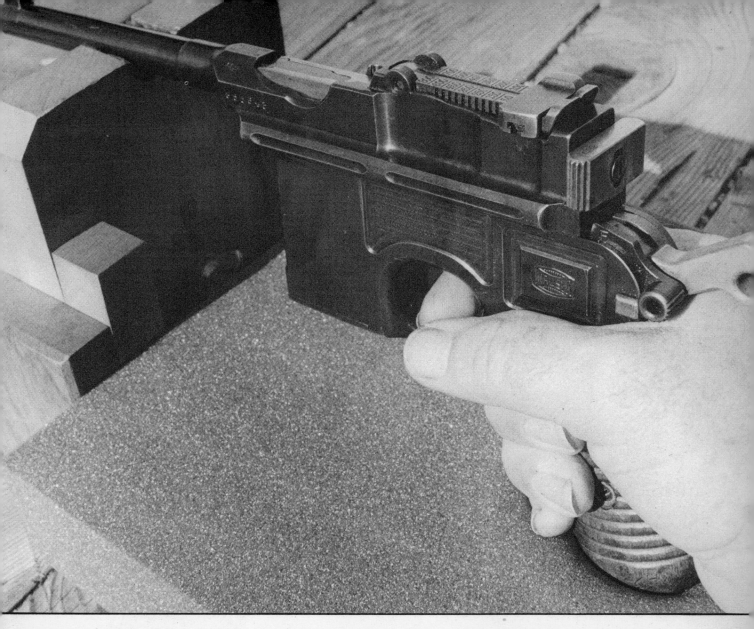

From the photo files, here's a view of a Model 96 Mauser I owned so long ago that it only cost $175 and I was grateful to recoup the exact purchase price a few years later. Today, it would bring a much higher figure, but I do not mourn it keenly, apart from that. Neither impressively accurate nor reliable in comparison to several other auto pistols, it had a most disconcerting habit of letting off two or three together, now and then.

by crowd were also killed as the assassin rolled on the ground under the blows of the guard, firing indiscriminately with a full-automatic pistol in each hand."

If you happened to see the film, *Star Wars* — I haven't — I'm told that some of the handguns brandished during the course of it are patently Model 1896 Mausers, thinly disguised, if at all. That suggests that it found its way, somehow, to "a Galaxy far, far away."

As a hopeless handgun buff, I've had my interlude of hard infatuation with the old spikenose Mauser and have come to grips with it and walked away sorely disenchanted. I would have to rank it far, far down the list of my personal preference. Nonetheless I'd be the first to concede

we owe it a debt of gratitude for preserving the doughty Sir Winston's resolute bacon to the day when we needed him badly and, in its own peculiar way, it represents the omega to the alpha of that first rock grabbed and tellingly swung. We have spanned a vast number of centuries and even millennia and this seems a fitting place to tie off the chapter. We have traversed from the earliest roots of the stone age to the era of the burp-gun and its autoloading counterpart that I tend to think of as the hiccough-gun.

From the dimmest origin of the race to the present, weapons have enabled your ancestors and mine to qualify for that distinction, spottily along the way. For my part, I'm grateful for that and I'm hoping you're the same.

CHAPTER 2

OPERATING PRINCIPLES OF
AUTOLOADING PISTOLS

Many Approaches Have Been Tried For Making Self-Loaders Work And This Discusses Some Salient — And A Few Unlikely — Examples

Something not too often seen: An absolutely unmodified Colt Model 1911 from the WWI era. Its doughboy liberator supplied a slip of paper that says, "American .45 automatic taken from an abandoned rolling kitchen of an unknown unit at Meuse Argonne." The M1911A1 appeared after the war, with a longer grip safety tang, arched mainspring housing, shortened trigger, modified hammer spur and crescent-shaped relief cuts on both sides of the frame to the rear of the trigger. Most of the changes are regarded as improvements.

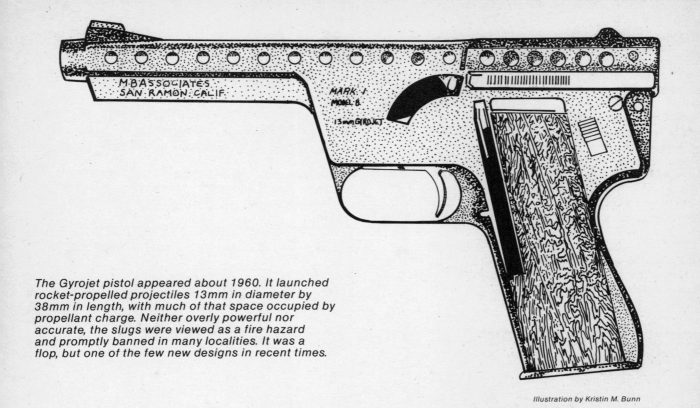

The Gyrojet pistol appeared about 1960. It launched rocket-propelled projectiles 13mm in diameter by 38mm in length, with much of that space occupied by propellant charge. Neither overly powerful nor accurate, the slugs were viewed as a fire hazard and promptly banned in many localities. It was a flop, but one of the few new designs in recent times.

Illustration by Kristin M. Bunn

T HERE IS a tendency, up here in the top end of the Twentieth Century, to think of the era between 1900 and 1918 in terms of bustles, button shoes and horse-drawn conveyances. A thoughtful associate once termed 1912 as, "the Indian Summer of modern civilization," and, for all I know, he may have been quite correct.

Whatever that period may have been to other aspects of human culture, it seems to have been the Golden Age of firearms development in general and of autoloading pistols in particular. Most of the handguns still in widespread use today trace their origins to about the first two decades of the present century. The appearance of nitrocellulose or smokeless powder and the self-contained cartridge, both legacies of the Nineteenth Century, seem to have galvanized the firearms designers of that era into thinking up nearly all the new ideas available in weapons development.

The Model 1911 Colt, for example, was so tellingly conceived that it is still a hard act to top after the traditional three-score years and ten. Compare it if you will, to a 1911 automobile, a 1911 camera or even a 1911 human being and you'll have to admit it bears its many birthdays with marvelous insouciance.

Autoloading pistols, then as now, utilized many different design principles to accomplish their given thing. The full census of such devices extends to a bewildering number of subvariants but most, if not all, either harness the force of recoil to operate the working parts or else tap a bit of the high-pressure gasses to accomplish something useful.

At the lower end of the scale, we have the tiny cartridges such as the .22 long rifle, .25 Automatic Colt Pistol (ACP), .32 ACP and .380 ACP, and most if not all guns handling those cartridges operate on a principle termed *full blowback:*

That means the mass and inertia of the slide, together with the compressive resistance of the recoil spring, team up to resist the rearward impetus of the fired cartridge sufficiently to hold the cartridge in the chamber until the bullet is out of the muzzle and the chamber pressure has more or less equalized with normal atmospheric pressures.

The high-pressure gasses from the burning powder push the bullet down the bore and out the muzzle. At the same time, they are pushing against the head of the now-empty cartridge case — from the inside, of course — with approximately equal force. The walls of the cartridge case swell outward under that pressure and are forced into tight contact with the chamber surface. The frictional resistance thus created is yet another factor in delaying the rearward movement of the case and bolt. The case serves the further purpose of obturating the high-pressure gasses, forming a gas-tight seal, in simpler terms.

The bullet emerges from the muzzle, followed closely by the powder gasses. Pressure within the bore moves rapidly downward to equalize with outside air pressure, which averages about 14.7 pounds per square inch (psi). The spent case and bolt, in the meantime, have been given a sharp impetus that is proportional to the energy imparted to the bullet. They are now free to move rearward, and do so, compressing the recoil spring in so doing.

The spent case is held by the extractor claw which continues pulling it rearward after the case mouth has cleared the chamber. A bit of further travel and the portion of the case head opposite the extractor collides with the ejector and, at the velocities involved, that hurls the case clear of the action, spinning rapidly.

The bolt continues rearward until its motion is arrested by contact with a mating surface in the receiver. At that point, the compressed recoil spring begins to drive the bolt forward again and, as it passes over the magazine, an area of its lower front surface encounters the upper perimeter of a cartridge head held in the magazine. Driven by forward inertia and the compressed recoil spring, the bolt strips the top round from the magazine.

The shape and design of the lips at the top of the magazine guide the cartridge and, together with the feed ramp at the lower rear of the chamber in the barrel, they deliver the fresh round into the chamber.

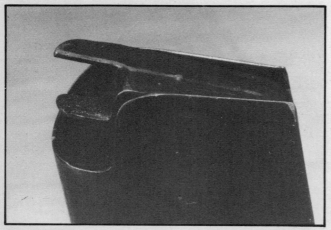

Magazine follower of the M1911 needs to be at just the right angle to work well. The lower finger at the front raises the slide stop to lock the action open after firing the final round and should look like this.

In the course of all this, some manner of disconnector mechanism designed into the gun will have repositioned the sear in such a manner that it will be necessary to let the trigger move forward some small distance before it can be pulled to fire the round that was just chambered. Lacking such a disconnector, the gun would fire until the trigger was released or until the magazine ran dry. The disconnector thus represents the distinction between an autoloading or self-loading pistol and a fully automatic design such as a machine gun.

In the early development of the Thompson submachine gun, it was believed that its action needed to be fully locked for a brief interval immediately after firing. For that reason, early models included a feature called the Blish hesi-

tation lock. Later, it came to be realized that the Blish lock served little or no useful purpose and it was omitted. By the time of World War II, most if not all Thompsons in service operated by the full blowback principle just described. When firing full-auto, the Thompson of that pattern was nothing more nor yet less than an internal-combustion engine and, if you hooked a connecting rod and flywheel to the rear of its bolt, the resemblance would have been complete.

When the trigger was pulled and held back, the bolt was free to move forward and did so under the thrust of the recoil spring, scooping a cartridge from the top of the magazine, carrying it on into the chamber and setting off its primer by means of a firing pin that was nothing more than an immovable nib, integral with the bolt face. That sent the bolt back again, ejecting the empty case and, if the trigger still held the sear out of engagement, the bolt lunged for-

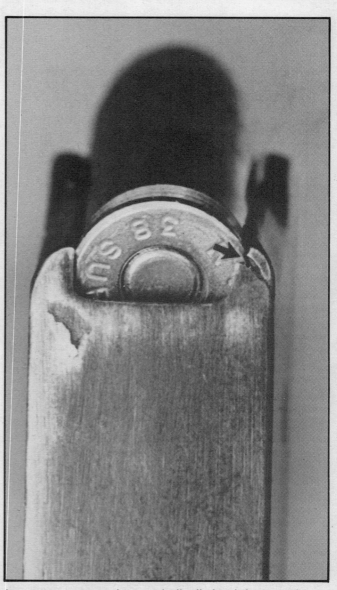

Inspect your magazines periodically for defects such as the separated weld at the upper right rear corner. It is sufficient to make the magazine feed unreliably.

Above, circle indicates tip of the disconnector of M1911. Arrow (left), below indicates the relief cut in the lower side of the slide. Rearward movement of slide forces disconnector down, disconnecting trigger from sear to assure just one shot per pull of trigger. Right (below) fixed firing pin of the Interdynamics KG-9 pistol.

ward again to repeat the process; all at a fairly high cyclic rate of fire.

The Thompson was one of those designs that fired from an open bolt. When the trigger was pulled, the bolt flew forward to fire the cartridge. As the bolt weighed a pound or so, its effect upon a steady sight picture was at least as disturbing as you might suppose. By positioning a three-way selector lever, the Thompson could be set to fire but a single round at each pull of the trigger, or full-auto, and the third position put it in safe mode, incapable of being fired until the selector was moved to either of the other two positions.

The design of the Thompson puts the axis of the bore rather high above the buttstock so that recoil creates a considerable amount of torque that is purely hellbent on boosting the muzzle upward. That, combined with the inertial

A pre-WWII Thompson submachine gun from the J. Curtis Earl collection. This one's chambered for 9mm Luger rather than the usual .45 ACP, thereby accounting for the curved magazine to accommodate the tapering 9mm cartridge cases. Thompsons of the WWII era had charging handles on RH side.

tumult of that furiously shuttling pound or so of bolt, combines to make it a depressingly to-whom-it-may-concern sort of weapon in the hands of most shooters and bursts of three to five shots are indicated for controlled delivery.

At one time, I would have covered modest wagers at even or favorable odds that no one could fire long bursts with the Thompson and keep them on a target of sensible dimensions, but I've modified my thinking on that. About 1969 I watched Lt. Dan Combs of the Oklahoma Highway Patrol stage a demonstration of gifted shooting and one of his more impressive feats was to come down on a silhouette target from fifteen or twenty yards and put an entire fifty-round drum of ammo into its gizzardly region in one continuous burst. He did it by firing from a slightly exaggerated crouch and had the gun about waist level, without using the sights, apparently guiding it like a garden hose by reference to the burgeoning holes in the cardboard. Nevertheless, it was profoundly impressive to anyone who ever grappled with Colonel Thompson's formidable trench-broom.

The full blowback principle, dampened solely by inertia of the bolt and thrust of the compressed recoil spring, is used with a few of the more powerful cartridges in guns large enough to incorporate a bolt of sufficient heft. In addition to the Thompson — which has been chambered for the 9mm Luger, .38 Colt Super and a few lesser-known cartridges in rare examples — there are several of what I think of as assault pistols in 9mm Luger that use the same

The 9mm Wilkinson Linda isn't compact, but it holds thirty-two rounds, fires from a closed bolt and, when fitted with the 2.5X Bushnell Phantom scope, can deliver remarkably tight groups, fired off a rest.

Curt Earl snapped this shot of me mooning enviously over his immaculately preserved caliber .30 water-cooled Browning — just what I need for the Honda!

approach. Examples include the Wilkinson Linda, the Sterling Mark 6 and the KG-9 or KG-99 from Interdynamics.

In order for a pistol of reasonable weight and dimensions to handle cartridges more potent than the .380 ACP, it becomes necessary to keep the breech mechanism locked up for a brief interval after firing. The usual term for that approach is *delayed blowback*.

Both the Borchardt and Luger employed a remarkably ingenious and effective design to keep the action locked for

a few milliseconds after firing. There is a fairly familiar bit of horseplay that involves coming up behind someone who is standing rather inattentively. Positioned closely behind them, the prankster juts both kneecaps forward to impact gently upon the rear of the victim's knees. Suddenly bent, the victim must tense leg muscles in panicked haste to keep from dropping to the ground.

In essence, that's the principle harnessed by the Luger and the Borchardt before it. Both have a toggle arrangement, resembling the human knee joint, which holds the action immovably close when in battery position. When the cartridge is fired, the entire breech assembly moves rearward for a short distance against resistance of a fairly powerful recoil spring. After a bit of travel, a projecting knob on each side of the toggle joint comes into contact with an inclined plane, deflecting the knob upward and "breaking" the straight alignment of the knee joint, thus permitting the residual thrust upon the fired cartridge case to force the bolt back at a much faster rate to perform the functions of ejecting the spent case and, upon return, gathering up and chambering a fresh round.

The familiar Colt Model 1911[A1] Government Model pistol does the same general thing, but by means of a slightly different approach. A pivoting recoil link is attached to the rear of the barrel, with its second hole secured by the pin of the slide stop. When in battery, the rear of the barrel is forced upward to engage a pair of locking lugs on the upper rear of the barrel with a pair of mating grooves in the top of the slide. Thus, at the instant of firing, the barrel is locked immovably to the slide and the vertical surface within the slide constituting the standing breech keeps the action firmly closed.

Slide is locked back on this Colt Woodsman .22 auto to simulate its appearance after firing. In normal mode, the slide would be driven forward by the recoil spring to chamber the next round from the magazine.

It's not too readily apparent but if you compare the rear of the barrel in both of these photos, you can see how the recoil link, passing over the shaft of the slide stop, raises and lowers the barrel with front/back movement. In so doing, the locking lugs atop the barrel engage and disengage mating grooves in the slide to lock the action.

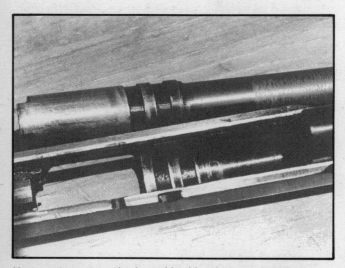

Here you can see the barrel locking lugs and mating grooves of the slide that interact as noted above.

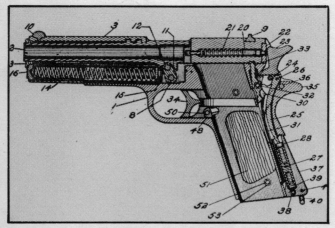

As a further clarification, this cross-sectional sketch shows the recoil link (11) connecting the link pin (12) and the slide stop shaft (8) to pull down rear of barrel.

As the bullet leaves the muzzle, the entire slide assembly is recoiling rearward. The slide stop passes through the receiver, which is not recoiling or, to be precise, it is not recoiling as vigorously as is the slide assembly. Since the recoil link is secured at its lower end by the crosspin of the slide stop, this acts to draw the rear end of the barrel downward, thus disengaging the lugs of the barrel from the mating grooves in the slide. That, in turn, releases the slide to continue its rearward travel until arrested by an accessory recoil buffer and/or immovable parts.

Thus the action of the M1911 is rigidly locked at the instant of firing and for a short time thereafter. When the pressure has eased to moderate levels, it has been transmuted to operation in a manner closely similar to the full blowback designs described earlier. It's the vital instant of hesitation that makes it work, hence the term, delayed blowback.

Although it has not been mentioned to this point, the rearward movement of the slide also performs the further function of recocking the hammer or resetting the striker in designs such as we've been discussing.

A different but ingenious approach to the delayed blowback was employed in the Thomas .45 auto that was made for a time and may be restored to production, according to reports that are circulating about. The Thomas had what any experienced shooter of the M1911 might take to be a grip safety. It was not that, however. When the gun was grasped in the usual firing manner, pressure on the "grip safety" cammed a pair of small lugs upward to engage mating notches, one on each side of the lower rear surface of the slide.

Under the rearward impetus of recoil, at the instant of firing, the push against the locking lever ("grip safety") was amply sufficient to maintain enough upward force on the locking lugs to keep the action locked shut until after the back-push began to fade. At that point, the recoil exceeded the locking effect and the slide came back to eject the empty case and feed a fresh round into the chamber. In the Thomas, however, recoil did not recock the hammer. Every round of the Thomas was fired by a full double-action pull of the trigger which cocked and then released

The Thomas .45 auto operated by means of novel locking lugs that operated when the lever at rear of the grip was pushed forward. All shots required full DA pull.

And here's fun-loving J. Curtis Earl, himself, about to ask, "And what did Santa bring YOU for Christmas?" Earl's address appears in a Chapter 1 caption.

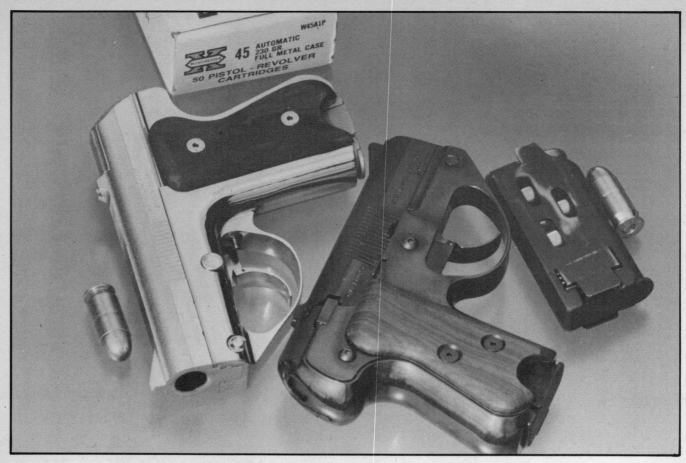

The Semmerling .45 was a manually-operated repeater of exceptionally compact dimensions. In use, after firing, the slide was pushed forward by hand to eject the fired case, then moved rearward to chamber the next round. The photo below shows it with the slide forward. With practice, it could be done one-handed.

the firing mechanism. It was an interesting concept and it functioned remarkably well, once you became accustomed to its modest vagaries and that didn't take long.

The Semmerling was/is [?] an even stranger breed of cat. Not an autoloader by any reasonable definition, it is a manually operated repeater. Like the Thomas, it fires by a long pull of the trigger such as usually termed double-action; a misnomer in this example, as in that of the Thomas, since neither offers the implied single-action mode to which the double-action is the usual counterpart.

After firing a round of .45 ACP ammunition, the slide of the Semmerling was shucked forward to eject the spent case and, upon being moved back into battery, it would chamber a fresh round, provided at least one remained in the detachable box-type magazine and another "double-action" pull of the trigger would set that one off.

The justification of the Semmerling's novel design was that it permitted the firing of the fairly potent .45 ACP cartridge out of a gun whose weight and physical dimensions were not much greater than that of a small revolver such as the Smith & Wesson Chiefs Special chambered for the less-potent .38 Special cartridge.

At the opposite end of the scheme of things, we had the

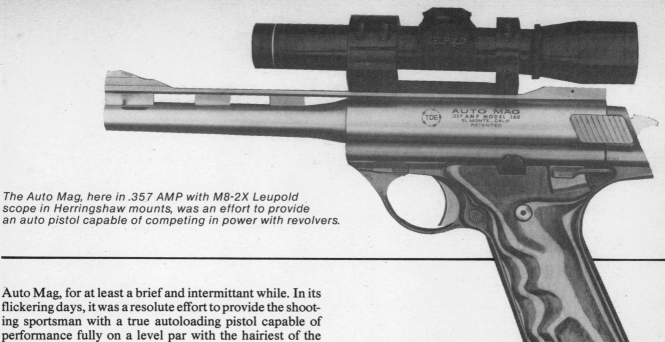

The Auto Mag, here in .357 AMP with M8-2X Leupold scope in Herringshaw mounts, was an effort to provide an auto pistol capable of competing in power with revolvers.

Auto Mag, for at least a brief and intermittant while. In its flickering days, it was a resolute effort to provide the shooting sportsman with a true autoloading pistol capable of performance fully on a level par with the hairiest of the revolvers.

In pure point of fact — digressing for a paragraph — if you wish to deliver the largest possible amount of kinetic energy from a handgun, the single-shot pistol is still King of the Mountain, as exemplified by the Thompson/Center Contender and the Remington Model XP-100, to cite but two examples. The XP-100 is a true bolt-action which can be and has been used in making up pistols to handle extremely large cartridges of the sort usually thought of in terms of bowling over elephants or the unexpected *Tyrannosaurus rex*. The special cachet of the T/C Contender is its omnivorous ability to switch barrels in a minute or so to go from the humble .22 CB cap up, up, and up to something such as the .460 Jurras, or even hairier.

But that's hardly Damon, nor even yet Pythias. We are talking about autoloading pistols in this book so let's get back to them, specifically the Auto Mag.

I take a size 10½ or 11 glove and have thumbs that are disproportionately long, even for such fairly large hands. That is a comment, not a complaint, since it's a welcome asset when it comes to firing handguns. Even so, I have about all I can manage to get my hand around the grip area

In a class all their own, in terms of power, the Thompson/Center Contender single-shot pistols, with their interchangeable barrels for many different cartridges, are capable of delivering well over a foot-ton of muzzle energy.

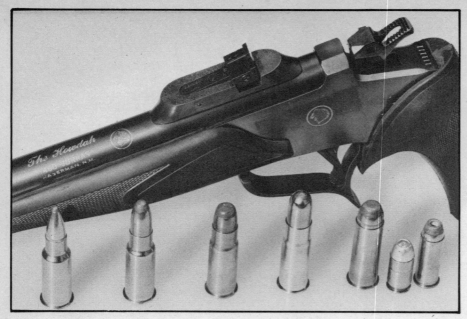

Lee Jurras, Box 680, Washington, IN 47501, built up a few of these mastodon-mangling monsters on the T/C Contender frame, calling them The Howdah. Cases were made out of Nitro-Express brass for bullets from .375 to .50 caliber. This one takes the .458-inch size, fourth from right, with a .45 ACP and .44 magnum looking rather diffident.

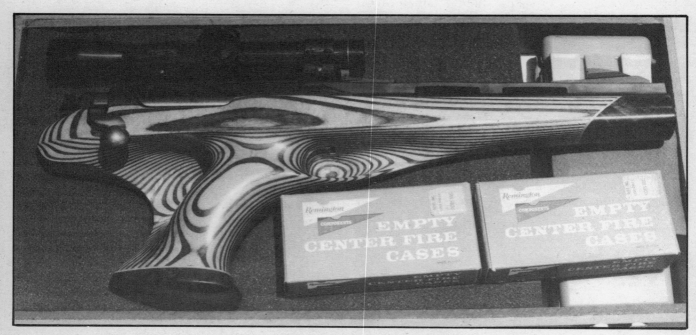

Another novel design, well ahead of its time, was the Remington XP-100 bolt-action, single-shot pistol of the early Sixties. Handling a small but hot center-fire .22 cartridge, the .221 Fire Ball, it was incredibly accurate, but clung to its place in the catalog marginally until the silhouette craze made it popular, at last.

of an Auto Mag and, encountering the Wildey, I feel even more inadequate. The latter has a staggered-column magazine that goes up through the hollow butt so it is not only long — as the handle of the Auto Mag surely is — but fat, as well. In an unlikely word, both are rather steatopygous, meaning beefy about the butt.

The Auto Mag was designed to handle a cartridge called the .44 Auto Mag Pistol or, as more commonly put, the .44 AMP. Later, it was modified to take the .357 AMP, the same cartridge necked down to accept .357-inch diameter bullets instead of the original .430-inch jobs. A further

variant was the .41 Jurras Mag Pistol or .41 JMP. All are of generous overall length, dictating a handle that is sprawly from front to back.

The Auto Mag was engineered to operate at peak pressures that are unusually high for handguns, even for magnum revolvers. Its design incorporates a multi-lugged bolt that rotates into mating locking recesses at the rear of the barrel, much in the manner of the Weatherby magnum rifles. This is provided to enable the Auto Mag to cope nonchalantly with peak pressures that would blow nearly any normal handgun into a burst of lethal shrapnel. It fairly

Another design slanted for the hunter and metallic silhouette competitor is the Wildey gas-operated auto. It handles the .45 Winchester magnum cartridge and, less commonly, the 9mm Win. mag, featuring barrels that can be interchanged. At right, from left, the .44 Auto Mag Pistol, .41 Jurras Mag Pistol and .357 Auto Mag Pistol, all for the Auto Mag.

well succeeded; that's the good news. In so doing, it dictated a price that not enough shooters were willing to disburse, so it went into and back out of production various times during its precarious career; that's the bad news.

As with the Luger or the M1911, the entire slide assembly of the Auto Mag moves rearward for a bit and then its distinctively multi-lugged bolt rotates to disengage from the barrel extension and that continues on through the operating cycle. It's a good design and it usually works nothing but great, yet the requisite level of sophistication sort of priced it out of the marketplace. It is another example of delayed blowback, albeit on a somewhat exalted plane.

There have been examples of blow-forward autoloading pistol designs, although no examples come to mind in current production. I have word of at least one such example presently going through birth-pangs on the drawing board but beyond that, my lips are sealed. If we think of the book at hand — as I do — as BAP-1, it may come to pass that we can discuss the nitty as well as the gritty of that particular gun in BAP-2 or perhaps BAP-3, assuming such works reach the moment of truth with the roaring presses. Until then, we must table the matter for an indeterminate while.

In the prior annals of the art, there have been some really remarkable designs for autoloading pistols. Quite early in

The Auto Mag with action locked open, shows the locking lugs at the front of the rotary bolt. This design feature makes it capable of withstanding a comparative high level of peak pressure.

the present [Twentieth] century, Sir Hugh Gabbett-Fairfax came up with an auto pistol he called the Mars. It was noteworthy for the fact that it delivered velocities and kinetic energies on a level so lavish they were hardly equaled until the appearance of the Auto Mag in the latter Sixties.

When you loosed a round from the Mars, the entire rather massive superstructure came lunging rearward and just stayed there until you released the trigger, whereupon it went lunging back forward to ready itself for the next shot. I have that on purest hearsay or, more precisely, on readsay, if I may coin the term. I've never held a Mars pistol in hand and have no recollection of having ever even seen one except perhaps so long ago that memories are hopelessly vague. I've seen pictures of it and will try to synthesize a sketch of sorts to convey the image of it along.

The gas-operated principle is a good one and it has been adapted quite tellingly for rifles in examples such as the Russian AK-47. The great beauty of gas-operation is its ability to handle loads across an incredibly broad gamut of power levels with suave savoir-faire. From the hottest and hairiest down to the most pallid and poopy, it tends to feed and fire them all.

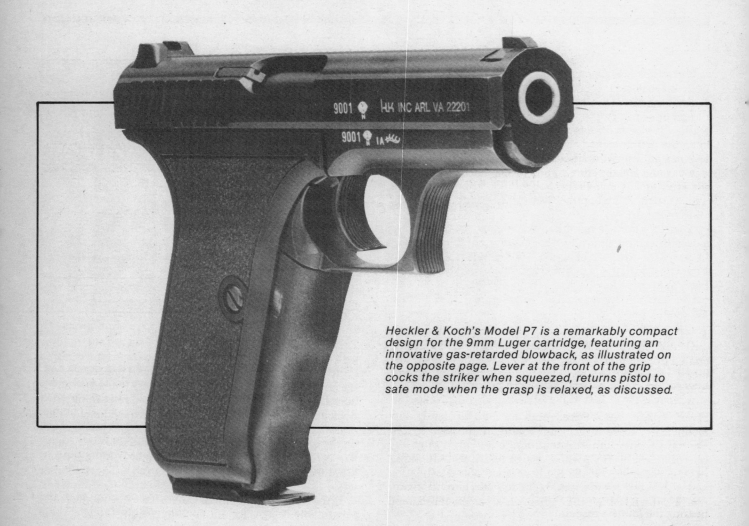

Heckler & Koch's Model P7 is a remarkably compact design for the 9mm Luger cartridge, featuring an innovative gas-retarded blowback, as illustrated on the opposite page. Lever at the front of the grip cocks the striker when squeezed, returns pistol to safe mode when the grasp is relaxed, as discussed.

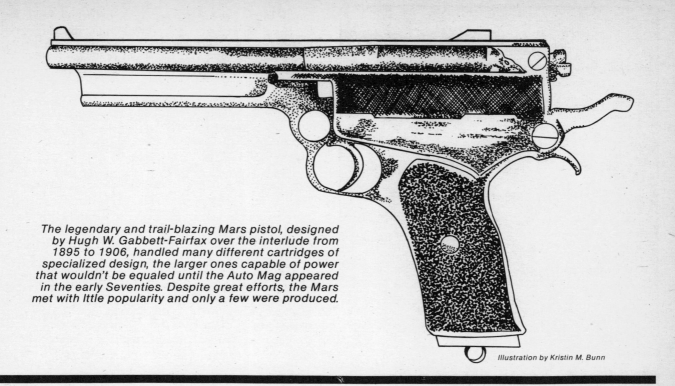

The legendary and trail-blazing Mars pistol, designed by Hugh W. Gabbett-Fairfax over the interlude from 1895 to 1906, handled many different cartridges of specialized design, the larger ones capable of power that wouldn't be equaled until the Auto Mag appeared in the early Seventies. Despite great efforts, the Mars met with little popularity and only a few were produced.

Illustration by Kristin M. Bunn

One of the few gas-operated autoloading pistols prominent on the current scene is the Model P7 from Heckler & Koch. Conceptually, it is something of a mutant since the design does not employ gas pressure to work the action. Rather, it bleeds off a bit of gas pressure and uses that to keep the action locked shut until pressures have more or less normalized with ambient air pressure, whereupon it unlocks and lets the slide go zinging back. In other words, the H&K P7 is a gas-retarded delayed blowback design and, as such, it is a commentworthy variant in the current state of the art.

The H&K P7 is a remarkably compact wee pistol, considerably smaller than any other counterpart in that caliber in current production. There is another auto for the 9mm Luger cartridge that's perhaps a trifle smaller than the P7, but it's still in prototype format from Detonics and little by way of hard particulars on it are to be had at date of writing, although a photo of it is on hand and should be included within a page or so of this mention.

Another novel design feature of the H&K P7 is its cocking system. There is a lever at the forefront of the grip area, pivoted at the lower end. When the P7 is grasped in readiness to fire, it is a natural motion to compress that lever, which cocks the striker. Given a remarkably light and crisp pressure upon the trigger, the striker drops and fires the chambered round. So long as pressure is maintained against the cocking lever, it requires but a release and further pressure on the trigger to discharge the next round, the one after that, and so on.

The test gun shown in the accompanying illustrations arrived with a spare magazine but without any paperwork bearing the faintest resemblance to an operator's manual.

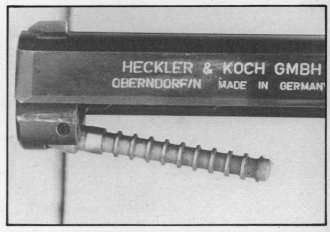

Ten flanges on the action rod of the H&K P7 move in a closely fitted cylinder. On firing, powder gas is diverted into the cylinder, flowing toward the muzzle to hold the action closed until pressure drops.

Coming to primal grips with it, I had the unsanctioned and, as it turned out, incorrect impression it would be necessary to squeeze the cocking lever and pull the trigger for each subsequent shot, somewhat in the manner of the Thomas aforedescribed. Not so! After firing the first shot, holding the cocking lever back and shifting my trigger finger slightly, I sent my second shot downrange to my mild discombooberation.

Other workers with the P7 have discovered and noted it's possible to pull the trigger, milk the cocking lever and get an unexpected shot off via that approach.

Under development by Detonics, this small 9mm pistol was displayed at a recent trade show.

The best feature of the H&K P7 is that, if it leaves your hand, inadvertently or by other means, it makes itself safe on the way to the ground. Under that rationale, it has no safety arrangements in the usual manner of other self-loaders and it probably needs none. In my humble opinion or, as I sometimes abbreviate that for convenience, imho, I think it might be a nice touch if the P7 were supplied with some manner of operators manual that spelled its peculiar talents and vagaries out clearly so the new owner/operator might be spared a few surprises on initial encountering.

The design of the P7 is faintly reminiscent of the Caraville Double-Ace accessory for the Colt M1911 and its conceptual ilk. They differ in that the C D-A put its operating lever at the rear of the modified M1911, pivoting from the top instead of the lower front corner of the grip area. The C D-A was a neat idea, imho, but it never really took the gun world by the throat and shook it savagely, sad as that may be to report.

With the Caraville Double-Ace installed on the M1911 chassis in accord with the clear and concise instructions supplied with it, a round could be chambered and, with the hammer fully forward, it was subject to no more than the usual hazards of the basic M1911 design. That's to say, if the gun were dropped from a height and landed on its muz-

Compressing the cocking lever at the front of the grip of the H&K P7 causes striker to protrude from slide.

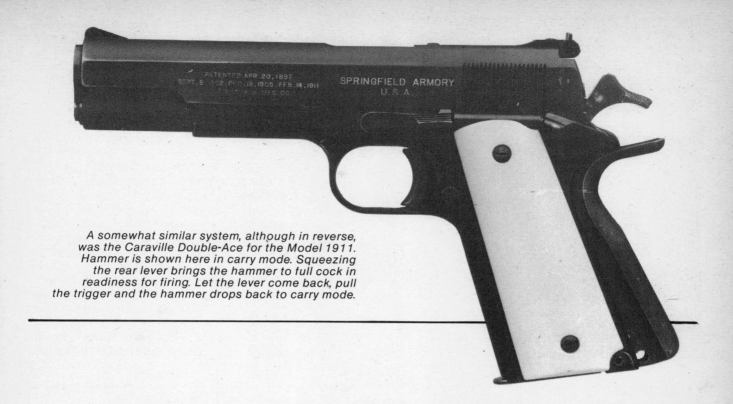

A somewhat similar system, although in reverse, was the Caraville Double-Ace for the Model 1911. Hammer is shown here in carry mode. Squeezing the rear lever brings the hammer to full cock in readiness for firing. Let the lever come back, pull the trigger and the hammer drops back to carry mode.

zle, sufficient inertial force might be applied to the firing pin to make it course forward and set off the chambered round. Apart from that, no sweat at all.

If you hauled the hammer of the C D-A-converted M1911 back to a position slightly farther than the usual half-cock, you put it into carry mode. At that setting, if you squeezed forward on the rear action lever, the hammer moved on back to firing readiness and, if you held it there and pressed the trigger, the gun would fire and continue to do so in autoloading mode until you relaxed pressure on the lever or the magazine ran dry.

To return the Caraville-modified Colt M1911 to the carrying mode just described, you relaxed pressure upon the cocking lever and, once it was fully rearward, you pulled the trigger. In so doing, the hammer dropped back down to carrying mode. Of course, the prudent operator would hook a thumb over the hammer spur to ease it down and, meanwhile, would keep the muzzle pointed in a safe direction so as to minimize any slight risk of mechanical malfunction.

If you're wondering about the source of the unusual designation, "Caraville" stems from the name of its inventor, Clarance A. Raville. Many question the wisdom of carrying the Colt M1911 in what is called "cocked & locked" mode; that is, with a round in the chamber, hammer back and safety up. Comes to that, there are those who disapprove of carrying a live round in the chamber, be the hammer back or forward. The reasoning behind that is — as noted — the risk of setting off the chambered round if the gun is dropped to land muzzle down. Under sufficient stress, inertia of the firing pin can overcome the resistance

Besides the C D-A, this pistol is assembled from unlikely parts such as Springfield slide with S&W rear sight and lightweight receiver by A&R Sales.

L.W. Seecamp conversion turns the M1911-type pistol into a double-action, as on this considerably modified Commander .45 ACP made up by noted knifemaker Bob Loveless as his personal pistol.

Another DA pistol is the Llama Omni, distributed in this country by Stoeger. Available in 9mmP and .45 ACP, this one is the 9mm featuring the novel magazine with partially staggered column, seen on facing page. Note the novel "mule-ear" shape of the hammer.

of the firing pin spring, allowing the pin to move forward and set off the cartridge.

It remained for L.W. Seecamp to design and perfect a conversion for the Colt M1911 to give it the capability of a full double-action trigger for the first shot, shifting to single-action for subsequent shots. Seecamp also adapted the design to the Browning 9mm Hi-Power pistol, but says he only converted two of the Brownings. One is in the mu-seum of the F.N. plant at Herstal, Belgium, and the other belongs to a retired lawman in southern Texas.

There have been and still are several auto pistol designs that incorporate what we might term the double-to-single-action trigger, one of the earliest examples being the Walther models such as the PP, PPK and PPK/S. Others include the Astra A-80, Star Model 28, the Llama Omni, Smith & Wesson's Models 39 and 59, and a small .22 long rifle

Smith & Wesson's Model 539 is a steel-frame version of their basic M39 design. Only a few were made in blued steel before phasing over to the M639, much the identical design, but made of stainless steel.

Astra Model A-80, here in 9mmP, is another recent DA design, likewise available in .45 ACP.

Browning's Model BDA-380, in .380 ACP, is a DA design with 13-round magazine, made by Beretta.

Another DA auto once imported by Browning was the SIG/Sauer in 9mmP, .38 CS and .45 ACP.

made by Iver Johnson along the general lines of the Walther. At various times, Browning has imported similar pistols such as one about the size of the M1911, made for them by SIG/Sauer as well as a smaller .380 made by Beretta.

The Bren Ten, nearing production as this book is being written, is reported to have the capability of being set, converted or programmed to fire its first shot by double-action or to delete that feature at the operator's preference. The Bren Ten was designed under the auspices of Jeff Cooper who is said to have termed the double-action autoloader, "A solution for which no known problem exists." Cooper is a staunch fan of the Colt Model 1911 and, comes to that, so is your present typist of the book at hand.

Heckler & Koch's Model P9S is another double-to-

The Walther Model P5, in 9mmP, is a design that is derived from Walther's wartime P-'38 pistol.

Iver Johnson's Model TP-22 is a DA design that's adapted from the Walther Model TPH, also in DA.

As noted elsewhere, the H&K Model VP 70Z is the chosen pistol of James Bond aka Agent 007 in a recent account of his intrepid deering-do and he considered concealing it to be no problem. Each round is fired by a full DA pull of the trigger and some models are adaptable for a shoulder stock that can be programmed to fire a three-shot, full-auto burst with one pull of the trigger. Jack Wood of H&K is showing me that, right.

single design but the H&K Model VP70Z employs somewhat the approach described for the Thomas .45 ACP in that it self-loads but requires a full double-action pull of the trigger for each shot. That is not the handicap you might suppose it to be. Many shooters find it distracting to make the shift from DA to SA modes without some sacrifice in accuracy with one or the other, or with both. We may have further discussion on that point later in the book, if all goes as presently planned.

The H&K VP70Z was designed originally for use with a highly specialized detachable shoulder stock and, when thus fitted, an arrangement integral to the stock enabled it to fire three-shot bursts at a single pull of the trigger. When the stock is removed, the VP70Z loses that unusual capability.

The usefulness of a shoulder stock on a handgun can be debated, and has been. It is one of those artifacts that requires payment of a $200 transfer fee plus some amount of red tape and folderol to own legally in this country under present law. Some other examples include such things as silencers, full-auto guns, sawed-off shotguns, cut-down rifles and smoothbore pistols. There are certain exceptions as in the instance of duly accredited curios exceeding a specified minimum age.

Presumably — and, again, some view this as debatable — there are aids to a steadier aim with handguns which are not prescribed by law and/or subject to the transfer tax and related formalities. One such device was a sort of shoulder stock with the distinction that its front end was strapped to the wrist of the shooting hand, not attached to the gun itself in any manner, not even touching the gun. Other approaches have attached small braces to the gun that are incapable of being put to the shoulder. Rather than that, a formed piece of rod — usually aluminum — comes back a short distance to fit over or under the shooter's forearm by way of taking some of the wobble out of the wrist joint. Others brace directly from shoulder to gun but are not attached to the gun, being held in place by the shooter's hand.

Exactly why the stocked handgun should be regarded as requiring tighter legal control than a stockless one is none too clearly apparent. If the objection is that it enhances the innate accuracy, even casual reflection shows that to be rather silly. There are handguns that will hold groups less than one inch in spread at one hundred yards and I know of at least two autoloading pistols that have held groups as tight as 1.7 inches or even 1.1 inches at fifty yards — all without benefit of any manner of shoulder stock, merely being fired off a benchrest.

Magazines of auto pistols are another design facet that have been the object of numerous approaches. As a usual thing, most such variants are attempts to increase the number of rounds that can be fired before pausing to replenish the supply. Toward this end, the staggered-column was introduced at least as early as the Browning Hi-Power, designed about 1935. Rather early in the Luger's career, a thirty-two-shot magazine was introduced for it, sometimes termed the ram's-horn or snail magazine.

The physical dimensions of the 9mm Luger cartridge have made it an attractive avenue for such experimentation. Others have attempted to increase the seven-shot capacity of the magazine for the M1911 Colt and one recent engineering triumph resulted in a magazine of the same size that holds the eighth round which, with one in the chamber gives it a total of nine rounds. Other approaches have let the magazine jut downward from the M1911 magazine well for a total capacity of twenty rounds or more, admittedly at the expense of ending up with a pretty unwieldy pistol. I should note the functional reliability of such extended magazines for the .45 auto is considerably open to question. I have one but have used it no more than rarely, having found it quite prone to produce feeding stoppages or jams in the usual terminology for such things.

The 1979 or eleventh annual edition of *Guns Illustrated*, published by DBI Books, carried an article by Darel Magee on collecting actions, specifically actions of autoloading pistols. In it, he listed no fewer than fourteen different categories of actions for autoloading pistols.

Illustration by Kristen M. Bunn

The Model 1900 Browning, in caliber .32, was the first of Browning's auto pistol designs to be made by Fabrique Nationale, of Herstal, Belgium.

Although the 9x19mm Luger/Parabellum usually is regarded as a cartridge for exclusive use in auto pistols, the S&W Model 547 revolver handles it well.

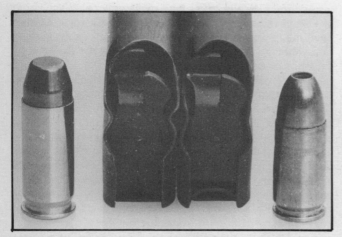

Magazines for the Colt M1911-type auto for the .38 Colt Super, left, and 9mm Luger, right. Note the small filler strip at the rear of the 9mm magazine.

The Webley-Fosbery "automatic Revolver" actually cocked its hammer and rotated its cylinder through action of recoil, but did not eject empty cartridge cases.

Refer to discussion of this incredible revolver in the text below. Note the speedy rascal has his right thumb on the hammer with flame still streaking out of the muzzle...and those flying spent cases!

Most of those, if not all, could be broken down in turn into further subdivisions based upon such considerations as whether or not the cycle left the hammer cocked and so on.

Magee makes a good case for the lure of collecting different design concepts and the interested reader is referred to his excellent (imho) coverage of the erudite topic. For my part, I've never thought of myself as a gun collector but rather as a gun user and accumulator. As a specialized subcategory of the delayed blowback principle, Magee mentions the momentum exchange system of the Remington Model 51 pistol in which the two parts of the breech block interact during the cycle to accomplish the necessary chores. Somewhat the same effect is achieved by the floating chamber of the Colt Service Model Ace, a pistol with the general size and appearance of the M1911, but handling the .22 long rifle cartridge. The separate chamber rides in the rear of the barrel and, on firing, powder gasses drive it back a small fraction of an inch to impinge against a small lug integral to the rear of the barrel. In so doing it amplifies the recoil effect sufficiently to work the slide and give somewhat the subjective impression that one is firing the .45 ACP, albeit at much lower cost per shot.

Magee mentions the automatic revolver, of which there have been a few, the best known of which is probably the Webley-Fosbery. In general appearance, these resemble fairly conventional revolvers except for the distinguishing feature of a zigzag pattern of lines milled about the outer surface of the cylinder. Upon being fired, the barrel and upper portion of the gun, including the cylinder, moves rearward on flanges and mating grooves, cocking the hammer and rotating the cylinder to bring a fresh cartridge beneath the hammer for the next shot. Other examples of what I would prefer to term self-cocking revolvers rather than automatics include the Union, a caliber .32 made in the United States and the Spanish Zulaica which, as Magee notes, is even rarer.

It should be obvious that such revolvers do not eject their spent cases in the manner of the true autoloading pistol. I don't think of myself as a collector, more as a sort of inadvertent accumulator, but among the things I simply can't resist, there are the examples of illustrations showing incredible firearms doing incredible things. Usually such affairs are paintings but one encounters the occasional photo which had to be retouched. A reproduction of a treasured specimen of such preposterous pistolry appears nearby, from the cover of a paperback western. It depicts a sorely beset gunslinger with a bloodstained bandage about his brow. He is wielding what is unmistakably a brace of percussion revolvers — one in each hand — and is blazing away like a sort of quad-fifty on two feet, teeth savagely bared in feral defiance.

One of the guns is being fired and the artist indicates that by a pencil-thin jet of red flame issuing from its muzzle. That is an artistic cliche heavily employed but quite without counterpart in the real world. The muzzle flash from any firearm, if visible at all, is in the shape of a freeform watermelon. What makes that edition of the book eligible for my collection is the presence in midair of several small objects that are about the size and shape of spent .38 Special cases. Presumably, these are hulls being flung from the brace of roaring sixshooters and, considering that the guns shown are of the cap and ball type that do not use cartridge cases in the first place, the entire effect is quite arresting and at least equally hilarious. I can only theorize that the guns are being fed from cartridge belts not readily visible from the viewer's viewpoint, making them a unique design not even familiar to Darel Magee.

The High Standard Model HD, here with 4½-inch barrel, had an exposed hammer and was quite accurate.

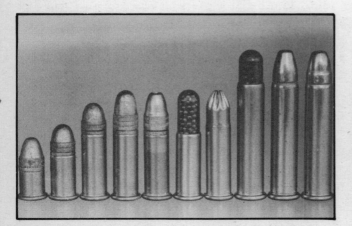

Left: From left, the .22 CB cap in its original shorter case; a .22 short; .22 long; .22 long rifle; .22 long rifle with hollow point bullet; CCI .22 long rifle shot load; crimped-mouth shot load for .22 long rifle; CCI shot load in .22 WMRF; CCI .22 WMRF with hollow point bullet and CCI .22 WMRF with solid bullet.
Right: From left, spent .22 long rifle case; spent CCI Stinger case; loaded CCI Stinger; Remington Yellow Jacket and the now-discontinued Winchester-Western Xpediter; all hyper-velocity in long rifle size.

CHAPTER 3

RIMFIRE AUTOS

Comparatively Easy On Noise And Recoil, Less Expensive To Fire, These Often Deliver Outstanding Accuracy As An Added Bonus

THE RIMFIRE CARTRIDGE was one of the earliest designs and it remains the most widely used in terms of the number of rounds bought and fired in a given year. In an earlier era, there was a vast profusion of rimfire cartridges carrying bullets of impressively large diameter. All of those have faded into limbo except for the .22 size, as exemplified by the .22 CB cap, short, long, long rifle and magnum. Of those, the long rifle is probably undisputed king of the mountain, particularly in the area of auto pistols.

There have been a few autoloaders designed to handle the .22 short, primarily for practice and competition in the Olympic rapid-fire event where rapid recovery and quick acquisition of the next sight picture is of vital essence. I have encountered a few autoloading actions that seem happy with CCI's high-velocity loading of the .22 long but that is purely fortuitous. If there are any autoloading pistols designed for the .22 WMRF/magnum, they have escaped my reasonably intent attention to the present. I'll admit I'm slightly astonished that none have appeared to date.

The CB cap, short and long, all share a bullet in the general weight class of about 29 grains and CCI continues to make a CB cap on a case the same length as that of the long and long rifle. The bullet of the long rifle, typically, weighs about 38 grains in hollow point or 40 grains in the solid version. All but the CB cap and magnum are offered in at least two power levels usually termed standard- and high-velocity or synonymous designations. In addition, since the appearance of the CCI Stinger load in late 1976, there has been a still more energetic long rifle variant called by such names as ultra-velocity, hyper-velocity, and so on.

Most if not all of the UHV (ultra-high velocity) long rifles carry bullets somewhat lighter in weight than the usual 38 or 40 grains and some — notably the Stinger — have cases slightly longer than those of the usual long rifle.

Designing autoloading pistols around the .22 long rifle cartridge is complicated somewhat by the fact that the cartridge came upon the scene some considerable while before much, if any thought, had been devoted to the autoloading concept. When fed up through a straight, single-column magazine of an auto pistol — as most if not all are — the presence of the indispensible rim of the .22 long rifle cartridge cranks in a problem, right from the start. It is larger in diameter at the head end than at the case mouth and bullet. Thus, when you put several of them together under the tension of the magazine follower, the cartridges are progressively less parallel to each other as the number of cartridges increases.

The fact that some really excellent pistols have been

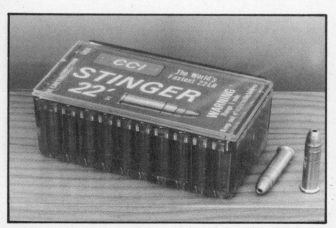 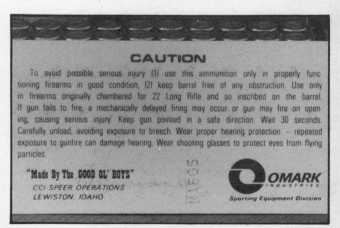

CCI terms their .22 Stinger load, "The World's Fastest .22 LR," and comparative chronographing with it and other striving loads indicates some amount of justification for such claims. The warning notice on the bottom of the Stinger box is reproduced at right. As discussed here, some pistols are not compatible.

Winchester's Xpediter long rifle was termed an xtra high velocity load with its 29-grain hollow point bullet and extra-length case; it's now discontinued. Remington's Yellow Jacket has a truncated cone hollow point bullet, a standard-length long rifle case and the distinctive headstamp visible here in lower right corner.

Several makers, including CCI, offer their .22 loads in plastic boxes of one hundred. Mini Mag, sometimes Mini-Mag, is their designation for high-velocity loads.

designed and developed to handle the .22 long rifle cartridge should, I think, burnish the renown of their designers to a brilliant luster.

Bullets for .22 rimfire cartridges are of the step-heel design, rarely encountered in center-fire cartridges. The .41 Long Colt is one of the few examples of the latter that comes readily to mind and is painfully obsolescent today. The step-heel designation means the bullet diameter is essentially identical to the case diameter and the mouth of the case holds the base of the bullet over a short area that is slightly smaller than the rest of the bullet; the step-heel of the designation.

The .22 long rifle cartridge is employed quite widely in rifle-length barrels as long as twenty-six inches if not more, as well as in handguns with barrels as short as two inches or even a bit less. That does not impose a handicap upon the handgun nearly as severe as you might suppose, particularly handguns with tubes of moderate length. Down the years the .22 long rifle has been produced in a bewildering profusion of different loads, carrying this or that powder in suitable charge weights.

While the myriad loads carry to some extent from one to the next, the general observation can be made that the majority of them hit their fastest velocities out of barrels ranging from about fourteen to perhaps as much as eighteen inches. Put simply, there is just not a lot of room for powder in the .22 LR cartridge and, by the time the bullet is sixteen inches or so up the barrel, the driving charge has achieved *brennschluss* — German, meaning approximately "burnout," a term coined by early rocket researchers of that country.

If you've ever had the woeful experience of getting a bullet from an undercharged cartridge lodged in the bore and had to dislodge it with a ramrod, you're familiar with the large amount of frictional resistance it presents, even in the example of the lowly .22 and its unjacketed bullet. When a bullet is fired, the same stubborn resistance is there and it must be overcome by the pressure of gas from the burning powder. When the powder burns out, the friction begins to gain the upper hand; just that clear-cut and simple. The trick is to position the muzzle right about past the point where the bullet is located at the instant of *brenn-schluss*. Any additional barrel beyond that point represents progressively greater loss of velocity due to frictional resistance.

By way of corroborating that, it can be noted, that in recent times I've been working with a stainless steel bull barrel made up by Arcadia Machine & Tool (AMT) as an add-on accessory for the Ruger .22 auto pistol. The barrel at hand measures about eight inches; unusually long for an auto pistol barrel although AMT has them out to lengths as great as twelve inches. The minimum length for rifle barrels is sixteen inches and the longest barrel usually found available in pistols is the fourteen-inch or Super-14 for the Thompson/Center Contender single-shot pistol. The latter is available in .22 LR chambering, I think. At least, I have one on hand and have been told that the factory plans to add it to the line of available barrels. The CCI Stinger loads comes sizzling out of the Super-14 Contender barrel at 1660 fps. From the eight-inch AMT barrel for the .22 Ruger Standard Auto, it averages about 1400 fps; still nothing in front of which to hold the unwary fingertip!

The interesting aspect of the .22 LR cartridge is that the better auto pistols chambered for it come pretty close to matching the best accuracy of any handgun. The Ruger receiver topped by the AMT barrel and a 2X Weaver

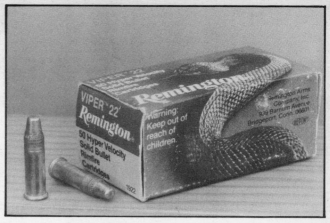

Responding to the popular acceptance of the Yellow Jacket, Remington introduced their Viper, much the same except for a solid bullet, U-headstamp.

Our daughter Bobbie Lynn is trying out my Ruger .22 auto with the eight-inch stainless bull barrel from AMT, with two B-Square Mono-Mounts to hold a 2X Weaver scope. With most loads, she can pot dimes at 25 yards.

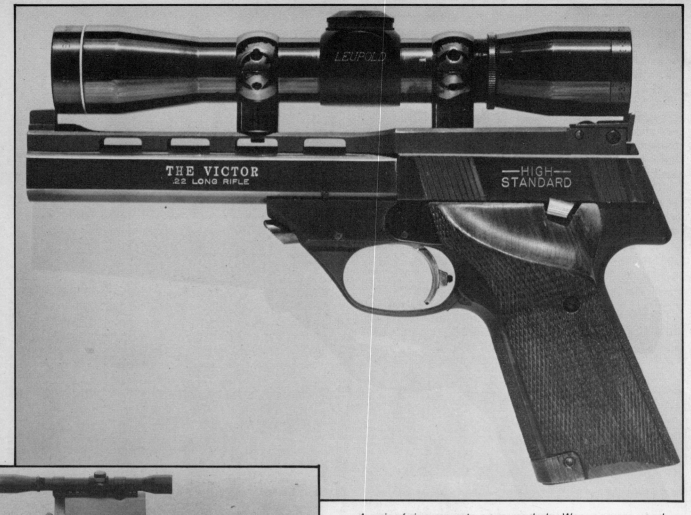

A pair of ring mounts once made by Weaver were used to attach this M8-4X Leupold scope to the 5½-inch High Standard "The Victor." Iron sights remain in place but you'll note it's a close fit. This particular pistol is exceptionally accurate, with iron sights or scope. Its grip angle, weight and general feel are a fairly close duplicate of the M1911 .45 auto pistol. Left, as discussed elsewhere, the Ransom Rest is a superbly accurate system for determining the best load for a given pistol. Here it's mounted on my "Robot Pistolero," with a scope to aim each shot.

scope can and has put five rounds of CCI Stinger into the paper at twenty-five yards so tightly that the entire group can be hidden by a dime. A High Standard Victor with a 4X Leupold scope can and has held hits inside the diameter of a quarter at fifty yards and, in so doing, has set a challenging standard for self-loading pistols.

As noted earlier, .22 rimfire ammunition is available in a variety of makes and the various manufacturers offer a further assortment under the given brand. One of the more

extreme examples of such diversification is the Italian ammomaker, Fiocchi, with their cataloging of something like two dozen different loads in .22 LR.

If you have some means to minimize the effect of the human element in firing, it quickly becomes apparent that any individual .22 rimfire auto has its own clearly apparent prejudices and preferences as to ammunition. As an illustrative example, one particular pistol may group significantly better with what we used to call the Western Xpert than with Remington standard velocity loads. Nowadays, Winchester is de-emphasizing the Western brand name so it may come to be Winchester Xperts in the near future.

Another fully comparable pistol may show at least as sharp a preference for the Remington loads over the Winchesters and either may display further fondness for other makes such as Federal, CCI, or one of the imports. The mere fact that some one single gun doesn't "like" a certain brand/make of ammo should not enjaundice you toward that load because somewhere down the line you're quite apt to encounter some other pistol that dotes upon the same load.

The important consideration is to obtain sample boxes of any and every different .22 LR load you can put hands upon, going on to test them in the gun at hand with all possible impartiality. If you encounter a promising candidate, by all means fire a few more groups with it to establish that its outstanding initial performance was not merely a fluke. Every bullet has to go somewhere and it does not lie outside the law of averages for even a mediocre performer to turn in one unlikely great group.

There are a few combinations of ammunition and pistol that are foredoomed from the very start. One of the more noteworthy is the Walther PP or PPK/S in .22 LR and the CCI Stinger cartridge. The Stinger is designed to provide good results in guns chambered to customary American standards. The Walther is not chambered to those dimensions. As a result, the longer case of the Stinger is quite cer-

A pair of well-aged boxes of Winchester's Super-X and Xpert loads in long rifle. Current trend is to phase out Western brand in favor of Winchester.

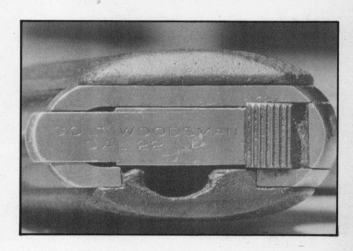

Butt of the 1936 vintage Colt Woodsman shows the magazine catch and rollmarking on magazine base.

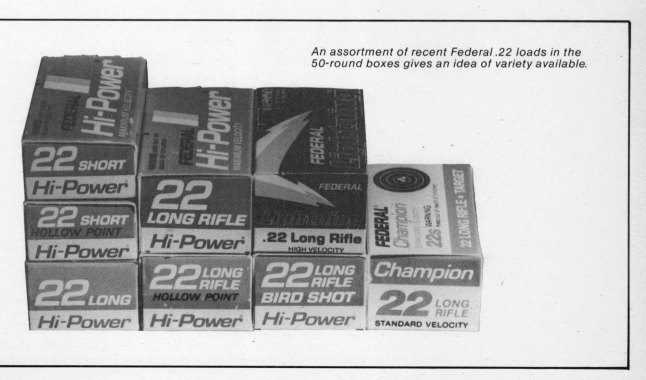

An assortment of recent Federal .22 loads in the 50-round boxes gives an idea of variety available.

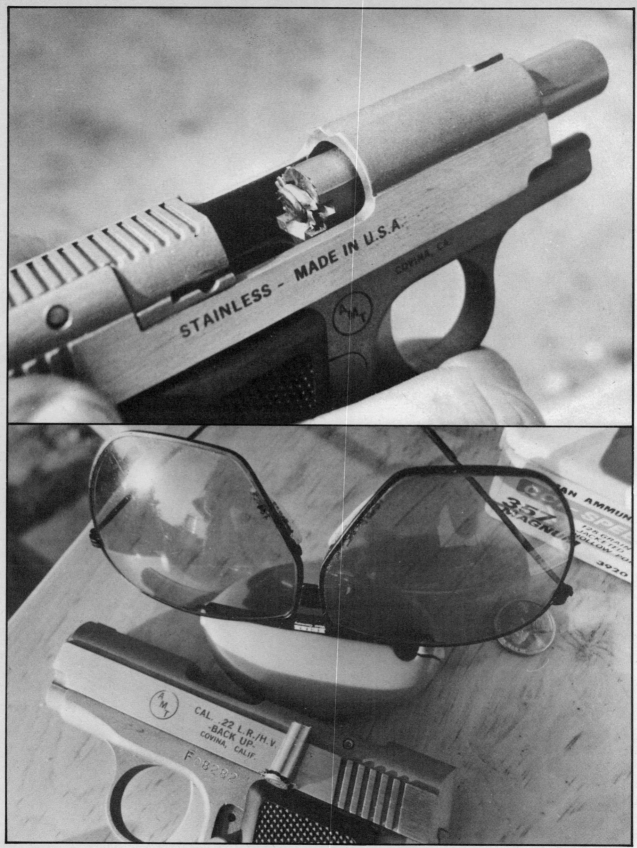

Not all auto pistols have chambers that are compatible with the extra-length cases such as the CCI Stinger. The AMT .22 Back Up above, Walthers and the Iver Johnson of the facing page are among those that should not be fired with such cartridges. Shooting glasses should be worn as an inflexible habit, whenever shooting.

tain to generate pressures beyond safe levels and it will usually rupture the case head. If that happens, you had better be wearing a good pair of shooting glasses.

There are other auto pistols that are highly incompatible with the CCI Stinger load and two other examples include the AMT .22 LR Back Up and the Iver Johnson TP-22. There may be others, but I cite those two on a basis of personal experience.

A few years ago, Winchester introduced an ultra-velocity .22 LR load they called the Xpediter, but that has been discontinued. Like the Stinger, its case was a bit longer than customary and the same general strictures applied to it.

Remington introduced first the Yellow Jacket, with a hollow point bullet, followed by the Viper with a solid bullet, both in the hyper-velocity category. These utilize a case of standard .22 LR length and generally seem to perform without the problems encountered when using Stingers or the discontinued Xpediters. I can report that both the Yellow Jacket and Viper feed quite nicely through the little Iver Johnson TP-22 and not only that but they grouped quite gratifyingly in the test gun I had on brief loan.

The AMT .22 LR Back Up can be a little confusing. The instruction sheet quite clearly specifies high-velocity ammunition for use in it, but does not go on to forbid the use of ultra-velocity, hyper-velocity or comparable terms. Most versions of standard-velocity .22 LRs will not function reliably in the little AMT and Stingers will rupture case heads in it. When asked, plant personnel say they do not want you to use Stingers, Yellow Jackets, Vipers or comparable .22 LR loads in the Back Up.

Federal, at the moment of typing this, has a new ultra-hot .22 LR load they call the Spitfire and, to present date, I've not put hands upon samples of it. If I can rectify that discrepancy before the last of the book is down, I'll try to inlay some comments on it; perhaps in the final chapter, which I usually reserve for such last-minute insertions.

A minor confusion of writing on this particular topic is that ammunition manufacturers are considerably prone to come up with some new item in a given year and then quietly drop it from their listing as years march forward, particularly if it does not sell at gratifying levels. Thus, the well-meaning gunscribe may wind up with samples on the back shelf that no longer have any discernible relationship to current state of the art. Yes, no one ever said it was supposed to be simple.

Iver Johnson's Model TP-22 seems to handle the Yellow Jacket loads quite nicely, as in this 5-shot group at twenty meters; one of its better groups.

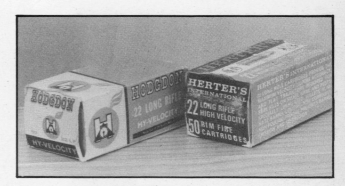

Many firms have marketed rimfire ammo over the years, making it a promising field for collectors.

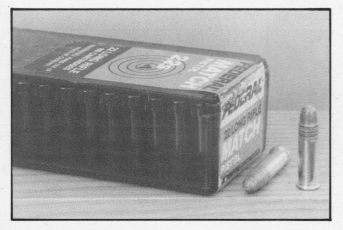

Federal's .22 long rifle Match load is packed in the 100-round plastic boxes and is exceptionally accurate.

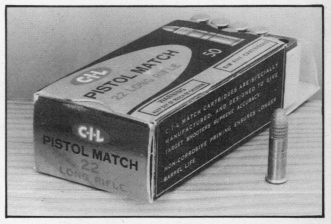

Here's a box of that Canadian-made C-I-L Pistol Match; a good performer in pistols and revolvers.

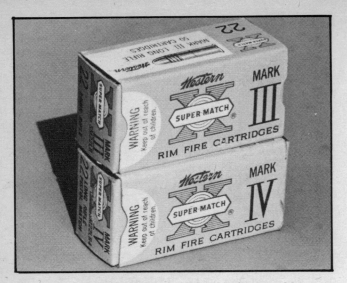

A few years ago, Winchester used to market two .22 long rifle match loads: the Mark III for rifles and the Mark IV for pistols and revolvers, as discussed here.

I mention that by way of providing prior explanation of minor contretemps wherein I may discuss and perhaps illustrate loadings of .22 LR ammo that cannot be found upon the display shelves of your friendly local gun dealer. My sole defense for this is that some of the obsolete stuff may still repose upon the shelves of shooters around the country and world, perhaps even on *your* shelf.

"We've mentioned that manufacturers like to turn out at least two, perhaps three levels of ammunition: standard-velocity, high-velocity and perhaps goshawful-velocity.

By way of injecting a little badly-needed charisma into the standard-velocity loadings, they are quite prone to designate them as target or match loadings. That's not hard to understand. Assuming they'll not blow an elephant's head clean off with a single twitch of the trigger, they need something else going for them and pin-point, tackdriving accuracy is the obvious second choice.

Since the .22 LR cartridge gets fired quite copiously in rifles as well as in handguns, it's only natural the manufacturers produce loads labeled for use in both barrel lengths and many of them do or have down the years. The clear implication is that Rifle Match loads have a slightly slower-burning powder that's better suited to longer barrels and vice, of course, versa for the Pistol Match loads.

I used the term, "American ammunition," and winced as I typed it because I'm keenly aware that our good neighbours to the north, up in Canada, take brisant umbrage to such arrant chauvinisms. Properly, it should be North American and I'm prone to employ a coined word — Usanian — to distinguish products of the forty-eight contiguous states beneath the fifty-starred banner.

There is at least one major ammomaker in Canada, C-I-L Dominion, headquartering out of Montreal, P.Q., and turning out a lot of good foom-fodder. I have no slightest intent nor desire to slight their efforts. I've not been in close touch with C-I-L in recent years, but back in the late Sixties they sent me a few test samples of their products, including some Pistol Match .22 LR and it certainly does perform uncommonly well in any number of handguns of that chambering in which I've tried it.

At one time the maker then known as Winchester-Western used to turn out Match Loads designated as Mark III for rifles and Mark IV for pistols. They may still do so; it's difficult to keep up with the status of the immediate quo on such matters. More recently, Remington or Remington-Peters produced Rifle Match and Pistol Match .22 LRs and, again, they may still do so.

Up along the western banks of the Snake River, in Lewiston, Idaho, amid the spoiling-cabbage reek of the nearby sulfite paper mills, the Good Ol' Boys [and at least equally Good Ol' Gals] of Omark/CCI-Speer continue to churn forth their uncommonly adequate rimfire ammo and, to the best of my knowledge, they've never yet discriminated between rifle-length and pistol-length barrels. Their usual standard-velocity stuff is designated Mini-Group, as contrasted to Mini-Mag for the high-velocity version. A further variant is labeled Green Tag and that appears to be a standard-velocity load that benefits from uncommonly intent attention to all the quality-control niceties and refinements.

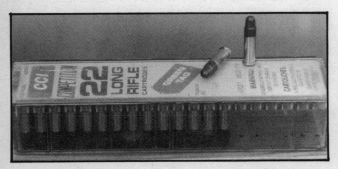

CCI's Green Tag load makes no distinction as to the barrel length, but performs exceptionally well in all. A newer Winchester load for match use is their Super Match Gold, for both rifles and handguns.

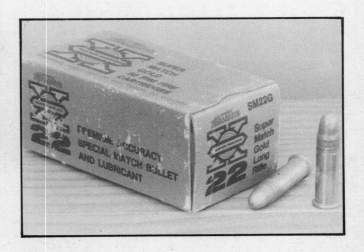

For reasons discussed here, I'm extremely partial to the pre-WWII Sport Model Colt "The Woodsman."

Rollmarked designation on the receiver was adopted about 1927. For its first 12 years, it was the .22 Target Model. Other changes were made later.

This I can say in calm confidence: If the springs and working parts of an auto pistol can compat and cohabit with standard-velocity ammo, the CCI Green Tag load is apt to perform quite well out of it. My High Standard Victor with the 4X Leupold scope atop it is dotingly partial to the CCI Green Tag load, as but one example. I've yet to find any other .22 LR cartridge that performs better out of it, although I keep trying, wistful would-be perfectionist that I assuredly am.

To this point, the discussion has focused upon both the auto pistols and, to a large extent, upon the ammunition they handle with greater or lesser competence. Let us now discuss a few salient examples of autoloading pistols for the .22 LR cartridge, with specific details of their assets and liabilities.

THE COLT WOODSMAN

Auto pistols come in a vast variety of shapes, weights and sizes and their adorability and capability varies to at least equal degrees. Everyone is entitled to a personal opinion and it is my own tautly-clenched opinion that the Colt Woodsman represents the outermost perfection and refinement of an auto pistol ideally designed and suited to handle the .22 LR cartridge. I'll go one stubbornly-prejudiced step beyond that and claim that the pre-WWII Sport Model Colt Woodsman with its 4½-inch barrel represents the high-water mark of achievement in that particular field to the present date. You may not agree with that and, if so, be my guest, Edgar!

Colt's The Woodsman, often termed the Colt Woodsman, made its debut in 1915 and, originally, it was designated the caliber .22 Target Model. About March of 1927/ serial number 54000 — commas are omitted in the serial numbers as they appear on the gun — The Woodsman became the adopted term, being roll-marked on the LH side of the frame, about over the chamber area.

Initially, the curvature of the Woodsman trigger was considerably less pronounced. At first, the more curvaceous triggers that came to be standard on later production were furnished as custom factory options, eventually being adopted for routine production. The curvier triggers

A pre-1927 with long barrel, no Woodsman rollmark and the straighter trigger of the original design.

Another pre-1927 from the J. Curtis Earl collection, fitted with a Maxim silencer: a bit cumbersome, but easy on the ears. Compare barrel taper to gun at left.

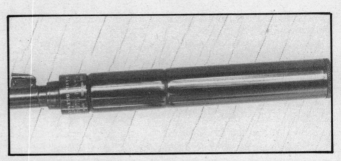

Above, a closer look at the Maxim silencer, which held a large number of small circular baffles to let the powder gas pressure diminish slowly. Left, the curvaceous trigger that was adopted in the early Thirties, having first been available as an option.

look, feel and fire better. James E. Serven's excellent and exhaustive work titled *Colt Firearms* is one of my primary reference sources for historical data on the auto pistols of that make and grateful credit is hereby freely given.

On page 291, Serven shows a photo of both the 6½-inch and the later 4½-inch barreled versions of The Woodsman, the latter frequently designated as the Sport Model and the longer barrel as the Target Model. Curiously enough, the Sport Model shown has the original, less-curved trigger; the only example of that combination I've ever seen, even on paper.

The Sport Model Woodsman is reported by Serven — among other authorities — to have been introduced in 1933, eighteen years after the appearance of the version with the longer barrel. It is my undocumented impression that the extra-curved trigger predated 1933. One theory is that the mysterious straight-triggered Sport Model in the Serven book is a rebarreled customization of an older frame.

On the same page is a third photo of a Woodsman with an extra-length barrel, an adjustable aperture or peep rear sight mounted on an extension tang, and a shoulder stock; the latter presumably detachable. Curiously enough, that one has the later, extra-curved trigger. Only a small number of such guns were made up and the Firearms Act of 1934 would have brought them under the requirement of licensing and payment of a $200 transfer fee, the same as machine guns, silencers, sawed-off shotguns and the like. Quite effectively, that sounded the doom tocsin for the long-barreled, stocked version and I note it all here, primarily in an effort to pinpoint the date of the change in trigger profile. Without sending to the corner druggist for a sack of radiocarbon, it appears to be about simultaneous with the introduction of the Sport Model; call it *circa* 1930 or so.

Just as the Model 1896 Mauser is known by such terms as the broomhandle or spikenose, the pre-WWII Woodsman in its Target and Sport Models, sometimes is referred to as the slope-butt Woodsman.

Those who've never had a hand-shaking acquaintance with the slope-butts may wonder at the intensity and fervor of my enthusiasm for the breed. Let me endeavor to explain and clarify that point.

Unique among all .22 LR auto pistols I've encountered to the present, the Colt Woodsman — and in specific particular, the pre-WWII Sport Model Colt Woodsman —

Rear sight of the Sport Model is adjustable for right/left compensation. Screw slot was burred that way by the previous owner. Knurled button is for takedown.

LH side of barrel is emblazoned with patent dates.

strikes me as having been designed around the cartridge it handles. It is not too small, nor is it too large; it is just right. Neither too heavy nor too light, but just right. The handle area may appear skimpy in comparison to contemporaries such as the High Standard or Ruger. Holding and firing The Woodsman cancels that false impression. I have rather large hands, with abnormally long thumbs — a great boon if you enjoy firing handguns — and the Sport Model fits either the right or left to total perfection. It is equally comfortable in smaller hands, or so I've been told.

I've encountered .22 LR auto pistols that were capable of better accuracy than I've been able to get from The Woodsman. High Standard's The Victor is a salient example of such designs. That presumes you've ample leisure to bed the gun into your hand with great care, sock it into a sandbag and take exquisite pains with sight picture and trigger squeeze. We'll get back to The Victor in a bit.

The great virtue of The Woodsman is that you can grab hold of its dainty butt, any old panicky which-way, stab its slender muzzle toward a selected small area, press its silky trigger through release and see the small hole turn up incredibly near the chosen point. More twitches result in more holes — up to eleven on a single loading — none of which will be much off the mark if you give it a reasonable effort.

The Guns Of August were well past the overture to WWI when the first Colt caliber .22 Target Model went from the gifted pen of John Moses Browning to the production line under the Onion Dome of the Colt works at Hartford, Connecticut, and the slope-butt reigned fairly well supreme through the lengthy but bygone interlude that terminated with the attack on Pearl Harbor; Sunday, 7 December 1941, you may recall. In 1938, near the end of that Halcyon era, it was joined by a modification called the Match Target Woodsman.

The Match Target retained the basic slope-butt frame in the grip area, but the wooden stocks usually jutted downward for added support, well beyond the point of hand contact. The added wood served little practical purpose, but it looked impressive and looks help to sell guns and build

A post-WWII Colt Match Target, vintage about 1969. None of the small Colt .22 autos are made at present.

volume. A few of the Match Targets carried stocks identical to the older version and probably grouped just about as well, perhaps even better.

Some lengthy while after V-J Day — the date that heralded the end of WWII — Colt came back with their post-war version of The Woodsman. In all, several variants were offered, along with models designated as the Challenger and the Huntsman, as well as post-war Match Targets in a choice of 6- and 4½-inch barrels.

The pre-WWII Woodsman design had carried the magazine release at the rear of the butt, but that was relocated to the frame behind the trigger guard in most if not all of the post-war versions, by way of matching the location of the same control on the Model 1911-pattern Colt Government Model pistols with which so many would-be buyers had become familiar in the then-recent global conflict.

Years came, years went and Colt finally dropped all of their .22 LR auto pistols, eventually coming back with their Service Ace — a dimensional lookalike to the Model

1911 Government Model — which remains the only .22 LR auto in that maker's line to the immediate date of writing. We will be discussing that design shortly, but before we lose touch with the slope-butts, let us set down the production in terms of serial numbers and years of production, as given in several sources including the February 1980 issue of *Gun World* Magazine, from which the following is quoted:

1915	1	1930	69000
1916	900	1931	77500
1917	3900	1932	84000
1918	5000	1933	85000
1919	6500	1934	88000
1920	12000	1935	93000
1921	23000	1936	98000
1922	27500	1937	107000
1923	33000	1938	123000
1924	37900	1939	126000
1925	42000	1940	135000
1926	45200	1941	144000
1927	51000	1942	156000
1928	57000	1943	157000
1929	65000		

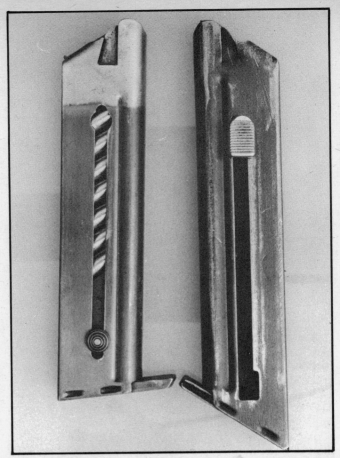

Magazine of the pre-WWII Woodsman at left, with the magazine from post-WWII gun appearing at left, here.

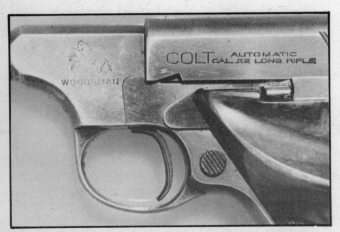

A post-WWII Woodsman had a dogleg trigger with the magazine release button behind it, in this manner.

The Sport Model at my elbow as I type this is number 99446, from fairly early in 1936, per the listing above. Likewise on hand is a copy of the No. 26 Stoeger Catalog from about the same point in time. On page 63, it displays

both the Target Model and Sport Model, both at a retail price of $32, with the caliber .25 ACP Pocket Model at $17 and the .32/.380 ACP Pocket Model at $20. If those prices boggle your credulity to the snapping point, I'd like to note that — having lived through that era at the dragging pace of 86,400 seconds *per diem* thirty-two bucks represented a vast sum of hard cash — for many wage-earners, it was equal to about one month's income. With that in mind, the sales volume for the highly engaging small pistols tend to fall into more realistic perspective, doesn't it?

The ammunition recommended for the early Woodsman pistols, as Serven notes, was "Lesmok or semi-smokeless, lubricated cartridges only." At serial number 83790 — late in 1931 — a design change added a mainspring housing that was modified to handle high-velocity .22 LR cartridges. A small area where the grip meets the web of the hand was distinctively changed to reflect the modification. Originally checked in a crosshatch pattern, the high-speed housings carried a series of horizontal lines to mark their ability to handle hot ammo.

The No. 26 Stoeger Catalog, on the same page, displays

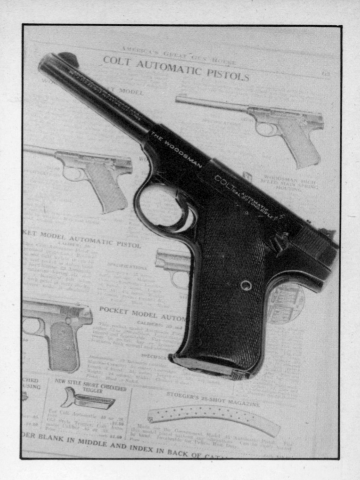

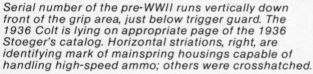

Serial number of the pre-WWII runs vertically down front of the grip area, just below trigger guard. The 1936 Colt is lying on appropriate page of the 1936 Stoeger's catalog. Horizontal striations, right, are identifying mark of mainspring housings capable of handling high-speed ammo; others were crosshatched.

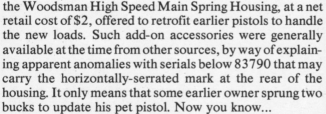

the Woodsman High Speed Main Spring Housing, at a net retail cost of $2, offered to retrofit earlier pistols to handle the new loads. Such add-on accessories were generally available at the time from other sources, by way of explaining apparent anomalies with serials below 83790 that may carry the horizontally-serrated mark at the rear of the housing. It only means that some earlier owner sprung two bucks to update his pet pistol. Now you know...

You may wonder if a pistol of that vintage will handle the hyper-velocity loads and I can only note that mine seems quite happy with them. I've never had any problems when firing CCI Stingers in it and the load it purely dotes upon is the Remington Yellow Jacket, which averages 1195 fps out of its 4½-inch barrel, meanwhile delivering excellent accuracy and impressive expansion in suitable target media.

My holster for the High Standard Victor was adapted by Safariland from one originally made for an Auto Mag, although it's slightly smaller and lighter.

HIGH STANDARD

High Standard Sporting Firearms (31 Prestige Park Circle, East Hartford, CT 06108) started out in New Haven, Connecticut, as a toolmaking firm manufacturing drills for gun barrels. That was in 1926 and, in 1932, they acquired Hartford Arms and Equipment Company. The latter firm had produced various pistols such as single-shots, repeaters and autoloaders. Not surprisingly, the first High Standard carried considerable resemblance to the Hartford but it was not long before a wide variety of dif-

ferent modifications were produced. All worked on the original straight blowback principle and the different models were designated alphabetically. The Model C fired .22 shorts. Many had a concealed hammer, similar to that of The Woodsman, others had an exposed hammer, as noted by inclusion of an H in the model designation.

Unlike many sporting handguns, High Standard continued to produce a .22 LR auto pistol during WWII. Used in military training, it was designated the Model H-D Military and it remained in production until 1951. At some point shortly before that, I managed to purchase a Model H-D with a heavy barrel measuring about 4½ inches. They sold for about $38 in those days and, generally speaking, it was quite satisfactory. Considerably bigger and heavier than The Woodsman, its rear sight was adjustable in elevation by means of a small ratchet arrangement and there were several sharp edges about that immediate area, making it a formidable knuckle-barker when packed in a holster on the right hip.

I kept the H-D until early in 1966, selling it for $35 to raise funds to wetback it from Wisconsin to California: A depreciation of three dollars in something like fifteen years is not bad. I purchased The Victor in 1971, discovering High Standard had made truly giant strides in the space of a couple of decades. Slightly larger and heavier than a Model 1911A1 Colt, the angle of its handle is the same as the Colt and it has much the same feel and balance. Terming its trigger pull exquisite hardly does it justice. Both front and fully-adjustable rear sight ride on a wide ventilated rib, all solidly anchored to the top of the barrel. That's in contrast to the usual procedure of putting the rear sight on the upper rear of the slide, and The Victor's approach keeps both sights and the barrel in Gibraltar-

When scoped, The Victor isn't overly compatible with holsters and I usually pack it about in a case or pistol rug-type carrier with supply of ammo.

A fairly recent photo of William Batterman Ruger, Sr., quite probably the outstanding designer and producer of firearms in the latter half of the Twentieth Century, in both quality and quantity.

solid alignment at all times. Beyond a doubt, that is a major contribution to the really phenomenal accuracy The Victor displays.

Officially designated the Model 107 Military, this one has a 5½-inch barrel which is removable in case you have barrels of other lengths and wish to swap them back and forth. Its hammer is concealed, its trigger gold-plated, with an adjustable trigger-stop to arrest rearward movement after release. The stocks are checkered walnut, with a thumb rest for the northpaw shooter. It can be fired from the left hand with no more than moderate discomfort.

Several years ago, the Weaver scope people came up

A well-worn pre-1951 Ruger .22 belonging to one of my neighbors. Note the emblem is on the LH stock with red hawk on a once-silver background.

Here's my bull barrel Mark I .22 Ruger with its iron sights and Safariland holster; a compact and highly competent pistol of good accuracy, vintage 1970.

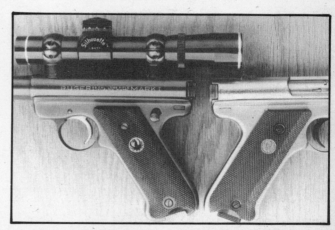

At some unrecorded point, the medallion was shifted from the LH to RH stock. Emblems went to black with the death of Alexander Sturm in 1951. Likewise, the emblem became silver against a black background. Pistol at right is from early Eighties, a special run of 5000 in stainless steel with return of the red bird.

with some neat little scope bases that could be mounted by drilling and tapping a single hole. I got a couple sets of those before they were dropped from the Weaver line and a friendly local gunsmith — since having gone into other activities — installed one set on The Victor and the other on a bull-barreled Mark I Ruger .22 auto. It was an extremely snug fit, but The Victor accepted a Leupold M8-4X extended eye relief scope within the space between front and rear sights.

If desired, it's a quick and simple operation to remove the scope and mounts, restoring The Victor to iron-sighted status or reinstalling the scope, whichever you prefer. Scoping the Mark I Ruger wasn't nearly as readily reversible since it involved cutting a dovetail in the rear mount base and installing it in place of the rear sight.

At present, High Standard continues to market several .22 autos, including The Victor with 5½-inch barrel an even flossier version termed the X Series Custom 10-X priced about $300 above The Victor's substantial $400+ figure. The lowest-priced HS appears to be the Sport King. Even that is nearly $300 and yes, that does tend to make me warmly appreciative of The Victor I have!

RUGER

The rise of Sturm, Ruger & Company into the ranks of firearms giants has been about as meteoric — perhaps skyrocketish is more aptly descriptive — as any other example that comes to mind readily; considerably more so than most. Much of their success pivoted upon pioneering in new production techniques. Traditionally, the receiver of a pistol has been milled from steel forgings or from raw steel stock and many still are. Conversely, the Standard Model Ruger .22 auto has a receiver that is made by welding a pair of steel stampings together. To be technically precise, it would be better to term that the frame because the receiver proper is a length of steel tubing which bears the serial number and it is attached quite rigidly to the barrel.

To the pistol-hungry gun world of 1949, the Ruger Standard Model was purely manna from heaven, and the price

The stainless pistols were shipped in the same "salt cod" boxes used for original production in 1949 era.

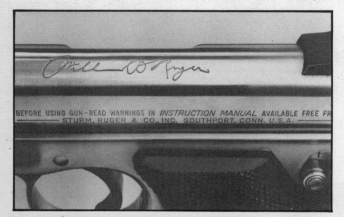

Each of the 5000 stainless steel .22 Rugers bears the signature of William B. Ruger on the receiver.

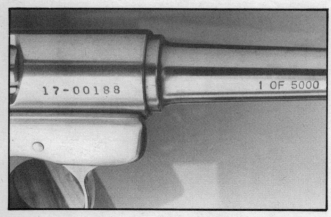

Serial numbers carry the 17-prefix and, as noted, the medallion is on the RH stock with the emblem in silver against a red enamel background. Right, the Rolls-Royce marque went from red to black in 1933, presumably in mourning for Sir Henry Royce. This early post-'33 is Fred T. Huntington's pride.

was right. Its appearance was by no means sharply unlike that of the German Luger — a gun that packs lots of charismatic clout, for reasons that have not always been clearly apparent to me — and even the names sounded quite familiar. The cute little pistols moved off the dealers' shelves with the notable alacrity of free beer at a German picnic. As Colt did not resume making their single-action until about 1956, and with the new medium of television pumping westerns out, SA revolvers were in urgent demand and old Colts brought fancy prices.

So, Bill Ruger came up with a neat little single-action revolver in .22 LR and, like the Standard Model auto, it captured the hearts and nearby giblets of the nation's handgun aficionados. Combine superb designing with diabolically efficient production to keep the cost down without a corresponding sag in quality — that's really all there is to it.

In an earlier work such as this, I commented upon the change from the red eagle — or is it a red hawk? — of the trademark to commemorate the untimely passing of Alexander Sturm in 1951. I likened it to the shift from red to black for the marque of the Rolls-Royce, but got the fine details sadly garbled. No one else noticed, but a crusty character in Tucson, Arizona, nearly bought the farm from advanced apoplexy. Permit me to set the records straight.

"Frederick Henry Royce made his first car in 1903 and ran the company with an iron hand until his death three decades later. His partnership with C.S. Rolls began in

1904 and ended with Rolls' death in an airplane accident in 1910. Originally, the car was called a Royce-Rolls and probably should have been always, but Rolls wanted to see his name first and he was putting up the money. [...] In 1933, the Rolls-Royce label was changed from red to black, presumably in mourning for Sir Henry Royce." The quotation is from an article by the late Ken W. Purdy, appearing in *Playboy* for May 1969.

That the Ruger .22 auto asked no favors as to intrinsic capability is more than amply evidenced by the fact that Jimmy Clark, the custom pistolsmith from Shreveport, Louisiana, gave his gifted ministrations to some that went on to terrorize the quaking daylights out of the smallbore competition circuits. At about that time, I came by one of the out-of-the-box Mark I jobs, with a 6½-inch barrel and used it to wreak moderate amounts of havoc upon parochial pistoleering circuits. I could tip some newspaper cuttings of that era, but modesty forbids. Suffice to say, the better Rugers were outrageously capable mechanisms, even without the magic Clark touch. Given that, they tended to boggle credulity.

My brother Ralph once owned a Mark I Ruger with a short but tapered barrel. Not many of those were made. As I still have a photo of it, I'll drop it in among the illustrations but I must note he no longer has it. I ran the photo earlier and some intrepid Ruger collector obtained his address from me and managed to ply him with blandishments sufficient to persuade him to part with it. Since that

James E. Clark, pistolsmith extraordinaire, of Rt. 2, Box 22A, Keithville, LA 71047, can turn the .22 Ruger into a tack-driving terrorizer of matches.

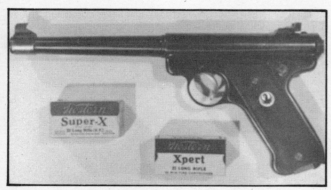

This is the long-barrel Mark I Ruger with which I terrorized a few matches in distant days, as noted. And here is the Mark I with shorter, tapered barrel once owned by my brother Ralph, but no longer, alas.

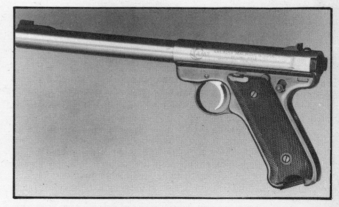

Arcadia Machine & Tool Co. (AMT), 536 N. Vincent Ave., Covina, CA 91722, offers a variety of tapered and bull barrels in stainless steel for Ruger .22 auto. The change involves a new serial number, as noted.

AMT barrel/receiver No. G00007 on Ruger Mark II receiver with a 2X Weaver scope in B-Square mounts is capable of putting five rounds of CCI Stinger into a 25-yard group that can be fully hidden with a dime, at average velocity of 1400 fps. For scale, AMT's Long Slide Hardballer and .22 LR Back Up are also shown.

Bob Loveless, man and bowie — well, not really. Here's the king of custom cutlers in a drowsy Buddha pose, with the Field Gun he sometimes modifies from the S&W Model 41; the ultimate handy little belt-gun.

Two views of the steel frame version of Stoeger's .22 LR Luger pistol, introduced in the early Eighties, with the toggle up and down. This is about the only Luger that actually carries the name, a Stoeger trademark.

time, other Ruger-stackers have assured me, given the details of the transaction, that Ralph let it go too cheaply. I merely note all this in hopes of saving you and me a bit of postal outlay.

SMITH & WESSON

Smith & Wesson brought forth a .22 LR auto pistol in 1941, designating it the Model 41, fittingly enough. That's one I've never owned and I can't even recall having ever fired one. Custom knifemaker Bob Loveless (Box 7836, Riverside, CA 92503) can turn a Model 41 Smith into what he calls the Loveless Field Gun, just the sweetest and neatest little gizmo ever to drive your salivary glands berserk. Later, a deflossed Model 46 version was introduced but that has been dropped. The Model 41 continues in production, with a 7⅜-inch barrel.

Here's the earlier Stoeger Luger .22 with aluminum alloy frame and fully-adjustable rear sight, dropped from production when the steel frame was introduced. Note the Stoeger Double Eagle trademark on the top.

STOEGER/LUGER

Stoeger Industries (55 Ruta Court, S. Hackensack, NJ 07606) has controlled Luger as a trade name for auto pistols in this country since way back in pre-WWII days when they used to distribute the renowned Pistole '08 on these shores. Some years ago, they came up with a pistol with a strong resemblance to the original Luger, modified into a full blowback design to handle the .22 LR cartridge. I think the usual term would be reasonably accurate facsimile. Actually, the Stoeger Luger .22 was accurate beyond any reasonable expectations and vastly more so than any of its 9mm Parabellum counterparts I've encountered to the present.

Made originally with a receiver of aluminum alloy, the pistol recently has been redesigned around a steel receiver. The alloy frame scaled just a thin tad over two pounds and the steel version adds about 10½ ounces to that. The alloy version on hand has a rear sight adjustable for windage and

elevation. The steel version has a fixed rear sight that tends to print the hits a bit left of the aiming point.

The cycling time of the Stoeger/Luger is just plain blindingly rapid. When the alloy version first appeared, Stoeger used to advertise that it was capable of discharging all eleven shots — one in the tube and ten in the hopper — in just one second, provided you could oscillate your index finger that fervently. A cyclic rate such as that does not compare too unfavorably with several machine guns.

The great *panache* of the original Luger has always been its uncanny feel, balance and pointing qualities, considerably marred by its incredibly wretched trigger pull. The Stoeger/Luger .22 retains all its forebear's virtues, adding a trigger pull that's remarkably decent. It is happily contented with pretty much any load you care to feed it and it really turns on with the Remington Yellow Jackets. The steel-frame version currently retails around the $200 bracket and the target-sighted alloy frame is no longer to be had. I'm sorry to have to say that.

This recent Colt Service Ace .22 long rifle sports a slide quite similar to that used on Colt's National Match Gold Cup models. The stocks are a set I whittled from yellow-gold Osage orange wood grown in Kansas.

Here's the breech end of the Service Ace barrel, showing the floating chamber that makes it work.

COLT ACE

At one time, before WWII, Colt marketed their just-plain Ace which was a dead lookalike to the Model 1911A1, but groomed to handle the .22 LR cartridge with impressive efficiency. It worked on the straight-blowback principle, as virtually all .22 LR self-stuffers do, and it was capable of accuracy sufficient to satisfy nearly anyone. Also available were .22-.45 and .45-.22 conversion units

so you could fit out your trusty thumb-buster to handle the rimfire fodder or modify your dainty paper-puncher into a bellowing bull.

Then along came Carbine Williams and his crafty subterfuge of the floating chamber and that begat the Colt Service Ace. In essence, the chamber is a small and separate component. Upon firing, high-pressure powder gas gets in between the front of it and drives the chamber rearward with vast vim and alacrity. That imparts a lot more rearward push to the slide and it even boosts the recoil. In theory, at least, you can fire the .22 LR cartridge with much the identical subjective sensations as if you were setting off full-patch .45 ACP loads.

The Service Ace remains in the Colt catalog to the present, their sole surviving .22 LR auto, as noted earlier. It is a sleekly handsome pistol, and great good fun to fire, but if you essay to use it on targets, you'd do well to make sure all the others are using the same gun. That's by way of noting its dispersionary parameters are concernably casual. Its cousin-German, the old Woodsman, will eat its lunch, every week in the world, as to tightness of group, and so will various other .22 LR autos.

There remain on the market various conversion units to enable one to operate a pistol of the Model 1911 pattern with .22 LR ammo and just about all of these have the floating chamber feature. Unless you observe certain crafty precautions, residues from burned powder will work their way into the interstices between mating surfaces and, rather quickly, the floating chamber floats no longer. It hangs up and so does the pistol. You can control that painful penchant by dousing and gooping the parts liberally in Break Free for a day or so, every now and again.

The foregoing by no means exhausts the concatenation of .22 LR auto pistols, be it cheerfully conceded. It serves merely to touch upon certain examples of the breed with which I have personal, first-hand acquaintance and familiarity.

There are other guns that could have been covered, and should have been covered; guns I wish I could have covered. To the present, those are the ones I've not been able to get my assessing meathooks upon. There are other guns I've tried out and hesitate to mention because you might buy one and I'd rather not have the guilt for that grinding upon my consciousness. There are still others that, more properly, deserve to be discussed in some other chapter by reason of their bulk or notable lack of it. The intended purpose of the chapter now a-dwindle has been to pass along some familiarity with the mill-run examples of the breed for you benefit and utilization.

It is a sadness that some of the best examples are not in current production, readily available for acquisition, given sufficient funds in the poke. Presumably, these may be findable in the used market and hunting is half the fun, right?

Break Free will go far to control problems with Ace.

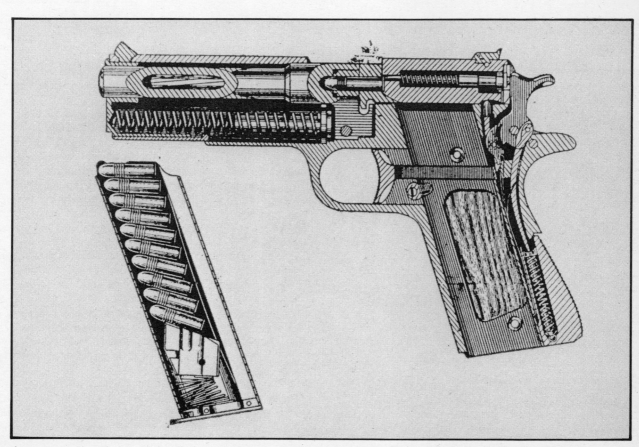

A cross-sectional view of the Service Ace, with details on its floating chamber. If not well saturated with Break Free in the breech and floating chamber, operation is apt to hang up with accumulated powder residue.

COLT'S PT.F.A.MFG.CO.HARTFORD.CT.U.S.A.
PAT'D AUG.25.1896 APR.20.1897 DEC.22.1903 JAN.25.1910

252860

COLT

Colt's Hammerless Vest Pocket Model was designed in 1908 and, in 1917, a magazine disconnect feature was added at serial No. 141,000. Chambered for the .25 ACP cartridge, it was discontinued about 1946.

Covina, Calif.
Diane 25 Cal.

The Wilkinson Diane, also in .25 ACP, shown here at the same scale as the Colt, is one of the most compact auto pistols currently being manufactured.

CHAPTER 4

COMPACT AUTOS

Neither The Most Powerful Nor The Most Accurate, Their Quality Of Being Available When Needed Is Perhaps Their Greatest Virtue

In Sweden, armed crime is a comparative rarity and these two Swedish policemen deemed the 7.65mm ample.

A S THE heading suggests, we are concerned with the itty-bitties of the breed. Most, if not all such pistols, fire comparatively small cartridges. The typical ammunition ranges from .22 long rifle up through .25 Automatic Colt Pistol (ACP), .32 ACP and .380 ACP. Metric designations are 6.35mm for the .25, 7.65mm for the .32 and 9mm Kurz/Corto for the .380 diameter. *Kurz* is German for short, and *corto* means the same in Italian. In terms of actual bullet diameter, the .25 is about .251-inch, the .32 is .308-inch, and the .380 is .355-inch, pretty close. Those dimensions apply to jacketed bullets, frequently used in such applications. Typically, cast bullets are sized to about .001-inch larger.

It is, I'll admit, no simple matter to categorize guns as compact versus military and police size. On a visit to

Sweden in the fall of 1974, I enjoyed a pleasant rap session with a pair of *Svenska polis* serving as bodyguards to HRH Carl XVI Gustav. Both were packing the Walther PPK/S, caliber 7.65mm — or .32 ACP, as we'd say — in cute little holsters crafted out of some manner of white plastic. Now, in my book, the PPK/S is a compact pistol but, in their book, it was a police — or *polis* — pistol. Different folks, different strokes, exactly that clear-cut and simple.

As a purely arbitrary line of demarcation, I have selected the .45 Detonics as the largest compact pistol for purposes of this discussion. It can be had in 9mm Luger, .38 Colt Super, .45 ACP and .451 Detonics magnum; an array by no manner of means to be viewed as picayune. There have been and perhaps still are a few ultra-tiny pistols for

Left, the AMT .22 LR Back Up above the Model '08 Colt and, right, the same Model '08 with current Colt Agent. Latter is an alloy-frame, six-shot, .38 Special; compact as revolvers go, but larger than M'08.

wee cartridges such as the various Kolibri numbers, but it is so unlikely to encounter them that they'll be ignored for the present discussion.

The Bauer, the Wilkinson Diane, and the Raven are about at the lower end of the size scale in the current marketplace. Of these, the Diane is probably the smallest, and a tiny bit more petite than the old Browning/Colt .25 auto that served as the role model for the vest-pocket pistol as a genre.

Some of these small pistols are available in .22 LR as well as .25 ACP. Indeed, I have here a slightly larger affair, the Plainfield 78 — no longer made — which came with a spare set of barrel, bolt and magazine so it could be cross-switched from the .22 LR to the .25 ACP, or vice versa.

Most ammunition for .25 ACP carries a full metal jacket (fmj) round nose bullet capable of nothing beyond drilling a quarter-inch hole to a depth governed by the tenacity of the target medium. These days, there are several loads available in .22 LR with lead hollow point bullets that can and will expand impressively, even at the modest velocities obtainable from a two-inch barrel.

A few years ago, Winchester brought forth a new load for the .25 ACP, their catalog No. X25AXP, with a 45-grain expanding point bullet. The actual bullet is of lead, copper-plated, with a small steel ball imbedded in its nose. These little rascals can and will expand at the velocities involved. In a stiff clay medium of the type I term duct seal, it produces a wound channel about .75-inch maximum diameter to a depth of about three inches. Transposed to living flesh, that would smart, sting and burn quite memorably, I think. The best of the hot .22 LR loads will do about as well in the same medium.

The long-term mortality rate of the .25 ACP cartridge is nothing to regard lightly. The wee round has promoted the sale of a great many coffins in its day. It is, however, rather random in its track record. There have been cases where one round of .25 ACP rendered the impactee — to purloin a phrase of friend Ferguson's that I admire — deader than canned tuna. There have been other cases in which the impactee soaked up the entire contents of a fully-loaded .25 auto and then, patience exhausted, vivisected the pistoleer with a shovel, resolutely swung. It tends to make you think, if you're contemplating pinning all your hopes for longevity on the .25 auto.

It is my humble but sincere opinion that the .32 ACP is perhaps the most totally useless and indefensible cartridge still surviving in the marketplace. True, it is slightly more

Left, revolvers come considerably smaller, however. Here the Freedom Arms .22 LR is contrasted to the Raven Arms, Colt and Wilkinson .25 autos. Right, .45 ACP Star PD above Heckler & Koch Model P7 in 9mm.

formidable than the .25 ACP and, by inference, than the .22 LR. The guns to handle the .32 tend to be about the same size as those for the .380 and the .380 strikes me as marginal, at best. It puts me in mind of Victor Borge's old line, "The trouble with pancakes is, in the first place, they should be waffles."

There are now a few auto pistols handling the 9mm Luger/Parabellum that are smaller than most if not all pistols handling the .380 ACP. I have seldom experienced drastic infatuation with the 9mmP cartridge but I certainly regard it with greater favor than I hold for the .380 ACP. In my handgunning career to date, I've encountered exactly one .380 auto that impressed me quite favorably. It was a Browning *Grande Modele,* manufactured by Husqvarna of Sweden. Originally, it had been chambered for the 9mm Browning long cartridge and, upon emigrating to these shores, some crafty gunsmith had sleeved the chamber to accept the shorter .380 ACP cartridge, the 9mm BL cartridge being rarely seen in the marketplace here.

In outward appearance, the gun resembled the charming Colt Pocket Model of 1903 — one of the prettiest pistols ever designed, I think — except that its barrel and slide were substantially longer.

As modified, it would chamber a .380 ACP factory load, and fire it, but it was highly unlikely the cartridge would generate sufficient energy to work the action. The amount of recoiling mass, together with the recoil spring, were still tailored to the 9mm Browning long and the gunsmith who'd sleeved the chamber hadn't done a thing to modify those.

Obviously, it was a case calling for the subtle if faintly demented expertise of the experimental reloader — an occupational specialty generally viewed with distrust by insurance actuaries. I got out my .380 reloading dies and commenced extrapolating. Du Pont's SR-7625 proved to be the powder that really got it all together, with a 90-grain bullet. By the time I'd inched my way up to dispensing enough propellant to work the action every time, those 90-grain slugs were issuing from the *Grande Modele's* king size schnozz at right around 1340 feet per second (fps) which, if you were about to ask, is good for about 359 fpe.

All that took place in late '69 or early '70 and for reasons not readily avoidable, I lost touch with that singularly interesting pistol soon after working up the copy on it and turning in the manuscript. Many times since, I've wished I'd been able to retain it, but that's not always possible.

Several years later, a fellow experimental ballistician in

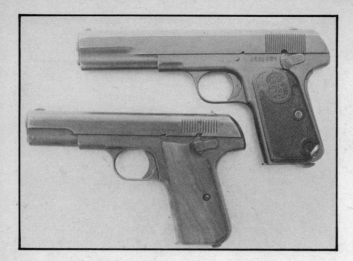

Top, the Husqvarna-made Browning Grande Modele converted to .380 ACP, as discussed here, with a .32 ACP version of Colt's 1903 Pocket Model auto.

The Star Model PD in .45 ACP with the ASP, made by Armament Systems and Procedures, Box 356, Appleton, WI 54911, from a S&W Model 39 in 9mm.

West Virginia came into possession of a small .380 auto that fired from a locked breech, rather than the usual full blowback mode. He quizzed me as to whether I had any knowledge of a load in .380 ACP suited for such a design that might enhance its performance beyond the usual pallid levels. I sent him a burn-copy of the story on the Husqvarna and he worked up to that load, writing to express great delight in its performance.

My West Virginian buddy lived near a substantial ballistic facility and knew some of the people who worked there. In the course of kaffeeklatsching with one of them, he happened to mention this new *wunderbar* .380 load he'd chanced upon. His friend in the lab wanted to try it out and arrangements were made so he could do so. The velocity was notably brisk, even in the somewhat shorter barrel. Then, the lab technician put the load in the pressure barrel and it read forth something on the order of 37,500 pounds per square inch (psi).

The industry maximum for the .380 ACP cartridge is 18,900 psi. In practice, commercial ammomakers and compilers of reloading books try to stay some percentage below such figures. Thus the hotsopple load was operating at right around twice the permissible maximum. I hope you'll understand and forgive if I don't specify the exact charge weight, hmm?

There is at least one compact pistol cartridge in the limbo between the .380 ACP and the 9mm Luger. It is known as the 9x18mm Ultra or the 9mm Makarov. It seems to have sprouted as an expedient in those countries forbidden by treaty to produce military pistol cartridges. The 9mm Luger aka 9mm Parabellum is also known as the 9x19mm. Thus we note the Ultra is — as the cigarette ads used to say — just a silly millimeter shorter than the ubiquitous Luger round. The Ultra is seldom seen on these shores as a cartridge, and guns for it are considerably scarcer. The .380 case, if you were about to ask, is 17.27mm

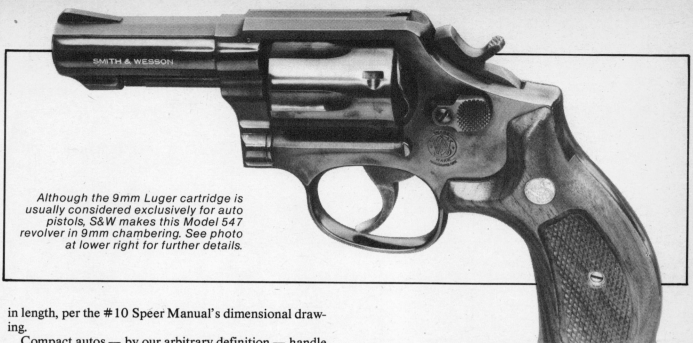

Although the 9mm Luger cartridge is usually considered exclusively for auto pistols, S&W makes this Model 547 revolver in 9mm chambering. See photo at lower right for further details.

in length, per the #10 Speer Manual's dimensional drawing.

Compact autos — by our arbitrary definition — handle cartridges across the fairly broad gamut from .22 LR/.25 ACP up through the .451 Detonics magnum; the latter a fairly feral beastie that will be discussed further in the chapter on wildcat cartridges for autos. To the present moment, no one has marketed a compact auto for the .45 Winchester magnum but, as the late Dorothy Parker observed, in another context, I wouldn't be a damned bit surprised. As you might suppose, burly cartridges of such credentials create quite a tumult in a pistol so petite.

The Colt Commander might have been a better choice as the outermost limit of dimensional limitations in the matter of compact pistols. In point of cold fact, I must admit I've never owned and no more than rarely fired a Commander, whether with the aluminum alloy or steel frame.

On the other hand, for the past several happy years, I've owned and operated a Star Model PD in .45 ACP and have come to regard it with undiluted affection. Its frame/receiver is of tough aluminum alloy, handsomely and durably anodized, and the weight is but a mere pittance. Despite that, it can/will/has handled loads to the upper .45 ACP specifications with dignity, elan and vast savoir faire. Not only that, it doesn't seem to muster nearly the recoil you'd expect and the accuracy is likewise amusing in its presumption.

In 1983, S&W introduced their Model 469, a pruned version of their Model 459 and extremely compact.

Model 547 S&W has a special firing pin to prevent pierced primers and a plunger above it to hold the 9mm round securely against the chamber ledge.

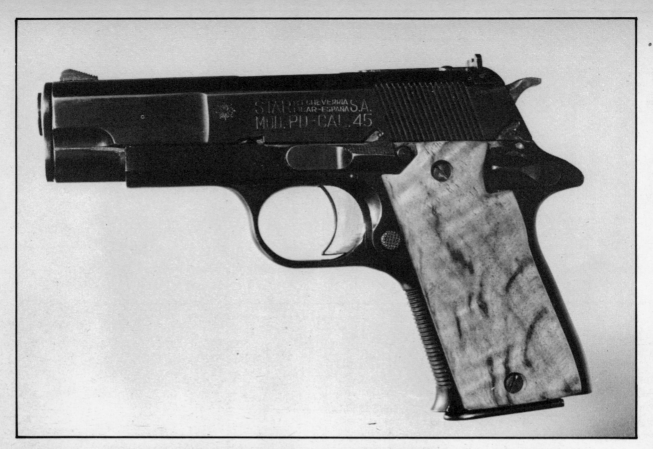

The Spanish-made Star Model PD — here in .45 ACP, also available in 9mmP — is extremely compact and, with its frame of tough aluminum alloy, weighs only 25 ounces, empty. Its rear sight is adjustable and it is surprisingly accurate and even more surprisingly easy on recoil; a thoroughly satisfactory one!

My Star PD is one of the earlier examples of the breed and it needed a touch of custom-tuning to cure it of an unpleasant trait. It tended to stop, its slide locked rearward, with some few cartridges remaining in the magazine. That was cured by gentle and patiently exploratory stoning away of small amounts of the metal on the inner nub of the slide stop. The object was to have the surface engaged by the rising magazine follower, not by protuberances and convexities of the loaded rounds moving up in prescribed sequence.

Let us speak for a short while on the matter of small pistols firing energetic cartridges and upon the lusty recoil generated by such combinations. It is relevant and pertinent to the discussion, I think, and I'm also going to beg the

Empty weight of the .25 ACP Wilkinson Diane is slightly less than 12 ounces. Its magazine holds six rounds with the option of carrying a seventh in the chamber. Photo at right compares its bulk to pack of cigarettes.

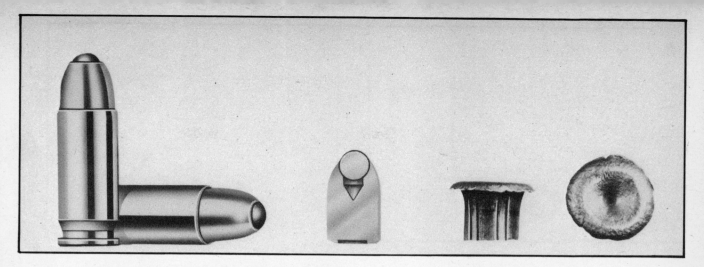

Winchester's expanding-point load for the .25 ACP is shown in cross-section and after expansion on impact.

Seldom seen on these shores, the 9x18mm Ultra is at left, with a .380 ACP and 9mm Luger/Parabellum.

Another compact .25 ACP auto is the Bauer, here in Presentation Grade, chrome plated, with pearl stocks.

Same gun in upper photo, from the other side and resting on top of its presentation case.

indulgence of the all-out purists and ask permission to veer from the assigned topic to talk about rifles and revolvers briefly.

It is, you see, largely a matter of the number of foot-pounds of energy (fpe) delivered per ounce of net gun weight. Admittedly, other criteria apply. Net felt recoil is an integration of bullet weight, gun weight, charge weight and other factors. Heavier bullets tend to create more recoil, even if the delivered foot-pounds are the same, all other conditions equal. Nonetheless, the foot-pounds of energy per ounce — are we ready for an abbreviation such as fpepo? — is a useful rule-of-thumb factor to consider.

The all-out meanest gun/cartridge combo I've encountered to date on that basis is the little Model 600 Remington carbine chambered for their intrepid but unappreciated .350 Remington magnum cartridge. It handles bullets up to the weight class of 250 to 300 grains and it launches them with incredible vim. The subjective impression, in firing such loads, is right in there with the time I got sweet-talked into trying a round with a Lahti anti-tank rifle. I still have one of the .350 R-mag Model 600s, admire it intemperately, and fire it frequently, but not with heavy bullets. What I load for it is the 140-grain Speer jacketed hollow point

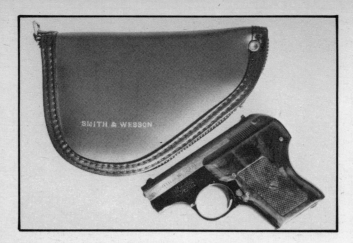

The S&W Escort, in .22 LR, was produced for only a short time and was extremely compact in size.

The problem with so-called "pocket pistols" is illustrated by the lady with an S&W Escort in her right hip pocket. Although about as small and thin as handguns ever get, its presence is quite obvious.

(JHP) ahead of 60.0 grains of Hercules Reloder-7 powder. That's good for around 3156/3097 at the muzzle and it groups within two inches at a hundred yards; an interesting recipe for non-edible varmints, whose pelts have no useful value. Recoil of that load is inconsequential...well, not *terribly* consequential.

The meanest handgun encountered to date? Probably the Jurras Howdah in .460 Jurras calibration and, hot on its heels, the Charter Arms .44 Bulldog revolver, tipping the scales at an empty weight of just nineteen ounces and firing the .44 Special cartridge. Now, the .44 Special — in the factory loadings — is a wee, sleekit, cowering, timorous beastie but, hand-filled with thin-lipped resolution, it can get on up there, and does so. I shall endeavor to include a photo or two illustrating the subjective effect of firing a .44 Special cartridge generating around 459 fpe out of the Charter Arms .44 Bulldog.

Coming in from the tangential departure, I recall but few auto pistols hailing from anywhere near the same ballpark. The .451 Detonics magnum conversion kit, installed in the Model 1911A1 Remington-Rand and fed with loads from

The Raven Arms P-25, in .25 ACP is another compact design utilizing die-castings for low-stress component parts. This one's in satin nickel finish.

The Plainfield Model 72, now discontinued, was a rather large design with the unusual feature of being quickly convertible between .22 LR and .25 ACP.

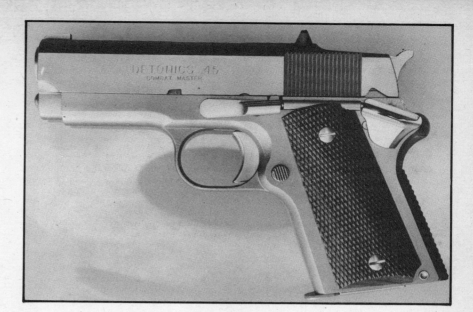

Current pattern of the Detonics .45 Combat Master in stainless steel.

An earlier Detonics .45 in the now discontinued blued finish, with a set of stocks in quilted maple, as made by Bullshooter's Supply, Box 13446, Tucson, AZ 85732.

the peak of the list probably comes as close as anything off the top of the memory. The wryly humorous aspect of all that was that I tested and wrote up the .451 Detonics mag conversion all in the same session with the new stainless steel .45 ACP Detonics and, as I recall, made much ado of the utterly kickless attributes of the latter.

I've fired the same gun a few times since then and, given realistic perspective, its recoil is reasonable but by no means as non-existent as I said it was, hot on the heels of soaking up the backlash from the warmer .451 D-mag loads. It is reminiscent of the old story about the chap who made a leap from the pier for a rowboat that was drifting away and came down astraddle its gunwales (or whatever rowboats have there). "Y'know," he remarked to a friend later, "for a little while along about then, my new false teeth didn't bother me the least bit!"

I have not, to the present, fired the Detonics auto fitted out for the .451 D-mag cartridge but I have an unwavering suspicion it would be a pretty memorable experience.

Quite a lot of attention has been devoted to pruning existing larger designs down into more compact contours. In Appleton, Wisconsin, Armament Systems and Procedures has been modifying Model 39 S&W autos into what they term the ASP and one such is shown here, before and after being...uhh...aspirated.

Having been built up from a Model 39-2, it retains the aluminum alloy receiver and, as a result, is a marvel of lightweight compactness. So far as I've been able to tell, the noteworthy operational reliability of the original design remains unimpaired and, as an added bonus, the translucent handle slabs of Lexan plastic let you see the rounds remaining in the magazine at any time.

It would seem the ASP was designed and intended for high-stress employment at close-in distances. The usual front and rear sights — not overly impressive in the Model 39-2 original — have been replaced by a single unit that Armament Systems and Procedures terms the Guttersnipe sight. That is a unit of black plastic, 2-1/16 inches

Two versions of the Semmerling, a manually-actuated repeating pistol in .45 ACP of extreme compactness.

The novel but discontinued Thomas .45 is at left, compared to a Model PP Walther in .22 LR.

long, with a three-sided tapering trough along the top, colored yellow on the sides and bottom. In theory, you set up a sighting image with it and fire in the usual manner.

It well could be it requires a knack I've yet to master. Suffice to say, all the firing I've done with it to date has been reasonable in right/left variance, but quite goshawful in up/down placement. Of a surety, within the final closing seven yards or so, it would pose no problem. At range that close, I pay little or no attention to the sights, anyhow.

The Heckler & Koch Model P7 is another compact and interesting design, chambered for the 9mm Luger/Parabellum cartridge. In size and weight, it is as small as or smaller than some of the .380 ACP offerings. Its rudimentary sights serve quite well for directing the holes to the points envisioned. By reasonable expectations based upon typical small autos of the same sort, its trigger pull is light, crisp and utterly admirable.

The P7 has an unusual feature in its cocking lever, which is quite like the Caraville Double Ace, except in reverse. With a round in the chamber, the P7 is quite safe from inadvertant discharge since its striker is not retracted (cocked). To take care of that, it is necessary to squeeze back on

Left, a closer look at the .22 LR Model PP Walther from facing page. "PP" stands for pistole polezei, or "police pistol," in German. A short-barreled version for plain clothes detectives was the Model PPK with the K standing for kriminalamt German for detective bureau. The PPK is not imported at present, but a specialized version of it, termed the PPK/S, S standing for special, as in engraved example at right.

The Walther Model P5 is in 9x19mm or Luger/Parabellum, and is a modification of their wartime military pistol, the P'38.

the lever at the front of the grip area. With that done, the chambered round can be fired by the aforementioned light pull of the trigger.

If you encounter your H&K P7 without any operating manual — as I did — do not assume you have to squeeze the cocking lever to reset the striker for firing the next round! No, indeed: So long as you hold the cocking lever rearward, all it takes is letting the trigger go forward a trifle, followed by another pull, and there she goes again.

The H&K P7 has a novel locking system in which gas pressure holds the action closed until in-barrel pressures have dropped off. I'm told that, on protracted firing, that will cause portions of the frame to overheat temporarily. To the present, I've not fired the test gun that intrepidly. I incline to doubt that most shooters would find this a severe problem.

From the standpoint of the reloader, the P7 has a further trait not entirely endearing. Its chamber walls are lon-

gitudinally striated, so as to ease the effort of dragging forth the empty hull, presumably. That exerts a somewhat traumatic effect upon the fired case, leaving it with lengthwise grooves. It is possible to reload fired empties from the P7, but continued use cuts rather heavily into their reloading longevity.

The magazine release of the H&K P7 is located on the lower rear corner of the grip area but, unlike most such devices, it is operated by pushing forward instead of to the rear. Once you become accustomed to it, you can drop the empty magazines free with notable alacrity, via a resolute

The Heckler & Koch Model P7 has no safety in the usual sense of the term and drawing rearward on the lever at the front of the grip cocks the striker in readiness for firing. If the grip is relaxed, the striker returns to uncocked mode.

The Iver Johnson Model TP-22, in .22 LR, is based upon Walther Model TPH and it's quite compact.

thrust of the heel of the free hand. The P7 comes with a spare magazine, as do most, if not all of the H&K auto pistols.

The P7 has no safety in the usual sense of the term, nor does it appear to need any such feature. Should the P7, held in the hand and ready to fire on the instant, be knocked from the grasp in any way, the spring-loaded cocking lever at the front of the handle zips forward and, with it, the striker is lowered without setting off the chambered round. Thus, you have an autoloading pistol that restores itself to safe mode as it drops from hand to ground. It locks the slide rearward upon firing the final round that came up out of the magazine and, as you fang the empty free and stuff a fresh one up into the well, as your firing hand closes to compress the lever up front, that releases the slide to bang forward and chamber a fresh round, all in readiness for immediate firing. It all strikes me as a remarkably thoughtfully designed system.

In the smaller compact auto designs, we have an example known as the Back Up — not "Backup," as it's done in two words on the LH side of the slide — and available in a choice of .380 ACP/Kurz/Corto or plain old vanilla .22 long rifle/LR. In the pictured examples, the .380 bears the circled OMC emblem while the .22 is from AMT. The latter stands for Arcadia Machine and Tool. I've been racking my recollection all in vain in futile efforts to recall what

Left, a Colt Commander in .45 ACP, as customized by noted knifemaker Bob Loveless to serve as his personal packabout pistol. He relieves all the sharp edges and corners and had Seecamp perform his double-action conversion on the action. Right, a stainless DA auto in .32 ACP; Sterling Arms' Mark II.

OMC stood for. I'm certain it's not Outboard Marine Corporation.

I can confide that the .380 Back Up is a right unforgettable lurcher-rearward when fired with just about any cartridge of those credentials. In its size and weight class, it is a leading contender for the goosed-mule trophy. If nothing else, it tends to give the shooter renewed and heightened respect for the .380 ACP as a cartridge. In other words, it comes pretty close to mustering about as much shazam as you can hope to crowd into that few a number of ounces and cubic centimeters.

Its .22 LR counterpart is more docile to fire, by a country mile but, at the same time, it is proportionally less formidable to the mass out in front of it. The test gun at hand in .22 LR has a rather demanding grip safety that needs to be grasped with the enthusiasm appropriate for strangling weasels before it will activate the trigger components to proceed with the firing cycle. With that done, it shoots respectably close to point of aim, and with generally impressive vigor.

The sight systems of either caliber of the Back Up are investment-cast into the top of the slide and acceptably precise for any of the sort of shooting apt to be pursued with either. Drawing it fine, the front sight is a tad wide in proportion to the width of the rear notch, with little or no daylight visible to either side in a normal sighting picture. Just a few whisks with a fine-cut file could improve that usefully. In elevation, the sights are dead-on with nearly any loads you can put through them. That results in somewhat more horizontal dispersion than vertical. It is not any big serious thing.

There are some few other compact autos that — being

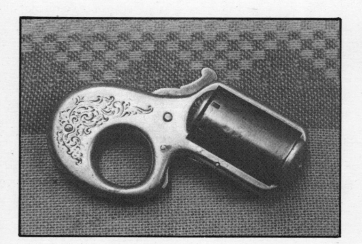 

The tiny antique at left was photographed in the Royal Swedish Army museum. Presumably, when its ammo ran dry, you reversed it and had a dandy set of brass knucks. Pistol at right is a reproduction of the Walther Model PP in .380 ACP, made under license from Walther in Turkey. As a brand name, it's a dubious choice!

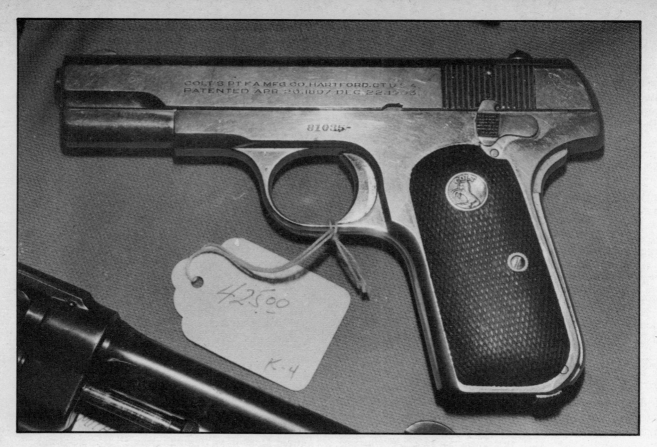

The Colt Pocket Model 1903 originally was introduced in .32 ACP and the .380 ACP version became available in 1908. At least five different design changes were made before it was discontinued in 1945 at serial 572,215.

An early Model 1903, with a four-digit serial and the checkered hard rubber stocks of that era.

A worker at the OMC plant, assembling pistols like the .380 Back Up that appears on page 93.

chambered for the .22 LR cartridge — could have and perhaps should have been covered in the rimfire chapter immediately ahead of this one. These include the aforementioned .22 LR Back Up and the Iver Johnson Model TP-22, as adapted and modified from the Walther Model TPH. The TP seems to stand for *taschenpistole,* German for pocket pistol, and I've no idea what the H signifies.

These seem to be pretty good little gizmos, that do about

all they can with the cartridge they're built to handle. Their accuracy, if not mindblowing, is far from execrable and any attempts to assess their punching ability do not reflect to their discredit to any great degree. At the same time, they seem decently reliable and there is no great discomfort as to noise or recoil.

We have a couple of sub-chapters coming up, touching upon such matters as the practicality of the pocket pistol and the realistic comparison between small autos and small revolvers. With no intention of muting the interest of either, I'd like to enter a few thoughts on the matters.

A dozen or more years back, S&W brought forth a petite pistol in .22 LR they called the Escort. It was about as svelte and unobtrusive as such things can hardly hope to get. I'll try to include a photo of a young lady, viewed from the south, with an Escort in the right rear pocket of her jeans. I trust you'll agree its aspect would levitate eyebrows in just about any quarter where packing iron is less than socially condonable.

At the same time, I'll toss in a few views of a fairly crafty affair run up by the folks at Safariland, made of heavy, heavy leather to accept small .25 autos. If the pistol is inserted and the entire assembly is planted in the left rear pocket, with the large rectangular surface outermost, the entire affair poses a reasonably convincing facsimile of a billfold being packed there.

With a rig such as that, you can probably get away with carrying a small auto in most circles. I incline to doubt if it would work with a small revolver. I'll try to include photos demonstrating the smallest revolvers are right in there with the tiniest autos, when it comes to unobtrusiveness. The

little Freedom Arms revolver, in .22 LR, can be had with barrels even stubbier than the one shown here. At the shortest, they can be had with a recessed belt buckle in which they can be packed with all the outward imagery of a simple decoration but, at the touch of a concealed stud, they spring free so as to be cocked and fired as desired.

The colloquial term for such buckle gats, as I trust you'll be fascinated to learn, is "navel destroyer." No, not naval, *navel!*

On the matter of efficacy *vis a vis* compact autos versus compact revolvers, it gets a bit difficult to muster much of a convincing case for the autos. In terms of cavity casts from the ultra-wee Freedom Arms revolver, the comparable casts from autos firing the same cartridge, and slightly larger in overall bulk, do not contrast favorably. The Freedom Arms popsquawk will handle loads up to and including the CCI Stinger without a sigh/without a prayer/with no betrayal of despair. The same cannot be said of the tinier autos, so far's I've been able to note.

Expand the dimensional limits ever so slightly and you soon arrive at a revolver capable of setting off the .38 Special cartridge without suffering irreversible ruptures. We have, or have had autos to handle the same cartridge, but

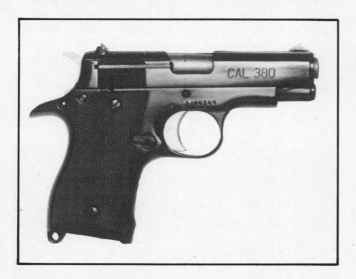

Introduced in 1983, the Iver Johnson Pony, in .380 ACP is a compact design firing from a locked breech.

Made by Beretta and imported by Browning, this DA .380 has a 12-round magazine, ambidextrous safety.

Although AMT doesn't recommend it, the .22 Back Up holds eight in the magazine and a ninth in the chamber.

A gun does the most good if you have it and keep it handy. A veteran southwestern lawman used to pack this small derringer inside the top of his boot with the aid of epoxied snaps, as shown above and below.

matching set of snaps and sockets to a small derringer and the inner surface of the top of one of his boots to pack the wee carronade adjacent to his shinbone. I see no obvious reason why the same approach could not be adapted to any small auto pistol, provided the idea turns you any kind of on.

In the last-ditch, final-twitch analysis, the great virtue of the handgun lies in its ability to be there when needed, inconspicuously. In that light, I recall an incident from several years back. I was sitting in on a shootfest hosted by a dealer in the southwestern part of the country. It was, as a matter of fact, the same session in which I was cozened into trying out the Lahti anti-tank rifle of formidable puissance. Not long after I got off my cringing round, someone else tried it and the projectile struck a spark off a rock, far up the side of a nearby mountain, igniting a small smoulder in a nearby patch of sage. As the outlying vegetation had the flammable properties of a freshly opened can of Hercules Bullseye powder, our problem was obvious. Everyone, self included, set out at flank speed for the site of the conflagration. Half-way up the side of the mountain, I began having sober second thoughts. What if I came brashly down with a foot about to trample a rattlesnake? Gee but I wished I'd thought to pack a gun along. And, with that, a recurring thump-thump on the right hip reminded me that I

vastly grosser in bulk and weight. Not long after S&W brought forth the Escort, they dropped it from production, much in the same way they deep-sixed the Ladysmith in an earlier era, perhaps for approximately the same reason, namely unfavorable imagery. Nonetheless, they continue to make their Model 36 blued Chiefs Special and its stainless steel counterpart, the Model 60. Metallurgical variances apart, both are five-shot .38 Special revolvers, of identical dimensions, typically with two-inch barrels or, less commonly, with three-inch barrels.

It does not lie within the titular limitations of the book at hand to delve too deeply into the innate capabilities of small .38 Special revolvers. It is freely conceded that some body of popular belief remains convinced the .38 Special cartridge is inherently inadequate in its own right. Be that as it may — or may not — be, the fact remains. If I were assigned to blow a hole of X-cc volume in a given medium, using a handgun that did not exceed a specified small weight and bulk, I probably could do better with a small revolver than with a small auto. In noting that, I'll concede I have access to some uncommonly hard-striving bullets that work better out of revolvers than out of autos, to this point.

In the matter of crafty and effective concealability, note the accompanying illustrations showing how a resourceful police officer in the southern part of the country affixed a

If you can put up with a bit of added bulk and weight, the small revolver such as this Model 36 S&W Chiefs Special packs a lot more authority than does the .25.

A bit larger than most .25 ACPs, the Model 1910 German Mauser was an early hammerless design.

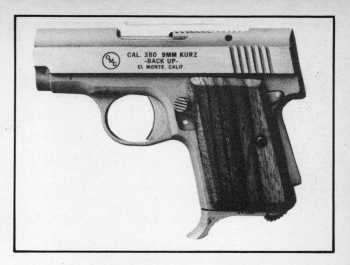

The Back Up in .380 ACP, now made by AMT, is a memorable kicker when firing that small cartridge.

did, indeed, have a Browning M-35 Hi-Power, stuffed to the top with the best loads I knew how to put up at that time — a 90-grain JHP slug going out the muzzle for around 1440/414 — at my needful beck and call.

So, I lengthened my stride and got to the trouble area first and scuffled sand to stifle the smoulder, all with the sunniest of outlooks. Any snakes around the area could cope with their own worries because humble self could strike with telling effect from fifty yards or any closer distance.

When a tried and proven handgun is on the hip and ready for business, its packer is prepared to cope with any reasonable eventuality. That, in my book, is the sovereign virtue of the breed.

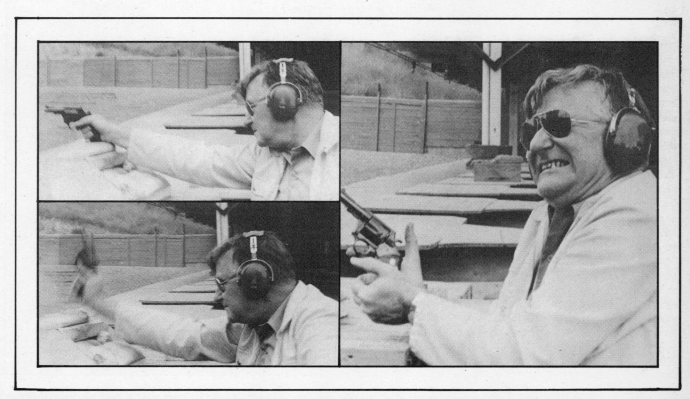

But for real "bump trauma," hardly anything equals firing warm .44 Specials in the 19-ounce CA Bulldog!

POCKET PISTOLS

Originally So Called Because They Were Carried In Pockets — Not Because THey Went "Pocketa-Pocketa," The Concept Has Become Slightly Obsolescent, As Discussed Here

What follows is a commentary on pocket pistols, their care and feeding, by Claud S. Hamilton, as told in his own words. Hamilton owns or has access to a number of makes and models of such things that are not available to me and I feel it offers a more comprehensive coverage of the subject. I've a few comments on Hamilton's comments, but I'll append those at the end of his discussion. — DAG

Here are four cartridges typically used in pocket pistols. From left, the .22 long rifle, represented by the exceptionally effective Remington Yellow Jacket load; Winchester's .25 ACP with a small steel ball imbedded in the nose of the lead bullet; the .32 ACP and .380 ACP, both with full metal jacketed bullets, round nose.

A Browning Model 1922, in caliber .380 ACP, modified from the basic Model 1910 Browning design in response to requests from police. Exceptionally trim and compact for its barrel length, Hamilton discusses the reasons behind the difficulty of obtaining such guns in today's slightly illogical marketplace.

"NECESSITY," a wise man once said, "is the mother of invention…" and this is certainly the case where firearms development is concerned. To explain the existence of modern pocket pistols, it helps to look at the environment in which they originated. Smooth, urbane, highly polished Continental Europe was, at the beginning of this century, the high point of civilization. Truly violent crime was rare by American standards. Those who felt the need to go armed wanted only the smallest and most concealable of arms. Since they did not encounter violent criminals — desperados, American style — stopping power was never a very important consideration even among European police. Often the mere threat of violence, not violence itself, was all that was needed.

The requirement, then, was for a very small, light handgun which could be carried comfortably and inconspicuously in the waistband, a pocket or madam's purse. It needed a very smooth profile so as not to catch on clothing. The cartridge need not be powerful — indeed should not be in so small an arm — and magazine capacity was no great thing. Pitched battles were rare on Continental streets, and in the stately banks, casinos and, yes, bedrooms. The primary weapons of conflict were wits not guns. The usual circumstances of combat when it did occur was about seven to twelve yards. It was strictly point shooting, and target sights were a liability, not an asset.

The picture that emerges is very nearly the antithesis of a good defensive handgun, American style. Our late 1800s history was still that of a frontier nation with Indians, Moros and hardbitten gunfighters to pacify. It is natural, then, that most pocket pistols were until very recently, made in Europe.

In America pocket pistols are "black hat" bad guys. They are viewed by our liberal politicians as having no "redeeming social graces." The Gun Control Act of 1968 excluded most of the best of the older pocket pistols from importation because of the "factoring" system which the Treasury adopted as part of enforcement. This system awards credit points for most of the very things that make pocket pistols unsuitable — target sights, length and overall size, target grips and the like. This is ironic when one considers that these pistols were long carried as uniform sidearms by many European police departments. One, the Model 1920 Browning .32 ACP, was designed specifically to meet police requirements. Today most pocket pistols here are made in the United States, or are assembled here from parts shipped in from Europe.

What *is* a pocket pistol? Typically, it is a small semi-automatic pistol in caliber .22 Long Rifle, .25 Auto Colt Pistol, .32 Auto Colt Pistol, or .380 Auto Colt Pistol (ACP). It is about five inches long, or less, and has a barrel length of about three inches. It will weigh twenty ounces or less and carry six cartridges in the magazine.

Most of these little pistols are of the simple blowback type described in detail elsewhere in this volume. They take advantage of the relatively low pressure of their small cartridge and depend upon the inertia of the moving parts to hold the action closed until the bullet has left the muzzle and the chamber pressure has dropped to that of the outside air. This eliminates the need for expensive lock work.

Pocket pistols may be striker fired or use a concealed hammer. In recent years, growing concern about safety has caused most to be made with exposed hammers, and a double-action feature is often added. Most recently, a tendency seems to have developed to add large capacity magazines although it is hard to see the need for them.

As I have said, ballistic performance was never a prime characteristic for pocket pistols, and the load statistics certainly bear this out. Here is a comparison of the four common pocket pistol cartridges with three commonly used American handgun cartridges:

Cartridge	Bullet	Barrel Length (inches)	Velocity (fps)	Energy (fpe)
Pocket Pistol Cartridges:				
.22 Long Rifle Rim Fire Hi-Vel	38-grain lead HP	6	1280	138
.25 ACP (6.35mm Browning)	50-grain FMJ	2	810	73
.32 ACP (7.65mm Browning)	77-grain FMJ	4	900	162
.380 ACP (9mm Browning Short)	90-grain FMJ	3¾	1000	200
Commonly Used American Cartridges:				
.38 Special +P	125-grain JHP	4	945	248
.357 Magnum	125-grain JHP	4	1450	583
.45 ACP	185-grain JHP, ST	5	1000	411

Here are bullets similar to those in the upper photo, with the noses turned in slightly to make them feed in the .380 ACP. They not only functioned well, but proved capable of impressive expansion in clay.

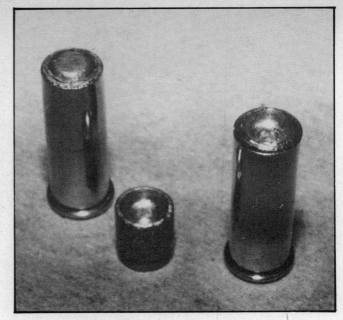

Hamilton was able to work up these examples of the Spelunker hollow point design, here loaded into .38 Special case. Originally intended for use in revolvers, Hamilton adapted them for use in autos.

Are pocket pistols safe as defensive arms? The .380 ACP is obviously the best of the lot, with the .22 Long Rifle rimfire probably a close second with its soft hollow point. Even the .380 is not up to the .38 Special, and we all know how that cartridge has been condemned in the United States in recent times as an inadequate man stopper. And yet, I am reminded of something friend Tom Ferguson, long of the San Antonio police, once told me; he said "Not many years ago we had a rather routine brawl in a downtown bar. An enormous 260-pound pro football player was involved. He was killed instantly by one shot from a .25 Auto..." There is no doubt about it. Any one of these little guns can kill you if the shot is placed well. But safe as a defense weapon by American standards? No.

For me, the Browning Model 1910 is probably the original standard of quality in pocket pistols. It is striker fired and has the smoothest profile and fewest protuberances to catch on clothing. It is just about as small and light as a gun can be made to handle the .380 ACP. Made by FN in Liege, its Belgian craftsmanship is unequaled. I had one for a number of years and found it absolutely reliable. It fed and fired my homemade swaged lead hollow points right along with the best FMJ factory loads. My only complaints were that even for my small hand the grips were hopelessly too short, and the thumb safety was too small to be used quickly and with safety.

After 1968, Browning could no longer import the .380 Model 1910 or the .25 Auto pistol. A brief effort was made to meet the "factoring" system by lengthening the barrel, adding a finger support to the magazine floor plate, installing large target sights and shaped, target grips...to create what was called the Model 1910/70. Of course, what you had by then was no longer a pocket pistol! It was soon discontinued.

In terms of pure popularity and widespread use, the

Martha Penso loads a Browning Model 1910 .380 ACP pistol in preparation for the test session. She would be wise to wear shooting glasses as well as earmuffs, due to the tendency of some auto pistols to eject empty cases into shooter's face.

Walther PP and PPK are no doubt the leaders. Originally made in 7.65mm (.32 ACP), they were later also chambered for .22 Long Rifle and .380 ACP. These were among the first of the double-action pocket pistols. "PP" stands for Police Pistol and these guns were widely used by European police. The PPK is simply a slightly shorter and lighter version made specially for undercover police use. In addition to having an exposed hammer for safety, they have a thumb safety which drops the hammer safely on a loaded cartridge in the chamber. Unfortunately, the European-style burred rounded hammer tends to catch on clothing.

The PP and PPK are highly thought of by many American shooters. My own experience was with a wartime gun probably made by slave labor which had a terrible, creepy, springy trigger. It did not feed too well, and before the first fifty rounds had been fired the ejector managed to come loose from the frame and jam the action closed. More recently I have used a new PPK/S made in this country which handled reliably and well. It is obviously a quality firearm.

Several years ago I inherited a Sauer 38 (H) from an uncle who "liberated" it in Europe in WWII. I had not seen one before; they are much less common than most of the others. This is a very advanced design and employs both a concealed double-action hammer and a special lever which permits the cocked hammer to be lowered safely on a loaded round in the chamber. I was unable to get my uncle's gun to feed any .32 ACP ammunition I could find. It would fire when loaded by hand. It was just my luck to have that little gun stolen before I had an opportunity to see what its "problem" was and try to have it corrected.

Probably the most interesting of the newer crop of pock-

Walther Model PPK/S is one of the best-known of the modern pocket pistols, made on a basic design that originated about 1929. These are now manufactured in the U.S. under license from the German maker.

et pistols is the Beretta Model 84. These beautiful guns feature double-action exposed hammers and a thirteen-shot magazine in .380 ACP. It is a bit large for a pocket pistol, being 6½ inches long and having a 3¾-inch barrel and a weight of twenty-three ounces.

A few weeks ago I was discussing pocket pistols with Steve Richards, of Hunters' Haven, in Alexandria, Virginia, and he suggested that I try out several of them against the requirement they were made to meet and write up the results. These few lines are the result of his suggestion, and he helped out with some of the needed guns, too. The test we devised involved an approach to the twelve-yard line on the range with the loaded pistol concealed in pocket or waistband, at the shooters' choice. On command, the shooter draws and fires five shots at a mansized silhouette poster paper target. Each shooter and gun would be graded on how fast the gun got off the first shot, the number of hits, and whether or not there were any hang-ups on clothing or mechanical malfunctions.

Three friends agreed to help. One is a former gunsmith, one an "average male citizen" without great gun experience, and the third a young woman who has done considerable

sport handgun shooting but is not familiar with pocket pistols.

The guns that Steve helped me test included:
A Browning Model 1910 in .380 ACP
A Mauser HSc in .380 ACP
A Walther PP in .380 ACP, and
A Beretta Model 84 in .380 ACP.
This little table tells the story:

| Shooter | Hits Per Gun: | | | |
	Browning M1910	Mauser HSc	Walther PP	Beretta 84
No. 1	5	4	3	5
No. 2	4	3	3	3
No. 3	3	3	2	5
Total Hits	12	10	8	13
Fastest Time From Draw	9 sec.	10 sec.	12 sec.	13 sec.

I concluded from watching, and the shooters agreed, that the Beretta is the easiest gun of the lot to shoot, but the one most likely to get hung up during the draw. The Browning and the Mauser had a pretty clear edge during the draw. Fortunately, we had no mechanical malfunctions at all.

Loading your own for pocket pistols is no easy matter. It is a fact that the smaller the cartridge the more difficult it is to reload, and the .22 Long Rifle being rimfire, is out for handloaders. These small center-fire pistol cartridges, the .25, .32 and .380, headspace on the mouth of the case and so it is essential that brass be selected or trimmed to the right length. The neck sizer die must be on the small side because such cartridges need to be hard and tough to work well through the pistol action. These cartridges are not crimped so the case needs to have a strong friction fit on the seated bullet. One must give close attention to overall cartridge length; cartridges that are too long will jam in the magazine, while those that are too short may not feed well. Charge weights need also to be measured very carefully. A very small overload in these small cases can cause disastrous increases in pressures. On the other hand, you must be sure not to load too lightly or the pistols may not cycle.

If you have a pocket pistol made in Europe and have the slightest reason to suspect that it may have been assembled by "slave labor" in German occupied Europe during World War II, my advice is that you keep it as a display piece and not shoot it at all. Some of these guns are dangerous. If you are sure that you have a well-made peacetime gun, here are some loads that seem to work well in the caliber .380 ACP Browning M1910s and the Beretta M84s that I have handled:

Bullet	Powder	Charge (grains)	Estimated Velocity (fps)
88-grain Speer JHP	Red Dot SR 7625	3.1 3.4	1030 1050
95 grain R-P JHP	Red Dot 700X	3.0 3.1	1000 900
100 grain Speer JHP	SR 7625 Herco	3.1 4.2	975 960
115 grain Hornady JHP	SR 7625 Red Dot	3.5 2.4	900 850

Beretta Model 84, in .380 ACP, has double-action trigger — shifting to single-action after firing the first shot — and a staggered-column magazine with a generous capacity of thirteen rounds of ammunition.

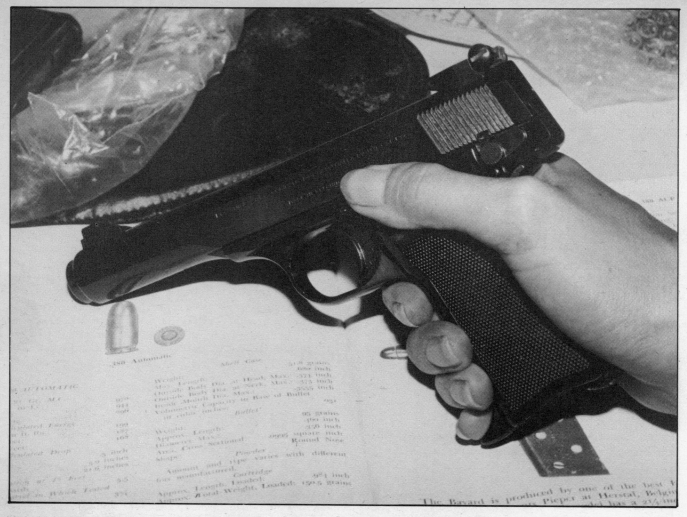

Little known and rarely seen, this is the Browning Model 1910/70 that was redesigned to get around the Gun Control Act of 1968 by adding thumb rest, target sights and so on. It was a resounding commercial flop.

These loads *work* well through the pistols, but they are marginally effective as far as I am concerned. While the jacketed hollow point bullet is probably the most effective conventional bullet we have today, it is not effective until an impact velocity of 1100 feet per second (fps) or more has been achieved. This is beyond what most .380s can do with bullets of reasonable weight. As a part of my shoot I decided to see if it might not be possible to adapt a new bullet recently designed by Dean Grennell for use in the .380. Dean's bullet, called the "Spelunker" because of the sound it makes on impact at the low velocities for which it is designed. It resembles a hard cast wadcutter but the nose contains a two-stage cavity making a compound-angle hollow point. Naturally, due to its design, he has recommended it for use only in revolvers thus far, for it is made to be seated flush with the case mouth. My thought was to make the best copy I could of Dean's bullet then see if a slight curvature at the nose might permit it to feed reliably through .380 pistols. The bullet would, of course, be seated

full out of the case to the normal cartridge overall length.

Starting with Lyman 105-grain cast lead bullets and Dave Corbin's bullet swaging dies, I came up with wadcutters containing the compound angle cavity of Dean's design. I then eased them *gently* into the nose forming die, just far enough to begin the curve process. The results were then lubed and loaded ahead of 3.8 grains of SR 7625 powder.

The alternative bullet Dean Grennell offers for use in pistols has a true conical point. This bullet, he cautions, needs to be driven at reasonably high velocity to assure useful effect. I decided to try this type of bullet also, in the event that my modified Spelunkers proved not to feed successfully through pistols.

This proved to be a real problem. No dies are made in this shape in .355/.357 diameter and I had no swaging equipment that could impart this nose shape. Finally I gave up and took Lyman 105-grain truncated cone lead cast bullets and filed them down by hand to sharp conical points. Then I lubed and seated them ahead of 4.2 grains of SR 7625 and, in the process, damaged all the noses and had to file them by hand again.

Using blocks of modelers' clay as a test medium, I tested standard factory jacketed hollow points against my two lead bullets. My control load was Federal 90-grain jacketed hollow points, and here is what I found:

Load	Bullet Weight And Type	Penetration In Oil Based Clay	Nature Of Cavity Formed
Federal	90-grain JHP	9 + inches	See photo below
Modified Spelunker 3.8 grains SR 7625	105-grain two stage lead hollow point	3 + inches	Pear shaped; about 1½ inch max. diameter
Conical 4.2 grains SR 7625	100-grain conical point lead bullet	9 inches	Very little; slightly enlarged "wound channel"

Not shown above was what happened to the bullets involved. The JHP was in every case completely undamaged when caught in polyester pillow stuffing placed behind the clay. The modified Spelunker expanded beautifully and retained ninety percent of bullet weight, plus or minus five percent or so. The conical bullet proved Dean to be correct; it does in fact need more velocity than the .380 is capable of giving. That bullet lost most of its nose but did not give much performance to show for the loss!

To my delight, the modified Spelunkers I made fed flawlessly through a Beretta Model 84 and a new U.S.-made Walther PPK/S. This brings to mind my experiences with the old Browning Model 1910. That little gun was always a marvelously smooth functioning little pistol. I cannot remember it ever malfunctioning except when being used for tests with marginal ammunition or when I was deliberately attempting to induce "typical" jams.

Tom Ferguson taught me some things about pocket pistols that are well worth knowing. They need frequent cleaning since there are few places more charged with small bits of dust and lint than your clothing. And, in cleaning, don't forget the magazines. These should be flushed out with a good solvent such as Gun Scrubber and then lightly lubricated inside and out to prevent rust. The less lube left on and in a gun when it is next carried, the less will be the lint and dust picked up. Even the best pistols can benefit from a little smoothing with crocus cloth at selected spots. The magazine lips, inside and out, the loading ramp and the

Federal's jacketed hollow point load in .380 ACP made a hole only slightly larger than the original bullet diameter, did not expand appreciably, and penetrated to a depth of slightly more than nine inches in the clay.

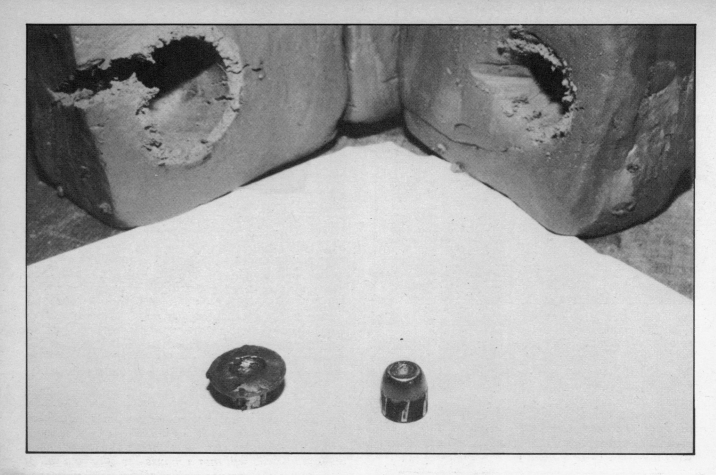

under surface of the slide need such attention. The under surface of the slide works back and forth over the top cartridge in the magazine; reduced friction here can improve reliability of function. Finally, Tom points out a possible source of danger. Some of these small pistols, notably the Walthers, have weak firing pin return springs. If the gun is dropped on the muzzle there is a chance it might fire.

I learned some things from our shoot that were unexpected. For one thing, it is no easy matter to carry a pocket pistol in a pocket. They are hard, solid and uncomfortable to carry in a pocket and are forever banging on something or giving themselves away by their characteristic shape. We tried several things that helped a bit. I rigged some stiff plastic envelopes cut to fill the pocket which supported the gun, blotted out its shape and made the draw easier, but we agreed that they were but a marginal improvement. Tom Ferguson is right when he states that the term "pocket pistol" is no longer valid. The clothing we wear these days is so much lighter and better tailored than that of fifty or sixty years ago that there is no comparison. It was relatively easy then to hide a pistol in a tweed jacket pocket! The solution that he recommends today is to cut away completely a trousers pocket on the inside. Lower on the thigh he would then wear a thin holster strapped to the leg and directly accessible through the slash of the pocket! Some judicious fitting of the pants would give good concealment.

For myself, I have found the waistband carry the best. I use a small inside-the-trousers holster made of the softest, lightest leather which attaches to my belt with a loop and

Above, modified Spelunker expanded well, holding its penetration to but three inches. Below, the homemade conical-point bullet. Lead was too soft and point too blunt for maximum effect. As discussed on opposite page, this design depends upon bullet diameter in order to achieve maximum effect.

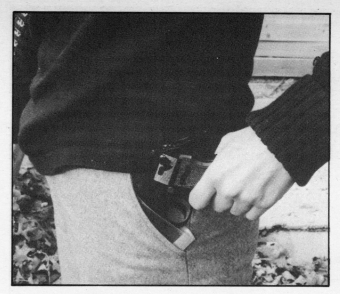

Pocket pistols are not easy to carry or conceal in today's garments. Plastic envelope in pocket is of some help. Hamilton prefers inside-waistband holster made of light, soft leather, held to belt.

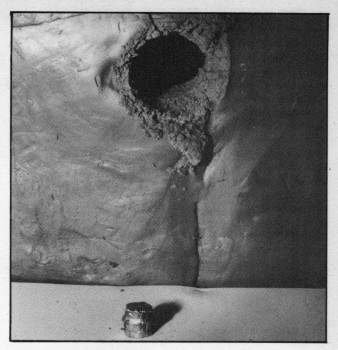

Conical-point bullet flattened its nose, but did not achieve the broader cavitation possible with a hard alloy in .45 size, fired at much higher velocities.

some snaps. With the gun in place, it hangs down far enough inside for complete concealment.

The quality pocket pistols available here these days are fun to shoot because of their light cartridges. Don't, however, expect great plinking accuracy with them. That's not what they were made for.

Author's footnote: *I think it's clarifying to add a few pertinent comments on the conical-point bullets at this point. A few years back, a French ammomaker introduced a load in several different calibers, known as the Arcane. It featured bullets with a conical point extending to about full bullet diameter and the bullets were turned from electrolytically pure copper.*

In exploring the potential of such a bullet design, I made up a few by casting bullets of suitable shape in hard alloy such as eighty percent linotype metal and twenty percent lead. The bullets were lube/sized in the usual manner, loaded into the cartridge and then chucked in the headstock of a metal lathe for contouring to final shape. The lathe, I should note in all haste, was operated at low speed to avoid heat buildup and, even then, I do not commend the practice to others.

Typically, the Arcane bullets appeared having a nose cone with an included angle of about seventy degrees — or whatever that works out to in the metric system... — and that was the angle I used for what I termed the ersatz-Arcanes. When fired into a stiff oil-base clay ballistic test medium that I commonly term duct seal — because that's what its maker calls it — a curious phenomenon was noted. The 9mm, .38 and .357 bullets made holes only slightly larger than the bullet diameter, but the .45 bullets with the same nose angle made holes up to three times bullet diameter at the entrance, gradually tapering as velocity was shed.

I tend to term that the "snow plow effect," and it appears to be much more impressive as bullet diameter

increases, even if the larger bullet is traveling at a lower velocity. Without going deeply into the matter, this seems to be controlled by what we might call the law of cubes. Consider if you will that a mouse can survive a fall of several stories to a concrete sidewalk with little more than minor discomfort. I've heard that a fall of but three feet can kill an elephant although I've never dropped one to verify that.

Somewhat the same factor appears to operate in the example of conical-point bullets on impact with a yielding, semifluid medium, such as duct seal. The increased diameter and frontal area of the .45 make a lot of difference in comparison to bullets down around .356-inch diameter, as used in the .380 ACP, 9mm Luger, et al.

The conical-point bullet was not envisioned nor designed to expand but, rather, to exploit the snow plow effect upon impact. Rather than making up .45 bullets one at a time on a lathe, it is now possible to order a #938 mould from Hensley & Gibbs, Box 10, Murphy, OR 97533. In the 80/20 alloy mentioned earlier, the H&G 938 bullet comes out about 174 grains. It feeds with remarkable reliability through a variety of typical .45 autoloaders, groups decently and can be driven to respectable velocities.

If friend Hamilton struck out on the conical-point design, he scored a homer with the adaptation of the Spelunker bullet design to the .380 ACP. The principle of the compound-angle cavity works so well in revolver loads, where the full-diameter nose poses no problem, that I had been meaning to see if it could be modified for use in auto pistols. Clearly, from Hamilton's results, it is not only possible but strategically advantageous. I plan to devote some R&R time to the project and any results thus obtained may be reported upon before we get to the end of the book at hand. — DAG

CHAPTER 5

MILITARY & POLICE AUTOS

Many Pistols Fit This Group, But The Choice Of Ammunition Is Sharply Limited

The Randall is another example of the trend to produce M1911-lookalikes, particularly in stainless steel, as here. The Randall has a ten-groove barrel and is quite accurate.

THIS CATEGORY, as you might reasonably assume, encompasses larger, more powerful pistols than we've discussed to the present. It is difficult to generalize on the topic without need for notable exceptions but it can be stated, tentatively at least, that military and police autos deliver a minimum energy at the muzzle of 250 foot-pounds of energy (fpe) and most examples are capable of exceeding that figure.

Curiously enough, the military forces of the world favor the autoloading pistol by a heavy margin, with many making use of the machine pistol having full-auto capability. Conversely, a large percentage of law enforcement units still prefer the revolver — usually chambered for the .38 Special or .357 magnum cartridges.

The basic reasoning behind that may be that the military recruit can be given more intensive training than is usually practical for the rookie policeman. It is simpler to acquire some rudimentary familiarity with the revolver than with the auto pistol and the wheel-gun tends to be slightly safer in inexperienced hands. My reasoning behind that statement — with which I'm certain some may disagree — is the fact the typical auto pistol, once fired, is all set to fire again at no more than a light pressure on the trigger. The typical DA revolver must either be cocked manually or its trigger given a long hard pull to fire further shots.

In the typical military situation — indeed, if there is such a thing — so long as the pistol wielder shoots someone in the uniform of the opposing force, little or no harm is done. In the police situation, the impactee is a fellow countryman and, unless the situation is pretty drastic, bullet holes in the suspect cause vast complications. Coupled with that, a great many law enforcement personnel care little if at all whether or not they become highly proficient with the handgun, nor do most of their superiors in the department. It would be nice if they did, but shooting the handgun is a tiny portion of the average cop's activities.

All that withstanding, there are and have been departments that standardized on auto pistols of various makes and types. The Model 39 Smith & Wesson and, less commonly, the same firm's Model 59 have been tried here and there. The Illinois State Police, for example, adopted the Model 39 several years ago and, so far as I know, still use it. So did the city department at Covina, California, and they still counted themselves fairly well content with it the last I heard. The nearby PD in El Monte, California, went to the Colt Government Model in .45 ACP back in the latter Sixties. The El Monte PD patrolled some fairly turbulent turf and the big Colts saw some amount of business use and, generally speaking, gave a pretty good account of themselves.

There is a further divergence between the viewpoints of military and police. The former feels anyone at all is automatically a bad guy if dressed in the uniform of the enemy. Any disabling wound that takes an enemy soldier out of action is all to the good. It's better to wound than to kill for the obvious, if somewhat cold-blooded reason, a wounded man ties up medical personnel and hospitals whereas a killed foeman requires only brief attention of their burial detail.

In the typical police shooting situation, the urgent necessity is to render a suspect incapable of further hostile action and to do so with all possible speed and celerity. A suspect, by that definition, is imminently endangering the life of the officer or some innocent other. If not stopped, the suspect

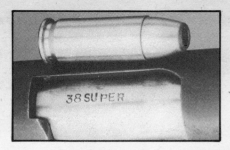

Speer's 200-grain "Flying Ash Tray," or #4477, left, above, is capable of expanding to extent illustrated at right, even at modest velocities down around 800 fps or less. The .38 CS, center, remains my favorite.

in all probability, will kill or seriously injure his victim. The clear need is for slam-bang, right-now stopping power, and lots of it.

There remains a serious shortage of guns/cartridges/ bullets capable of the obviously desirable maximum stopping capability. There are a few bullets that fail better than hardly anything else to be had, but these tend to work better in revolvers than in the auto pistols. The reason is quite simple: The extra-effort bullets have hollow point cavities extending across virtually the full bullet diameter. Such a bullet presents considerable problems when it comes to feeding through the action of an auto pistol.

The ideal bullet to assure utmost reliability in the auto pistol is the round nose full metal jacket (RN FMJ) design and that is the bullet the designers of most if not all military auto pistols had in mind when drawing up the initial blueprints. Sadly, the RN FMJ bullet is about the poorest of all possible designs in terms of stopping power. Its chief forte is penetration and, in an urban police situation, too much penetration poses a major problem. If the bullets goes completely through the suspect, hardly even slowing down, and goes on to hit some innocent bystander, the legal problems become all but unbearable.

Cartridges for auto pistols, carrying bullets capable of expansion, were all but unknown prior to the early Sixties when Lee Jurras launched the Super Vel Cartridge Corp., in his hometown of Shelbyville, Indiana. Jurras commenced his production with lightweight, jacketed hollow point and jacketed soft point (JHP, JSP) bullets loaded to the upper practical velocities and the idea gradually took hold in the fancy of the shooting public.

Today, every major domestic ammomaker carries some amount of loads for both auto pistols and revolvers with bullets capable of expansion. Winchester has them from the diminutive .25 ACP on up. Friend Claud Hamilton has the conviction you need upward of 1000 feet per second (fps) velocity to assure expansion of a JHP bullet in typical medium. I believe he makes that statement, *passim* in some of his contributions to the book at hand. I did not choose to edit or modify such comments because I felt the man was writing under his name and thus was entitled to state his sincere convictions. Here, writing under my name, I will note that some caliber .45 JHP bullets will, can and have shown excellent expansion velocities well down into the three-digit levels.

The salient example of that, in my experience, is the caliber .45 JHP made by Speer in a weight of 200 grains and marketed as their catalog #4477. The same bullet is

put up in loaded ammo and marketed as the CCI-Speer #3965 load, in plastic boxes holding twenty-five rounds.

Some while ago, working with the stainless steel version of the Detonics .45, I had chronographed the CCI-Speer load out of its 3½-inch barrel at average velocities of 859 fps/328 fpe and was pleased to note it functioned through the action of the little pistol as dead-reliably as anyone might ever wish.

As a ballistic test medium, I customarily use a stiff, oil-base, claylike material its maker terms duct seal. It is considerably more resistant to penetration than common modeling clay, hence better suited for the purpose. Six or eight inches of duct seal usually stops nearly any handgun projectile and it affords at least a comparable evaluation of a bullet's expansion capability, if any.

So, I fired one of the CCI-Speer factory loads out of the Detonics into a block of duct seal by way of finding out what it would do. What it did was to leave an entrance opening about 1¼ inches in diameter, shading upward to about 1¾ inches in maximum diameter and penetrating to a depth of slightly over six inches. The bullet upon being recovered, had disintegrated into several good-sized fragments and the jacket was almost perfectly flattened, with most of the fragments having come to a stop nearby.

It appeared the Speer bullet probably would have expanded usefully at velocities substantially lower than that. It should be noted the centrifugal force of the bullet's rotation is a heavy factor in encouraging expansion. In an earlier test, using modeling clay as the test medium, the spiral markings in the impact crater, caused by the rotation of the bullet, were clearly apparent.

Some refer to that 200-grain Speer JHP as the "flying ash tray," perhaps with some justification. Certainly its nasal crater is of awesome aspect, but you will note it puts no soft lead core in contact with the feed ramp, hence it tends to feed quite reliably through any of a great many .45 autos in which I've tried it. By the same token, it delivers accuracy in most autos beyond reasonable expectation. All around, I regard the CCI-Speer 3965 load as probably the most effective and satisfactory factory load for the .45 ACP available in the current marketplace.

In the 9mm Luger/Parabellum, the factory load with which I've had the best overall results in a number of different pistols is Federal's #9BP, carrying a 115-grain JHP bullet. It is accurate and feeds with admirable reliability in every action chambered for that cartridge. Few, if any factory loads, deliver a greater amount of muzzle energy.

Military/police pistols need not be huge and heavy, as witness Heckler & Koch's chunky little P7 in 9mmP.

In the .38 Colt Super, the traditional bullet is the 130-grain FMJ, irreproachable as to functional reliability, capable of high penetration — sometimes too much penetration, as discussed earlier — but any hope for expansion has little basis in realistic fact. Only Remington and Winchester produce .38 CS factory loads at present, both offering the 130-grain FMJ bullet as their mainstay. Remington now has a 115-grain JHP load, their catalog #R38SU1, rated in the charts at 1300/431.

Winchester recently added their #X38ASHP load, with a 125-grain Silvertip JHP bullet, presumably to replace their earlier #38A3P load with its 125-grain JHP bullet. The latter had a considerable amount of exposed soft lead at the nose and was considerably prone to stoppages. The new version with the Silvertip bullet puts jacket metal in contact with the feed ramp and its reliability is right in there with the RN FMJ bulleted loads. I have not as yet had an opportunity to try out the Remington JHP load in .38 CS but, pending comparison, would give the nod to the Winchester Silvertip load.

The three cartridges just discussed appear to constitute pretty much the entirety of the current offering in military and police auto pistol ammunition. True, there is the 7.65mm or .30 Luger, the .30 Mauser and assorted European numbers rarely encountered on these shores, but they constitute a minor factor in the overall state of things. The Bren Ten pistol and its cartridge fall within the general category of military and police pistols but, at date of writing, hard data on the Bren Ten remains unattainable.

As for the guns handling the 9mmP, .38 CS and .45 ACP, there are several and I offer comments on some of the more outstanding examples. The Heckler & Koch Model P7 is an adaptation of the same firm's Model PSP that was developed expressly for adoption by the West German police. The P7 was discussed in the previous chapter under compact pistols, which it certainly is. At a suggested retail price in the neighborhood of $600 per copy, I do not foresee its widespread use by U.S. police departments, even with departmental discounts.

Heckler & Koch also have a somewhat larger pair of auto pistols, the Models P9S in 9mmP with nine-shot magazine and .45 ACP with seven-shot magazine as well as the Model VP 70Z in 9mmP with a fairly cavernous eighteen-shot magazine. The Model P9S features a novel sliding roller lock action with stationary barrel and is DA for the first shot, shifting to SA for subsequent shots. The Model VP 70Z requires a full DA pull of the trigger for each shot. Recently I bought and read a book called *For Special Services,* by John Gardner, featuring the intrepid James Bond aka 007, as originally conceived by the late Ian Fleming. Getting to page 24, I was amazed to find he was now packing a VP 70 [no zed mentioned] as his new duty gat and, "...Bond had to admit that the weapon posed no problem as far as concealment was concerned." Tantalizingly enough, Gardner didn't say exactly *where* Bond concealed the massive pistol. I'd think a gun of that bulk would cause telltale bulges, even if one went about clad in a muu-muu.

At one time, Browning imported the SIG-Sauer Model P-220 DA auto pistol, available in 9mmP, .38 CS and .45 ACP, and sold it under the Browning name. The same gun is now imported by Interarms under the SIG-Sauer name, priced at $650 or so. During the Browning era, I had the opportunity to wring out one gun apiece in all three calibers and found it the most unswervingly reliable feeder I've ever encountered. In the course of several hundred rounds in all three chamberings, with a broad variety of factory loads and reloads, the .45 ACP chambered but failed to fire one round. As it turned out, that one was a reload in which a friend and associate had seated the primer backwards. Every single other round went through the guns snorp-boom with total Teutonic efficiency; remarkable!

If imitation is the sincerest form of flattery, the basic Colt Model 1911 design is being fair flattened with flattery these latter days. I hesitate to say just how many firms are producing autos with substantial resemblance to the M1911, as I'm sure I'd overlook a few. Some incorporate numerous innovative features, such as the Detonics, while others produce pistols hardly differing in any respect save for perhaps the material — stainless steels are much in evidence — and, of course, for the stamping on the side of the slide.

One of the first of these was the Hardballer, currently produced by Arcadia Machine & Tool (AMT), in .45 ACP only, with the standard five-inch barrel or an option for the special version called the Long Slide with seven-inch barrel and slide to match. The latter is a fine piece of pistol. I have one and admire it intemperately but note it's rather difficult to find a holster to fit it.

The Llama Omni DA autos, in your choice of 9mmP with thirteen-shot magazine or .45 ACP holding seven shots is a capable performer, quite close to the M1911 in overall bulk and weight, but with a 4¼-inch barrel, same as the Colt Commander. The .45 ACP version features a well-designed adjustable rear sight not available on the 9mmP model.

The O.D.I. Viking, in 9mmP or .45 ACP, choice of 4¼- or 5-inch barrel length, is in stainless steel and features the DA trigger system invented by L.W. Seecamp.

The Arminex Trifire pistol bears at least a casual resemblance to the M1911, is available in 9mmP, .38 CS and .45 ACP, all with five-inch barrels and its special *schtick* is that you can change it back and forth to any of the three calibers by swapping the barrel, magazine and recoil spring. Available in blue, electroless nickel, and stainless steel it is singular by contemporary standards in that it does not have a DA trigger.

Vega, Crown City, Auto Ordnance and Randall all produce pistols in pretty much the exact M1911A1 pattern, Vega and Randall favoring stainless steel. At the Colt works in Hartford, they have a strong union — fittingly enough, the United Auto Workers — and I've heard it said, but can't vouch it's true, that the union has put up stiff resistance to any proposals to switch production to stainless steel, claiming its more difficult machining qualities would cut seriously into piecework rates. Be that it as it may, a version of the Colt Python revolver appeared in 1982, made of stainless steel, so perhaps we may yet see a stainless M1911 carrying the familiar rampant Colt trademark.

The exact value and desirability of stainless steel as compared to nicely blued chrome-moly alloys is a moot point that has been discussed extensively without much agreement being reached. Mindful of the phenomenal performance of the stainless steel barrels by Bar-Sto — see Chapter 18 — there can be no denying stainless steel is capable of accuracy at the upper levels of attainment. The AMT stainless barrels for the Ruger .22 LR auto pistols likewise leave hardly anything to be wished for in tight-grouping ability. Not all other stainless barrels perform quite as well and, for that matter, it is by no means unknown to get wretched groups from blued steel barrels.

The exact degree of impregnability to corrosion damage varies to surprising extents from one alloy of stainless to several others and there a great many "stainless" alloys, each with its own set of traits and characteristics. As many have discovered to their chagrin, there are even some nominally stainless steels that will rust with more enthusiasm than a comparable part that has been treated to black oxide finish, the finish usually termed blue.

As was noted, the choice of ammunition for military and police auto pistols is rather limited. In the present state of the art, we have the 9mm Luger aka Parabellum, the .38 Colt Super and the .45 Automatic Colt Pistol. Hardly visible in the stage wings at present, we have an emerging cartridge for the Bren Ten, which may carve a niche for itself or may not.

Offered my personal choice of the major three, lacking any familiarity with the Bren Ten round to the present, my odds-on preference would be for the .38 CS, assuming a barrel length of five inches. In shorter barrels, the .38 CS loses some of its edge over the 9mmP and .45 ACP.

The hard truth, however, is that few others share my maverick fondness for the .38 CS and you can't fight majority opinion with much more hope for success than you can fight city hall. Comes a hard choice between the 9mmP and .45 ACP and, again it's my immovable opinion a good big cartridge will out-punch a good little cartridge, every week in the world. I am well aware the 9mmP musters paper performance closely on a par with the .45 ACP, by reason of operating at nearly twice the peak pressures of the latter. The 9mmP has a flatter trajectory and retains its striking force better at extended distances. In guns of comparable weight, the 9mmP is easier to control because recoil is heavily influenced by projectile weight. The guns

An auto I'm still itching to try is the Coonan in — would you believe? — .357 magnum caliber!

chambered for 9mmP usually hold more spare rounds in the hopper than do those in .45 ACP.

All that notwithstanding, I just cannot seem to shake this dogged conviction I have that the 9mmP is hardly more than a .380 ACP with delusions of grandeur and I've never encountered but one .380 for which I could kindle any small amount of fond regard. That, of course, was the funny old modified Husqvarna discussed in the previous chapter.

All of which is somewhat relevant because there have been some amount of subalimentary rumblings and general borborygms toward the notion the U.S. of A. should clasp to its national bosom the 9mmP cartridge that is so universally adored in most of the other nations we regard as on our side in the matter of global teeth-gritting, snarling and face-making.

That figures, I guess. It's logical that this country — nearly the last shaky strong-hold of the inch, the pound, the quart and similar anachronisms — should cling with sentimental tenacity to a pistol initially designed for cavalry use when that arm was still king of battles. In point of fact, by the year 1911, progress is weaponry had already relegated cavalry to the same low level of practicality as the quinquereme, but that may be irrelevant. Coming up is a subchapter on the matter of the 9mmP *versus* the .45 ACP and I'll turn you over to that in just another paragraph.

Meanwhile, for the delight of fellow .38 CS aficionados, I'll note there seems to be a growing ground-swell of interest among steel plate-plinkers in the .38 CS because it sends the plates clanging better than does the 9mmP and it's quicker to get back on target than the .45 ACP. All this just possibly could serve to reprieve a remarkably capable cartridge from untimely transition to the limbo of obsolete rounds. I dare to hope so.

Will The U.S. Stay With The .45 ACP Or Switch To The 9mm? Here Are Notes On That And Other Related Subjects.

IN 1980, at the annual conference of the United States Marine Corps Combat Correspondents Association, a spokesman for Marine Corps headquarters told the gathering of active duty and past correspondents of the Pentagon's plan to replace the venerable old 1911A1 service automatic with a new 9mm pistol.

This spokesman made the declaration that "the 9mm is better" and immediately aroused the questions of numerous members who possibly knew more about ballistics than the lieutenant colonel delivering the address. Among them were Jack Lewis, editor of *Gun World* and author of numerous books in the Gun Digest lineup; Bill Haynes, a hunter, shooter and reloader; along with Tom Baker, who does all of those things and runs a gunshop as well.

The Marine Corps spokesman, who seemingly knew more about his speech than the handgun he was touting, retired as quickly as possible, somewhat embarrassed.

For years, there has been talk of replacing the .45 auto with the 9mm and it was on the verge of happening, until President Reagan put a stop to it temporarily in an effort to hold down the budget. However, like the Phoenix, the 9mm will rise from the ashes once again, we're certain. One of the basic reasons for the United States Armed Forces' ultimate adoption of the 9mm lies in the fact that virtually all of our Allies in the North American Treaty Organization — NATO, when mentioned in your morning newspaper — are armed with the European-favored cartridge. To have the United States using the same caliber would do much to simplify manufacturing and supply problems. It would mean that our ammo would be interchangeable with that of the other NATO countries and we wouldn't be standing out there all by ourselves with an orphan cartridge that none of the other countries use.

From a supply and manufacturing point of view, I'm sure this makes a high degree of sense, but I — and a lot of

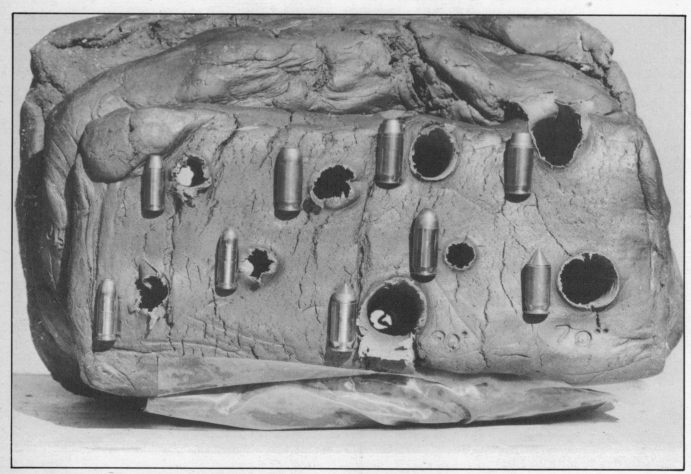

The three 9mm loads — JHP, FMJ/FN and FMJ/RN, as well as the .45 ACP FMJ/RN all left entrance holes in the duct seal medium of hardly more than bullet diameter. Each bullet appears to the left of the hole it made.

A Hensley & Gibbs No. 292 bullet was loaded into the .45 ACP case and recontoured to a 70° conical nose to approximate the bullet profile of the French Arcane loads. Its hole is lower-right, on the facing page.

others — are not all that convinced of the wisdom, when it comes to combat use.

First, of course, comes the question of just how valuable is a handgun of any type in modern-day combat. Jack Lewis, who has managed to wander through three wars to date, says he never has seen a handgun actually used in combat, although he is aware of several situations in which it turned out to be a handy item. During World War II, there was a move to replace the .45 auto for the most part with the .30 M1 carbine and most of us agree that wasn't much of a trade. I know of at least one bayonet charge in World War II that was led by a captain armed with nothing but a .45 Model 1911A1, but I suspect if he'd had his druthers, he'd have used a Garand rifle or a Thompson submachine gun.

Lest one think I'm getting emotional about the continuing threat to the .45 by the 9mm, let's take a more scientific look at what it's all about.

For the sake of logistics and uniformity, the cartridge that was recommended for our services before the Reagan freeze was the 9x19mm Parabellum, which also is known rather commonly as the 9mm Luger.

In discussing the comparison with Claud Hamilton, a retired colonel of field artillery, he made note that handguns were logical weapons for the horse cavalry, along with sabers, but cavalry charges became outmoded rather abruptly with the introduction of the machine gun.

Rather than the pistol, the NATO allies appear to be thinking more in terms of what is the most suitable cartridge for submachine guns; there is little doubt that this is a far more effective military weapon than an autoloading pistol, no matter what the bullet's measurements.

There are some old-timers around, the aforementioned J. Lewis, Esquire, included, who swear by the Thompson submachine gun of World War II and earlier notoriety among the gangsters of the Twenties. Lewis loves to tell of his disgust with the .30 M1 Carbine; after a bad night on a Korean hill, he stuck the barrel of his carbine in the crotch of a tree, bent it into a metal U and threw the wreckage into a nearby creek. He then confiscated a Thompson that had been captured from the North Koreans, who had received it from the Chinese Communists who had captured it from the Chinese Nationalists, who earlier had received it as a gift from the United States Government, when we phased it out of the inventory. If that sentence seems somewhat confusing, it's not surprising, but that is the manner in which the gun came into use on our side in Korea, according to Lewis. And it still worked well, although he admits "it took three men and a boy to carry ammo for it. But that problem was negated by peace of mind."

When one stops to consider the need for automatic weapons by the Pentagon and the NATO Forces, one can do little to defend the .45 Automatic Colt Pistol (ACP) cartridge as the ideal submachine gun round. To start with, the difference in weight between a drum of .45s and the 9mm is startling. There also is the modern-day approach to warfare which seems no longer to involve accuracy, but is a matter of firepower: how many bullets can you get out there in a given amount of time? There is little doubt that in an automatic weapon the 9mm Parabellum cartridge is easier to control for the average shooter, although I've known those who can hold the Thompson submachine gun on a target for extended bursts of fire.

Under the terms of varying treaties and international understandings, the military wants a jacketed bullet for its smallarms. This factor alone, it would appear, gives the .45 ACP an edge in that particular direction, as there is likely to be little if any expansion upon impact.

For those who have made no great study of the matter, it should be pointed out that, to a great extent, a bullet's

From left, .45 Winchester magnum; .45 ACP; 9mm Winchester magnum and 9mm Luger/Parabellum. All carry the rather inadequate FMJ/RN bullet that delivers minimum impact shock.

effect depends upon its cross-sectional area. The 9mm bullet has an area of .099 square-inch, while the .452-inch bullet used in the .45 auto has a cross-section area of .1605 square-inch or sixty-two percent more area. At the other extreme, the 9mm Parabellum tends to have more penetration power, if that's what is sought. The reasons for this involve a smaller frontal area and higher velocity; these tend to offer longer effective range and a flatter trajectory. I don't see many people feeling that a submachine gun is effective at two hundred yards; most soldiers, in my experience, tend to miss a lot at that distance with a rifle. But, it should be noted for the record that the drop of a .45 ACP hardball load, carrying a 230-grain bullet, is about fourteen feet at that two-hundred-yard range!

Let's take a look at the 9mm for the sake of comparison. A 125-grain bullet in this particular persuasion has a muzzle velocity of about 1200 feet per second (fps). At that speed, it will drop roughly 8½ feet at 250 yards. Thus, the drop of the 9mmP is roughly half that of the .45 ACP at the two-hundred-yard mark.

Still comparing, the 9mmP, leaving the muzzle at 1200 fps, has slowed to about 850 fps when it gets out to 250 yards, retaining about 200 foot-pounds of energy (fpe) at that range. On the likely assumption that muzzle velocity of the .45 ACP bullet is about 800 fps, calculations show that after traveling 250 yards, muzzle velocity would be 635 fps, with 206 fpe for a 230-grain bullet.

Our calculations thus show that the 9mm bullet has a slight advantage at close ranges, with the balance shifting to be about equal to extended ranges.

While adoption of the 9mm Parabellum is on hold for the moment with the Department of Defense, there was an earlier report that a threaded area at the muzzle was being considered by the military for simple attachment of a sound suppressor — or silencer as it is often called. While such a device tends to sound more like a need of the CIA, there no doubt are times in a combat situation when a silenced handgun would be of use.

If one were in need of sound suppression, the .45 ACP would make things much more simple, since the majority of loads for the 9mm exceed the speed of sound at the muzzle.

This declaration probably deserves a bit of explanation: At a temperature of 70 degrees Fahrenheit, the speed of sound is 1124 fps. Any bullet exceeding that speed makes a good deal of noise simply in passing through the air; it can be compared to a lesser-scale sonic boom.

Thus, even if the report of the gun is suppressed at the muzzle, the sound of the bullet's passage is something that is not going to be ignored, until flight slows to the point that the bullet is traveling at less than the speed of sound.

As indicated, virtually all of the standard 9mm loads are traveling at supersonic speeds as they leave the gun's muzzle. At the other hand, were loads to be reduced to subsonic velocities, the 125-grain bullet would be somewhat reduced in its effectiveness. The answer to this would be to load with a heavier bullet when sound suppression is a combat necessity. This has been done with a moderate amount of success, but if the overall length of the 9mm cartridge exceeds 1.160 inches, it is too long to feed through most magazines.

It would seem that the obvious requirement here is greater seating depth, moving this heavier bullet back into the case to meet the requirements of overall length, but this presents still another problem. There isn't all that much space in the 9mm Parabellum case and that space is needed for powder if the round is to be at all effective.

Armor-piercing bullets are manufactured for both the .45 ACP and the 9mmP and the latter has a definite advantage due to its smaller cross-sectional area and its higher velocity. The matter of penetration has been given some deep thought by some of our allies on the European side of the Atlantic and, as a result, a new line of cartridges was introduced a year or so back in France. This specific design is called the Arcane, the name being drawn from the Latin word, *arcanum,* which translates as meaning secret.

These French bullets boast a conical nose profile and are turned on a lathe from solid, electrolytically pure copper. The pressures, I'm told, are what might be termed downright adventurous and bullets are being made in .45 ACP, 9mmP, as well as several other calibers including .38 Special and .357 magnum.

While I've not had an opportunity to check out this French design personally, photos have been taken of wound channels produced in clay by the Arcane loads. Compared to those created by more conventional ammunition, the Arcane bullets show much more extensive cavitation as well as impressive penetration in heavy aluminum plate. As nearly as I can gather, both of these properties are created in large part by the conical shape of the bullet, while the pure copper composition of the bullet lends aid to the penetration factor by resisting distortion.

The round nose bullet has been somewhat traditional for autoloading handguns around the world, but the French are not the only ones who are thinking these days in terms of variation. Hornady, for example, has departed somewhat from the norm with a full metal jacketed (fmj) configuration for both the .45 ACP and the 9mm Parabellum that features an area of flat tip. In checking out these bullets, I've found that both feed through auto actions with a high degree of reliability and, upon impact, the flat tip tends to send up shock waves when fired into clay. The bullets seem to force this target material outward from the cavity, moving the material perpendicular to the line of flight of the projectiles.

A rather basic concept of warfare is that it is better to wound an enemy soldier than to kill him. This theory is less humanitarian, perhaps, than practical in that it requires two men and often four to depart the line of battle as stretcher bearers with the wounded soldier. To this point, the comparison of the .45 ACP and the 9mmP has been based upon that concept.

But, if one is a private citizen who is considering the purchase of one or the other of the autoloaders for his own use, including self-protection or home defense, there are other considerations that are less political and less logistically oriented. The average citizen is not too likely to be concerned with whether the ammunition for his handgun is interchangeable with that of his neighbor. And when it comes to the costs of factory ammo, there isn't that much difference between the two.

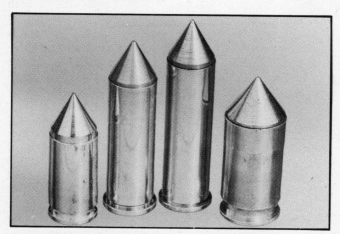

Grennell's "Ersatz Arcane" loads for 9mm, .38 Special, .357 magnum and .45 ACP cartridges. The last two have enhanced impact effect in duct seal.

Bullets and loads for the 9mm Luger, left, and the .45 ACP. Although smaller, the 9mm delivers paper ballistics on a par with the .45 due to higher pressure.

In firing, the recoil of the 9mm is somewhat less than that of the .45 ACP, while the noise level of the two batters the ears in about the same degree. However, if firing on a range, I'd say that adequate ear protection is a definite necessity for both.

When one considers bulk for bulk and weight for weight, the 9mm usually offers a greater number of rounds in its magazine. This is particularly true of the guns that feature staggered-column magazines that offer increased ammo capacities.

It has been my own experience, and that of others with whom I've shot and conferred, that the .45 is apt to have a slight edge over the 9mm when it comes to accuracy. However, if one is firing on silhouettes or other targets of large dimensions, the accuracy of either is more than adequate. And if it is an expanding bullet you want, such bullets are made for both calibers today, which was not always true.

It is for the reloader that the .45 ACP offers a definite edge in that he is able to realize more shooting for his dollar spent. First off, reloading the .45 ACP is relatively simple; rebuilding rounds for the 9mm is considerably more difficult and demanding. With any of the 9mm autos available these days to civilian shooters, functioning reliability requires stiff loads of top quality. The .45, on the other hand, tends to be more forgiving.

I would like to think that, should the Armed Forces of these United States ultimately adopt the 9mm as a means of cooperating with our European allies, the supply of military .45s would be made available to civilians through the National Rifle Association as was the case years ago. In view of the current anti-gun efforts, I doubt that any of us ever will see this happen.

As an admitted fancier of the .45 auto, I have attempted in this chapter to remain as impartial as possible. But one thought still comes to mind. If the .45 is still with us in the year 2011 as the standard military gun, it still will not be as ancient in caliber as some would have us think. Those who insist that adoption of the 9mm Parabellum for military use is a step forward in modernization should be reminded that this round is even older than the venerable .45!

Smith & Wesson 9mms May Be
The Most Accurate Service Arms Around

(Author's note: As a footnote to the earlier discussion of the results I obtained with the steel-frame S&W Model 539 auto pistol, I'd like to add these comments by Claud S. Hamilton on a rather extensive program of comparison testing he carried out. By virtually eliminating the human element from the firing system, the Ransom Rest shows the exact capability of the firearm and its ammunition. Hamilton's selection of the load for his final tear-and-compare session is a canny one, I think. I've used a lot of the Federal 9mm cartridges with the 115-grain jacketed hollow point (JHP) bullet — No. 9BP in the Federal catalog — and it was a top grouper in nearly every gun through which it was fired. I will note further that I've had thoroughly discouraging results when firing the S&W Model 59 handheld, even off a sandbag rest, and hereby turn the discussion over to friend Hamilton. — DAG)

A fairly early Model 39, in the 69## serial range was one tested for this report.

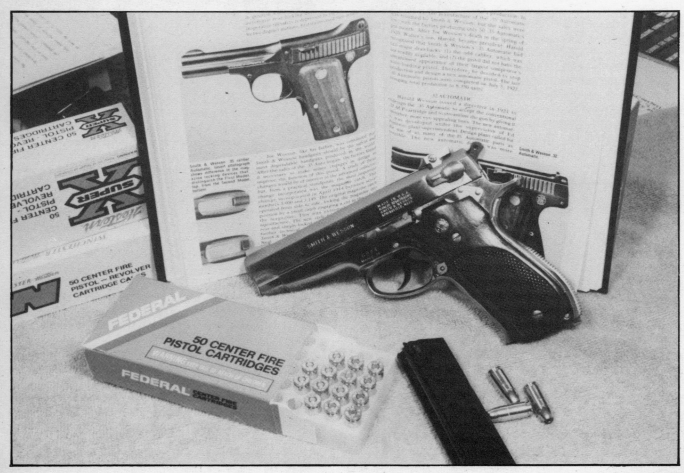

A still-earlier Model 39, with the old style wide extractor.

SMITH & WESSON'S Models 39 and 59 9mm autoloaders are probably the most accurate out-of-the-box service pistols made in that caliber today.

Now that I have gotten your attention, and possibly incurred your wrath, let me tell why I say this. I bought my first service pistol in 9mm — a Model 39 — in El Paso in 1956, the year after they came onto the market. In those days I wasn't doing much serious pistol shooting, but I did burn some powder with this gun then and later while stationed on Okinawa. I was pleased with the results I got. Dumb me, I gave that gun away to a friend some years later.

In 1964, S&W brought out the Model 59 with its large capacity staggered column magazine. In the late 1960s I managed to buy a pair of these, but soon found myself on the way to Korea again so they went into storage for several years.

My first serious experience with the Smith 9s came

about three years ago when I got a Ransom Rest. My first project was to see for myself just what sort of accuracy we can reasonably expect from modern handguns. I spent the summer and fall of that year shooting groups at twenty-five yards with every gun I could beg or borrow, and find a grip adapter for. The calibers ranged upward from 9mm through .38 and .357 to the .41 magnum and .45 ACP. I used both handloads and commercial ammunition of both target and full house types. I also used the complete spread of bullet types.

After some eight months of this pleasant research, I took a week off to look over the targets. I found that my two best groups had been shot by an old S&W Model 28 Highway Patrolman using a pair of my handloads. They measured .45 and .65 inch on centers. My worst groups were in the four-inch-plus range and were almost all made by the two Model 59s! The overall average group size for all guns came out as 2.4 inches.

This, as you can imagine, left me with a sour taste in my

Pat Wald tries a handheld group with one of the Model 39s.

mouth for the Model 59s and the 9mm Parabellum cartridge. And that wasn't all. Both of these pistols developed a habit of latching the slide open when the magazine was still about half full! This, it seems, is a problem with the M-59, and both of my guns had been sent back to the factory for the corrective work-over that S&W did some years ago. It did not seem to help them.

At about this time, a friend, the late Bill Corson, called my attention to the Devel Corporation, of Cleveland, Ohio, that specializes in work on the Models 39 and 59. They have three levels of modifications they do, the two more extensive fall into the category of what I call "chop jobs." The first level is referred to simply as a function and reliability treatment. All important springs are replaced and a permanent bushing is installed, and the gun comes back satin chrome finished. I sent both my 59s off to Devel in the hope that they might be improved.

The poor performance of the two Model 59s still bothered me. I asked dealers and friends who shot the 9mm more than I, and found that the groups I was getting seemed to be considered about par for the course. I was asked over and over again why I expected to get better accuracy out of service pistols? This got me to thinking about service guns in

general and what we really expect of them. Of the qualities we want in them, where does accuracy rank? I jotted down some ideas; here is what I arrived at on a scale of 100 points:

Durability; the ability to stand up to rough use, falls, scuffles, etc. 38
Reliability; must shoot the first time every time 34
Accuracy; have a very high first shot hit probability 25
Firepower 2
Cost 1
_____
100

You may agree or not. Accuracy is important if you keep in mind what a fair standard of accuracy is for service pistols. I believe that it would be reasonable to require that a service pistol be able to keep all its hits on a man-sized target at fifty yards. By that standard I guess my pair of Model 59s would pass, though certainly not *magna cum laude...*

An acquaintance at the club where I shoot has a new,

Ed Presler takes his turn at firing a Model 39-2 off the Ransom Rest.

One of the Model 39-2s shot a group that measured .94-inch. The hole above the group was used to seat the gun in the grip adapter of the Ransom Rest. A few such settling shots are necessary for best results.

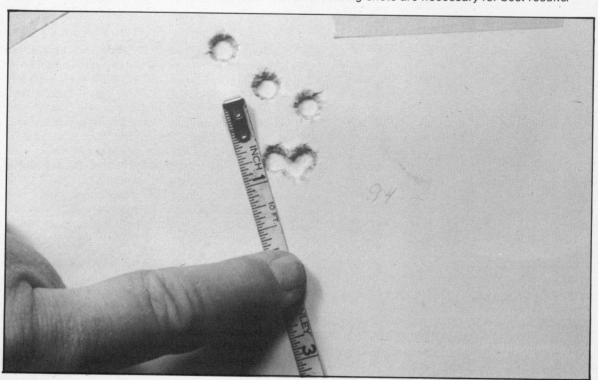

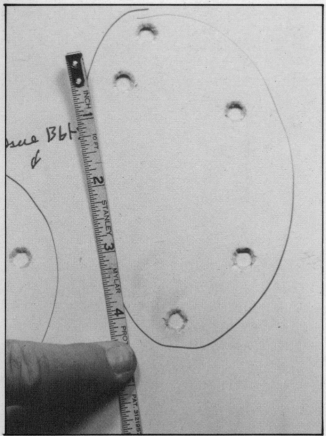

Browning Hi-Power did not beat the Model 59s.
Left, in early tests, best M59 groups were in the
4+-inch range. Opposite, Pat Wald and Ed Presler
examine some of the guns assembled for the test.

post-war Walther P'38. I couldn't help wondering how his gun might group and he jumped at a chance to see what it could do off the Ransom Rest. It could not match my Model 59s, as it turned out. I admit that I wasn't much impressed. The P'38 is a wonderful example of engineering and design, but is so loosely fitted that it would be a real challenge to a gunsmith to get one to shoot good groups.

I still wasn't satisfied and next turned to what many consider to be the cream of the 9mms, the Browning Hi-Power. I tried three in all; the first was a pre-war Belgian model with leaf rear sight and the prettiest blue finish you've ever seen. The other two were new guns of recent Belgian manufacture. These are beautiful guns and I like the way they handle, but not one of the three would shoot groups better than my Model 59s.

Bob Smith, who helps me with photo processing, has a Model 39-2 which he asked to shoot off the Ransom Rest for groups. Working on something else, I was only half paying attention as he shot his groups — I had even furnished him some old handloads of mine to burn up to free the brass for reloading — when I noticed that his gun was turning in nice, tight, 1½- to 2-inch groups, one after another! That started me wondering. Could I be wrong basing

Examples of the M59s tested included the new nickel-plated gun, above, and the Devel modified one below.

my appraisal of the accuracy of the Smith 9s on just my two M59s? They might be lemons, that sort of thing happens to the best of guns sometimes. Well, it seemed that there was only one way to find out; assemble as many as I could and see how they shot.

Checking around, I managed to locate six Model 39s and 59s and, as luck would have it, my pair of 59s came back from Devel so that my test sample went up to eight. They were a good spread, too: two older Model 39 pistols; two newer Model 39-2 pistols; two Devel modified Model 59s; two new nickel finish Model 59s of recent manufacture.

To eliminate as much uncertainty as possible, I decided to use just one lot of good commercial ammunition for all the shooting. I chose Federal 115-grain JHPs, Lot 24A 7147. All targets were unmarked white poster paper and all groups were shot at twenty-five yards. I put five rounds through each gun to seat it well in the grip adapter before going for the record.

Except for my two Devel Model 59s, none of these guns had been fired more than one hundred times, and none had been worked over or touched by a gunsmith. They were, in effect, out-of-the-box, and this was literally true for the two new nickel plated Model 59s.

Gun	Groups Size (inches) at 25 yards		
	Largest	Smallest	Average
Devel Model 59	3.02	1.80	2.29
Devel Model 59	3.76	2.63	3.12
New Nickel M59	1.60	1.27	1.43
New Nickel M59	1.84	1.50	1.69
Model 39	2.67	2.19	2.38
Model 39	3.31	2.79	3.01
Model 39-2	2.65	.94	1.79
Model 39-2	2.47	1.37	2.01
		Average	2.21

The cost of ammunition being what it is, all I could afford was five groups per gun, so you can see that there really isn't too much statistical value to my test. But, for what it is worth:

Six of the eight guns shot better average groups than the 2.4-inch average of my all-gun shoot, which had included some fine target guns!

The guns worked over by Devel managed to decrease their groups by twenty-five to fifty percent even though the Devel people do not claim theirs is an "accuracy job."

I had not one single malfunction with any of the guns tested.

Please note that I have made reference to the fact that the two new Model 59s were nickel finish. The Devel guns also returned that way. I have no proof whatsoever of this, but a strong impression that nickel plating may well make for a tighter fit and a slight improvement in accuracy.

Since my shoot I have fired the new H&K 9mms and the Browning Double Action, though not off the rest. From what I have seen, I remain convinced that the Smith & Wesson 9mm pistols, if not the most accurate service 9mm pistols out-of-the-box available today, are at least as good as the best.

Service pistols — here exemplified by AMT Hardballer — are better known for ruggedness than accuracy.

119

Air Force Personnel Produce Custom Combat Auto At Virtually No Cost To The Taxpayer!

The parent Model 1911A1 pistol and the OSI modification.

The same pair of pistols, as viewed from the RH side.

From top, Government Model, Commander, OSI pistol and a stainless steel version of .45 Detonics.

(Author's note: Chuck Karwan turned up with this account of modifications on the basic Government Model pistol. I find it not only absorbing in its own right, but an attitude on the part of government employees that merits encouragement and emulation. — DAG)

AS THIS is written, the U.S. Air Force Office of Special Investigations (OSI) is re-arming its personnel with .45 M1911A1 pistols modified to a configuration much like those customized by our top pistolsmiths.

A standard .45 magazine protrudes ½-inch from the OSI .45. Each pistol is issued with one shortened magazine and two standard ones, all function-tested and serial-numbered to match that particular pistol.

The OSI is a law enforcement arm of the Air Force that has the dual missions of counterintelligence and criminal investigation. Most of their work is done in civilian clothes requiring them to be armed with a concealable handgun. Previously they were armed with two-inch-barreled, light-framed .38 Special revolvers. The new .45 auto they have adopted is a marked improvement.

Thanks to the cooperation of Colonel Douglas Wickman, the OSI Commander of District 5 at Wright Patterson Air Force Base, Ohio, I was able to handle and shoot an example of the OSI .45 that had just arrived from Lackland AFB, Texas. When Colonel Wickman handed me an OSI .45 to examine, it didn't take me long to get enthusiastic over this little beauty. What I saw was a .45 auto that was smaller than a Colt Commander, yet retaining virtually all the good features of the original M1911A1. In addition, it had several excellent features not found on its parent M1911A1.

For some time, the OSI had not been satisfied with the two-inch .38s they were issued. Several years ago General Curtis E. LeMay, now retired but still a knowledgeable shooter and gun enthusiast, suggested that a cut-down .45 be investigated as a possible replacement. Several designs and approaches were investigated. Tom Krcmar, the foreman at the Air Force's Lackland Weapons Maintenance Section, is largely responsible for developing the modifications to the M1911A1 to meet OSI requirements. The Lackland Weapons Maintenance Section is the Air Force's one and only gun shop. They handle the repair, maintenance, and modifications on all of the Air Force's smallarms. Shop foreman Krcmar has a staff of seventeen other gunsmiths and machinists and all the work on the OSI .45 is done in-house by them.

Starting with a standard M1911A1 .45, the slide and barrel are shortened .75-inch. This results in a barrel and slide length identical to that of the commercial Colt Com-

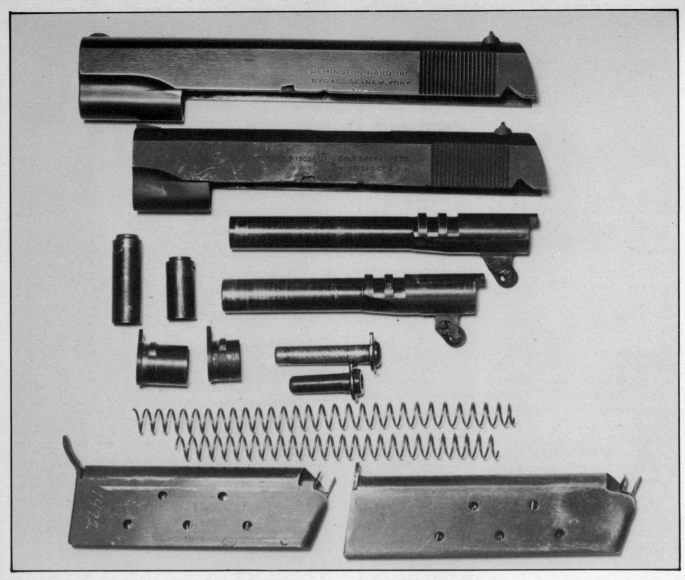

Here are the slide parts and magazines that are shortened in the OSI .45 conversion.

bat Commander model. There is also a corresponding shortening of the barrel bushing, recoil spring guide, recoil spring plug and recoil spring. The frame is shortened .5-inch in the butt with a similar shortening of the mainspring housing, grips and magazine.

The lower grip screw bushings are moved to a higher location. The trigger guard is squared and checkered, a modification first popularized by custom pistolsmith Armand Swenson to aid in a two-handed hold. The hammer spur is shortened to eliminate any pinching of the web of the hand and to minimize the possibility of snagging clothing when the pistol is drawn.

The magazine chute is beveled to aid in making fast magazine changes. A wide ramp-type front sight is installed and the rear sight notch is widened to match. The result-

ing sight picture is quite excellent for fast work, yet the low sight configuration minimizes the possibility of a hang-up on the draw. The front strap and mainspring housing are stippled to give a secure grip.

The shortened magazine is fitted with a finger spur to give support to the little finger, particularly for people with large hands. Finally an ambidextrous safety, made in-house of bar stock, is fitted. The latter feature is primarily for those OSI operatives that are left-handed.

The auto is finished in a dark matte military finish offering a remarkably business-like appearance. The resulting pistol is noticeably lighter and handier than the standard M1911A1 or even a Colt Combat Commander. It looks more like the product of one of our better pistolsmiths than government issue.

Finger spur on the magazine aids in taking a solid hold. Squared trigger guard is for off-hand index finger when firing the OSI .45 from two-handed hold.

Colonel Planchon takes aim with the OSI .45. Note position of left index finger on the trigger guard.

The OSI .45 in full recoil. Col. Planchon found it quite controllable, compared to standard pistol.

Five full magazines, at 25 yards, fired by five different shooters, each using a different brand of ammo in semi-rapid mode kept all in the 8-ring.

Sizewise, the OSI .45 has the same length slide and barrel as the Colt Combat Commander (4.25-inch barrel) which makes it .75-inch shorter than the M1911A1, but still about .75-inch longer than the Detonics .45. This length was chosen as a practical compromise for concealability, ballistic performance, and ease of conversion. The butt of the OSI .45 is .5-inch shorter than the M1911A1 or the Colt Combat Commander, but still about .25-inch longer than the Detonics.

Again, this choice was a compromise for concealment, control when shooting and ease of conversion. It was amazing how much difference in concealability there was with the OSI .45 over a standard M1911A1. The .5-inch difference in the butt seems the most significant factor. Also the OSI .45 was more comfortable and controllable than the Detonics .45 when they were shot side-by-side. It

Colonel Planchon said, "This is the way the .45 should have been made in the first place!"

Colonel Douglas Wickman, OSI commander of District 5 at Wright-Patterson AFB, Dayton, Ohio, with the newly developed OSI .45 auto pistol.

would seem that Tom Krcmar and the OSI came up with a winning combination.

I was accompanied to the shooting range by Colonel Gus Planchon, a longtime friend and an excellent shot with rifle and shotgun. Though pistol shooting is not his prime forte, he is no slouch with a handgun.

I was interested in getting his impressions of the new OSI .45. We both found the OSI .45 quite comfortable to shoot. Any increase in recoil over the standard .45 was negligible and handling characteristics were excellent. It was noticeably more comfortable to shoot than the Detonics .45, the .25-inch longer grip and magazine spur making a significant difference particularly for my thick-fingered hands.

The accuracy acceptance standard for the OSI .45 is three inches at twenty-five yards, which is more than adequate combat accuracy on a par with the issue M1911A1 .45. We found that it was easy to keep all hits inside the 9-ring on the police silhouette target firing rapidly at twenty-five yards.

We were accompanied to the range by a couple of novice pistol shooters including Planchon's 18-year-old son, Carl. We had him, two other shooters, Gus, and myself each fire one magazine full at a silhouette. To make things interesting, we used a mixture of .45 ammunition that included recent military .45 National Match, WWII steel-case .45, some recently made military hardball .45, some Winchester commercial .45 hardball and a few rounds of Winchester Silvertip .45 hollow points.

To my surprise, the combined group for all five shooters was well centered with most hits in the 10 and 9 rings. Only a few rounds strayed out into the 8-ring with one touching 8 in the 7-ring. Had our target been a bad guy, he would have been one sick hombre.

Any pistol that can be handled with such good effect even by novice pistol shooters is an excellent design. All shooters fired semi-rapid fire using a two-handed combat hold except for a few one-handed shots taken by myself and one other shooter. The fact that the trigger pull was a nice crisp 4- to 4½-pound pull was a substantial factor in our success, I'm sure. Also commendable was the fact that the OSI .45 operated perfectly with all of the types of military hardball and commercial ammunition that we tried, including the Winchester Silvertip hollow points. Colonel Planchon's enthusiasm about the OSI .45 was reflected in his comment: "This is how the .45 auto should have been made in the first place." Obviously he liked the improvements and features added by the Lackland gunshop.

Each OSI .45 is thoroughly function-tested before it is released by the Lackland gunshop. This includes function-testing with the shortened magazine accompanying each pistol and with two other standard-length magazines. All three magazines are numbered to the pistol and issued with it. The intention is that the OSI operative carry his .45 with the shortened magazine in the pistol, retaining the two standard-length magazines as spares.

The shortened magazine has a capacity of six rounds giving a fully-loaded capacity for the OSI .45 of seven rounds when one round is placed into the chamber. If an operative has to empty his pistol in a shootout, it is felt that the fact that he reloads with a magazine that protrudes .5-inch from the bottom of the pistol is of no importance. However, the extra round in the seven-shot standard maga-

The butt, mainspring housing and stocks are shortened ½-inch on OSI receiver, at bottom here.

Although the .45 Detonics, lower, is smaller, it is not as controllable or comfortable to shoot.

zine might be a definite asset. I concur with that thinking.

One of the most amazing things about the OSI pistol project is the cost factor. Tom Krcmar estimates that the conversion cost of each pistol is less than $100 with most of the cost being attributed to labor. The .45 M1911A1s used in the conversion are taken from a lot of about nine thousand procured through the Defense Property Disposal Office at no cost to the Air Force. These were pistols released by the Navy as surplus or not worth rebuilding. Many were in poor condition. This did not present a problem to Krcmar's staff as each pistol had to be torn down to start the modifications from scratch anyway.

Instead of being chopped up or torched, these surplus .45s are being put to excellent use. As a result, for less than $100 per pistol, the Air Force OSI has an excellent handgun of which the commercial equivalent would cost the Air Force $350 to $400 per copy. Actually the less than $100 cost quoted by Krcmar is probably a little deceiving because the Lackland shop overhead costs, including pay for the workers, would be paid by the Air Force if they were converting .45s to OSI specs or not. No additional funds had to be procured. Looking at it this way the Air Force is procuring these excellent handguns virtually for free! I doubt if there has ever been another weapons procurement as cost effective in the history of the U.S. military. This is particularly commendable in the light of the OSI .45's excellent characteristics, i.e., powerful, accurate, reliable, concealable, and ambidextrous. It is truly an excellent handgun for concealed carry by any standard.

In light of the proposed adoption of the 9mm Parabellum cartridge as the standard pistol cartridge for the U.S. military, the OSI's adoption of a .45 ACP handgun may seem strange, but it really isn't. First the project started several years ago before all the current hoopla over adopting a 9mm. More importantly, the 9mm handgun adoption is actually a two-stage program. The first stage is the testing and adoption of a 9mm service handgun. The second stage is the testing and adoption of a concealable 9mm handgun for use by CID, OSI and other people in the military that need a smaller, lighter handgun.

Since the first stage hasn't even gotten off the ground, it will be many years before a small 9mm will be available for issue. Until that time comes, if it ever does, the OSI .45 will fulfill the role superbly.

I found the OSI .45 to be such an excellent piece of ordnance that I could find little to criticize. I am not too enthusiastic about the ambidextrous safety, preferring the commercial Swenson or Colt versions. Instead of every OSI .45 having an ambidextrous safety, it might be better to just issue left-handed agents pistols so equipped. Admittedly my criticism is minor.

One improvement I would investigate is getting seven rounds into the shortened magazine. Since Detonics gets six rounds in a magazine .25-inch shorter still, and eight rounds into a standard-length magazine, it would seem possible to get seven rounds in the OSI magazine through the use of a different follower and spring.

Regardless, when all is said and done, the Air Force can be proud in having the good sense and resources to bring this project about. The OSI now has the most effective concealable handgun issued in the U.S. military or anybody's military for that matter. To do all that with so small a procurement cost is truly remarkable.

An earlier photo of Chuck Karwan, before he lost several pounds and gained the moustache.

CHAPTER 6

THE BIG AND FANCY AUTOS

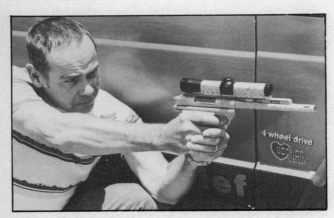

Lee Jurras, with a highly gussied-up Auto Mag.

As Autos Go, These Are The Counterparts Of The Rolls-Royces And Ferraris; No Cadillacs Need Apply

Massively-ribbed M1911 at Bianchi Cup Match.

RECENT TIMES have seen considerable changes from the days when the National Rifle Association's bullseye course was about the only competitive game in town. We now have such events as handgun metallic silhouette, bowling pin shoots, steel plate challenges and the annual Bianchi Cup Match, to mention only a few. Some of these are fired for heavy cash or merchandise prizes so it's hadly surprising most of the guns in use have been considerably improved, modified, customized and otherwise gussied-up from their original, out-of-the-box status.

In fact, it is quite possible to get well into the four-digit price brackets when setting up an auto pistol that will do its helpful best to aid the shooter in placing top-gun in some of the modern competitions. You can run up a tab of that magnitude without even including stock slabs of exquisitely carved jade.

The favorite starting point for such marvels of latter-day pistolsmithing appears to be that staunch standby of this country's military services, the Model 1911 Colt in its several versions and calibers, as currently produced by assorted makers in addition to the Colt works. True, some of the guns hopefully intended to dominate the competition start out as S&W Model 39s or 59s and the Browning M'35 Hi-Power is by no means neglected, but the M1911 still charms the majority of the shooting public's fancy.

The possible modifications of such guns span a gamut so broad as to defy hopes of exhaustive listing, but some of the commoner improvements include custom barrels — such as the Bar-Sto barrels discussed in greater detail in Chapter 18 — heavy sight ribs, muzzle brakes and/or Mag-na-porting, taking up of unwanted slack between moving parts, tuning the trigger pull to the owner's finicky preference,

Extended safety slide stop, by Bob Loveless. Note modified hammer loop on Commander.

custom stock slabs and almost anything else you can suggest, perhaps stopping just short of a built-in custom stereo rig and I'm not absolutely positive even that can be ruled out. As further tongue-out-of-cheek examples, ambidextrous safeties and extended slide stop levers seem to be favored widely. Most such modifications are viewed as painfully incomplete if the front surface of the trigger guard

Here's my Long Slide AMT Hardballer; a nice pistol, for which I can't find a suitable holster.

Tom Ferguson also photographed this M93 Beretta at the Bianchi Cup Match: foregrip, folding stock and 3-shot burst capability!

has not been either straightened or perhaps concaved, with its surface grooved or checkered to provide a slip-free anchoring point for the index finger of the free hand in the two-handed holds now so widely favored.

The Gun Digest Book of Pistolsmithing, by Jack Mitchell and *The Gun Digest Book of Combat Handgunnery,* by Jack Lewis and Jack Mitchell, both from DBI Books, provide extensive, in-depth coverage of details on the customizing of competition pistols and the interested reader is referred to one or both.

HUNTING/HIGH-PERFORMANCE AUTOS

Interest in this particular field is somewhat more narrow spread than in most others. Handgun hunting is quite popular and its popularity shows marked signs of healthy growth potential, particularly as more and more jurisdictions sanction the use of handguns for hunting. There's no denying it has been a long, uphill battle to legalize handguns for hunting in many places and a vast amount of dedicated effort has been expended to make it possible.

The probable reason for the relatively small percentage of auto pistols used in hunting is that a goodly number of revolvers and single-shot pistols have long been available, capable of delivering velocities and quantities of foot-poundage quite a bit in excess of the popular autos. More, the price tags on such guns are quite a bit more seductive than those on the few auto pistols approaching their performance potential. For about $300 to $400, you can assemble a Thompson/Center Contender single-shot in a caliber such as the .357 Herrett or, for a bit more, you can set up one of J.D. Jones' hand cannons, based upon the T/CC action. For a starting cost around $500 to $600, you can scope a long-barreled Smith & Wesson Model 29 or a Ruger Redhawk, both in .44 magnum, to end up with a six-shot repeater capable of taking game to the size of deer or somewhat larger, at ranges out to 150 yards and perhaps a bit beyond.

The large auto pistols such as the Auto Mag or the Wildey muster quantities of delivered energy approaching — though hardly exceeding — that of the all-out .44 magnum revolvers. The hangup lies in the fact that assembly of a comparable setup based upon either of those is going to involve cash outlay to the tune of $1500, probably substantially more.

The Auto Mag — as one gun book commented — has

Two views of the near-legendary Wildey, now said to be in limited production.

used up manufacturers with almost as much avidity as some guns consume ammunition. Its production has been quiescent within recent times, but there are rumors going about that it's about due for another courtship of the shooting public, perhaps to be available in .45 Winchester magnum this time in addition to prior cartridges such as the .357 and .44 AMP.

After a decade or so of struggling, the Wildey is reported to be in limited production, as indicated by advertisements in some of the trade papers. The Israeli-made Eagle, in .357 magnum, is being displayed at trade shows complete with interchangeable barrels in assorted lengths. The Coonan auto, likewise handling the .357 magnum, is gearing up for production. Several years ago an auto called the Kimball was set up to handle the caliber .30 carbine cartridge. It did not generate a vast amount of interest amid the shooting public, perhaps because many viewed the cartridge as submarginal, even if fired from the longer barrel of the GI carbine.

Screenwriter/photographer Magali Akle, with the Sterling 9mm folding-stock, semi-auto carbine.

A later version of the Sterling is this Mark 7 pistol, with a choice of 34-round or 10-round magazines.

ASSAULT PISTOLS

The term is my own private one, not apparently sanctioned by the makers of such armament. Given a shoulder stock and full-auto capability, such specimens would be termed assault rifles — provided they handled a cartridge nominally intended for use in shoulder guns/shoulderguns; select the spelling of your preference.

The ability to own and operate full-auto weaponry legally is somewhat contingent upon place of residence in this country, even if you're prepared to slog through the registration fee of $200 and attendant red tape complexities.

A lot of shooters are disinclined to go to quite that much expense and bother, even if they reside in tolerant states. This has led to the introduction of semi-automatic, but otherwise closely comparable versions of several submachine guns/machine pistols — two synonymous terms for full-auto weaponry designed to handle nominal handgun ammo. If you refer to such things as burp-guns, you're welcome to adopt my favored term for the autoloading equivalents: hiccup-guns.

The foregoing considerations have led to the reintroduction of the Thompson Model 1927, an autoloading counterpart of the legendary tommy-gun, as a stocked carbine or, sans stocks, as the last-most auto pistol in all the world that the fictional sleuthess Honey West might be expected to pack in a garter holster; particularly with a drum magazine.

Beauty, it's been observed, is in the eye of the beholder. This particular beholder has long felt the old Thompsons had considerable quantities of svelte charm and outright elegance, especially the old pre-WWII production from Colt, with their exquisite workmanship and finish. An entire new school of thought has sprung up, it would appear, resolutely rejecting any such poppycock and balderdash.

Tom Ferguson has theorized that modern designers of assault weaponry seem to be operating on the tacit assumption that, almost any year now, a Nobel prize will be established and awarded to the given year's most ugly-revolting assault-weapon and its designer. I'd never considered it in that light but, by golly, once it was brought to my attention, it seemed to make a lot of solid sense.

This leads us to the Israeli-designed/built Uzi, which I'd term purely hell for capable, but no great shakes for cute. Uzi carbines have been on the market for a fair while now, firing but one round of 9mmP per pull of the trigger and, when the trigger is released, it can be pulled again to fire a further shot. In more recent times, a stockless pistol version of the same basic action has hit the market.

The British Sterling has been exported to these shores in several different subvariants. In its original forms, it is the current issue submachine gun of the British Commonwealth and, as such, it cackled, chortled and sewed stitches in the Falklands Fracas of the early Eighties. One of the subvariants incorporated a silencer or sound suppressor. Being chambered in 9mmP, you'd suppose that would require use of subsonic ammo in order to function but not so. The suppressed Sterling incorporates a craftily vented barrel that bleeds off powder gas as the bullet moves downbore, channeling it through the same set of baffles and mazes, so as to reduce the velocity to subsonic levels, no matter how lusty a load went into the chamber in the first place. Clever, these Britons!

I can report on that particular gun from first-hand experience. Attending an exposition of police weaponry at Los Angeles in early 1983, the representative for the U.S. importer packed a magazine full of torrid NATO 9mmP

Interdynamics KG-9, left, fired from an open bolt. Later, improved, KG-99 version, right, fires from a closed bolt, a vastly more accurate system. The foregrip on the '99 may require special registration.

If you can live with a bit of weight and bulk, the 9mm Wilkinson Arms Linda is one tack-driving sweetie!

loads — considerably more zesty than SAAMI specifications sanction — and let me revel in a second or so of pure glory. I can confide that — to my decibel-deadened tympani, at least — the sound-effects can be accurately likened to those of a runaway sewing machine. At the same time, it is incredibly easy to control in full-auto mode.

An autoloading carbine version — unsuppressed — with a folding stock has been imported and marketed and, more recently, a stockless pistol version, likewise autoloading, has joined the domestic offering of the Sterling. Its effective concealment would still pose a considerable challenge to Honey West, even with the ten-round magazine in place of the usual thirty-four-rounder. It will accept and work well with either magazine. Fire it one-handed, in the classic NRA offhand stance — ? Well, Chuck Karwan — who is built like a brick smokehouse, only a trifle sturdier — might bring it off, but I'll confess I can't. Even finished in black-crackle paint, it is not a promising candidate to back in the all-out-ugly sweepstakes, but given another five centuries, it might kindle an appreciative gleam in the eye of Buck Rogers.

Another gun designer and maker who has hardly any chance at all of carting off the hypothetical Nobel prize for repugnant repeaters is Ray Wilkinson. His is the drafting pen that gave us the Wilkinson Linda, Diane and Terry, all named in honor of Wilkinson family members, with only Mr. W. himself left uncommemorated. One day the Raygun may appear, but best not to hold the breath, okay?

The Linda pistol is considerably too heavy and bulky to be concealed by Ms. West — or, comes to that, the burly Bertha Cool — but it consumes the 9mmP cartridge with voracious, unhesitating appetite, it delivers its projectiles close to the point of aim and, in general appearance, it looks unmistakably gunnish, rather than like a few parts that fell off a roto-tiller. In the category of today's assault pistols, that sets it quite radically apart from the main body of its contemporaries.

Apart from the section of perforated gaspipe snood up front, the Interdynamics KG-9 and its successor, the KG-99, also look fairly gunnish and probably will claim no top awards for ghastlitude. The KG-9 was a slam-fire design, meaning it fired from an open bolt. Pull the trigger and a

pound or so of bolt lunged forward to scoop the top round out of the magazine, chamber it and, via an integral nub on the face of the bolt, fire it. The distracting effect upon the sight picture can be readily and accurately imagined. Threatened by King Kong on the far side of a card table, you had a fair chance of pinking the awesome ape. Any adversary smaller than that, or farther away, enjoyed attractive odds in favor of escaping unscathed.

The KG-99 was a matter of "back to the old drawing board," and it emerged modified so as to fire from a closed bolt. The improvement as to grouping capability was most gratifying. At a distance of twenty-five yards, the KG-99 has a good chance of hitting a playing card, whereas, at the same distance, I'd not care to wager a Confederate penny I could pot the top of a pingpong table with the KG-9.

The exact parameters of practical utility for all such weaponry are much open to conjecture. Some have theorized that an assault pistol with oodles and oodles of Darth Vader ambience may be capable of pacifying a sticky situation without need for firing a shot. That, in itself, may aid in validating the Ferguson Theory previously mentioned. In certain examples, such as the now-discontinued KG-9 and other slam-fire designs, the owner will do well to hope the looks of the gadget frighten the adversary into whimpering submission because, as noted, if you have to fire the madly lunging things, your chances of scoring a helpful hit are about on a par with garnering top award in the Irish Sweepstakes. Most such guns, it can be noted in conclusion, are efficient devices for converting live rounds into empty cases; you have to give them that, at least.

CHAPTER 7

THE IVY'D HALLS OF LFI

Schoolday Memoirs Of A Student At Massad Ayoob's Lethal Force Institute

Ayoob keeps an alert eye on the firing line as his students give the silhouettes what-for. Much of the firing is from about the distance shown here, thus putting a premium on speed and reliability over pure accuracy.

IN MARCH of 1983, Roger Combs and I sat in on a highly compressed cram course in what our mentor and guru chooses to term *stress management*. It is a most absorbing concept, as I can attest and I have no doubt it merits all the attention you can give it. In the normal routine of things, I view firearms — specifically auto pistols for purposes of the discussion at hand — as fascinating gizmos embodying varying degrees of excellence in design and fabrication. Long ago, I had to resign myself to the hard reality I'll never be as skilled with firearms of any sort as I'd like to be. Nonetheless, they hold an unbreakable Circean enchantment for me and I continue to make gallant efforts to get better with them. Virtually all of my firing is done at paper targets or the occasional tin can,

making certain of adequate backstops and adherence to prudent rules of safety.

Despite all that, in a time of hard stress, auto pistols and other types of firearms can be invaluable allies. They can preserve your beloved health and well-being, if employed properly. I view that as incomparably preferable to the alternative. I've never had to fire a shot in anger or alarm. It's my sincere and devout hope I never have to.

How-EVER...Should fate or whatever's in charge maneuver you into a clutch where you have to engage in serious social shooting, two vital considerations apply:

First: It is starkly imperative that you survive the encounter and it's ice cream on the pie if you do so unscathed.

Our genial guru, left, with yours ever so humble and truly, during one of the brief breaks in the intensive training course.

Second: It is of the keenest essence you comport yourself so scrupulously as to avoid any messy and unpleasant legal aftermaths stemming from the encounter. In our current social matrix, the police do not drive up, survey the scene of the shooting, vindicate what you did and shake your hand with the jovial assurance Matt Dillon would've been proud of you, driving away after that, leaving you to police up your spent hulls for return to the reloading bench.

No indeed, it's by no means that simple. I had long been aware there were complexities involved but, until I'd gone through what Ayoob terms his Gravest Extreme Course, I really didn't realize things were quite *that* complicated.

Massad Frederick Ayoob, founder and director of Lethal Force Institute, Inc., has been a frequent contributor to the firearms press for the past many years. He served for seven years as a part-time sworn officer with the Hooksett, New Hampshire, police department and was the departmental firearms instructor for most of that time. His other qualifications and teaching credentials cram nearly two pages of single-spaced typing and I do not propose to quote all of them here. I regarded him as redundantly qualified before taking the course and, having done so, my conviction is reinforced.

The Lethal Force Institute was organized and incorporated in October of 1981. Based out of New Hampshire, Ayoob conducts courses in areas that include Florida, California, the Midwest, the Northwest and Canada. Pertinent information as to dates and locations of upcoming courses can be obtained on request to Lethal Force Institute, P.O. Box 122, Concord, NH 03301; the phone is 603/224-6814.

Tuition for the Gravest Extreme Course — as offered for civilians in the judicious employment of deadly force — is $400. That includes the supporting paperwork: a copy of Ayoob's *In The Gravest Extreme,* together with almost the equivalent of another book in supplementary material. Prospective students must furnish proof of their bona fides

and good character such as a permit for carrying concealed weapons (CCW permit), or references from their local chief of police, sheriff, judge, et al.

If accepted for the course, the student must bring a gun of the sort they might plausibly use for self-protection, a suitable holster, at least two functional reloaders — magazines for autos, speedloaders for revolvers — carriers for same, ear protection, eye protection and five hundred rounds of what might reasonably be considered full-power combat ammunition. For example, if using a .38 Special revolver, mid-range wadcutter loads would not be regarded as acceptable.

I will sidenote that LFI courses are held in two basic formats. You can attend for eight hours a day over the course of five weekdays or you can put in two ten-hour days over two consecutive weekends. Combs and I chose the latter and it may be relevant to note you can get by with about two hundred rounds the first weekend and three hundred the second weekend. The three hundred rounds for the second weekend are designed to get you through your final qualification firing, with enough ammunition in reserve to enable a second pass through the course if you don't qualify the first time. As I made it comfortably on the first pass, I brought back a quantity of leftover loads I've not gotten around to expending to the present.

Devout reloaders can be advised that opportunity is given to retrieve the spent cases. Until reassured on that score, I was giving serious consideration to running the course with the Sport Model Colt Woodsman and a generous supply of Yellow Jackets. If the shooter next to you is firing the same cartridge you are — and one of mine was — you can negotiate an equable division of the spoils. Rest easy on that point.

Each class is limited to twenty students, accepted in order of application. Ayoob notes the average student is upper-middle-class, about eighty-five percent male, at an average age of 30 to 50. In descending order by occupation: physicians, high-risk retail merchants — such as

"The gun is the tool — the MIND is the weapon!"

gunshop owners and liquor store personnel — airline pilots, civil engineers and attorneys. The last are there not only to sharpen their own skills but to pick up information on the dynamics of violence they can utilize in court cases.

The odds are not attractive that anyone sufficiently interested in shooting to have purchased a copy of this book still retains keen and perfect hearing acuity. If you are the exception, congratulations to you. I can hear sounds, but have vast difficulty in deciphering much sense out of them. Personally, my hearing is utterly pediculous — a gentle euphemism for lousy — and I had more difficulty than I really needed in auditing the high-speed jetstream of information directed our way over the four sessions. As with many born and raised in the northeastern corner of this country, Ayoob's normal speech pattern is a runaway staccato. Hetalkssortoflikehewastypingandkeptforgetting-tohitthespacebar. Sometimes the ends of the words seem to overlap a bit, but I do not propose to tax our typesetting department with rendition of that effect.

More, his sound system is downslope from the pinnacle of sophistication and, at the time we attended, he was using some tape cassettes of a brand I regard as the most wretched to be had in the marketplace.

Still more, the classroom was scant yards from the firing line of a public range in Long Beach, California. As a result, the daytime lectures were stochastically punctuated by an unfaltering background of crump-snap-boom as local shooters did their happy thing. Stochastic means

occuring without discernible pattern, in a random manner. It's a neat word, I think.

I had asked if I could tape the lectures and had been told I could not, due to legal considerations of copyright status and the like. No big thing. Listening to a tape of all that would have snapped the composure of a granite Buddha. The topical flow was of sufficient interest, however, that I listened with the intentness of a starving terrier at a likely rat hole. It must have worked, because I have my certificate right here.

As clumps of information go, it was amply capable of choking a Strasbourg goose. I made no pretense of reproducing it all in the space available here. I will try to pass along a few salient highlights for your contemplation.

The laws of this land — with the firm stipulation they vary significantly from state to state — do not sanction nor condone killing or endangering the well-being of another person unless circumstances make it clearly apparent — "in the judgment of a reasonable man" — that that person is about to cause death or severe personal injury to yourself or to another innocent victim.

The hypothetical assailant must have AOJ: Ability, Opportunity, Jeopardy. He — or she, since the female of the species isn't always all that innocuous — must have the ability to inflict grave bodily harm, along with the opportunity to do so and the assessment of jeopardy must be clearly apparent. Again, that litanical phrase, "in the judgment of a reasonable man." The reasonable man/woman can be thought of, amplified twelve-fold, as the jurors at the impending trial.

Ayoob relies heavily upon audio-visual training aids. There were two really outstanding reels of training film — produced by Motorola, as I recall — in which the students in turn were handed a cap-pistol and told to face the screen. A situation would unfold in which the student had to make a shoot/no-shoot decision in just a few split-seconds after a signaling beep had come over the sound system. Something like that tends to get your full attention, as might a cobra obviously infected with rabies. I sailed through all my turns doing the right thing at the right time or even a trifle sooner, but I'd be the first to admit it was sheer good luck. Even while watching the other students take their turn, it was impossible to stifle the neural impulse to the trigger finger and I'll admit I wrong-guessed a few: Immensely educational!

Some of the cinematic sequences got damned stark. It is not a course the tender of stomach and outlying viscera are apt to sit through shruggingly. If you happen to have serene faith in the stopping power of handguns, one film carries pungently clinical details of a malefactor who stopped or at least slowed down thirty-some hits by 9mm Luger hollow points, plus a few blasts from 12-gauge police shotguns. True, the deceased was sustained by a massive ingestion of PCP or angel-dust, but even so...

By way of lending perspective to the relative lethality of various weapons, the visuals include victims of knives, blunt instruments, attack dogs and perhaps other hazards. Should you ever come under attack by a knife wielder and feel reluctance to defend yourself with a firearm, due to ethical qualms that you have your foe out-weaponed, those photos will disabuse you of your unsupported fancy.

If all this has an undertone of gross violence, I am sorry

and I apologize. The hard fact remains that shuddersome things happen to innocent victims and they happen regularly, unceasingly. Within the past week, within not too many miles of where I'm typing this, four lives were snuffed out in the messiest *Grand Guignol* manner imaginable. It happens all the time, to some luckless souls. If you're utterly certain you're so lucky you never need worry about such sordid things, you're free to skip along to the next chapter, right here and now.

Me, I have no slightest trifle of such calm certainty, for I doubt I'll ever forget an evening when I missed departing this vale of tears via a faceful of buckshot and windshield fragments by a margin of perhaps twenty minutes. Like Ayoob, I was a sworn, part-time officer in a tiny-town police department. You don't have to wear the badge of a big department to get killed pretty dead, as I've seen along the way. As a matter of fact, I was badge number six in a five-man department and, really, that's the story of my entire life, right there in a neat nutshell.

We only had one patrol unit, but it went by the name of Car 73, please don't ask me why. My partner's name was Ernie and he was driving that evening. We usually knocked off and put Car 73 to bed around midnight in hopeful assumption that crime would stalk slowly if at all from then until dawn. Most nights, we were correct on that score.

In that mini-metropolis there was a firm called Schaetzel Oil situated up a lengthy driveway from the main drag and we always made a point of checking it out just before we called in and terminated our patrol. We did so that night and I've vivid recollection of our cheerful ebullience. We had served our community's welfare for some number of hours and, in the fullness of time, come payday, we were due to get two dollars for each and every hour thus put in, minus deductions, of course.

Schaetzel Oil was serenely inviolate as we completed our circuit. Ernie and I were harmonizing handsomely on "Gimme cracked corn and I don't care," and I recall wishing I could've recorded it. We called in to our dispatcher — a gent called Tony I never met, who had a fascinating way

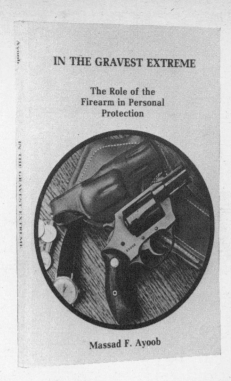

IN THE GRAVEST EXTREME

The Role of the Firearm in Personal Protection

Massad F. Ayoob

Massad Ayoob's book will go a long way to keep you out of deep, dark trouble, hence cheap at twice the moderate cost. Address is in text, write for price.

with the more or less English language — and garaged Car 73 in its assigned niche in the local fire house. Exchanging parting farewells, we got in our own cars and called it a night.

Well before sun-up, the phone by the bed went berserk. It was Freddie, our revered chief of cops, who foremanned a crew of tree trimmers dayside. We were all part-timers in those days and that place.

"Get down here to Schaetzel Oil. Bring your camera stuff."

I was the only member of the department who knew which end of the camera got aimed toward the intended subject. I will spare you the memoirs of a police lensman and for that, you owe me a bit of gratitude.

Schaetzel Oil had been well and truly busted and ravished during that brief interim. The assistant chief of the department drove a truck for them dayside. He'd just bought a new car and, being in the midst of an upper-midwestern winter, had driven it into the truck area, washed it and left keys in the switch in case a fellow driver needed to move it. The blaggards took the assistant chief's new Pontiac as part of their getaway fleet.

Night-firing exercises and my fellow .38 Colt Super fan shows what a muzzle flash really looks like. In point of fact, I held the camera shutter open through the entire magazineful to produce this. Easy? No.

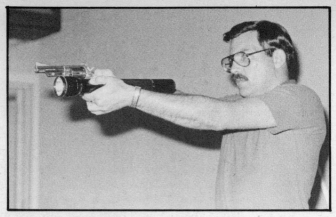

Classroom demonstration included technique for use of handgun and flashlight for night use. Below: "In a matter of hard choice, I'd rather have a cheap gun and the best damned laywer in the whole wide world!"

With empty hands for safety's sake, Roger Combs practices concealment behind barricade with another student — a highly educational experiment, I thought.

Quite a bit later, their outlaw luck frazzled out and they were picked up in Las Vegas. In the course of the debriefing interrogation, they made free admission they'd popped Schaetzel's right after midnight and, while the rest of the crew were busily engaged, one had stood atop the desk in the front office to keep vigil out the window, with a sawed-off 12-gauge double in his hands. Thus, in a remote and roundabout way, I encountered my almost-killer, the chap who nearly managed to cause the lettering on my tombstone to read 1923-1965. I can still see those muddy footprints.

To the moment, I continue maintaining an open hyphen after the first four digits and you can bet your sweet bippy I like it that way. Thus ends the tangent from the nominal discussion. If I seem a trifle glacial, you may now be able to understand the reason behind it.

Toward the end of each of the four afternoons, the lectures stopped and we all trooped out to put in the fun part or cap-snapping phase of the curriculum. On the first Saturday, I selected a small revolver I think of and refer to as Li'l Montgomery. It started out as a Smith & Wesson Model 10 in the usual .38 Special calibration. It benefited hugely from the skillful ministrations of a gifted pistolsmith by name of Chuck Ward, down in Raymore, Missouri. With the aid of a brace of Safariland speedloaders, it performed

nothing at all short of superbly. That was all very well, but I was keenly mindful I had the manuscript for the book at hand to get out.

There was no objection to changing horses — or, for that matter, colts — in midstream so for the Sunday afternoon session I made the switch to a Government Model Colt chambered for the .38 Colt Super cartridge. I had a modest but ample supply of Remington factory loads along with the 130-grain FMJ/RN bullets. The auto did its part with impeccable *savoir faire* and even a touch of *sang froid*.

I've been on friendly terms with the genial and voluble Ayoob for quite a number of years, but for the duration of the session considered myself merely one more of his students, under his direction, not presuming upon past friendship; well, no more than I could readily control, anyhow. One of our first sessions at the silhouettes were practically at powder-scorch distance and I was amusing myself innocently, I thought, by lettering my initials in bullet-pocks in its solar plexus, firing from the hip. The familiar down-east twang came from behind, modulated to get through my Lee-Sonic earplugs: "Please, Dean — go along with the gag and use the sights, okay?" I did so, meekly and humbly.

For practically all of the shooting sessions, the emphasis was upon rapid reloading and the really *heavy* emphasis

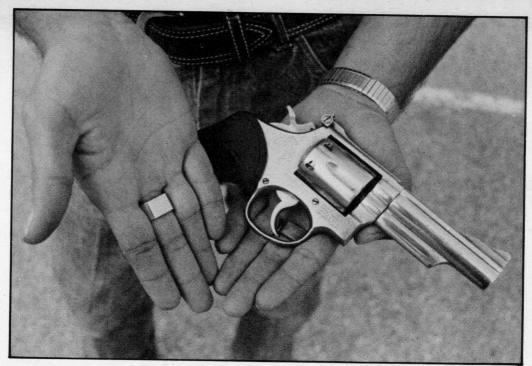

Apparently, I'm not the only one sometimes given to bestowing names upon guns. Ayoob refers to this S&W Model 66 as "Fluffy." Unless held in a hand wearing one of the special samarium magnet rings to deactivate the lock, it's absolutely inert and cannot be fired. Until hoods start wearing such jewelry, that sort of helps.

was upon letting the blasted empties drop to the ground and not worrying about them. There was excellent reason for that. The usual tendency to stash the spent hulls for later reloading has cost some embattled officers their lives and their remains have been found with a handful of empty cases. So it was a matter of stabbing the empty cases free of revolvers, jamming in the speedloader and letting that drop in turn, or dropping the empty magazines of the auto pistols with blithe abandon.

By the time the second weekend session came up, I no longer had any remaining supply of .38 CS factory loads I cared to expend, so had set up the bench and knocked forth about three hundred reloads. Ayoob counsels against use of reloads for serious social shooting and my experience underscored the validity of that. I had four failures to either feed or fire in the course of about two hundred shots the second weekend. True, I cleared the stoppages *muy pronto*, being redundantly familiar with the M1911 system, but the fact remains: What if that particular shot had been of the gravest extreme in importance? Tough breaks, Dino!

Not that the performance was all that wretched. I copped second highest score in the class and was reminded of the title of Bill Jordan's highly pertinent book on the fine points of ongoing survival through pistolcraft: *No Second Place Winner.* Of a possible six hundred points, I got 527 and the high gun for the group bagged 544, skunking me by seventeen. He was also firing a Government Model Colt in .38 Colt Super, with the rest of the class using .357 revolvers, .45 ACP and 9mm Luger autos. I viewed it as gratifying vindication for my favorite pistol cartridge,

which Ayoob holds in well-bred disdain. "The .38 Super is pretty much a bummer," is about the way he put it. He didn't say why he thought that and I neglected to ask.

The shooting sessions are only part of the LFI curriculum, albeit the most enjoyable and interesting. A lot of the nuts-and-bolts nitty-gritty can be absorbed by reading Ayoob's book, *In the Gravest Extreme,* which can be ordered for about $8, postpaid from MFA Publications, Box 122, Concord, NH 03301. I recommend it without reservations, feeling some of the chapters are worth more than the asking price of the entire book.

The crucial point, I think, is that Ayoob sees the broad overall picture, from extensive personal experience as a witness for either the prosecution or defense in countless courtroom trials. He knows, all too well, the final curtain doesn't come down when the last shot is fired. A brief excerpt from *Gravest Extreme:* "...while almost everything in print on the use of a gun for self defense begins with the draw and ends with the last shot, you have to understand that when it comes to court, the judge and jury will be looking at flashbacks from *long* before you went for your pistol, and the whole ordeal won't end for months or years, if ever." That's from page 93.

Matriculation from the LFI Gravest Extreme course tends to make you a peace-loving citizen of the devoutest sort, mindful of a great many lurking pitfalls to which you never gave a passing thought before. Get and read the book, by all means, audit the course, if you can. Either way, it could extend the longevity of your one and only bacon and that's much to the good, in my humble opinion.

CHAPTER 8

ACCESSORIES FOR AUTOS AUTO MAGAZINES IMPROVING THE BREED CLASSIC AUTOS

In Which We Speak Of Many Things Pertaining To Auto Pistols

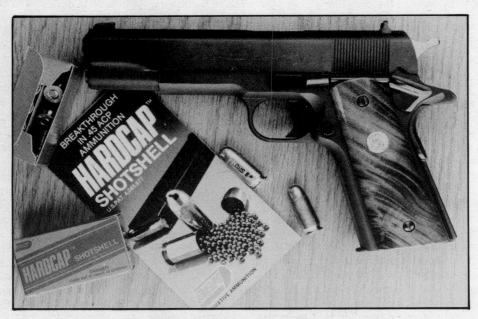

Colt's Combat Government Model, in .45 ACP, was introduced in 1983 with modifications discussed here. Those did not include the set of handmade stocks, complete with medallions the gun now wears. Refer to facing page.

BY ITS VERY nature, the auto pistol stands painfully ready to benefit from a number of helpful gadgets. As but one example, a reader named Frederic R. Bennett, of 277 Luce Road, Williamstown, MA 01267, sent me a handy and ingenious small item crafted of stainless steel. You hook it over the button of the magazine follower of the magazine for the .22 auto Ruger, pull it down and secure its built-in catch to the bottom of the magazine. With that done, you can proceed to fill the magazine with elegant ease. I believe he will

undertake to make one of these for several popular makes of .22 autos, if approached by an interested party.

I've never experienced serious difficulty in loading most .22 auto magazines, but some of the 9mm jobs are a trifle trying. On occasion, I've whittled out small loading aids from wood so as to serve to shove the rear of the previous case down into the magazine far enough to start the next one beneath the magazine lips. Such things are helpful if you don't lose track of them.

An area where further research and development might

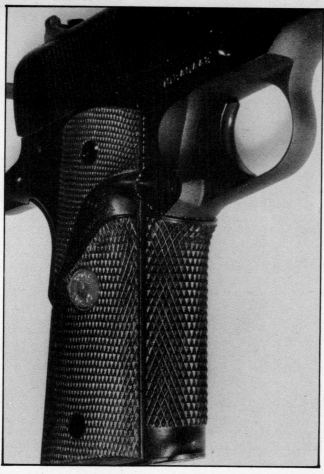

This set of Pachmayr rubber grips is as furnished on the Combat Government as standard equipment.

prove helpful — making no guarantee it would be profitable — is that of maintaining some semblance of control over the ejected empties. Even if you don't reload, fired center-fire brass is worth a nickel apiece and up, as can readily be verified by a visit to your local gun store.

I had hoped to include a discussion in this book by a good friend of mine by name of John D. Ellison, who lives in Plymouth, England. Ellison is an enthusiastic handgunner, owning and operating a Model 1911A1 Colt, a Model 19 S&W, and I forget how many other hip-howitzers. Many Usanians have a firm belief it's impossible for a British subject of good character to own and use handguns. Not necessarily so, although it's more heavily fraught with complexities than it is here, in most places. That was what I'd hoped to have Ellison discuss for us but, as I write these lines, the deadline fuse for this book fizzles spookily short and the remaining space is all spoken for. An explanation, not an excuse, please? This is the last chapter of the book through the typewriter and I need to cover four topics originally outlined for a chapter of their own. For that, you have my sincere apologies.

What brought Ellison into the discussion is that his shooting club fires at a range where the ground is covered with medium-length grass much like a typical lawn. As you'd suppose, it makes ejected empty cases from autos terribly hard to retrieve. As their solution, some club member scrounged up an old parachute and they spread the canopy evenly about the shooting area and, on completion of firing, simply lift the outer edges and virtually all the vagrant brass is neatly decanted into a suitable container. Clever, these Britons and I wish I'd thought of that.

It's a project I've had gently simmering on the back burner for some while to scumble together some manner of hanging baffle, perhaps a large if scruffy bath towel that could be suspended from suitable supports to gently arrest the flight of the hurtling empties and drop them in a neat windrow beneath it. I had discussed this with a shooting buddy and he turned up for a strafing session with a large

Lower extractor is as installed on the Combat Gov't. at factory. Arrow indicates critical area that must be radiused to assure proper ejection direction. Top extractor is the old one I put in its place which, as noted, works in the manner wistfully desired.

sheet of thin plastic. That didn't work at all. The cases come out hot enough to melt their way at least part-way through the plastic and it's terribly hard to get the fused plastic back off the cases.

Speaking of improving the breed, Patt Bogush of the Colt works recently sent along one of their newly introduced Combat Government Models. Essentially, it's a fairly standard M1911A1 except it has the straight mainspring housing of the M1911 pattern as well as the longer trigger. It also came with a fine set of Pachmayr rubber grips. I think those are immensely practical but as a purely personal foible, I care little for the feel and even less for the looks, so I took them off and replaced them with a homemade set in Osage orange, from a tree that grew in my native Kansas.

With that done, the Combat Government turned out to be a really impressive grouper with several different loads, including the pointy-nose #938 Hensley & Gibbs. That was just great, I thought, but it had one serious flaw: Each and every spent case was hurled with insensate violence, smack between the eyes of the shooter.

I confided my problem to old friend Johnny Adams, currently head honcho of Saeco and he offered a promising solution. Merely radius the lower end of the hook on the extractor. With that done, when the empty case collides with the ejector, the curved surface on the extractor deflects the case in a different direction. It seemed worth a try. Rummaging through the old cigar box of .45 parts, some few of which were salvaged from the ordnance dump at Tonopah AAFB, long ago, I found an extractor with a promising contour in that area and merely substituted it for the one supplied.

Trying it out, Adams' hypothesis was validated thoroughly. The replacement extractor flips the empties to about 4 o'clock in the traditional manner of the pistol we know and love. If you have the same problem, give it a try and drop Adams a thank-you note if it works as well for you as it did for me.

Bullshooter's Supply, Box 13446, Tucson, AZ 85732, makes these highly effective custom stocks for the .45 and other pistols; they also have kits for making colored front sight inserts that are of high quality.

I had hoped to include some discussion on the techniques of making replacement stocks for the M1911-pattern pistols. Alas, we squandered the space on other matters and I regret that, also. For what it's worth, I covered the matter in considerable detail in another title I did for DBI Books: *Pistol & Revolver Digest, third edition.*

If space permits, I'll include photos of the two extractors, giving a close look at the working surfaces of the hooks. If just a bit more room can be shoehorned, I'll include a shot of the Combat Government sporting its jayhawk woodwork, along with a box of .45 Hardcap ammo. That's really novel stuff and I meant to discuss it in Chapter 9, but it sort of slid off the top of my head.

The Hardcap load is a shot load and can be had in small boxes of ten rounds, in a choice of pellet sizes — #6s and #9s, to the present — but, from the outside, it looks exactly like a round of 230-grain military-type hardball. More, it generates enough recoil to work the action of any M1911 I've tried in it to date, and quite reliably. That's to say you can fire seven or eight rounds of it in rapid-fire cadence. It's strictly a short-range proposition. At six feet, the pattern is about eighteen inches in diameter, evenly distributed about the hole made by the nose cone. The Hardcap load is made by BBM Corporation, 221 Interstate Dr., W. Springfield, MA 01089 and should be available through your local dealer.

A cross-sectional view of the .45 Hardcap shot load for the .45 ACP. A special barrel is available from BBM Corporation to improve its pattern tightness.

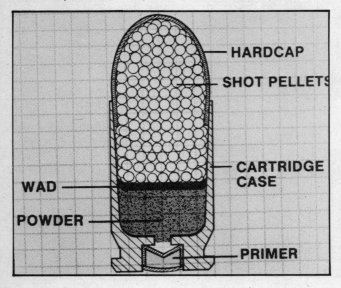

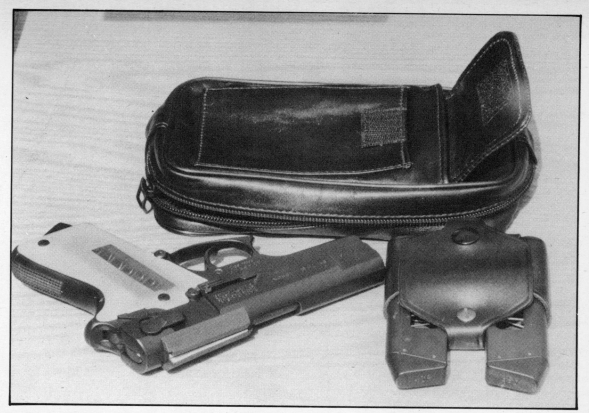

Armament Systems and Procedures markets this carrying case for their ASP modification of the Model 39 S&W pistol, with Velcro-fastened pouch for the carrier that holds two spare magazines.

The exact strategic value of such shot loads in a combat situation can be debated and has been. Some — self included — feel a round or two of shot coming first under the hammer serves a useful and distracting effect and, further, they're not apt to penetrate thin building partitions the way solid bullets might, thus endangering innocent bodies. Others, including Massad Ayoob, see no valid reason for it whatsoever. Put down your money and take your choice. Meanwhile, inside of three feet, the .45 Hardcap looks like the snake-tenderizer of all time. Will Hardcaps be made available in other calibers? Only the maker knows for sure.

A contented magazine makes for an efficient auto pistol and vice, for sure, versa. The magazine is one of the most vital links in the chain that delivers reliable performance, along with the ammunition. Over the course of four decades grappling with the M1911, I've managed to accumulate a cigar-box full of magazines for it, for which I've been grateful countless times. If I encounter feeding problems with a given pistol — as sometimes happens — I take it to the range with the box of magazines and proceed to try the load at hand through this one, that one, and all the rest. I have never failed to find one out of the box that serves the purpose pretty well. I'm not sure if I regard this as the ideal solution, but it's at least one promising approach.

Candidly, I've never had a great amount of success in modifying magazines to improve their functional efficiency. My favorite auto, a venerable M1911 Colt of 1918 vintage, which I refer to as "Old Loudmouf," seems to have an exceptionally skinny magazine well. Most magazines will not drop freely when the magazine release button is pressed. There are various approaches to correcting that problem. Some advocate compressing the sides of the magazine in a bench vise, using extreme care not to overdo it so as to interfere with the cartridges moving up from within. If you don't object to marring the finish, you can fasten a sheet of about 320-grit Wet-Or-Dry abrasive paper to a flat board and patiently work both sides of the magazine on it until you've ground off enough high spots to permit its easy insertion and ejection.

In the original outline for this book, I'd also planned to devote an entire chapter to what I termed "classic autos." Like so many well-intentioned plans, I suddenly find I've used up the space for it and again, I'm sorry about that. Many consider the Broomhandle Masuer and the Luger/Pistole '08 to be classic designs and perhaps they are, but I'm not certain I could sing their praises with a straight face. Both are quite fascinating; that, even I could not deny. The specimens of them I've encountered have not impressed me sufficiently so as to find a sample of either in my present control and possession — if that tells you anything.

There are a number of guns heavily swathed in lore and legend and I've tried out quite a few along the way. It's a tossup if the account of my encounter with the renowned Springfield rifle would break your heart before you died laughing so I'll not risk either chance. Suffice to say, I had my moment of destiny with the Luger so long ago I got the

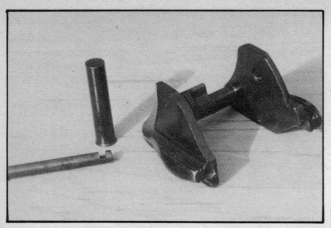

Colt's Custom Shop, same address as for the main plant, is the source of this ambidextrous safety kit for the M1911 and numerous other accessory add-ons.

Commander. I have a blued .45 Detonics and a Star PD and, as far as I'm concerned, they fill my needs for compact .45 autos quite nicely. It's pertinent to note the Detonics functions quite well with the standard seven-round M1911 magazine and, at the same time, provides a place for you to anchor your little finger.

In the Government Model size, I have a fairly complete run of the variants available, from the .22 LR Service Ace through the 9mm, .38 Colt Super and two .45 ACPs. I have the better part of a cord of spare barrels that will work in one or the other — rarely both — of the .45s to handle cartridges such as the .38-45 Clerke, .41 Avenger or .451 Detonics magnum and that adds to the general interest, too. In the specialized line of what we might call king-size Government Models, I have one of the Long Slide Hard-ballers, likewise of .45 ACP persuasion and I like that quite well, also. I'd like it even better if I could find a holster to fit it.

I farmed out the holster discussion coming up in Chapter 11 to my friend and business associate, Roger Combs, on the plausible grounds that he had just completed a full-length treatise on holsters for DBI Books and thus had more expertise still clinging to his fingertips than I could hope to latch onto. Pressed to name my favorite holster for my favorite pistol — the Colt *Guvmint Model* — I wouldn't hesitate for a nanosecond. It's the Model 55 Safariland, going away and out of sight. Nothing else, in my humble opinion, fails anywhere close to half so well. I have a Safariland M55 for all my Government Models except, of course, for the Long Slide Hardballer — sometimes referred to with irreverent affection as the Horrid-Bawler — and I'm still trying to chevvy Rudy Herman into adding a ver-

DWM product with matching numbers, spare magazine and military holster for $25, no sales tax. I bought some factory loads, tried it out, took it back and turned it in for $25 credit on future purchases at Elwood Gosse's gun emporium in Sheboygan, Wisconsin. True, I could've kept it and increased my investment by twenty-fold or so. Are you prepared to believe I still do not regret it?

My sentiments on the Colt Woodsman are recorded elsewhere — Chapter 3 — rather redundantly, perhaps. Apart from that, the old M1911 and its various modifications has an unbreakable option on my heart. As elsewhere noted, I've never owned and only rarely fired the

Harlan Rust, a photographer from Conrad, Iowa, made this set of scope mounts: "I bolted together two blocks of cold-rolled steel, using four 10-24 cap screws with a 1/32-inch spacer between; bored two 1-inch holes, 1½ inches on centers; and parted in the center to make two blocks, each ¾-inch wide. Rear block fits nicely between rear sight and ejection port. Have had no functioning problems. Another time, I'd use hard aluminum."

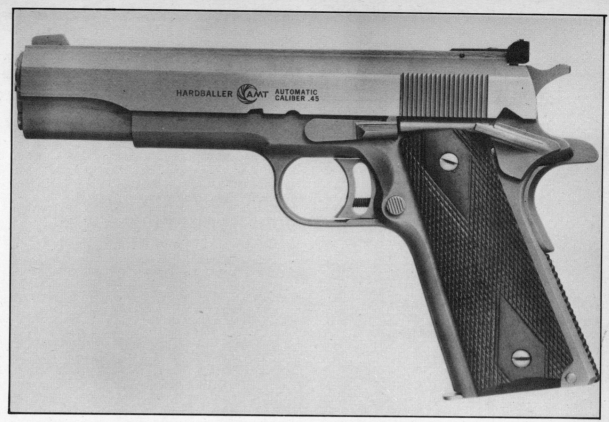

Here's the AMT Hardballer with the standard five-inch barrel, target-type rear sight, adjustable trigger stop and straight mainspring housing. Stainless steel is increasing in its popularity.

sion for that to the Safariland catalog. If you have an LSH, you can wish me luck, no?

An accessory for autos that once had some popularity but hasn't much any longer is the trigger shoe. In theory, at least, you fastened one of those to the front of the trigger and it gave you added area for the trigger finger to squeeze against; thus giving the subjective impression of a trigger pull considerably lighter than its actual weight. They performed pretty much as advertised, but posed a big problem by getting hung up on the holster now and again if the pistol was shoved into the holster cocked and unlocked. It could fire the round in the chamber, with consequences best imagined. Exactly why anyone would contemplate holstering a pistol in that mode is not clear to me, but it seems to have happened with messy consequences.

Are there other classic pistols? I'm sure there are. Classicity — if, indeed, there is such a word and, if not, why shouldn't there be? — like beauty, is in the eye of the beholder. The S&W Model 39 and its latterday variants are a strong contender for such honors, I think. As to the steatopygous (a high-falutin' word meaning beefy-butted) Model 59, I'm not so charitably inclined. You will find a staunch champion for the M59 in Claud Hamilton. As his hands are considerably smaller than mine, that baffles me utterly.

Is the Auto Mag a classic? I see no reason to deny it that status. It is unique among pistols and, in its own specialized way, it went about as far as it could go. Any pistol that meets those credentials is a classic, *ipso facto*. The

Pachmayr recently introduced .22 LR conversion kits for the M1911, M39 S&W and M35 Browning autos. Retail price is reported to be about $300.

thing is, I've a .357 AMP Auto Mag, but it's not had a live round in the chamber over the past half-decade. On the other hand, the Colt Government Models seldom enjoy much leisure. To me, they are a joy and a delight to fire, rather than a challenge and they always perform gratifyingly well. The late Colonel Townsend Whelen said it for me and for many of the rest of us: "Only accurate guns are interesting."

Perhaps if that long-ago DWM Luger had grouped a bit better, I might be the howling Luger buff of all time to the present. It didn't, so I'm not. Classic is as classic shoots and groups, in my humble opinion.

CHAPTER 9

AMMO FOR AUTOS, INCLUDING WILDCATS

A Pistol Isn't Much Use, If You Don't Have The Proper Fodder For It!

John A. "Bo" Clerke — pronounced Clark — is the designer and developer of the .38-45 Clerke cartridge. This is a wildcat in the sense that the ammunition is not available commercially.

AT THE TIME of making up the first outline for this book, it was planned to include a separate chapter on wildcat cartridges. Those are not readily available through commercial channels and have to be made up via handloading. During the course of producing the book, it became apparent the wildcats would be handled more conveniently — from the viewpoint of the reader — if they were included with the factory loads in natural sequence of size and power.

For one thing, there are not a great many wildcat cartridges for auto pistols. More, the exact status of some is open to doubt and question. Some have been produced as factory loads but are not in current production.

Rather than the customary cross-sectional drawings, I've chosen to illustrate the appearance of the various cartridges with photographs and every reasonable effort will

be made to present them at twice lifesize. Should there be any productional slips in that area, I'll also note the maximum overall length for each round, as that's fairly important to assure they'll feed out of the magazine properly. For the sake of uniformity, I will quote the overall cartridge length as given in the Lyman Reloading Handbook No. 46, or LRH-46, as it's sometimes abbreviated. The other abbreviations for similar sources, as used here, are:

Speer Manual No. 10 . . . . SM-10
Sierra Manual No. 2 . . . . SM-2
Hornady Handbook No. 3 . . . . HH-3
Hodgdon Manual No. 23 . . . . HM-23
Hercules Guide . . . . HG
Du Pont Guide . . . . DPG

.22 Short/Long Rifle

Both of these are factory cartridges, not reloadable. The short is considerably lower in power, available as standard or high-velocity, with solid or hollow point bullets. The long rifle is longer in the case — see Chapter 3 for further details — with a power choice of standard-, high- and ultra-velocity; the last sometimes termed hyper-velocity. Typical bullet weights are 29 grains for the short and 37 to 40 grains for the long rifle. Typical overall lengths are .682-inch for the short, .981-inch for the long rifle.

.25 ACP/6.35mm

Designed prior to 1908, the .25 ACP carries a 50-grain bullet of .251-inch diameter and the typical performance in the usual two-inch barrel is 810/73 — fps/fpe in the customary format. Winchester markets a .25 ACP load with a small steel ball embedded in the nose of a copper-plated lead bullet and it's capable of modest expansion in suitable media. Hornady markets a 50-grain fmj/rn bullet that's about the only factory bullet presently available for reloading. Lyman's #252435 mould produces a cast bullet weighing about 51 grains, intended to be sized to .251-inch. Sizing dies of that diameter are available from Lyman or Saeco. The HG has load data, as does the LRH-46. Reloading the tiny case is a touch nettlesome, but buying factory loads is even worse, due to the surprisingly substantial cost. Maximum cartridge length: .910-inch. HH-3 has load data for their 50-grain fmj bullet.

7.62mm Russian Tokarev

Said to be closely similar to the caliber .30 or 7.63mm Mauser, some brands of that load will work in the Tokarev. The only current source I know of for the .30 Mauser factory load is Midway Arms, Inc., 7450 Old Highway 40 West, Columbia, MO 65201. Make note of that address as they specialize in supplying scarce cartridges, put up in Boxer-primed cases that are reloadable. Maximum cartridge length: about 1.381 inches.

.30 Mauser/7.63mm

As was just noted, this cartridge has been discontinued at nearly all U.S. ammomakers, with Midway Arms the sole domestic source. RCBS, Box 1919, Oroville, CA 95965, can supply die kits for making .30 Mauser cases out of empty .223 Remington brass. They and several other makers of reloading dies offer die sets for the .30 Mauser.

LRH-46 offers load data for Bullseye, Red Dot and Unique, using their 313249 cast round nose bullet, to maximum performance of 1243/288. A typical factory load delivers about 1410/380 with an 86-grain bullet. Maximum cartridge length is 1.381 inches.

.30 Luger/7.65mm

Vastly less popular than the 9mm Luger, the .30 Luger case is .850-inch as compared to .754-inch for the 9mm, fairly well precluding hope of forming the .30 from 9mm brass. Remington no longer lists the .30 Luger in their current catalog, but I believe Winchester still may have a supply of loaded ammo. Most makers of reloading equipment can furnish loading dies. Head dimensions are nearly the same as those for the 9mm and shell holders interchange. LRH-46 has load data, but few other sources do. Lyman shows a maximum of 1171/283 for the 93-grain jacketed bullet; 1244/289 for the 84-grain cast 313249 bullet. Maximum cartridge length: 1.175 inches.

.32 ACP/7.65mm

Still in abundant production by Federal, Remington and Winchester, the .32 ACP delivers a 60-grain bullet from a four-inch barrel at 970/125 and the LRH-46 has data for a 71-grain fmj at 945/141; a 77-grain cast Lyman 311252 at

940/151. HG lists data for a 71-grain fmj bullet with their Bullseye through Herco powders to a maximum 880/122 for 3.2 grains of Herco at a pressure of 13,500 copper units of pressure (c.u.p.). Case length: .680-inch; maximum cartridge length: .984-inch.

8mm Nambu

Until fairly recent times, owners of WWII souvenir pistols of this caliber had to rely upon a few dedicated custom loaders. Now Midway Arms, Inc. — address given in the third entry here — can furnish Boxer-primed cases and fmj bullets of 102 grains and .320-inch diameter, as well as recommended load data. Cartridge length is about 1.200 inches.

.380 ACP/9mm Short, Corto, Kurz, etc.

For this one, you'll find loads listed in virtually all sources covering handgun data. Industry maximum pressure for this cartridge is 18,900 c.u.p. (SM-10) and that source lists data from a 4½-inch barrel for their 88-grain jhp bullet to 1060/220 and 975/211 for their 100-grain jhp. Some sources list deliveries slightly higher and the .380 does not suffer shamefully in comparison to the .38 Special from revolvers. Factory loads are readily available, delivering about 1000/200 with a 90-grain bullet. Case length is .680-inch; maximum cartridge length, .984-inch.

9mm Luger/Parabellum/9x19mm

Domestic ammomakers decree an absolute maximum industry working pressure of 35,700 c.u.p. for this cartridge and routinely load commercial cartridges to some percentage below that figure. European ammunition may exceed the quoted maximum figure and, as Claud Hamilton discusses here, the Luger or Pistole '08 may not function reliably with domestic loads. The Winchester factory load with a 115-grain Silvertip jhp bullet is rated to deliver 1255/383 and that is about the upper level of factory load performance for the 9mmP cartridge. The hottest load listed in the SM-10 puts their 100-grain jhp bullet out of a four-inch barrel at 1438/454, using Blue Dot powder. That should be regarded as the impenetrable ceiling for reload performance and it should be approached cautiously, if at all.

The 9mmP is extremely popular and factory loads, reloading components and load data are abundantly available from a broad variety of sources. The powder with which I've had the best results in 9mmP is Hercules Herco, but not all data sources list loads for Herco. Hercules lists loads for it using bullet weights of 95, 115 and 124 grains, all of the fmj type. It is noteworthy that the highest pressure they list for the 9mmP is 29,500 c.u.p., rather than the maximum figure mentioned here.

Nominal case length for the 9mmP is .754-inch and maximum cartridge length is 1.169 inches. As the case is slightly tapered, it is essential to assure a secure grip of case neck against bullet base to prevent the bullet being shoved back into the case at the time of chambering. Such deep-seating tends to increase peak pressures substantially and many of the loads listed for the 9mmP are so close to the top that any further increase is clearly hazardous.

.38 ACP

Dimensionally identical ancestor to the .38 Colt Super, but restricted to lower peak pressures, this is no slouch and factory loads will operate the typical pistol chambered for the .38 CS, more often than not. They usually carry a 130-grain fmj bullet delivering about 1040/312. The DPG for May 1983, for the first time, listed one set of data for the .38 ACP, using the 115-grain Hornady jhp, to maximum pressures of 22,900 c.u.p. and performance of 1015/263. About the time of that listing, Sierra added a 130-grain fmj bullet of the suitable .355-inch diameter for use in this and the .38 CS; the first such bullet commercially available in some while. HH-3 carries a section of load data for the .38 ACP, as does the HG. Most other sources ignore this one to the present. As few if any pistols have been chambered for the .38 ACP since the late Twenties, this is hardly surprising. Maximum cartridge length: 1.280 inches.

.38-45 Clerke (Wildcat)

Cases have to be formed from .45 ACP brass, using forming die sets available from RCBS or C-H Tool & Die Corp., possibly from other sources. The two firms mentioned can supply loading dies, also. Bar-Sto Precision — see Chapter 18 — can supply barrels and fit them to M1911-pattern Colt autos. The cartridge was developed by John A. "Bo" Clerke — pronounced "Clark" — about the early Sixties, with the intent of providing owners of M1911-pattern .45 autos with a simple and economical center-fire conversion to a smaller bullet diameter. Interchanging between the .45 ACP and .38-45 C is a simple matter of substituting barrels. The magazines and all other components handle either cartridge.

As may be noted elsewhere, the .45 ACP operates at an industry *maximum* of 19,900 c.u.p. and there is absolutely no basis for assuming the .38-45 C can be pushed beyond that level with any pretense of safety. The Achilles heel of either cartridge is the crescent-shaped area around the lower head of the chambered case, where it hangs out over the feed ramp, quite unsupported, with nothing but a modest thickness of brass between the high-pressure gas and the internal parts of the action. If the head should rupture at that point, pressures on the order of three or four Cadillacs per square inch are blasted into the top of the magazine. Obviously, that's a disaster much better avoided.

With the foregoing understood and accepted, the challenge is to concoct a load that will generate enough recoil impulse to work the action without exceeding the permissible peak pressure. As the genie remarked to Aladdin, that's where the rub comes in. There are few if any pressure barrels in .38-45 C so it's impossible to state the peak pressure developed by any given load. As many have produced barrels for this wildcat round, over the years, a considerable variation in chamber dimensions can be encountered. I have two .38-45C barrels; a Bar-Sto and an early one by Clerke. The headspace on the latter is about .023-inch greater than that of the newer one. Thus, a load marginal for the Clerke barrel would be excessive in the Bar-Sto barrel with its substantially smaller internal capacity. It is the variation in chamber dimensions that makes it unwise to offer suggested load data for this cartridge. A load working reasonably well in one barrel could be dangerous in another barrel.

If you have a .38-45 Clerke barrel and are determined to try to make it work, and are willing to accept the fact that the project involves some amount of personal hazard, the procedure I would follow in tracking down a custom load for it would involve a cautious approach from the lower side, making up a load, trying it and, if necessary, making up a slightly heavier load, trying it, until you reach the level at which it locks the slide back fairly reliably. At that point, discontinue further experimental development and do not exceed that charge.

To clarify: Make up the test load, put it into the magazine — just one round — shove the magazine into the gun, chamber the round and fire it. Mindful you need recoil to work the action and bullet weight has a heavy effect upon recoil, use bullets in the 124- to 130-grain class. As a starting point with each new bullet, I'd suggest around 7.5 to 7.8 grains of Hercules Blue Dot powder, increasing by hardly over .1-grain (one-tenth-grain) increments until you reach the point where it drives the slide back far enough to lock it.

With the stipulation that these are *not recommended loads*, I'll note that the 125-grain Sierra fmj/rn bullet, in my Bar-Sto barrel, delivers 1010/283 on 8.5 grains of Blue Dot and 1186/391 on 9.3 grains of Blue Dot. Note that just .8-grain more powder adds 108 fpe and it should be apparent why I urge such small incremental increases in the test loads.

At the bottom line, if you feel a need for that much power, or more power than that, I'd strongly recommend you buy an entire Government Model Colt chambered for the .38 Colt Super cartridge. In doing so, you gain access to a lot of reliable load data and you raise the ceiling of permissible performance to a substantial extent.

I've devoted considerably more space to the .38-45 Clerke because so little information is available elsewhere for it. Cartridge length: about 1.275 inches.

.38 Colt Super

Many of the comments made concerning the 9mmP apply with equal force to the .38 Colt Super. Its industry maximum working pressure is 35,700 c.u.p., exactly that of the 9mmP and, again, it is much the wiser course to stay well below that level. With its greater powder capacity and identical pressure range, the .38 CS enjoys a good edge in performance over the 9mmP in barrels of five inches in length. In shorter barrels, the difference is less apparent.

The traditional bullet for the .38 CS is the 130-grain fmj/rn and Remington loads that to 1215/426, Winchester to 1280/475, according to current ammo charts from each maker. Winchester rates their load with the 125-grain Silvertip jhp bullet at 1240/427 and Remington their 115-grain jhp at 1300/431.

The SM-10 lists load data for their 88-grain jhp bullet at a top of 1652/533 and 1475/483 for their 100-grain jhp; the 125-grain jsp bullet is taken to 1299/468 and the round nose lead bullet by Speer to 1303/471. The SM-2 takes the Sierra 90-grain jhc bullet to 1550/480 and their 1150-grain jhc to 1500/575. The higher performance levels quoted here should be approached with great caution, if at all.

Case length of the .38 CS is .900-inch and maximum cartridge length is 1.280 inches.

9mm Winchester Magnum

Developed by Winchester as one of the two cartridges to be used in the Wildey gas-operated auto pistol — along with the .45 Winchester magnum — little is available in the way of hard data on the 9mm Win. mag to the present. In appearance, it resembles a slightly obese .30 M1 carbine cartridge and the sample factory load has a case 1.155 inches long with a cartridge overall length of 1.565 inches. Head diameter at the neck is .3754-inch. Winchester's current cartridge charts list the .45 Win. mag, but not the 9mm version.

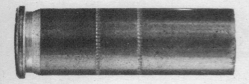

.38 AMU

This is a semi-rimmed version of the .38 Special, developed for some customized target pistols used at one time by the Army Marksmanship Unit. The head of a sample fired case mikes .404-inch, compared to the nominal specification of .440-inch for the .38 Special and the extractor groove ahead of the rim has a depth of about .340-inch. Bullets of the traditional 148-grain wadcutter design were seated flush with the case mouth and loaded to moderate mid-range velocities typical for .38 Special target loads. Little if anything has been done with the .38 AMU in recent years and it is listed here more in the light of a curiosity than as a working cartridge. As all other dimensions are substantially identical to those of the .38 Special,

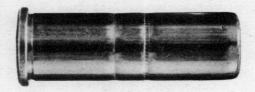

the .38 AMU cases can be fired in .38 Special revolvers and perhaps in target auto pistols such as the S&W Model 52 or the Colt .38 Special National Match/Gold Cup that was introduced in the early Sixties and discontinued some few years later. Cartridge length: 1.155 inches.

.38 Special

Although usually considered a cartridge for revolvers — and an enormously popular number for such use — a few auto pistols have been developed to handle the .38 Special with varying degrees of success. The bullets must be seated with the nose flush to the case mouth and the 148-grain wadcutter is the usual choice, with or without a hollow base. Most mid-range factory wadcutter loads work fairly well in such autos and, in reloading, best performance is apt to be obtained at velocities from about 700 to hardly more than 850 fps. Maximum cartridge length is 1.155 inches, the same as the nominal length of the .38 Special case.

.357 Magnum

As with the foregoing entry, this is essentially a revolver cartridge but it is included because at least two auto pistols have been designed to handle it: the Coonan and the Israeli-built Eagle. Presumably, both will handle cartridges with some amount of bullet protrusion beyond the case mouth. Further details are not available at present. Illustrated cartridge is 1.568 inches long.

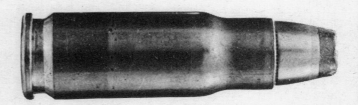

.357 Auto Mag Pistol/AMP (Wildcat)

Super Vel, when operating under Lee Jurras out of

Shelbyville, Indiana, produced small quantities of the .357 AMP as a factory load, perhaps disqualifying its wildcat status. Nonetheless, any current consumption of this cartridge must be made up on the loading bench, hence the designation here.

The ninth edition of the Speer Manual, or SM-9, carried listings of load data for both the .357 and .44 AMP, but both were dropped when the SM-10 appeared. The .357 AMP can be loaded with 9mm bullets of .355-inch diameter — provided the loading dies give the requisite tightness of case neck against bullet base to prevent bullet movement during chambering — but the .357-inch diameter bullets are the usual choice. Case length of the .357 AMP was listed as 1.298 inches in the SM-9 and Super Vel factory loads have a cartridge length of 1.639 inches. Top performance, as listed in the SM-9, ranged close to 1000 fpe with the bullets weighing 110, 125, 140 and 158 grains.

.41 Avenger (Wildcat)

Developed in the early Eighties by J.D. Jones of SSK Industries, Route 1, Della Drive, Bloomingdale, OH 43910, the .41 Avenger is essentially the .45 ACP case necked to accept bullets of .410-inch diameter as used in the .41 Remington magnum revolver cartridge or the .41 Jurras Mag Pistol. Case forming is quite simple, consisting of a pass of the parent case into the regular full-length resizing die of the .41 Avenger reloading set.

At the same time, the .41 Avenger can be made up from stronger parent brass such as the .451 Detonics magnum or .45 Winchester magnum cases. The latter must be trimmed to a case length of about .95-inch, the approximate length of the .451 D-mag case and somewhat longer than the nominal, .898-inch length of the .45 ACP case. It is also possible to form .41 Avenger cases from rifle cases such as the .30/06, .308 Winchester and any of several others having the same basic head dimensions. Any of the parent cases mentioned in this paragraph are substantially stronger in head construction than are .45 ACP cases, permitting loads to pressures well above the 19,900 c.u.p. ceiling of the .45 ACP.

Jones has load data for use with the .41 Avenger in both the .45 ACP and heavier cases. Loads for the latter should not be put up in ACP brass for painfully obvious reasons. In .45 ACP cases, 10.6 grains of Blue Dot behind the 170-grain Sierra jhc bullet averaged 1120/474 in the five-inch barrel with good accuracy and a high degree of functional reliability. The bullet was seated to 1.200 inches overall length. That is the load I've settled upon for this cartridge. A six-inch barrel is available, with the extra inch projecting ahead of the barrel bushing of the M1911 pistol. A moderate amount of fitting may be required on the conversion barrel as received.

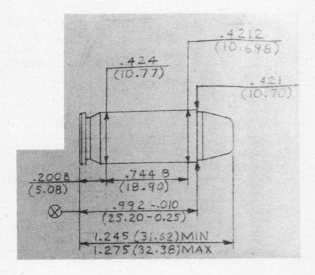

Bren Ten

A true caliber .40, the Bren Ten cartridge takes a jacketed bullet of .400-inch diameter; .401-inch in lead bullets, with a bullet weight of 200 grains. Suggested charges for either bullet are 11.7 grains of Blue Dot or 7.0 grains of Unique. Case length is .800-inch, maximum cartridge length is 1.275 inches and it takes the large pistol primer of .210-inch diameter. Case head diameter is .428-inch, tapering to .421-inch at the neck of the loaded round.

No loaded rounds of Bren Ten ammo were available to photograph as the deadline for this book came up. A last-minute report from the gun's designer stated that they plan to hold the factory load at a velocity of 1150 fps from the five-inch barrel for 587 fpe. The bullet is described as a jtc — jacketed truncated cone — and has a broad flat tip, radiusing to the tapered sides. The lead bullet maintains the same profile.

.41 Jurras Mag Pistol/JMP (Wildcat)

This was a specialized variant made up for the Auto Mag by Lee Jurras, currently getting his mail at Box 680, Washington, IN 47501. He recalls approximately one hundred barrels were made up for it in assorted lengths. He preferred the 170-grain Sierra jhc bullet and, with some unspecified amount of Winchester 296 Ball Powder, he was able to drive it to velocities in the neighborhood of 1850 fps for 1292 fpe. Although the exact charge weight was not readily retrievable when I called him on it, he recalls the load was moderately compressed. Cartridge length would be about the same as for either the .357 or .44 AMP rounds.

.44 Auto Mag Pistol/AMP (Wildcat)

The great majority of all Auto Mags produced to date handle this cartridge. Factory cases were manufactured at one time by Cartucho Deportivos de Mexico — sporting cartridges of Mexico, approximately translated — and headstamped CDM. For a brief time, the Swedish firm of Norma also made .44 AMP cases. Except for those two sources, cases needed to be handmade from rifle brass such as the .308 Winchester by trimming to a length of 1.298 inches and reaming the inside of the necks to a depth equal to the seating depth of the bullet to be used. RCBS offered forming die kits, including the necessary reamer and reaming die. The SM-9 carried listings of load data for this as it did for the .357 AMP and the current Sierra Manual or SM-2 still has a listing for the .44 AMP, but not for the .357 AMP.

At the time I was working with a .44 Auto Mag on loan for testing, the load I came to prefer was 20.0 grains of 2400 powder behind the 240-grain Sierra jhc bullet. That is .8-grain over the maximum as suggested by Speer, but .5-grain below the maximum Sierra listing. In the 6½-inch Auto Mag barrel, the load delivers about 1350/971 and, when it goes off, you are aware of it at once. Maximum cartridge length is 1.610 inches.

.45 ACP

The official military handgun cartridge of this country since 1911, the supply of military cases in .45 ACP is plentiful and varied. Few if any such carry the .45 ACP desig-

nation in the headstamp. Usually, they show an abbreviation indicating the maker and a number for the year of manufacture. Prior to WWI, military cases also included the month of manufacture. As an example, I've one old-timer in the collection headstamped FA over 1 14, indicating it was made at Frankford Arsenal in January of 1914. Shortly after that, only the year was given, usually the final two digits and, less commonly, the final digit.

The age of such loads is highly pertinent because, prior to about 1952, all military .45 ammo used corrosive primers, thereby requiring prompt and thorough cleaning immediately after firing. Some of the military cases have the primer stamp-crimped in place to prevent it from backing out when fired in submachine guns and such crimps need to be removed when being reloaded, so as to simplify seating of the new primer. At one time, Frankford Arsenal (FA) used a slightly smaller primer, about .206-inch diameter instead of the standard .210-inch. It is difficult to impossible to reload FA brass of that era and best to cull them out and set them aside.

The traditional bullet for the .45 ACP is the 230-grain fmj/rn as used in the military "hardball" loads. In recent times, all of the commercial makers have offered assorted loads carrying jhp bullets and the one I consider most effective is the CCI-Speer #3965 load carrying the 200-grain Speer #4477 jhp bullet. It feeds reliably, it's accurate and it expands awesomely in typical media at velocities as low as 859 fps; the average velocity from the 3½-inch barrel of the .45 Detonics. I use the same Speer bullet extensively when reloading, favoring a charge of 10.6 grains of Blue Dot, slightly below the maximum SM-10 listing of 10.9 grains for 1003/447. As a cast bullet load, I prefer the Hensley & Gibbs #68, a semi-wadcutter design weighing about 190 to 200 grains, with 4.5 grains of Bullseye for velocities in the low 800 fps brackets. Case length of the .45 ACP is .898-inch, maximum cartridge length is 1.275 inches.

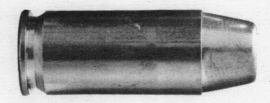

.451 Detonics Magnum (Wildcat)

The .451 D-mag case is somewhat longer than that of the .45 ACP — about .945- to .947-inch, as compared to .898-inch — but otherwise identical in external dimensions. It is more heavily constructed in the area around the case head so as to enable it to withstand peak pressures considerably higher than the 19,900 c.u.p. pressure ceiling of the .45 ACP. I've heard the figure quoted for the D-mag's ceiling, but refrain from mentioning it here.

The .451 D-mag was developed by Detonics Manufacturing Corp., Firearms Division, 2500 Seattle Tower, Seattle, WA 98101, for use in their compact auto pistol and it is also available as a conversion kit with five-inch barrel to install in Model 1911A1 Colt .45 ACP pistols of modern construction in good condition. The conversion kit includes a special dual recoil spring, a different firing pin spring and extractor. Unprimed virgin .451 D-mag cases are available from Detonics in boxes of fifty and the kit is accompanied by a reloading manual and instructions.

Judiciously reloaded, the .451 D-mag is capable of delivering performance up to around 1216/657 for the 200-grain Speer jhp bullet and that is not far from double the 800/327 delivery that's fairly typical for the 230-grain fmj military load. The recoil of the old G-Model pistol with an all-out D-mag load is calculated to fairly crumble the mind. As with so many comparable cartridges, Blue Dot is the powder most apt to succeed. The supplied reloading manual for Detonics max's out with a 185-grain bullet at 1353/752 and 1275/722 for the 200-grain bullet. Bullet length should not exceed .558-inch and maximum cartridge length is 1.220 to 1.235 inches, depending somewhat upon the nose contours of the given bullet.

Above, a round of .41 Avenger carrying a pointed fmj bullet made by reswaging the 170-grain Sierra jhc bullet. Below, the .45 ACP Hardcap, discussed in Chapter 8. This one contains number 9 shot.

.45 Winchester Magnum

Refer to listing here for the 9mm Win. mag for further details. The .45 Win. mag was developed for use in the Wildey gas-operated auto pistol — a gun I've photographed but never fired to the present. About the time of the cartridge's introduction, Thompson/Center Arms came up with ten-inch bull barrels of that chambering for their single-shot Contender pistol and I've worked with that, to a moderate extent. I also loaned my barrel to Dave Andrews of the Speer ballistics lab for use in developing the load data for the .45 Win. mag as published in the SM-10.

With the lighter bullets, Blue Dot is the going-away winner and, with the heavier numbers, Winchester 680 Ball powder is the most effective canister powder available to date. The maximum SM-10 listing for their 260-grain jhp is 1435/1189 and 1640/1195 for their formidable 200-grain jhp; 1524/1160 for their 225-grain jhp. That puts the .45 Win. mag pretty much on the same level as the .44 Remington magnum cartridge out of long-barreled revolvers and gives the .45 Win. mag plausible claims to being the most potent auto pistol round available to the present. Case length is 1.198 inches and length of the Winchester factory load, with 230-grain fmj/rn bullet, is 1.563 inches.

I think this is some kind of goshawful gully-gouger of a cartridge and if anyone comes up with anything harrier, my enthusiasm for firing it would be under some amount of restraint. It comes pretty close to where I draw the line.

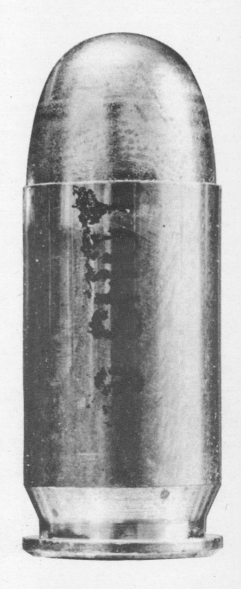

CHAPTER 10

SIGHTS FOR AUTOS

No One Ever Said It Was Supposed To Be Simple — And It Isn't!

THE USUAL provision on a pistol for steering the bullet to the desired point of impact consists of a front sight and a rear sight. In use, a sighting picture is acquired in which the front sight is centered, left/right, in the notch of the rear sight. The upper tip of the front sight is aligned level with the top of the rear sight and the intended point of impact is brought to rest just at the upper tip of the front sight. With a jar-free manipulation of the trigger, a hole will appear in the target or whatever, more or less precisely coinciding with the point of aim.

If all does not work out as hopefully envisioned, various recourses are available. If the bullet struck three inches to the right and two inches high, you can take aim for the next shot at an imaginary spot two inches low and three inches to the left, hoping for the best. The technical term for that is "Kentucky windage."

If one of the sights — customarily the rear one — is movable for adjustment and correction, the operative rule is to move the rear sight the way you want the holes to move. If the shot struck low, you raise the rear sight and, if it went to the left, you move the rear sight a judicious distance to the right and so on.

It's rather common for auto pistols to have sights that are not readily movable. Perhaps the rear sight rides in a dovetail so it can be drifted a trifle to right or left to correct for gross discrepancies in azimuth (right/left), but with no

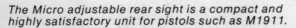
The Micro adjustable rear sight is a compact and highly satisfactory unit for pistols such as M1911.

The Aimpoint superimposes a tiny dot of red light in the same plane of focus as the target for effortless precision in aiming. James E. Clark makes the mount.

ready route for correcting elevation (up/down) vagaries. If you're really desperate, you can attack a fixed-sight system with a fine-cut file and all the delicacy you have at your disposal. Removing a touch of metal from the upper tip of the front sight will raise the point of impact correspondingly and taking some off the rear sight will lower it. The resulting battle damages can be somewhat concealed with touches of cold-blue solution; an unsatisfactory solution at best, since most such preparations operate by an inclusion of copper sulfate, which deposits a microthin coating of copper on the steel, plus some other chemical to darken the

A competitor at the Bianchi Cup Match uses an Aimpoint sight on steel plates. Such sights are gaining in popular use. (Tom Ferguson photo.)

copper wash to a color not too far from that of blued steel. The wearing properties are about what you'd pessimistically imagine. Put briefly, if you can avoid filing the sights, avoid filing the sights.

As an alternative solution, consider the fact that different loads tend to "print" to different points of impact, with the sight picture unchanged. Conduct some intent research to find out if there is some other available load that will be delivered onto the point of aim or, failing that, slightly closer to it.

The open iron sights, front and rear, have an in-built handicap about which little of a constructive nature can be done: It is virtually if not absolutely impossible for the human eye to hold three separate points in sharp focus simultaneously. One can be sharp, but the other two will be more or less blurred. The customary strategem is to focus the aiming eye upon the front sight and let both rear sight and target blur as they will (and do). The really amazing thing is that, even with this haphazard approach, some amazingly fine groups get fired, year after year.

There are at least two other possible approaches that work, and work well. That's the good news. The bad news is they both add large increments to the pistol's topside bulk, turning it into a cumbersome and specialized instrument, no longer conveniently packable in a conventional holster or even a fairly unconventional one.

With some pistols, such as the Colt Model 1911 or the Auto Mag, you can affix a mount to the slide, with rings on that to hold a scope having an extended eye relief so it can be used and aimed at a typical distance of fifteen to twenty-three inches from the aiming eye, rather than the customary two or three inches of eye relief of scope sights intended for use on rifles.

The added weight and mass of the mount, rings and scope attached to the slide may have a serious effect upon the functional reliability of the pistol upon which they are installed. If the gun is recoil-operated, the extra weight dampens the recoil and may increase the probability of stoppages.

A way around that is to install a specialized type of grip panel that juts upward, out and around to position the scope just above the slide, but not attached to it in any way. With this approach, you encounter an increased problem from parallax. The line of sight is some significant distance above the axis of the bore so that the sight must be adjusted

Rear sight on High Standard "The Victor" carries helpful markings to aid the memory as to which way to move. Moving the rear sight moves point of impact in the same direction; an easy matter to remember.

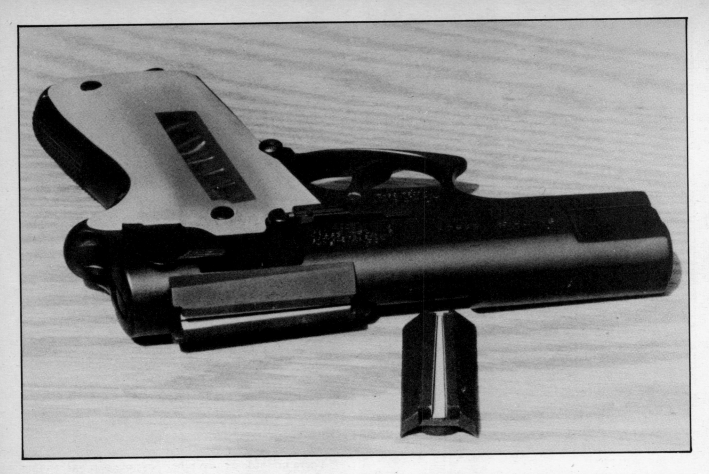

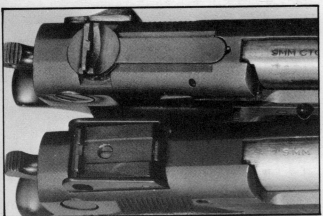

Armament Systems and Procedures installs the novel "Guttersnipe" sight on their ASPs. The tapering trough is lined with bright yellow for fast sight acquisition.

Original rear sight for S&W M39, top, was adjustable only for windage. On M439 and later designs, fully adjustable rear sight was used, as on lower pistol. Right, .45 ACP version of Llama Omni has this sight.

into precise congruity at some specific distance.

Pretty much the same can be said for electronic sights, as exemplified by the Aimpoint. When the switch of the Aimpoint is turned on, internal batteries power a small light-emitting unit that projects a tiny red spot onto a pellicular mirror. As a result, the target can be viewed with the red spot superimposed upon it. Since the placement of the spot is controlled by adjustments for elevation and azimuth, the Aimpoint can be adjusted to put the holes right where they were aimed and it has the same happy

to bring both together at some given distance. At shorter or longer ranges, the departure gets correspondingly greater.

All that notwithstanding, the telescopic sight has one stellar virtue in that its crosshairs or reticle — when properly adjusted — will be seen by the aiming eye in sharp and effortless focus, simultaneously with the aiming point. More, the built-in adjustments of the scope make it a simple and easy matter to bring the points of aim and impact

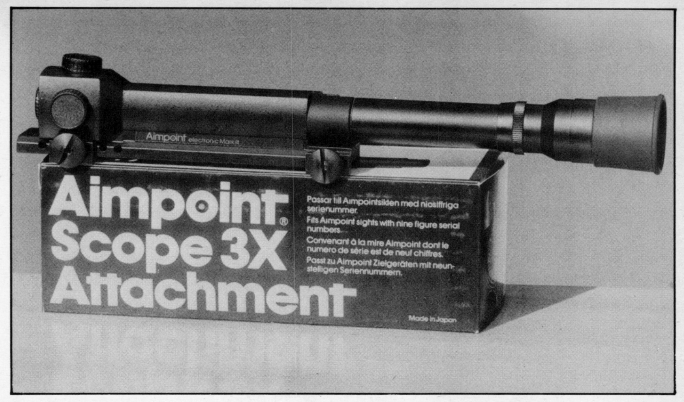

Perhaps not overly practical for use on auto pistols, but available if needed is this accessory 3X scope unit for installation on the rear of the Aimpoint. It is readily removable when the owner/shooter desires.

quality as the scope for keeping all the viewing in one easy plane of focus.

Installed as it comes from the box the Aimpoint does not magnify the viewed image, but an accessory attachment is available to provide a 3X magnification.

One further modification is the laser sight that projects a pencil-thin beam of intensely bright scarlet light to put a highly visible spot upon the target. When suitably adjusted, if the trigger is pulled, the bullet makes a hole right where the red spot glowed. The laser beam travels in a dead-straight line, rather than the somewhat curvaceous

Standard Aimpoint is lightweight, fairly compact and does not magnify the sighting image as viewed. It is adjustable for windage and elevation via the turrets.

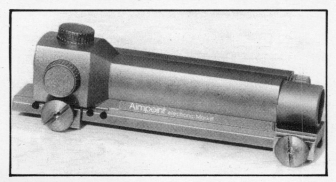

trajectory of any projectile whatsoever. More, it requires a heavy, bulky battery pack to power it and the basic gizmo is far from petite. On top of that, it's not your ideal aiming system for conditions of total darkness. You can push the button and project the tiny scarlet beam but, when it's pitch dark, you've no way on earth of telling just what it is the red spot is impinging upon.

The great asset of the laser sight is its psychological effect, provided the would-be impactee is aware of what it is. Upon perceiving the little red spot on personal real estate, there is a strong tendency to become extremely docile and anxious to please.

The telescopic sight that performs so superbly when mounted on rifles has yet to win widespread popularity for use on auto pistols, although it seems to be doing quite well on single-shots such as the Thompson/Center Contender and, to a lesser extent, upon high-performance revolvers.

The Aimpoint has carved itself a noteworthy niche for competition in those events where its use is permitted. It has aided in the winning of various national championships by means of its unquestionable assistance in acquiring a sharp and precise sight picture.

In the meantime, for all practical purposes, the two-way adjustable rear sight remains alive and prospering by the inescapable fact that it's about the only system that doesn't louse up the pistol, eight ways from the jack, from the standpoint of packing it about in a holster, dragging it out and pumping lead in a telling manner when the chips are down.

153

CHAPTER 11

AUTOLOADING PISTOL HOLSTERS

No Matter The Size Or Intended Use, There Is A Holster For Every Pistol

For the law enforcement types armed with the auto pistol, an important consideration is preventing unauthorized draw. Lethal Force Institute's Jerry Chin, left, and Massad Ayoob demonstrate the safety factor built into Bianchi's Auto Draw police holster.

FOR EVERY autoloading pistol, no matter how large or how small, there is sure to be a holster in which to carry it. Autoloaders may be packed on the hip, under the arm, up high or down low, in the small of the back, on the ankle, in plain sight or concealed, in a holster made of leather or one made of heavy-duty nylon. The choice of holsters is larger than the choice of pistols by a factor of five or ten, as the most popular autoloaders are accommodated in several holsters which are designed to be carried in any of the selected locations or modes.

For those who prefer the Colt .45 Government model pistol, most manufacturers offer holsters that permit the gun to be carried cocked-and-locked; the holster design includes a safety strap which is snapped or secured across the gun, under the hammer. Many will have a thumb-snap release at the safety strap, for a quick, safe draw from the holster, without danger of an accidental discharge.

Not many, but some police departments in the U.S., issue or permit the officers on the force to carry an autoloading pistol as the duty sidearm. Others allow their detectives or undercover officers to arm themselves with the auto in .45 or 9mm. For them, the choice of leather gear is particularly large.

For the law enforcement officer, an additional requirement is that the gun must be carried not only securely but must be as snatch-proof as possible. Unfortunately, a large percentage of officer shootings are the result of the firearm somehow being wrested from the holster or hands of the officer and used against him or her by a felon. Holster makers have, and continue, to research and refine their designs to all but eliminate holsters from which the gun may be drawn by anyone other than the armed police officer. A major consideration for police, this is given top priority by designers and law enforcement officials.

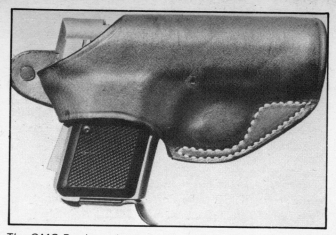

The OMC Backup pistol chambered in .380 ACP has proved popular for off-duty police wear, as well as its intended backup duties. Safariland's adjustable thumb-snap holster carries the gun well concealed.

During the past several years, the price of good leather has risen faster than the inflation rate. Demand from foreign buyers, inventory building and monetary fluctuations have caused the price of American cowhide to skyrocket. Thus, it has become common for a holster rig to be priced at a hundred dollars or more. While many people are willing to pay such an amount for the best leather products, the cost has put some holsters out of reach for some buyers. The gap is being filled by holsters and belts made of nylon. These nylon holsters have proven to be lightweight, long-wearing, protective to the gun, and often less than half the price of a comparable leather holster. They are available in various colors, such as black, brown and various shaded camouflage patterns.

The makers of the popular Backup pistol, AMT, are distributing a wallet-like small holster for their AMT .380 autoloader. It is made of tough nylon and closes with a Velcro fastener. It may be worn inside or outside, either side or in a pocket, concealed. Matching magazine pouches are optionally worn vertically or horizontally.

Assault Systems is one of the newer companies to concentrate on holsters and cases of nylon material. Their holster line includes shoulder rigs, both concealable and not, hip holsters and ankle holsters for small autoloaders. All are constructed of black ballistic nylon, nylon harness straps and Velcro-type safety strap closures. The concealable model carries the autoloader in a horizontal position under the arm, while the so-called military shoulder holster puts the gun in a vertical carry. There are enough adjustments to fit most any autoloader with different human body shapes and sizes. The all-black belt holster also may be matched with magazine pouch and nylon web belt with a durable Fastex quick-release buckle. Assault System's holster line is completed with two ankle holsters (large or small autos) featuring padding and Velcro closures and straps.

Armament Systems Products (ASP) produces holsters primarily intended for undercover police or other concealment carry. The Tightrope model is worn in the center of the back by those for whom speed of draw is not as important as concealment. The holster is made for medium-frame semi-autos and small revolvers. Large frame semi-

autos are accommodated in SP's Pro Speed Slide holster, which carries the gun high and tight, with a minimum of leather. Another concealable pistol model is the Undercover Silhouette, worn inside the trouser band, high and close. For the Walther owner, the UWS scabbard has no stitches, carrying the gun high and tight for maximum concealment. The ASP pistol magazine carrier has a magnetic retention system and is available in sizes for the .45 ACP, 9mmP or .380 ACP. The carrier is said to be fast enough for combat competition.

Frank Behlert is well-known among pistol shooters for his custom conversions and accurizing work. To go along with his fine gunsmithing, Behlert and JGS Leather have come up with some new holsters designed for the IPSC competitor, as well as for concealed wear. Generally, the Ultra Hide-Out model rides low; the Victor rides high. Both are of heavy leather and hand-moulded to fit the specific handgun for which each is designed. The adjustable tension screw on the Victor allows the holster to be worn without the safety strap, as the wearer prefers.

There would seem to be no holster manufacturer with a variety of styles and designs larger than Bianchi. The sheer number of holsters is almost staggering. But it means that there are almost no pistols made in the United States or regularly imported in any numbers from overseas which cannot be carried by Bianchi holsters. And they may be carried on police duty, concealed or revealed, in a shoulder rig or on the ankle, left side or right, crossdraw or strong side, carried high or low, in brown, black, plain or basket-weave leather. Everything from the smallest caliber .25 autoloader, through Walthers, Mausers, Heckler & Kochs, up to and including S&W autoloaders, Colts, Brownings and Hardballers will find a home in Bianchi holsters.

The on-duty police officer armed with a semi-auto pistol will find complete rigs in plain or basketweave black, in traditional silver-colored hardware or in the newer hidden hardware, with no metal visible. The holster may be of the Border Patrol style, riding lower on the hip or Auto Draw, riding high on the belt. The Auto Draw holster design was eight years in development, and is considered by many police to be the most nearly snatch-proof holster available. Matching key holsters, handcuff cases, baton rings, keep-

In black basketweave leather, the Bianchi Auto Draw holster matches police rig of belt, keepers and magazine pouch. Basic holster design is available in plain brown finish for the combat competitor.

ers and magazine pouches are available for all police rigs.

The sportsman, too, will find a Bianchi holster to match the pistol he or she owns. Many will have the Bianchi Sight Channel built in to protect the front sight blade on the larger autos. Some of these sight channels are steel reinforced; all are hand finished. The combat pistol competitor is not forgotten, with four Bianchi autoloading models from which to choose. The same Auto Draw design for police is also available in plain brown finish for the combat match shooter. Newest of these is the International holster, belt and magazine pouch set which features a variable tension adjustment screw to fine-tune the holster and pistol.

Other Bianchi models include clip-ons, slide holsters, thumb-snap designs, ankle holsters, the inside-the-trousers Pistol Pocket, shoulder rigs in horizontal or vertical carry modes, for the largest to smallest auto pistols. Extra accessories include belts, magazine pouches, rubberized grips for some guns and an excellent leather maintenance kit.

The J.M. Bucheimer Company is an old-line manufacturer with considerable experience in producing holsters for the military-issue Colt .45. The full-flap .45 holster you were issued in Korea or Vietnam may have been stamped with the Bucheimer label. They still produce a line of pistol holsters, particularly for the law enforcement trade and/or concealment wear.

Cobra Gunskin, headquartered in New York state, manufactures holster designs licensed from famed Andy Anderson for fast-draw competitors. Cobra also has a line of autoloading pistol holsters intended for the handgun

hunter, sportsman, off-duty police or the plainclothes detective.

The Cobra Sidewinder is an unusual Andy Anderson design in that it has a swivel arrangement, yet is a clip-on, inside-the-belt holster. The gun butt may be tilted to the rear or the front, straight up or worn cross-draw; it is designed for medium or large autoloaders. The Stingray holster, also meant for medium or large autos, has the familiar appearance of the Pancake type; a double side-slotted, high-riding design. The thumb-break safety strap is steel reinforced.

Cobra has three shoulder holsters to accommodate automatic pistols: The Comvest rig, Puma and X-Caliber. The three holsters are interchangeable on the various harness rigs. Other Cobra automatic pistol designs include the Grabber, held by a metal spring clip for inside-the-trousers wear; the Combo, which is a clip-on or belt-slot model; and the traditional high-ride belt holster called Easy Rider. Cobra has the usual quality line of belts, magazine pouches and police leather gear.

G. William Davis, a small custom leather outfit, produces holsters primarily for the pistol competitor, the PPC and IPSC shooter. But the Davis product lineup is ever-changing and offers at least three designs for the security officer or the sportsman: inside, outside, and cross-draw holsters.

There are times when even the largest autoloaders need

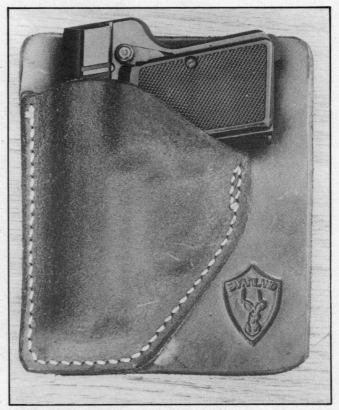

Safariland's pocket holster is designed to carry the .25 Auto Colt concealed in hip or breast pocket.

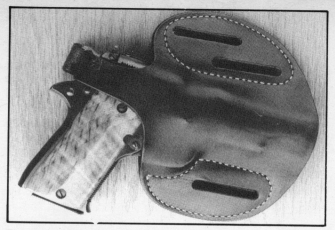

The original Roy's Pancake holster design has proven popular for years; three belt slots vary the carry.

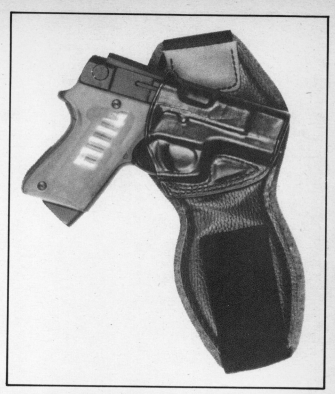

Ken Null's ankle holster shows close moulding to pistol shape, padding and Velcro closure system.

to be carried in a shoulder rig, concealed or not; this sometimes presents a problem in bulk for the wearer. DeSantis Holster and Leather's solution to the problem is their swivel shoulder rig. The gun is carried under the arm in the traditional upright position. The holster, a pivoting scabbard design, is held in place by a snap device that is released with the draw; the butt of the gun tilts forward and out for easy withdrawal by the shooter. DeSantis also has a more conventional slant shoulder rig, which carries the pistol at a slightly butt-forward and down angle. On this model, the pistol is held in place partly by the reinforced thumb-break strap and the moulded fit of the holster itself. Both shoulder harnesses will accommodate several magazine pouches and handcuff cases in their design. The company has a new competition-style holster and belt rig, but most of their other pistol holsters are intended to be carried concealed, on belt loops or via metal spring clips inside the trousers. A new concealed model, the Silent Partner, places the pistol just to the rear of the hip, in the natural hollow at the kidney location.

Another outfit that seems to specialize in concealment holsters is Fury Leather. Their shoulder rigs for small, medium, and large autoloading pistols place the gun at a slightly butt-down, muzzle-rear-and-up position, with the extra magazine slotted onto the harness just above the holster.

Jackass Leather is reported to have passed through a change of ownership and control and is now known as Galco Gun Leather. Galco concentrates on concealment holsters but does have a competition-type model, the Crossfire, for autoloaders. For the right-hander, the Crossfire may be worn in the crossdraw position, as the name implies, or on the right side, high on the hip with the muzzle raked forward. Galco offers a pancake design, called the High-Jak which features a metal reinforced thumb-break with a countersunk, leather-covered snap on the safety strap to protect the gun from being scratched. One Galco design that is unique is the Inside Hooker. This holster is worn inside the trouser band in almost any location the wearer may prefer. A J-shaped metal clip loops under the belt, holding the holster in place when the gun is drawn.

Galco's shoulder rigs are all leather, using no elastic bands to position the gun and magazines. The model SS2 carries the pistol in the butt-forward, angled-upward muzzle position in a moulded leather holster. The Big Game Auto puts the gun in a vertical, muzzle-down mode, requiring a trouser belt to stabilize the rig.

The Don Hume organization in Oklahoma, finds most of its customers in the law enforcement field. They produce an extensive line of holsters and associated police leather gear, including belts, pouches, loaders, badge holders and similar equipment. Several of their pistol holsters perform well for the handgun hunter who prefers an autoloader, as well as the on- or off-duty police officer. Hume's Model 724 is designed to carry the pistol cocked and locked under the spring-loaded thumb-break safety strap. The Model 725 has a more obvious safety strap passing over the hammer to snap on the outside of the holster. Hume also offers a number of swivel designs as well as concealable models for the pistol shooter.

John's Custom Leather has a couple of holsters for the smallest autoloaders and one for medium and large autos. The #116 is a concealment holster for the bigger pistols. Designed to be worn inside the trouser band, at the kidney area, it is lined with smooth calfskin. John's also has a pair called the Mini-Auto and Mini-Auto leg holster for smaller automatics. Their Wallet holster design permits the little pistol to be fired while still in the holster. The Wallet holster fits in the hip pocket and is drawn out with the gun.

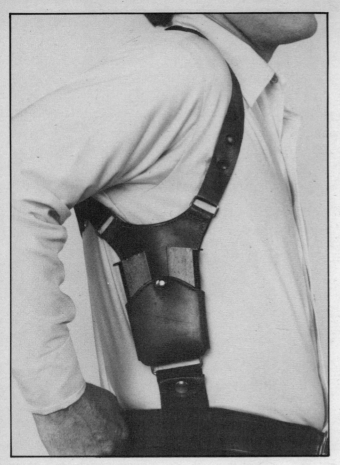

As part of the shoulder holster rig, the Bianchi 13C spare magazine pouch features a tension adjustment screw to carry two .45, 9mm or .380 magazines. Scorpio system fits most autoloaders.

Early, two-snap version of Bianchi Pistol Pocket has given way to newer single, swivel-action snap.

Down Texas way, Joe Kirkpatrick operates two holster outfits: Kirkpatrick Leather and American Sales & Manufacturing. American Sales features mostly fast-draw and competition revolver belts and holster rigs, but does have several automatic pistol designs in the lower price range. Pistols accommodated include most models from the Ruger .22 through the Browning Hi-Power and Colt Combat Commander. In the Kirkpatrick line, the choice is somewhat wider, including a plain black model for police uniform wear for the .45 and 9mm autos. The Model 245 features what Kirkpatrick calls "no sight-drag construction," with a channel to protect the front sight from excessive bluing wear and drag.

Kirkpatrick has a series of holsters featuring the Rolled Edge, wherein the full leather lining is extended up and over the upper edge of the holster, visible around the gun. Light in color, the lining is attractive, practical and different. The outfit also offers a paddle-type concealment holster for medium and large automatic pistols.

Kolpin has been producing quality rifle and shotgun cases, bow cases and archery and shooting accessories for years. Recently, the firm moved into the holster market with a couple of nylon models for autoloaders: one is for belt carry, the other a shoulder rig. The belt model is a full-flap padded design available in black or camouflage. The shoulder holster carries the pistol in a horizontal position, holds medium- or large-frame autos with two- to four-inch barrels, is padded and also is offered in black or camouflage. For autos with barrels up to six inches, Kolpin recommends their vertical carry shoulder model. An ankle holster, clip pouch and a variety of pistol cases round out the Kolpin handgun protection line.

The George Lawrence firm in Portland, Oregon, is an old-line leather company, more than 120 years in business. They produce a number of special leather designs such as saddlebags and rifle scabbards for the hunter. For the automatic wearer, though, the Lawrence FBI style, and their numbers 31 and 52 models are offered. The #52 is a concealment holster with an attached magazine pouch sewn onto the rear edge of the leather.

Michaels of Oregon, also known as Uncle Mike's, is best known for black powder shooting accessories and rifle and shotgun sling swivels. Lately, however, Michaels has begun selling a line of nylon Cordura holsters to fit most handguns, including autoloading pistols. The holsters, padded with foam and lined with nylon, are available in left- or right-hand models. The holsters may be ordered in either camouflage pattern or in black with matching brown or black nylon web belts.

Ken Null is a small manufacturer who produces holsters and accessories primarily for the law enforcement market, most of them in a concealed manner. Null holsters are moulded to the pistol model for which they are intended. Most offer a fast draw and firm grip; a couple of Null's designs are finding favor with the combat pistol shooters, particularly in the Southwest.

Old West offers a full line of holsters for revolvers as well as autoloaders. Among the more recent designs is the Model 1180 shoulder holster system which is constructed without rivets or fastening screws. The shoulder strap harness is of wide leather for comfortable wear. All accessories and parts are interchangeable with snap adjustments and optional elastic strap. Normally the 1180 rig carries the pistol in a horizontal position, but the adjustments permit the system to be converted to an upside-down shoulder holster. The company recently changed its corporate name to Viking Leathercraft.

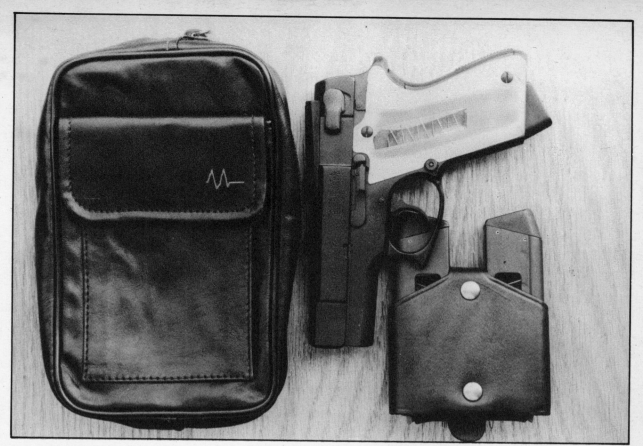

Armament Systems Products (ASP) are intended for the professional law enforcement or undercover market. Using leather or man-made materials, double magazine carrier, at right, features magnetic retention system.

In addition to a full line of holsters, pouches and other leather goods, Rogers sells bullets, timers, grips, and associated gear for the police officer and competitive handgunner. Founder Bill Rogers is a former FBI agent and is now a serious competitor, which is reflected in his holster line. Most of the leather products are intended for police or combat competition work. Many of the top pistol champions use Rogers holsters, especially IPSC shooters.

Bill Rogers spends a great deal of time designing and evaluating his designs before putting them into production. He seeks and receives considerable input from autoloading pistol shooters regarding what a holster ought, and ought not, be on the firing line. Rogers also has done considerable exploration into leather substitutes for some of his product line.

Roy's Custom Leather is best-known for the Roy's Original Pancake holster design, still being made, still popular with shooters, competitors and police, and available to fit small-, medium- and large-frame auto pistols. Generally, the Pancakes are available in russet or black, plain or basketweave, lined or unlined. Roy's has expanded their product line to include an efficient shoulder harness and holster system, called the Hidden Thunder, for large-frame pistols. This comfortable system features suede lining, a dual-suspension harness, belt tie-down straps on both sides of the rig and a wide range of size adjustments to fit the

individual wearer. In addition, Roy's offers two ankle holsters for small- and medium-frame autos, and a snap-on conealable holster intended to be worn between body and trousers, just above the kidney.

Safariland, another giant of the industry, has an extensive line of autoloading pistol holsters designed for law enforcement, the sportsman, hunter, or the competitor who may carry guns of various sizes and configurations.

On the law enforcement side are plain or basketweave finish holsters to accommodate pistols from the smaller Walther P-5, the Colts, the Smith & Wessons, SIG-Sauers, Brownings, through the larger Berettas and AMT Hardballers with five-inch barrels. Safariland offers holsters lined or unlined, made of leather or of their newest leather substitute, Porvair.

Porvair is a man-made product, closely resembling patent leather in appearance. The Porvair is laminated onto leather, but easier to maintain than plain leather. It has become popular with several law enforcement agencies, according to Safariland. The high-riding Model 2, Model 9 large auto swivel holster and the Model 254 large auto Border Patrol holsters are all available in either black leather or Porvair.

One of the most popular Safariland police holsters is their forward-cant Model 55 for the AMT, Browning Hi-Power, Colts and S&W autoloaders. The unit's adjustable

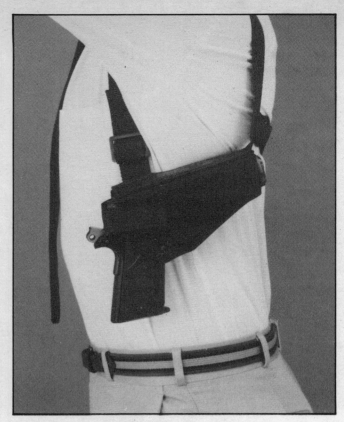

Heavy-duty ballistic nylon fabric is the material used by Assault Systems for their line of holsters and other shooting accessories. Hook and loop closure adjusts to fit most pistols. Right- or left-hand models available.

safety strap is designed to carry the Colt autoloader in the cocked and locked hammer mode. It, too, is optional in Porvair.

For those who prefer to carry a gun in a shoulder holster, the Safariland Models 7 and 53 will accommodate small- and medium-size pistols, while the Model 100 is designed to carry large autoloaders. Specifically for the police officer, the Model 1000 by Safariland may include optional extra-magazine and handcuff cases attached to the off-side of the rig and help balance the load on both shoulders. The Model 1000 is available for left- or right-hand shooters.

For those who do not enjoy the shoulder and back harness, Safariland's Model 550 rides close and high on the off-side, with a retaining spring opening for security and fast draw. Small or large pistols will carry in the Model 530 Klipspringer holster, with a spring steel retaining spring instead of belt loops; fast and easy to put on and take off. The Klipspringer does not require a belt. Similarly, the Safariland Hip Hugger is a fully-adjustable paddle-type holster which may be placed in cross-draw or standard location at any angle the wearer may desire.

Medium-size autoloaders such as the Beretta, Detonics or Walther are easily carried in the high-ride position in the Model 8. Colt .25 autos and Walther PP models are positioned high and tight by the Model 15. Two other Safariland concealment holsters are the Model LS-28 (LS for low silhouette) and the LS-27 belt slide holster. The

Model 3 Hi Ride is used on the pistol competition range by many favoring the big autoloaders. Safariland's Sight Track, which keeps leather off the front sight blade for minimum wear and faster draw, is standard on this holster.

The sportsman will find Safariland's Model 6 Large Auto holster just right for his AMT, Browning Hi-Power, Colts or S&W autoloaders. For the Ruger .22 autoloaders, each of the three barrel lengths is accommodated by the Model 4. Incidentally, Safariland is one of the few makers offering holsters for the Ruger .22 pistols. For larger autos, the Model 4 has been popular for several years. The Model 75, also designed for large autos, has a clip pouch mounted on the face of the holster. Both models feature Safariland's Sight Track.

Tex Shoemaker, who founded a leather business in 1936 in San Dimas, California, was a law enforcement officer for thirty-three years. Not surprisingly, much of his gear is designed for police work. For duty wear, Shoemaker offers at least eighteen designs, including those for various 9mm or .45 autoloaders, for the Colts, S&Ws, Brownings, Berettas and Heckler & Kochs. The list includes high rides, swivel holsters, full-flap models, break-front models, thumb-break Jordan styles, shoulder holsters and military styles, as well as matching full accessory rigs for the uniformed officer.

For the off-duty or plainclothes police officer, Shoe-

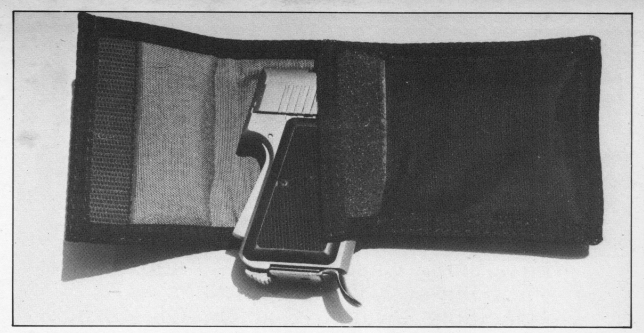

AMT distributes newest small concealable nylon pocket holster for Backup .22 pistol, featuring Velcro closure.

maker offers holsters for large and medium pistols, ranging downward to include styles for small autos such as the Colt .25, Beretta Jetfire and AMT .380 Backup. Other models include a clip-on that is worn inside the trouser band and a paddle-type design with an inside thumb-break to fit most medium or large autoloaders. High-riding huggers and shoulder models also are included in the Shoemaker line-up. The police officer also has available an extensive line of duty and off-duty leather accessories.

Smith & Wesson produces more revolvers than auto-loaders, thus one might assume they would also produce more holsters for revolvers than for pistols. Not necessarily. The S&W holster factory in North Carolina also makes leather goods for such diverse autos as Beretta, Bernardelli, Browning, Colt, Ruger, Star, Walther and others.

Styles include two with spring clips, one for wear inside the trouser band and one outside. The Model 21 Blazer has proved quite popular and will handle medium- and large-frame autos, while the Model 22 is a higher quality, lined holster that puts the gun on the belt with the butt slightly forward. It is favored by S&W Model 439 and 459 pistol owners. The AutoBelt Strap carries automatics with barrels of up to five inches with the muzzle exposed. This affords maximum concealment in minimum space. Other models include a closed-trigger guard style, a thumb-break, a cross-draw and a shoulder holster.

Wessonhide is S&W's leather substitute material which is less expensive than real leather. It has the look, feel, and smell of leather. It is impervious to heat or cold, won't absorb moisture, and is said to be maintenance-free. Holsters and other products made of Wessonhide cost about one-half the price of a similar leather item.

A new outfit called Tabler Marketing offers an adjustable holster that is said to fit all medium- and large-frame autos up to and including Broomhandle Mausers and Auto Mags. Gun bluing is protected by a sheepskin lining; sizes are adjusted through use of the five belt slots in the simple

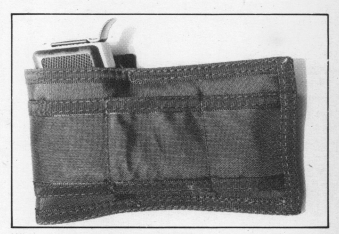

When not carried in pocket, AMT holster offers optional-position belt loops sewn into back of pouch.

design. The Tabler may be changed for left- or right-side wear, cross-draw or standard, or in the middle of the back.

Krasne's Triple K of San Diego has found a rather large market for their police leather gear, from full-duty rigs to small concealable holsters. Such leather usually is finished in black with a basketweave finish; there also is plain-clothes shoulder rigs.

For the sportsman, a couple of high riders, called Speedster and Tornado have slightly different trigger guard coverage designs. Both are offered in black, cordovan, walnut oil or what Triple K calls gold oak. They are plain or basketweave, with suede or leather linings. Triple K also has a lightweight belt slot model, and the Partner, which includes a built-in extra magazine pouch in the design.

CHAPTER 12

RELOADING FOR THE AUTO PISTOL

Those Empty Cases Can Be Turned Back Into Perfectly Good Cartridges, At A Respectable Saving In Cost Out Of Pocket!

The RCBS Green Machine is a progressive loader that can load 50 rounds in about six minutes. It's available in 9mm and .45 ACP, other calibers. It's always a good idea to wear eye protection when reloading.

GIVEN the equipment, components, suitable load data and a moderate amount of know-how, it is a simple and rewarding operation to reload center-fire cases after they've been fired and, in most examples, a given case can be reloaded several times before reaching the state of mandatory retirement. It is not practical to reload rimfire cases, once they've been fired.

Reloading for the auto pistol encounters one basic problem, right at the start: By its very nature and design, the auto pistol ejects its spent cases with considerable enthusiasm, thereby making it somewhat of a challenge to recover them entirely. The auto pistol shooter who reloads quickly learns to direct the fallout from the ejection port to an area where the elusive hulls will be fairly easy to spot. By the same token, the thoughtful shooter will take along a container of some sort for the purpose of fetching the recovered brass back to the loading bench. An emptied milk carton, thoroughly rinsed, with its top cut off, works well for such purposes.

If the cases are stored for an extended period before reloading, it is a good idea to inspect them before proceeding with the other steps. When writing earlier books in a similar vein, I've made reference to watching out for dead grasshoppers entombed in the spent hulls and some have viewed this as overly facetious, and have let me know their views on the matter.

Only a few months ago, I decanted a batch of 9mm Luger hulls from their container in preparation for their planned resurrection and was bemused to note that one had the *derriere* of a good-sized beetle of some sort protruding from the mouth. True, it was not a grasshopper: point conceded. Entomology is not one of my strong suits but I took pains to photograph the hapless critter *in situ* and, having dislodged it from its brazen sarcophagus, snapped an overall view of it for the sake of any who wish to identify it by the proper Latin moniker. Apparently, it

Here's that reloading bench with the adjustable feet, able to be leveled up on practically any uneven area. It takes apart for transportation or storage, easily.

Details of the clench-lock on the downhill side of the bench. Section of threaded rod is anchored on the side of the foot not visible here; loosen and move it!

crawled in and then couldn't back out; an extreme example, true, and quite obvious. The sneakier pitfalls are the spiders who deposit their eggs in the cases and cover them with webbing, not to mention the occasional hunk of gravel that can lodge inside the case and snap your decapping pin, if undetected.

In addition, you need to check for frazzled case mouths, split sides, incipient case separations, head bulges, enlarged primer pockets and — if obtained from other than your personal firing — you've got to watch out for what I like to term Berdan-primed cases of foreign extraction.

There are two basic priming systems for center-fire cartridges: Boxer and Berdan. Named for their respective inventors, Boxer was a Briton, Berdan an American. Curiously enough, the Boxer system is almost universally used in ammunition made here or intended for export to the U.S. The Berdan system is widely used in other parts of the world. Berdan-primed cases can be reloaded, but it takes specialized equipment and, of course, primers of the proper sort, making it a vastly more complex and trying process than reloading the Boxer-primed cases.

The primary difference is that the Berdan-primed case has its anvil integral to the case head, with two small flash holes offset from the center of the head. The Boxer primer carries a small anvil inside the primer and has a single, larger flash hole in the center of the head. Domestic reloading dies carry a single decapping pin, centered in the die, for the purpose of entering the flash hole and punching out the spent primer as one of the first steps in reloading the case.

In the process of inspecting the cases, it's my usual custom to sort them by headstamp to compensate for small but significant dimensional differences between one make and the others. The 9mm Luger is an extreme example of such variation, but there are several others nearly as bad. In the .45 ACP, for example, the cases with an R-P headstamp, for Remington-Peters, usually have preceptibly thinner case mouths than do most other makes. Some makers offer reloading dies specifically tailored for the R-P cases in .45 ACP and, lacking such a die, you may find the base of the bullet to be insecurely held after the bullet has been seated.

Curiously enough, in the instance of the .38 Colt Super cartridge, exactly the opposite is true. In that size, the R-P cases have nice thick necks that hold bullets of .355-inch (9mm) diameter quite securely, while the W-W — Winchester-Western — cases have the thinner mouths.

It is highly desirable — fairly well mandatory — for the case mouth to grip the base of the bullet with considerable tenacity in the reloaded round, be it for the auto pistol or for revolvers. Reloads for the latter must resist working forward under the impetus of recoil and reloads for the auto pistol need to hold the bullet tightly enough to keep it from being driven back into the case upon meeting the feed ramp. Any increase in seating depth beyond the intended amount will boost the peak pressures developed at the time of firing. The faster-burning powders are more sensitive to this effect than others, but it's proportionally true of all of them.

As a simple but effective test of the immovability of the seated bullet, I sometimes put one base-down on the bathroom scales and use a piece of wood against the tip of the

Lee Precision turret press has three stations and a remarkably painless price. A recent feature is auto advance for the turret and automated powder drop. Mounting stand here is a homemade production.

brass between the burning powder and the space at the top of the magazine. If the reload develops pressure excessive for that particular cartridge, there is a severe risk the case head may rupture, venting powder gas at pressures on the order of 20,000 to perhaps 50,000 pounds per square inch (psi) against the top of the magazine. The danger of setting off a chain explosion of cartridges still in the magazine is obvious and, even if no cartridges are present, it's likely to cause damage to the gun mechanism and/or the shooter's hand.

I've had that memorable experience exactly once, and I much prefer not to experience it again. No, it was not a dubious reload, but a perfectly respectable factory round, but it was fired in an experimental barrel I'd been given to test. I was lucky in that I didn't even have a magazine in place, so the gas was free to vent down the magazine well. Even so, the force was sufficient to shatter a pair of sturdy stocks on the gun and, nearly fourteen years later, my right palm still tingles at the recollection.

A little earlier, we mentioned checking fired cases for head bulges. Having reviewed the conditions that apply, it can be explained that you're watching for visible convexities in the area immediately ahead of the extractor cut in the head of the case. If you don't catch such bulges on initial inspection, you may note a slightly greater effort is required to work the case up into the resizing die and, on being withdrawn, you may be able to see a burnished and detectably brighter area at that point. If so, that should be regarded in exactly the same light as the warning whir of a disturbed rattlesnake, for much the same reason. The previous loading in that case generated too much pressure; quite a bit too much.

If desired, the cases can be cleaned/polished by using a tumbler. It hurts nothing and it certainly makes the finished loads look nicer although it's debatable if they perform any better. As an alternate approach, you can make up what I call a K-Spinner, which is a small mandrel dimensioned so its tip is a friction-fit in the case mouth. Put into a drill press or electric drill and set to spinning, the case mouth is pressed over the mandrel tip and a tuft of fine steel wool is used to clean the outside of the case. If the primer has been punched out, you can twist another small tuft of steel wool onto the end of a small wooden dowel and press it up into the primer pocket to remove any firing residue present there. When done, just pluck the case off the spinning mandrel, pop another in its place and keep going; no need to shut it off and turn it back on.

If you are using standard steel reloading dies — specifically, the full-length resizing die — it is necessary to apply case sizing lube to the case before resizing and, with that done, it is equally necessary to remove the lube before going on with the remaining steps. The K-Spinner and a bit of paper towel make quick, easy work of that chore.

The other route is to purchase a die set having a resizing die with an insert of tungsten carbide — or titanium carbide, in the example of dies made by Redding-Hunter — whereupon you can forget about the resizing lube entirely, thereby saving much time and avoiding a somewhat messy pair of chores. The t-c dies cost a little more, but they are richly worth the difference. The pistol reloading die sets from Lee Precision (4275 Highway U, Hartford, WI 53027) are furnished solely with t-c resizing dies in the straight-

bullet to press downward, watching the dial to see the amount of static push needed to make the bullet move. If it breaks loose at anything under about thirty pounds, in the example of the .45 ACP, its seating tenacity is unacceptable. Smaller cartridges, having less bearing surface between case neck and bullet base, may break loose at a lower weight, meanwhile being satisfactory for use. Another way to check is to eject a round after it has cycled through the action and compare its overall length with that of a round of the same batch as loaded. If the chambered round comes out shorter, you still have a problem that needs correcting.

Another problem peculiar to the auto pistol is that a portion of the case head hangs unsupported over the feed ramp when the cartridge is locked in the chamber and ready to fire. That means there is nothing but a modest thickness of

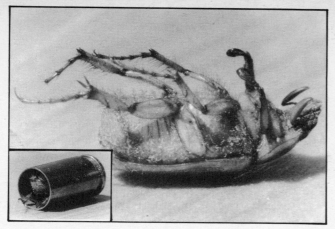

Cases need inspection before loading because you've no idea what may turn up in them, as shown here!

The K-Spinner goes in a drill press or hand drill to spin cases by friction fit for cleaning, de-lubing, or polishing. Note partly-polished .45 case at right.

Lyman's Turbo tumbler is a speedy way to polish a lot of fired cases all at once. Run only one caliber at a time or small ones will lodge tight in big ones!

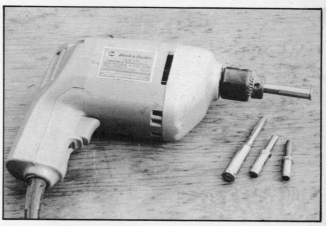

A K-Spinner in an electric hand drill. Cordless drill can be used to good advantage if no wall socket is available. K-Spinners aren't commercially available.

walled numbers and, within recent times, they've been working on a t-c die for the slightly tapered 9mm Luger case. The price of these Lee sets is remarkably modest, even so, and I've used them in several different calibers with a high degree of satisfaction.

Most die sets for reloading pistol cartridges consist of three dies, sometimes four, and the basic arrangement varies somewhat from maker to maker. The first die, for example, may resize the case full-length, and that's all. In that example, the second die positions an expanding plug to bring the resized case neck to the desired inside diameter (ID) meanwhile flaring the case neck slightly and punching out the spent primer with a decapping pin located at the lower end of the expanding plug. The third die seats the bullet and may — or may not — crimp the case mouth around it. The fourth die, if present, is a taper-crimp die that serves to iron out the flare at the case neck to assure smoother feeding. Most die sets by Hornady-Pacific are as just described.

The other common approach is to put the decapping pin in the resizing die on a support rod smaller than the ID of the case neck. The second die carries the expanding plug

and the seating die is as described before, with the option of a taper-crimp die for the final finish. Die sets from RCBS, for example, follow this pattern.

The reasoning behind either system is that the resizing die will bring the fired case down to an ID that is just slightly too small, whereupon the expander plug will bring the ID back up to precisely the desired dimension, regardless of minor variations in case neck thickness. Usually, the final ID will be about .002-inch smaller than the diameter of the bullet to be seated, resulting in the desirable friction fit of case neck to bullet base.

The expander plugs furnished with Lyman die sets have a novel but quite admirable feature. The main portion of the plug is of a diameter slightly smaller than the bullet diameter and, at the end of the stroke, the case mouth goes over a shallow collar that is about .001-inch larger than bullet diameter. Thus there is no extravagant mouth belling, yet the processed case — with the expander plug suitably adjusted — accepts the bullet base quite nicely, permitting the bullet to be seated without scraping or other deformation of the bearing surface.

When reloading lead or cast bullets, it is highly important to avoid any mutilation of the bullet sidewalls or bearing surface. If you can see a thin sliver of shaved lead around the mouth of the loaded round, you're doing something wrong and you can be certain that load will not group as well as you'd hoped it might.

Personally, I'm extremely partial to taper-crimp dies and use them by strong preference over the roll-crimp type. Given the necessary couple of thousandths of friction fit between case neck and bullet base, you've all the holding power you need. If you don't have that, even a heavy roll crimp will not take the place of it. In using the taper-crimp die, the trick is to adjust it so the cartridge going up into it meets only modest resistance, as felt by the hand on the press handle. All you really want to do is to iron-in the flare at the case neck. If you taper-crimp excessively, you will reduce the effective diameter of the seated bullet just a bit and, on being withdrawn from the die, the brass case — being somewhat elastic — will spring outward slightly, while the notably unelastic lead will not expand correspondingly. In so doing, you will have reduced the tenacity of the fit between the bullet and case and, with it, the potential accuracy of the reloaded round.

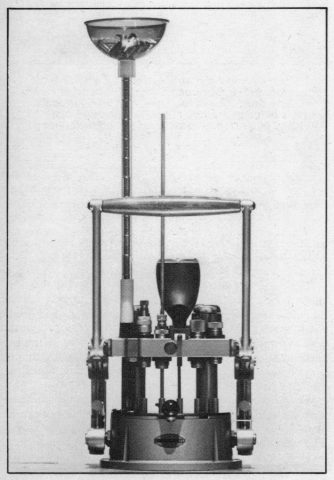

Ransom Grand Master is a progressive reloader made by C'Arco, producers of the Ransom Rest. Installed here is their automatic case feeder.

Accuracy is certainly an important factor in ammunition, be it reloads or factory fodder, but the functional reliability is of equal or considerably greater importance for loads to be used in auto pistols. A stoppage — "jam" — can cost you points in a match that you'd much prefer not to lose and, should you have the bad luck to get involved in a serious social shooting situation, a jam could be a great deal more costly.

Feeding reliability is the end product of several interlocking factors, any of which can gum up the works. First of all, the load must generate sufficient power to work the action, perhaps with a little margin to spare but certainly not to excessive levels. If it's too poopy, it won't work the action and if too zesty, it may wreck the mechanism.

Secondly, the overall length of the loaded round must be such to permit it to be loaded into the magazine and come back up out of it smoothly, without hanging up at any point. The overall length of the cartridge, combined with the profile of the bullet nose and the coefficient of friction of the bullet tip, interact to produce either a smooth feed or one that is unreliable.

The auto pistol at hand can be expected to have its own individual prejudices as to ammunition and it can be relied upon to demonstrate them unmistakably. If a round is too short — for that particular gun — feeding will be marginal and jams the order of the day. The movement of the cartridge from magazine to chamber is a highly kinetic process, somewhat guided by inclined surfaces along the way in the shape of the feed ramp and/or the barrel shroud, magazine lips and its attitude in a limited amount of free flight.

There are some pistols that can and will feed empty cases out of the magazine and into the chamber with excellent reliability but even such remarkable devices may not feed any and every loaded round. Putting a bullet up front changes its center of gravity. When the ledge on the lower surface of the slide strikes the upper portion of the case head, it may induce a turning moment that has the effect of making the tip of the bullet nose down slightly. That can cause the tip of the bullet to butt up solidly against a point rather low on the feed ramp, coming to a sudden stop and turning the autoloading pistol into a manually actuated repeater of dubious credentials.

Much the same applies if the bullet has any substantial area of dead-soft lead at its tip. Many pistols have feed

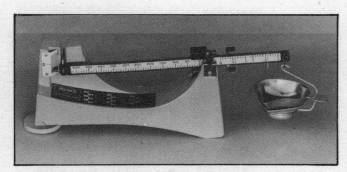

A good powder scale is indispensible for the job of reloading, being used to adjust powder measures, weigh bullets, etc. This is the RCBS Model 5-0-5.

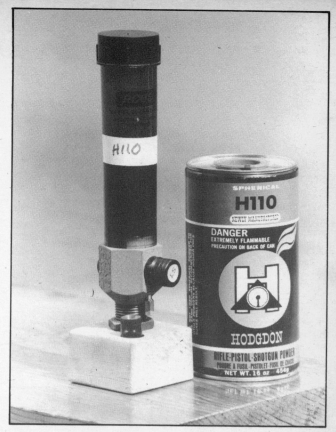

Dillon RL-450 press is manually-moved progressive, here at left, with a four-position turret; a good unit for making quantities of loads for a given cartridge. Above, a piece of drafting tape on the reservoir of the RCBS Little Dandy helps to identify powder held.

ramps that are comparatively steep, designed for optimum functioning with round nose, full-metal jacket (RN/FMJ) bullets. The sliding qualities of soft lead against such a surface at the angle involved is not good at all. Even if it feeds — as may happen — the bullet tip will have been deformed to unsymmetrical contours with a degrading effect upon the resulting accuracy.

It is possible to obtain an impressive level of feeding reliability along with gratifying accuracy with cast bullets in auto pistols. The No. 68 design by Hensley & Gibbs (Box 10, Murphy, OR 97533) is an excellent example for the .45 ACP cartridge, but even that one won't work nearly as well if cast of a soft alloy or of pure lead. The same maker has another mould, their No. 264, that performs exceptionally well in the 9mm Luger or .38 Colt Super, both as to accuracy and reliability. These and several other designs will be discussed in greater detail in the chapter on bulletmaking, but they are mentioned here as a significant factory in producing satisfactory reloaded ammunition for the sometimes temperamental auto pistol.

Some of the factors affecting the reliability of auto pistols are inherent in the basic design of the gun, imposing a limit as to what can be done at the reloading bench. I have encountered a few examples of the breed that functioned poorly, if at all, on factory ammo and hardly any better, if as well, on reloads. The logical recourse, with such a specimen, is to horsetrade it off as cannily as you can manage and quest about for a replacement, with fingers crossed in hopes that it will do better.

We have touched upon several points of special significance in reloading for the auto pistol. That there are some unmentioned here, I've no doubt. After some thirty-three years of pretty intent interest in the matter, I've even less delusions I know all there is to know on the subject and even less hope I'll ever find out all of it. Let us now add a few thoughts and comments upon the generalized aspects of reloading cartridges, with the firm *caveat* that space does not permit an exhaustive coverage of the topic. The reloader of modern times has access to a library of excellent works on the subject that hardly were dreamed of in 1950 and several such works will be illustrated here. Meanwhile, I will add what I regard as noteworthy notes.

Quite early in my reloading career, I came to regard it as a stand-up operation. After considerable trial-and-error experimentation, I determined that the ideal height for the working surface — top of the loading bench — was even

Spare rotors for the RCBS Little Dandy measure, are stored in plastic case for shotshells, numbered with colored pasters for easy identification of size.

An assortment of primers by Federal, Remington, CCI and Winchester. They're available in large and small sizes, standard and magnum priming mixes.

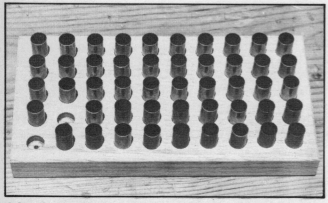

A handy cartridge loading block for 9mm Luger was made by laying out spots on ⅜-inch centers, then drilling ⅜-inch holes to a fairly shallow depth.

with the upper edge of the reloader's belt. It is also pretty close to the distance from the point of the elbow — with forearm held horizontally — to the floor. For my own five-eleven frame, that works out to forty-two inches, floor to bench-top, but it's a simple matter to custom-tailor it to your own dimensions.

Within fairly recent times, goaded by occasional problems of sore feet after lengthy loading sessions, I conceded a point and built a three-legged stool to perch upon when operations do not require unduly strenuous exertions. Its upper surface is thirty-three inches off the floor, nine inches below the bench surface, or just one inch less than the proper inseam measurement when ordering a pair of pants, if that's any helpful guidance and I'm pleased to report it works out quite nicely.

Most reloading presses exert substantial torque upon their mounting surface in operation, making the preferred thickness for a proper bench top on the order of 1½ inches; the thickness of nominal two-inch planks. A fairly recent project was to design and build a lugabout loading bench that usually reposes in a secluded corner of the front porch. It can be picked up and carried out to the driveway without vast exertion. Once on that sloping surface, a few minutes with a spirit level and its built-in adjustable footing, leaves you with a sturdy, dead-level working surface that can cope and has coped with the considerable stresses involved in swaging bullets. Put an electric melting pot on it and you have the pluperfect setup for casting bullets, with all the ventilation in the world, quite literally. Attach the little clamp-on ledge to the left front corner and you have the pinnacle of luxury for the otherwise patience-trying chore of lube/sizing cast bullets. The undercarriage bolts to stubs at the top so it can be disassembled and portaged in the car, if desired.

The distance from the uphill edge to the ground is, of course, forty-two inches. The clench-lock design of the base takes every last bit of jiggle and wiggle out of it and it sits as steady as a camera tripod.

An earlier session of head-scratching resulted in the reloader's mini-bench that worked out well in general principle, if not in fine detail. Its base is T-shaped so that it will shrug off the heaviest stresses with nary a rock nor tilt. The major tactical error was in covering it with Formica applied with contact cement. It would have been better to have left it bare wood, with a few spray coats of Varathane to ward off attacks by the elements. More, the top didn't need to be that thick. As it is, mounting a press to it requires a large C-clamp and, even so, it is inclined to slip under stress. However, it is a capable bench that weighs about twenty-three pounds and costs small change for materials. It can be held out at arm's length without coloring your face much beyond pale mauve. Try that with any other loading bench!

There are at least two basic and contending schools of thought in reloading. One feels the way to go is to take a single spent case and put it through the works to emerge as a reloaded round, then do the same with the next, and so on.

The second and diametrically opposing school believes the thing to do is to bring the cases to load-ready status, put them in a loading block, drop the powder charges into each, scan them keenly for uniformity of powder level, put bullets into the flared mouths and then go on to seat the

RCBS Model A4 press is rugged and powerful. This one carries a short handle I made for convenience in reloading handgun cases where effort is minor.

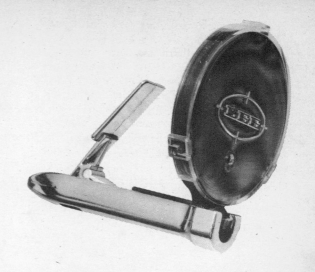

Lee Auto-Prime offers speedy seating of primers, fed by gravity from the drum reservoir visible here.

bullets, perform the crimps, package and set aside for eventual consumption.

Much can be said in support of either contention. Much has been said and I doubt that the end is at hand. I can say that I subscribe to the second school, as listed here. If you are absolutely certain that there are no absent-minded genes in your ancestry for a thousand generations back, you may find happiness and satisfaction in the first or spent-case-to-loaded-round school.

If you have doubts about that — as I most certainly do! — you may incline to favor the second or batch-through-steps approach.

I have one of the fine old Hollywood turret presses here, and love it with a pale puce passion. It is eminently capable of turning a spent case into a live round in just a few flicks of the turret and strokes of the handle, once properly set up and programmed. Doing so assumes the operator to be undistracted the whole while. "Assume," it has been observed, is a word that makes an ass out of "u and me."

On my door at the office, I have an elegant poster of an oriental warrior doing his sanguinary thing, ballooned with a caption: "Interruptions by appointment only!" It cuts absolutely no detectable ice, whatso-a-tall. People interrupt me without compunction, without first or second thought. Any profound concept I may have been formulating with all loving care goes into a glittering heap of shards and shambles. Who could care less, apart from me, that is?

Reloading is performed in the shop at home and there, it's even worse. The phone rings. The neighbors come up to the door, needing to borrow dado saw blades or a metric crescent wrench. Stray dogs come marauding up and helicopters roar overhead. Sirens keen past on the nearby freeway like berserk banshees and any ten solid minutes of peaceful productivity is on an approximate par with a winning ticket for the Irish sweeps. So it goes and yes, you're right: It's better than nothing.

With a subjective *status quo* such as that, any attempt to produce a sequence from spent case to loaded round in one fell swoop is doomed at the outset. Panics march up like the tireless beat of surf on a sandy beach and the beat never falters. Sooner or later, you leave the powder out of one — ba-aa-ad! — or, still worse, you make up for it by double-dosing some other case. No, thank you.

To my way of thinking, there is nothing half so comforting as to see a whole platoon of load-ready cases set out in their loading block, and to dispense the charges, one and one-only, into each in turn, and to get the light over my shoulder to block-check the entire small lot, followed by insertion of a bullet into the mouth of each case in turn. With that done, the bullets can be seated and interruptions can come and go, as they always have and forever shall, world without end.

I apologize for bending your ear this way, but it is one of the relatively small number of things upon which I have fiercely held convictions.

Reloading presses can be categorized into two groups: single-station and multi-station, with yet another variant termed the progressive. The single-station designs are described by different alphabetical letters. If the press is open at the front, it's a C-type; if it is braced by an integral upright at that point, it's an O-type and if the bar carrying the shell holder slides up and down on a pair of columns, it's an H-type. The little Decker press, currently made and sold by Huntington Die Specialties (Box 991, Oroville, CA 95965) is unmistakably a W-type.

The multi-station presses may have an upper turret holding the dies and rotating to put the desired die above the single shell holder. Others have up to four shell holders and the four dies are held immovably above the shell holders and aligned with them. In other such presses, the dies are stationary and the shell holder moves from one to the other. The basic purpose of such designs is to get away from the time-consuming chore of taking dies out of the single-station presses and putting other dies in their place. Being able to pop the case back and forth from one die to the next saves a lot of time.

The progressive presses are designed to perform several different steps simultaneously, so that a complete loaded round is produced with each stroke of the press handle. The cases move from station to station automatically, actuated by working the press handle — as in the example of the RCBS Green Machine — or the shell plate may be moved manually, as with the Dillon RL-450.

Progressive presses are purely the cat's pajamas if you need to produce a large quantity of cartridges in a short space of time, but they are not each and every reloader's first-choice cup of tea. That's to say they sometimes require a bit of inspired adjustment and further fiddling about and you must, repeat MUST! keep your eyes open and your full attention on what you're doing. In that vein, illustratively, I wish I could avoid recalling the time I was cranking out loads on the RCBS Green Machine at a merry clip, only to notice at length the reservoir of the powder measure had run bone dry. Have you ever inertia-pulled three hundred bullets to segregate those with powder behind them from those without? Take my solemn word, it is a trying task, but it tends to make you keep a wary eye on the powder level, henceforth!

Much of the secret of success at running reloading presses lies in proper installation and adjustment of the dies. Let's discuss that briefly. In nearly every instance, the full-length resizing die is installed so the upper surface of the shell holder makes positive contact with the lower edge of the die. Run the ram — with shell holder installed — to the top of its stroke and leave it there. Turn the die down into the station at the top of the press until it touches the shell holder. Back the ram down and turn the die on in by perhaps a tiny trifle and move the ram back up. When it's just right, you'll feel a gentle but discernible "snick" in the handle as it tops out. Tighten the locking ring on the die and secure it in its setting with the small screw on the side of the ring to save time when making future installations of that die.

If the resizing die also carries the decapping pin, the tip of the pin needs to project beyond the bottom of the die just far enough to punch the spent primers out, each and every time. Typically, that's about .25-inch or so.

A sidenote here: Several years ago, it was customary for ammomakers to make the flash hole from the primer pocket into the case body slightly smaller in diameter than the current practice. If you work solely with modern cases, that will pose no problem. If you have a few ancient cases in the stock bins, or if you accept occasional donations of brass, you may encounter cases that will grab the decapping pin in a death-grip and wrench it from the holding collet as the ram goes back down. As this is a problem I bump against every now and again, I put a No. 45 or 46

drill bit in the press and — with great care — ream the flash hole out with that. Once attended to, that case will present no further problem. Old .38 Colt Super and .38 ACP cases are notorious offenders in this respect.

If the second die carries the expander plug and decapping pin, or the plug alone, the usual procedure is to turn the die body down until it touches the ram at the top of the stroke, securing the locking ring at that setting. Turn the expander plug well up in the die body. Put a resized case in the shell holder and run the ram to the top. Turn the expanding plug down until it touches the case, as indicated by feel. Turn it still further — if possible — until you feel the expanding shoulder touch the case mouth. Back the ram down a trifle and turn the plug on in just a bit farther. Run the ram up to the top of the stroke, run it down and remove the case. You want to have the plug set so it puts just the barest minimum amount of flare in the case neck, so as to permit the base of a bullet to start into it. Excessive flare is a problem and so is insufficient flare. Use the bullet base as your test gauge.

A good way to install and adjust the seating die is to put a factory load in the shell holder, run it to the top, back out the seating stem of the die and turn the die body down until it makes snug contact with the case mouth of the cartridge, securing the locking ring at that setting. Then turn down the seating stem until it touches the tip of the bullet and secure it in that setting with the small knurled collar around it. By so doing, your reloads will approximate the dimensions of the factory round and, as may be necessary, you can make minor adjustments from that trial setting.

RCBS Model RS-2 press is a light, handy, economical unit capable of reloading nicely.

Reload-A-Stand is a take-down support from Accessory Splty. Co., 2711 S. 84 St., W. Allis, WI 53227.

If you are using a taper-crimp die as the final step, it should be turned up or down until the loaded round enters it with no more than moderate resistance, as was discussed earlier. You want to turn the neck flare back in and straight with the body of the case, but not much beyond that.

On dispensing powder, there are at least two accessories more important than the powder measure, itself. First, you need at least one — preferably several — manuals or handbooks for reloading or handloading — two pairs of mutually synonymous terms, there — in which you can look up the proper amount of the given powder to put behind a bullet of that weight in the specific cartridge. Next, you need a good powder scale to check the weight of the charge of powder you propose to use.

Beyond that, there are several devices for the actual dispensation of the powder charges. These range in complexity and sophistication from the small dipper-type measures sold as a kit by Lee Precision on up to flossy electronic affairs with digital readouts, at around five hundred bucks a throw. Between those extremes, we find rotary measures with interchangeable fixed-cavity rotors and other rotaries with adjustable cavities. Either of the last two need to have their charges checked against a good powder scale.

About the early middle Sixties, when Pacific operated out of Lincoln, Nebraska, they came up with a cute little measure that operated with fixed-cavity rotors that were

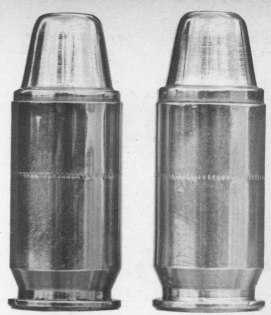

Bullet seating depth is important! Load at left works perfectly; load at right won't quite let the action close. Check (with great care) to be sure it fits the chamber.

A set of RCBS dies in .38 Colt Super, with resizing die equipped with tungsten carbide insert to avoid the need of lubricating cases and cleaning after resizing.

available in several cavity sizes. They would also furnish blank rotors you could drill to your own specifications. It was an addictively fine and handy gizmo, marred solely by the fact that the little plastic reservoir was painfully — uhh — pervious to deterioration when in contact with double-base powders. The nitroglycerin in the DB powder would leach out and attack the plastic, darkening it and replasticizing it, unless you remembered to empty the reservoir the instant you finished using it. Being set up the way I am [sigh!], I didn't always manage that. Thus, my original Pacific measures ended up painfully shopworn in the reservoirs after extensive use.

It was, as I've said, addictively handy and I nursed by two or three of those, with their little rack of rotors, for years after they'd been dropped when Hornady bought out the Pacific operation. Nominally intended for use with

Bullseye powder, they could be hand-calibrated for use with any other suitable powder by a simple and straightforward procedure. For example, if you wanted to use it with Du Pont PB powder, you poured some into the reservoir, dropped ten charges all together into the pan of your powder scale, weighed it, divided the figure by ten and you had the average drop for that powder with that rotor. If you noted the figure on a chart, and didn't lose track of the chart, you could tool up in a fast jiffy to drop the same charge at any future time.

As a spinoff of the extensive research that went into development of the RCBS Green Machine, RCBS developed their Little Dandy powder measure and put it on the market. The Little Dandy serves as the powder dispenser on the Green Machine and, as a separate unit, it can be had with twenty-six different fixed-cavity rotors to dispense a bewildering number of charges of this or that powder in the same number of different weights.

It is at least as handy and useful as the original Pacific measure and, as I can attest, even more addictive. While it can be used advantageously with the smaller rifle cartridges, up to around .223 Remington, it is at its best for reloading handgun cartridges. Its great virtue lies in the utter repeatability of its performance. Two years ago, today or a decade down the road, you can put in a given rotor, fill the hopper with the proper powder and it will deliver X.XX grains of it, every time you actuate the rotor.

What about uniformity? Glad you asked. I've used it to meter out charges that have grouped under .5-inch center-to-center spread at a bit over one hundred yards; less than one-half minute of angle (MOA). That was in a rifle, fired off the benchrest, but it serves to illustrate the capability of the Little Dandy.

Keeping track of all those rotors was a bit of a challenge, but the solution turned out to be quite simple. Twenty-five

Lyman T-Mag press, left, is a rugged four-station turret design. Right, operator's view of the RCBS Green Machine. Placing a bullet in the seating die opening is its only manual operation, besides working the handle.

can be put into a MTM carrier for 12-gauge shotgun shells, with the twenty-sixth installed in the Little Dandy. The identifying number is stamped in the end of the rotor and none too readily visible. I took care of that by applying .75-inch self-adhesive pasters and lettering the number on them with a pen.

A bar chart is available for use with the Little Dandy measure, covering the drop weights for several typical powders. You need to verify the accuracy of those figures by metering the powder you have into the pan of your scale and weighing the resulting charge. Usually the chart figure is quite close, but individual techniques and manufacturing tolerances crank in slight variations. Thus, I've made up my own chart and prefer to go by that.

I've also fitted my Little Dandy measures with finger-turned stop-screws to replace the slot-headed ones supplied with the units originally. I find that a great convenience as I endlessly take this rotor out and put that one in; no need to stop and rummage for a screwdriver.

If you work with several different powders, it's an excellent idea to use some system to identify the powder that's in the measure reservoir at the given time. My solution to that is to apply a small piece of white drafting tape to the tube and write the name of the powder on it. When changing to another powder, the tape can be peeled off and stuck to the can for future use.

The plastic used for the tube on the Little Dandy seems entirely impervious to the effects of double-base powder and most powders will not stick to the sides. When changing powders, it's quite important to get the last few granules of the old powder out before putting the next powder in, lest they change the burning characteristics of the next powder by finding their way into some of the charges.

The Little Dandy comes with a warning notice that it is not to be used for dispensing black powder and that caution should be observed, lest it set off the powder in the reservoir with acutely distracting effects.

The primers used in reloading ammunition pack an impressive amount of power and need to be handled with sensible respect. Left in their original packing trays, they are as safe as almost anything you care to name. Dispensed onto a plastic pickup tray, a few lines at a time, they present little or no hazard. They should never be dumped from the trays in bulk or roughly handled when out of the tray because that can set off a mass explosion of them, and has done so in certain instances, with serious injury and damage resulting. The little wafer of priming compound deteriorates if exposed to oil, so take care not to pick them up with oily fingers. Several presses feature some manner of automated primer feed and the feed tubes need to be handled carefully against the risk of setting off a chain explosion of the primers. Wearing shooting glasses or

Seven powders from Hercules, all more or less suitable for reloading auto pistol ammo. Bullseye, at left, is the fastest in burning rate, 2400 the slowest and the ones in between are ranked in progressive order.

Winchester Ball Powders, of which 231 is the one most apt to be used in auto pistols. Never use any powder unless guided by a reliable data source. Seven Du Pont powders are at right; not shown is their 800-X type.

safety glasses while reloading is an excellent practice and should be followed at all times.

The small plastic ammunition boxes, such as the MTM Case-Gard, are an excellent way to store reloaded ammunition until it's used, but it is highly desirable to affix some manner of label to identify the load as to amount and kind of powder and so on. Unless your memory is awesomely eidetic, you will soon find that such vital details have slithered off the mental surface. Reloaded cartridges without identifying details on the load are of dubious value and represent a painful waste of components. Worse, if they turn out to shoot extremely well, you'll wish you'd preserved the recipe for future use. A reader of one of my earlier books offered a suggestion I consider a good one. He writes the particulars of the load on the box with a grease pencil, then applies a short strip of clear sticky tape over it to prevent the marking from rubbing off. In putting on the tape, he leaves one end folded under slightly to enable the tape to be removed easily. The lettering is easily removed with a facial tissue and perhaps a few drops of lighter fluid.

Both powder and primers present hazards if handled foolishly. Restrict your supply to moderate quantities and do not store them together. It is a good idea to keep the cans of powder in a case or cabinet that can be picked up and evacuated quickly in case of fire, and the primer supply in a similar but separate container. Smokeless powder will not explode violently unless confined — black powder, including Pyrodex, will do so. If ignited in the open, smokeless powder flares up in a hot flame that can ignite nearby flammables. Obviously, it's extremely poor practice to smoke while reloading or near reloading components. When casting bullets, be aware that a splashed droplet of lead can land in an exposed quantity of powder and set it off. Instances of such catastrophes are a matter of record. Electrical reloading equipment such as melting pots or case tumblers should not be left unattended with flammable material nearby.

Several of these precautionary considerations seem obvious and they are so, but they are noted here to help keep readers out of trouble. A bit of judicious common sense is perhaps the most useful of all components about the reloading bench.

Loads To Make The Luger Work

Claud S. Hamilton has given us his thoughts and observations on several topics pertaining to auto pistols and he now proposes to narrate his experiences in producing reloads capable of functioning reliably in the Pistole '08 aka Luger aka Parabellum. As he notes, factory ammunition made on this side of the Atlantic may — or may not — function reliably in that picturesque old pistol. I insert the following discussion not without some amount of qualms and misgivings. That is because I'm reasonably familiar with the outlook of your typical reloading pistoleer, being one of those myself.

Such folks, I've noted, tend to take any printed word as gospel and proceed to make up any hot-and-hairy load recipe they encounter. You should not do so with the loads listed here. These are extra-effort loads and are by no means suitable for use in each and every Luger. Remind yourself some of those guns are well into their second half-century and probably have seen a prodigious number of rounds go up the barrel.

If you can see no alternative to trying out these loads, please do two things first: Have the pistol you plan to use checked and inspected by a competent gunsmith, telling him what you plan to do. Follow his advice, whatever it may be.

Secondly, do as Hamilton did: Start well below the loads listed here and work up with great caution, from the underside. When you reach the point at which the given load cycles the action reliably, STOP AT THAT POINT. Make no further increases in powder charge, even if you have not yet reached Hamilton's listed charge weights. Further cautions appear in the text and may seem redundant. Not every reader reads every word and I think it's important to get this message across.

You have been warned... — DAG

This pistol, used by Hamilton in his tests, as reported here, is patterned after the Swiss Model, without the small curved area at the lower front of the grip. It was made by Mauser and termed the Parabellum.

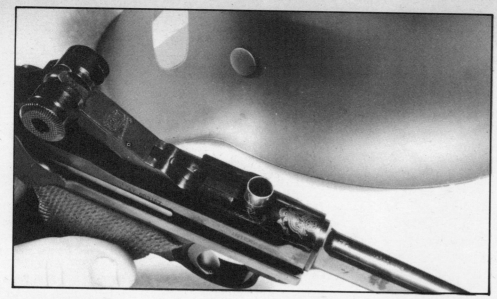

A typical "stovepipe" jam: Load had insufficient power to eject the empty case, which was trapped by the returning bolt to cause a stoppage.

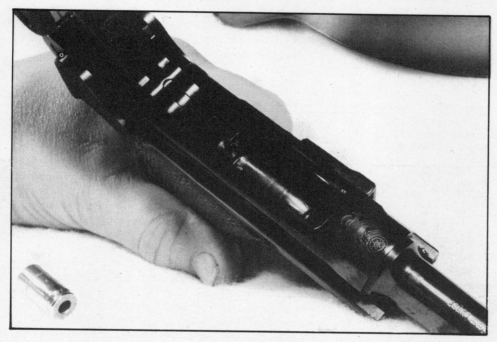

Even if the cartridge has enough power to eject its empty case, the bolt may not be driven back far enough to pick up a fresh load from the top of the magazine.

WHAT IS A "Luger load?" Simple: It is a load for the 9mm Parabellum cartridge that functions reliably in the Luger pistol. Next question: Well, don't they all? No. They don't.

I fired a Luger pistol for the very first time on a summer Saturday afternoon at Fort Benning. It was not long after the end of World War II. After returning from the Philippines, I had been assigned to a battalion of field artillery of School Troops at the Infantry School. A friend, fresh back from Europe, had liberated a fine, pre-war Luger and we took it along to shoot, together with several pet guns not much used during the war years. We found a deserted creek bend way out on the reservation and spent several happy hours plinking at clods of dirt, bits of floating wood, tin cans, and suchlike. To me, that Luger was a beautiful

pistol, and a joy to shoot, but it just wasn't a particularly reliable performer. It jammed on nearly every other shot.

Often since then I have read articles comparing 9mm service pistols and it seems that the Luger is always being faulted as unreliable. It's a bum rap.

The Luger — which Mauser prefers these days to call their "Mauser Parabellum" pistol — is unique in several ways. For one thing, its unusual toggle-lock action has never been copied to any serious extent in any other large production pistol. For another, it got its start as a "cart before the horse." When it came along the German Armed Services were not aware that they needed a new pistol, and they took their own good time getting around to adopting it.

As a result, the factory and Georg Luger personally, spent a great deal of time and effort out-selling the new pis-

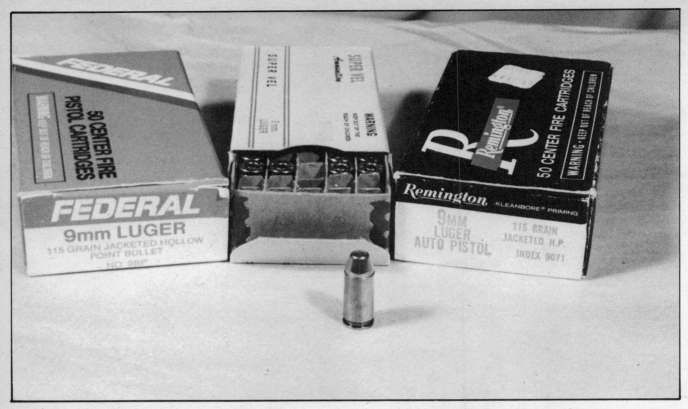

Hamilton was unable to obtain reliable operation of his "Lugers" with U.S. loads such as the three here.

Off the Ransom Rest, Hamilton's pistols grouped quite well, having bypassed the dubious trigger pulls.

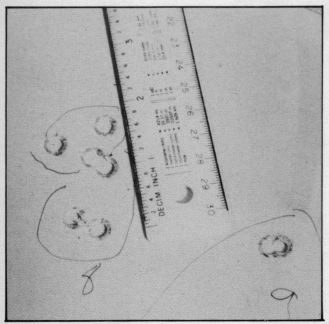

tol to anyone who might be interested. Many small orders came in which led to many small production runs having special features and markings, and almost innumerable variants. The result: a collector's delight!

The Luger was not well known in this country until the end of the First World War when returning servicemen brought them home in droves as war trophies. Understandably, American ammunition makers responded by increasing output of 9mm ammunition, but thy did not load it to German standards. At about the same time a number of cheap Italian and Spanish pistols and revolvers were also entering the country. While some of these could chamber and fire the 9mm Parabellum, they were not sufficiently strong to handle it safely. The U.S. makers agreed upon a lower pressure level and that has since been formalized by the Sporting Arms and Ammunition Makers' Institute (SAAMI).

Two types of malfunction are typical in Lugers when American ammunition is used. In the first, recoil energy is insufficient to eject the empty case and it is caught by the closing bolt in the classic "stovepipe" position locked between bolt and breech face. In the second case, a little more recoil energy is present and the case just manages to eject. The bolt, however, does not travel far enough to the rear to clear the top round in the magazine and so the action closes empty.

Recently I managed to gather together five of the new Lugers produced some ten years or so ago by Mauser and

Hamilton's shooting companion, Martha Penso, tries an offhand group with one of the longer-barreled guns.

The Swiss pattern Parabellum, next to a Government Model Colt. Note that the Parabellum has a grip safety, a feature not often encountered.

For best reliability, Hamilton found that loads need to be made up to overall length of 1.169 inches.

several older "shooting" Lugers and shot them off the Ransom Rest using a number of different bullets and loads. My purpose was to find the "break point": that load level below which Lugers cease to work reliably. I also wanted to find out if there was a basis for the often-expressed opinion that Lugers are highly sensitive to ammunition, and demanding of uniformity if they are to work well.

Several friends and I took the Lugers to the range on three different occasions. We fired all of them from the Ransom Rest as well as freehand and used both American

U.S.-made guns for the 9mmP cartridge, such as the Colt or Smith & Wesson, should not be fired with the heavier loads listed in the accompanying article.

BULLETS	POWDERS								
	BLUE DOT			UNIQUE			HERCO		
	grains	fps	fpe	grains	fps	fpe	grains	fps	fpe
125-grain Speer JSP	8.8	1250	434	6.1	1270	448	6.8	1285	458
115-grain Remington JHP	9.6	1300	432	6.2	1295	428	7.1	1400	501
100-grain Speer JHP	10.1	1410	442	6.3	1330	393	7.7	1430	454
88-grain Speer JHP	10.8	1440	405	6.4	1350	356	8.0	1500	440

NOTE: Velocities measured from a four-inch barrel.
CAUTION: Peak pressures of these loads may exceed accepted American standards. The authors, editors and publishers of this book cannot and do not accept any liability, express or implied, for use of load data given in this book. Use of such load data is at user's risk and discretion. U.S.-made guns for the 9mmP cartridge, such as those from Colt or Smith & Wesson should NOT be fired with these loads.

commercial ammuition and handloads I put together. Some of the things we found were predictable, such as the fact that none of the guns reacted in precisely the same way. The older guns generally would function with lower pressure ammunition, probably a sign of weakened springs and smoother actions.

We agreed that the break point would be that load level which would empty a magazine without a single malfunction. For the guns we shot, it seemed to lie somewhere in the range of 390 to 410 foot-pounds of energy (fpe). The shorter four-inch barrel guns required more energy than the six-inch guns, which was to be expected since the longer barrels generate more muzzle energy and recoil. The dynamics involved are not simple, but their usual results seemed to be that heavier bullets require a little less power to cycle the action than do the lighter ones. It turned out not to be the simple matter I had expected; a physicist could probably do a small book on Luger functioning!

It comes as no surprise to find that most commercial ammunition loaded in the United States generates between 330 and 390 fpe. While some of it will operate the Lugers in the Ransom Rest because of its stiff resistance to recoil, almost none would work when the guns were handheld.

On my last visit to the range we took along a series of my handloads carrying a graduated series of powder charges arranged to increase 0.1-grain at a time from the 400 fpe level. I wanted to see if the Lugers were supersensitive to pressure. We quickly found that they are not. While I certainly do not recommend experiments with heavily loaded 9mm Parabellum ammunition, I found a number of loads that worked well in the Lugers. While they were all "hot" by American standards, none showed excessive pressure signs. Here are some of these:

These are, or are very close to, maximums even for Lugers. It has been said often but it bears repeating, do not experiment with these loads. Approach them cautiously from the low side; your gun and those I tested do not necessarily handle pressures in the same way.

Are loads at these pressure levels safe in other 9mm pistols? The Browning Hi-Power and Walther P-38 were made for European ammunition. The American Smith & Wesson 9mms, however, were developed on our loads. I would say that the Luger loads are probably safe in good, well-made modern pistols. They are too heavy, though, and will cause pounding and eventual damage if used continuously in American 9mms.

CHAPTER 13

BULLETMAKING FOR AUTO PISTOLS

You Can Buy Your Bullets, As Many Do, Or You Can Build Your Own, At A Gratifying Conservation Of Cash-Flow, And Have Fun Doing It!

Probably the most efficient design for cast bullets in .45 ACP is the Hensley & Gibbs #68, weighing about 190 grains. Termed a semi-wadcutter, it's exceptionally accurate and remorselessly reliable in feeding and functional reliability.

BUYING BULLETS is relatively simple and easy, if you have a nearby dealer, but it is not overly cheap. Typical small jacketed bullets go for around eight cents or a dime apiece. Unclad lead bullets cost significantly less but, even so, you can probably turn them out for a useful saving in cash spent. That is particularly true if you are prepared to write off your person-hours as expended in recreational manners.

There are two basic ways to produce bullets, both reasonably practical from the do-it-yourself standpoint; they are termed casting and swaging. Casting involves making up an alloy of lead and certain other metals, melting the mixture, and decanting it into bullet moulds. As the alloy solidifies, the unwanted excess — the sprue — is separated by knocking a cutting plate — called the sprue cutter — aside. The bullet thus produced needs to be lube-sized by passing it into the appropriate machine which puts lubricant into the groove(s) provided and, at the same time, renders it perfectly circular in cross-section, at the precise desired diameter. In order to engage in bullet casting, you will need a supply of lead and the alloying additives, a facility in which to melt and dispense the alloy, one or more bullet moulds, a lube/sizer, and a supply of cast bullet lubricant.

Swaging — pronounced "SWAY-jing" — involves the cold-forming of lead, lead alloy and/or a jacket material under fairly respectable pressures. It requires a press capable of applying and withstanding the considerable stresses involved, along with the appropriate dies, some lead wire or cast cores, perhaps some jackets and, if jackets are not used, a lubricant capable of keeping the formed bullets from fouling the bore when fired.

Both methods will be discussed here, in moderate detail. Each technique has its advantages and disadvantages. The ideal situation is to acquire the capability of using both methods, since they tend to interlock usefully. If you can cast bullets, you can also cast cores: a handy capability when swaging bullets. If you can swage bullets, you can remanufacture cast and lube/sized bullets into some exceptionally intriguing formats and we'll be discussing that, too.

Suitable bullet alloy can be melted and mixed in a pot or perhaps in a discarded frying pan by using the family kitchen range as a heat source, be it gas-fired or electric or, for that matter, wood-burning. In a pinch, a gasoline-fired camp stove can be used, or a propane torch, or a gasoline blow torch, or a hibachi grill fired with charcoal. I have cast bullets over all the mentioned sources except the last, generally with good results. The important thing is to assure lavishly adequate ventilation, particularly with the charcoal because it produces a quantity of carbon monoxide in burning and that can prove fatal if inhaled in excessive quantities, or highly debilitating in lesser amounts.

Lead, you must realize and accept, is a toxic material. Introduced into the human system, it is eliminated very slowly, indeed if at all. Lead rubs off onto the fingers handling it and, if those fingers get into or around the mouth, you ingest lead orally. It can also be absorbed through the skin and, when melted, some amount of it can and may become airborne to be absorbed through inhalation. That's the reason for stressing the need for ventilation; *lots* of ventilation. When lead bullets are fired in indoor ranges, the abrading effect of the bullets on the backstop can and often does put quantities of airborne particles into the air you breathe for further hazards. If you know all that and observe suitable precautions, it's no big threat to your well-being, which is why it's being discussed here.

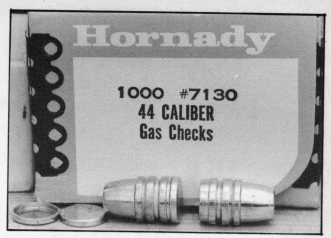

For the higher velocities, some mould designs use gas checks, such as these by Hornady for Lyman's No. 429215 design in .44 at a weight of 215 grains.

Brownells markets this thermometer for checking temperature of the alloy used in casting bullets.

Corbin's Core-Bond can be used to bond the core to jacket wall, as discussed.

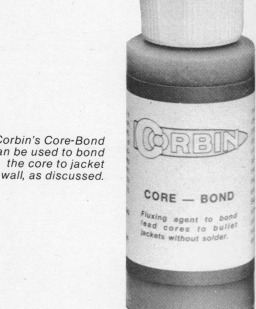

Steps in making a swaged JSP bullet in .410-inch diameter, starting with a core cast of pure lead, core-swaging, drawing jacket from .44 to .41, seating the core and the final nose-forming step.

Factory-made ingot moulds for bullet alloys from Ohaus, Saeco and Lyman: All turn out pigs that weigh about one pound each.

My own preference is this old top from a stainless GI mess kit. If filled, each kidney-shaped pig weighs about six pounds and is a convenient size for working with electric melting pots. A felt-tipped marker can be used to record any data desired.

Lead and tin alone can be used to produce a satisfactory bullet alloy. Adding tin hardens the resulting castings up to a certain point, beyond which more tin has no further effect upon the hardness. One part of tin to twenty parts lead — usually stated as a 1:20 ratio — is about the practical maximum. Melted together, the two metals form an intimate and homogeneous blend and remain in that state as they solidify.

Lead and antimony alone do not make up a satisfactory alloy for casting bullets. Due to its considerably higher melting point, the antimony begins to solidify and crystallize as the temperature falls, while the lead remains fluid until a considerable amount of further cooling has taken place. This results in pure lead filling the spaces between the antimony crystals and the bore-fouling properties are little better than pure lead alone, although the apparent hardness may seem higher.

By adding even a relatively small amount of tin to the mixture of lead and antimony, the lead remains mixed with the tin until both have solidified fully, resulting in cast bullets capable of excellent performance.

There are several sources of raw material for casting bullets. One of the most readily available and inexpensive is the wheel weight used in balancing automobile wheels after installing a tire. Customarily, the old weight is pulled off and tossed into a container for salvage. They are rarely if ever used again. Most garages, service stations and tire stores accumulate wheel weights and it may be possible to obtain a supply for moderate cost. Melting them down to get rid of the steel clips and surface impurities is a messy and malodorous task, best performed outdoors. Dump the weights out where you can inspect them visually as you put them into the melting pot because there's no telling what may be mixed in with the lot — wads of chewing gum, bits of rubber, tar and perhaps the random rimfire cartridge.

Any time you are working with molten metal, eye protection is absolutely mandatory. Wear shooting glasses, safety glasses or a good face shield. Some would add

Another good design from H&G is their No. 292 for the .45 ACP at about 235 grains. It's quite similar to the FMJ bullet developed by the USAF in cooperation with Hornady.

gloves and a long-sleeved shirt as additional necessities, and they certainly wouldn't hurt a thing, ambient temperatures permitting.

Linotype metal remains with us — that gorgeous stuff — although it gets scarcer and harder to find with each passing year. When available, a pound of linotype metal will produce superb cast bullets when diluted with as much as four or five pounds of wheel weight metal. Used straight, linotype metal also makes dandy bullets but that's a little like saying lobster makes highly palatable cat food, I think!

Occasionally there will be bullet metal available through commercial channels. I know of no such sources at present, but there have been at least two within the past few years. Such endeavors do not prosper impressively as a rule because most bullet casters can obtain something reasonably adequate at well below the retail price of tailor-made alloys.

Some of the larger public shooting ranges routinely mine their backstop areas and melt down the reclaimed metal for resale, often at fairly attractive prices. It is strictly a Hobson's choice proposition and the only thing of which you can be certain is that all of it was made up into bullets and fired — at least once. If you buy some and try it out, I'd sug-

The business end of the Saeco lead hardness tester, a handy device for verifying the hardness of a batch of bullet alloy. A cast bullet is installed, as at right here, and tensioned until the two lower lines coincide. At that point, the numbered line from 0 to 10 that aligns exactly with a line beneath it is the tested hardness.

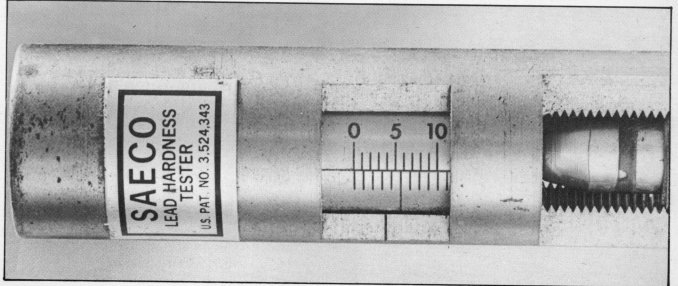

I designed this bullet for Hensley & Gibbs, in .45 size at about 174 grains, as a much more convenient means of producing loads similar to the Arcane. In photo at right, you're looking at the entrance of a hit in a block of duct seal, illustrating what I prefer to term the "snowplow effect," upon initial impact.

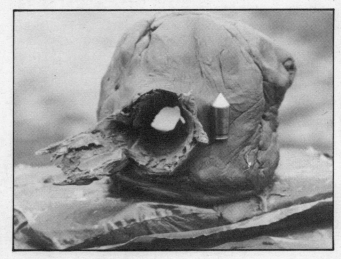

gest using it strictly as received, not adding it to a quantity of alloy known to be good.

Be advised there are a few metals that can find their way into lead alloys and, when present, they can change the flowing characteristics of the molten alloy to about the consistency of cooling oatmeal porridge. When that happens, about all you can do is cast them into fairly large ingots and use them as gluing weights, boat ballast, or similar employments. Label them clearly to keep them from getting mixed into other batches of good metal.

If you reside in an area where plumbers still remove old systems from existing installations, you may find they have quantities of lead pipe and — even better — the wiped joints used in joining sections of lead pipe. Plumber's wiping solder, as I recall, is about 35:65 lead/tin and a beautiful source of that vital ingredient. Plumbers salvage the pure lead and use it for caulked joints in cast iron pipe, but they cut off the wiped joints and set them aside because that is too hard for purposes of caulking. As a result, you can — or at least used to be able — to purchase the wiped joints at interesting prices.

Cable sheathing is mostly pure lead, and usable as such if properly alloyed. Be alertly suspicious, however, of the solder used to join sections of sheathing because it may contain some of the undesirable adulterants that can and will ruin whatever quantity of alloy you melt up with them.

Old, replaced beer coils usually are pure "block" tin and great stuff if you can get them. I note that, not having encountered a beer coil in the marketplace over the past quarter-century. For all I know, it's been supplanted by plastic and I would not be a bit surprised.

I have tried several different types of equipment for casting bullets, usually with fairly good results. As was noted, the alloy can be melted in a discarded frying pan atop the kitchen range, being dipped up with a ladle and poured into the mould. If done in the winter, with all the windows closed, this tends to permeate the entire house with offensive odors and thus requires a high order of tolerance on the part of other family members.

There are a number of excellent electric casting furnaces available today, most with a valve-controlled bottom delivery design and I tend to consider that the best of the several approaches. Most such electric furnaces feature a thermostatic heat control that can be adjusted to keep the alloy at any desired temperature across a range of about 550 to 800°F. Given that option, the canny thing is to set it at the lowest temperature that produces an acceptable bullet. If you set it too high, you burn away some of the tin; an obvious tactical error.

The alloy, once melted and blended to taste, needs to be fluxed so as to bring the solid impurities to the surface to be skimmed off and discarded, also to mix the various ingre-

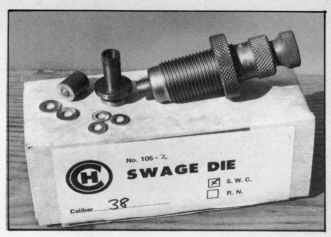

C-H Tool & Die's 105-Z swage die for swaging up bullets with a zinc washer on the base. A wadcutter is shown, but semi-wadcutters can be made, as well.

A most handy arrangement for lube/sizing puts a detachable tray in front of the lube/sizer to save surplus motions in picking up the as-cast bullet and performing the required operations upon it.

dients thoroughly. I used to use beeswax for the purpose but, in recent times, have discovered a material called Marvelux that performs beyond my fondest dreams. It's sold by Brownell's, Inc. (210 South Mill, Montezuma, IA 50171) in one-pound cans. A can that size will see you through a lot of casting sessions.

Most bullet mould blocks continue to be made from ferrous alloys — cast iron, cast steel, Meehanite, whatever — and some of the others are made with blocks of aluminum alloy. A few are made of brass and some amount of research is going into production of moulds with blocks of a suitable type of stainless steel. With any of these materials, the first step is to eliminate any and all tiny traces of oils, greases and similar hydrocarbons that may have been used in production or as a rust preventive coating after the previous casting session. So long as even a few random molecules of hydrocarbons remain in the block cavities, cast bullets will drop out of them resembling little silvery raisins; quite unsuited for your needs and desires.

Once you acquire a set of mould blocks — and the suitable handles with which to use them — you have at least theoretically an endless supply of bullets in that particular design, needing only the ingredients for the casting alloy.

That presupposes you care for the mould blocks properly, for they are heartbreakingly vulnerable to rust, corrosion and similar problems. The ferrous blocks are much more so than the ones made of aluminum, but even the latter are by no means incorruptible.

RIG Products (P.O. Box 1990, Sparks, NV 89432) markets a pair of products that are especially well suited for preserving bullet mould blocks against danger from corrosion damage and for removing such protective coatings when getting ready for a casting session. RIG 2 is the preservative and RIG 3 is the degreaser. You will need quite a lot more of the RIG 3 degreaser than of the RIG 2 oil lubricant since it only takes a quick whisk to oil it for storage but it takes some amount of scrubbing with the RIG 3 to get the last of the oil out of the cavities. A judicious warming with a hand propane torch is likewise helpful in getting the mould blocks ready to go, after spraying them with degreaser. The RIG 3 degreaser is non-flammable, but use it with copious ventilation since the fumes are unhealthful if inhaled.

Since my Southern California habitat is moderately

A small electric fan, blowing a stream of air across the top of the mould is a great convenience and time saver with large bullets being cast in hot weather. Always-always use eye protection when casting!

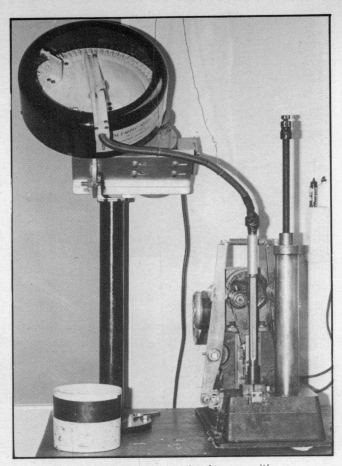

Walt Stephenson, of S&S Precision Bullets, buys Marvelux casting flux in the large economy size for use with their Magma automatic bullet caster. Their auto lube/sizer, right, processes slugs at a prodigious rate.

warm outdoors most of the year, I do the bulk of my bullet casting outdoors, with the RCBS Pro-Melt casting furnace resting atop the lugabout loading bench described in the previous chapter. It's pretty much a stand-up operation and having the working surface even with the upper edge of the belt buckle is about right. As a precaution, I secure the base of the furnace to the surface of the bench with one or two C-clamps by way of insurance against the risk of having it tipped over. If it looks as if it's going to rain, I postpone the casting session or cover the top of the pot.

You are hereby advised that even a tiny droplet of moisture, falling onto the surface of the molten bullet alloy, flashes into steam with violently explosive effects. Friend Tom Ferguson — whose contributions appear elsewhere here — recalls he once made a visual check of the alloy level in the pot on a hot day and a drop of sweat trickled off his brow onto the hot stuff, triggering a reaction comparable to a scale model of Mt. St. Helens — or did he say Krakatoa? At any rate, it blew sizzling globules of molten metal up into and onto his face and he is most grateful to have been wearing shooting glasses at the time.

On one occasion I'd sooner forget, the level of lead in the pot was running low and I decided to recycle a cardboard boxful of bullets in a size and design I use but rarely. They'd been setting about the shop, gathering dust, for a

long while. With my mind on other matters, I decanted the entire shebang into the pot and *KER-BLAMM!* Like Ferguson, I had the luck and good judgment to be wearing a pair of shooting glasses at the time and there were silvery spatters solidified on both lenses, right in front of the pupils of either eye. My only regret is that I didn't think to photograph them before scraping the lead off. It would have made a great illustration to tip in, right about here.

In cleaning up the resulting mess, I was bemused to discover the spent hull of a .22 short cartridge lying on the driveway. Closer examination showed it bore no indent of a firing pin. A bit of elementary ratiocination suggested that, prior to being set off, it had somehow fallen into the box of orphan bullets and worked its way down among them out of sight. When dumped into the lead, the priming mix and powder had gone off spontaneously. Since then, before reclaiming unwanted bullets, I dump them out onto a tray or table for intent scrutiny before dumping them in the pot and I recommend you do the same.

Most of the producers of bulletmaking equipment offer neat little ingot moulds for use when you melt down and mix up your alloys, reclaim wheel weights and so on. I have various examples of such things but usually prefer to use the upper half of an old stainless steel GI mess kit. In use, it produces two kidney-shaped pigs at each filling, weighing

garbage plywood beneath the pot to keep spatters from discoloring the finish on the bench. I pull the business end of a heavy-duty extension cord out of the shop and plug the pot into it, making certain its on/off switch is turned on.

It takes about twenty minutes for the RCBS Pro-Melt to get hot and melt any alloy left in it from the previous session. Specifications as to the prior mix can be jotted on a scrap of paper or piece of white tape to aid your memory. If, on the previous session, I'd been casting swaging cores from pure lead, it's necessary to get that melted and drained out before stoking up for the session at hand. Run it into the mess kit and, when it cools, identify it with the marking pen.

While waiting out the warm-up phases, you can get out

roughly six pounds apiece. After cooling, the resulting pigs can be identified as to composition and date of production, using a felt-tipped marker and they are of a convenient size for storage and later use.

With preliminary discussion attended to, let's talk about the procedure of setting up and launching into a casting session. I tote out the bench, using the spirit level to get its work surface level in both directions. I set the melting pot on it and clamp it down, usually putting a small piece of

C-H Tool & Die Corp. markets the canneluring tool at left as a means of performing a knurled crimp-line or cannelure such as the one in the swaged JSP bullet in photo above. The two bullets were swaged in the Corbin Bullet Press, using Corbin's dies.

Left, Rust Free, applied with a cotton swab, is highly effective for removing rust from mould cavities. It will not, however, do anything about pits left by extensive rusting. Right, here are two prototype bullets I designed for S&S Precision Bullets by turning them from cold rolled steel in the Corbin/Jet metal lathe. Walt sent both to Magma and they used sophisticated tooling to produce a cherry with which to cut mould blocks in fairly close duplication of the design for the S&S casting machine. Both designs are performing quite well in firing tests.

the mould(s) you plan to use. Mould makers such as Lyman or NEI offer blocks that can be put onto or taken off of the handles and you may need to install the desired blocks onto handles. That done, knock aside the sprue cutter and rap out the bullets if you left the blocks filled after their previous use. Grab your can of RIG 3 and give all the working surfaces of the blocks and sprue cutter a light spray, allowing it a bit of time to commence dissolving the preservative oils, then give it a longer, more vigorous spray-down. A few blasts with a dust-remover gun — available in photo stores and handy as pockets on a shirt — will dry the highly volatile degreaser from the surfaces.

Fire up your propane torch and give the blocks a preliminary warming. That's about the last thing you do before filling for your first cast. Don't overdo the torching. Meanwhile, if the alloy is slow in melting, you can hasten that along with the torch played against the still-frozen ingots. Always remove the torch head from the bottle of gas before putting it away and your fuel will last a lot longer.

When I can get linotype metal, I'm not in the least reluctant to cast that up in dainty little pigs, using one of the ingot moulds. With the pigs of lino' weighing a pound or less, you can feed one of those plus a six-pound kidney of wheel weight metal into the pot and anticipate production of some pretty decent cast bullets.

When you've assembled the ingredients and gotten them melted nicely — having set the thermostat in the neighborhood of 650 to 700°F for starting purposes — it's time to skim away the dross and flux the mix. The scaly oxides and random crud that rises to the top of molten alloy have no detectable value and are not apt to reduce back to usable metal so skim them off and get rid of them.

This is hardly a moment too soon to warn you not to attempt casting bullets out of metal salvaged from old automobile batteries. Within fairly recent times, makers of such batteries have changed the composition, adding some amount of calcium and/or arsenic and assorted whatnottery. As a result, battery plates, if melted down, can lead to production of toxic gas that is extremely deadly. Even if

the battery plates are not contaminated, they can sometimes contain small pockets of encapsulated electrolyte which, as it melts, explodes like you can hardly believe.

I use an old, retired tablespoon for skimming and the stainless steel handle off a long-defunct ladle for fluxing and stirring. The Mavelux flux needs to be kept tightly covered when not in use. Prying the lid off with the ladle handle, I use the tip of the handle to scoop out a squinch of the crystalline powder, dropping that onto the surface of the alloy and then stir it thoroughly into the mix...*with eye protection.*

As you stir, you may note an increasing liquidity of the alloy, almost approaching the fluidity of skim milk only heavier, of course. At this time, the mould cavities can be warmed moderately, using a small propane hand torch, mindful the hottest part of the flame is at the tip of the light-blue inner cone. Turn off the torch, removing and setting aside the burner head, if removable (prevents gas leaks, saves fuel). Take the mould to the casting furnace and hold the conical hole in the top of the sprue cutter against the tapered nozzle of the furnace outlet and ease the valve lever open.

You do that for at least the first few castings. It's known as pressure-pouring, as opposed to air-pouring; the two basic casting techniques. As the blocks and sprue cutter warm up, you may be able to get good bullets by holding the cutter about half an inch below the nozzle, letting the silvery stream funnel down through the opening.

Most bottom-delivery pots have a locking adjustment to regulate the opening of the valve and a spot of fine-tuning on that will prove most helpful in getting the rate of delivery just-so.

We now have ambidextrous reloading presses but I know of no comparable lead pots. The valve lever is worked with the right hand and the mould handles are grasped in the left. To the left of the pot, there are two shallow trays, the nearest to catch the sprues, the one at far left to receive the newborn bullets. From time to time, the accumulated sprues are dumped back into the pot.

Depending a bit upon the working temperature of the

When pressure-casting, you may encounter cavities in the bullet base such as the one beneath the sprue cutter at left here. As a matter of routine, such bullets should be rejected and recycled back to the pot.

you save a small amount of production time with a two-cavity set of blocks, but do not expect to turn out twice as many bullets per minute or hour with the latter. With a good set of four-cavity blocks, skillfully handled, your output will be gratifyingly higher and, in time, the muscle tone in your left wrist will beggar belief. Moulds are available with six, eight, ten or more cavities. Years ago, a friend owned a ten-cavity Hensley & Gibbs mould for their #50, a wadcutter for the .38 Special. He used to loan it to me now and again. The recollection of its production rate remains indelible in memory through the years: one hundred bullets every six minutes, pretty close.

More defects, caused by mould blocks too far apart, improper pouring or a looseness in the sprue cutter above the mould blocks. Such problems can be controlled by suitable adjustments.

alloy, as determined by the thermostat setting, the Marvelux flux is good for about twenty minutes of working time. Brownell's — address noted earlier — can furnish a neat little dial thermometer for checking the actual temperature of the alloy within close limits, by way of verifying the accuracy of the thermostat calibration. If you've got to run it up around 700°F, the flux needs renewing more frequently.

If you're casting tiny bullets, say for the .25 auto, the small amount of heat passed along to the blocks with each new bullet is just about radiated away between fillings. If you're casting big lunkers for the .45, the heat transmitted to the block with each fresh fill will build to excess, particularly on a sunny day with ambient temperatures in the nineties. Such a state of affairs will be signaled by bullets that have a frosty, crystalline surface. That is largely a cosmetic flaw, as they'll still perform fairly well.

More serious is the delay in cooling/solidifying of the sprues. If you knock the cutter aside too soon, with portions of the alloy still liquified, you'll build up curving, silvery streaks across the top of the block and those will keep the sprue cutter away from intimate contact with the block.

The solution to that is to utilize any manner of small cooling fan to jet a stream of air down onto or across the upper surface of the sprue cutter after having made the pour. As you watch, you'll note a distinct change in the appearance of the sprue when the last of the alloy components solidify. The use of a sprue-cooling fan is particularly helpful when working with multi-cavity moulds.

Single-cavity mould blocks are the basic standard and

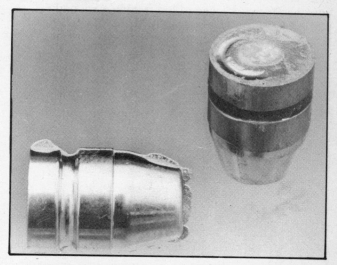

A valuable accessory for casting bullets is a suitable tool for knocking the sprue cutter aside. It must be non-marring, to avoid battering the cutter, but tough, to avoid battering the artifact itself. For a long time, I used to employ a large screwdriver with a plastic handle, but it slipped out of my hand one day to land in the frying pan of molten alloy and departed this vale of tears and sorrow with truly spectacular pyrotechnics. After that, I substituted about a nine-inch length of heavy-duty maple flooring and that mid-wifed pehaps 100,000 bullets, becoming a touch shopworn in the process.

Currently, I use and appreciate something I term my "super-artgum mallet." It was made up and presented to

A sort of Semi-Spelunker for the .45 ACP is as far as I've gotten into that area of research to the present. The mould here is a modified version of Lyman's 452460 mould, minus one base band and grease groove. That is no longer available, but a comparable operation could be performed on the standard 452460 cast bullet. A custom nose punch was made up for use with the Corbin Bullet Press and bullets were modified after lube/sizing. They fed nicely through Old Loudmouf (shown) and expanded to about dime-size diameter at around 1000 fps when fired into duct seal.

me several years ago by a friend who worked in a plastics shop at the time. The head is made of some variety of polyurethane, attached to a handle of .75-inch diameter hardwood dowel. I'd guestimate it has delivered over half a million bullets and it is only now commencing to appear faintly used. That's the good news. The bad news is that such artifacts are notably absent from the marketplace. I've shown it to any number of friends who are in the business of purveying goodies for bullet casters, but they just shrug and their eyes glaze over.

There are firms that make up and market robot bullet-casters of remarkable capabilities. A local friend produces cast bullets commercially and he has one. I'll try to include a photo of it in intrepid action. The maker of the device can produce tooling to turn out a bullet of your fancied contours and specifications, given a pilot sample at lifesize dimensions.

The friend — who goes by the name of Walt Stephenson — expressed a sharp hankering for bullet designs of several precise specifications and I jotted them down to serve as projects on the metal lathe I acquired a few years back. I plan to include pictures of several such primal prototypes; crystallizations of bullet designs I yearn for, non-existent in the real world to the present. As this is typed, Walt tells me the heavier design for the 9mm/.38 Super is reported to be moments from completion and about due to be shipped.

There was a time, in the long-long ago, when various other mouldmakers would produce a set of blocks to your custom specifications for comparatively paltry sums out of pocket. Few make a pratice of that anymore, although some will consider making up a mould to custom designs if they are assured of orders for a substantial number of sets in that design.

A few years ago, the Hornady folks collaborated with personnel from the USAF in developing a new shape of full metal jacket (fmj) bullet. Rather than the traditional round nose, it has a broad truncated cone point, with generously radiused frontal shoulder. Hornady has gone on to produce this shape in both 9mm (.355-inch) and .45 sizes and both perform exceptionally well. Hensley & Gibbs came up with a .45 design matching the basic Hornady/USAF contours, terming it their #292, at a weight of around 235 grains in typical alloys. Saeco introduced a closely comparable mould design, their #377, in 9mm size, weighing about 122 grains. Both of these are excellent

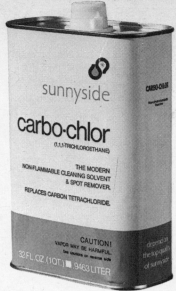

In .30 Luger, use the 84-grain Lyman 313249, sized to .309-inch diameter. Load data can be found in the LRH-46 and in a few other places. The same comment applies to the .30 Mauser/7.63mm Mauser, except you size that to .311-inch diameter.

In .32 ACP/7.65mm Browning, try the Lyman 311252 at 77 grains, sizing it to .309-inch diameter. Quite a bit of load data can be found in the LRH-46. Most other sources ignore this little cartridge.

In the .380 ACP/9mm Corto, try Lyman's 358242, available in a weight choice of 92 or 121 grains.

In 9mm Luger, I like the Hensley & Gibbs #264 mould design, as well as the Saeco #377; both about 122 grains.

In .45 ACP, the Lyman 452374 at 225 to 230 grains is a close duplicate of the fmj bullet used in the standard service load and the LRH-46 data tables take it to a peak of 964 fps/464 fpe, which outperforms virtually all of the fmj hardball loads. Its feeding ability is good, but its grouping prowess may prove disappointing in some pistols. If accuracy is your major goal, favor the Lyman 452460 or the Hensley & Gibbs 68, both semi-wadcutters (swc) at around 190 grains and superb from the standpoint of feeding reliability.

If you care to try cast bullet loads in the .44 Auto Mag — most tend to prefer jacketed bullets in that one — you'll want a gas check design and you're not apt to do a vast lot better than the Lyman 429215, at a typical weight of 215 grains.

Cast bullets are sized to the desired diameter and lubricant is put into their grease grooves at the same time by means of a lubricating sizer or lube/sizer. That is necessary to keep them from lead-fouling the bore of the barrel to a fare-thee-well. There have been explorations in recent times into the possibilities of merely dipping the bullets in a drying lubricant and firing them as-cast, thereby saving a lot of time. This seems to work respectably well, so long as you do not push the bullets thus treated to unduly giddy velocities. That's to say the dip-and-dry lubes function fairly well up to paces around 1150 fps or so.

performers in their respective cartridges. They not only group well but show outstanding functional reliability in most pistols.

The Saeco 377 bullet is likewise an impressive performer in the .38 Colt Super cartridge. With 5.0 grains of Bullseye, its average velocity in the five-inch barrel is 1220 fps for 404 fpe (1220/404). That particular load packs a trifle more punch than any .38 Super factory load I've checked to the present, and its accuracy compares favorably with most factory loads.

Let's mention a few likely choices of bullet moulds for the various popular cartridges. In .25 ACP, I'd recommend Lyman's #252435; just about the only game in town for that size, to be sized to .251-inch diameter and loaded to data given in the Lyman Reloading Handbook #46 or the current booklet from Hercules. The cast bullet weighs 51 grains or, if you fancy the fmj bullet, Hornady now markets an excellent one at 50 grains. Use the Hercules data for loading that.

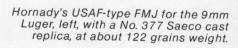

Hornady's USAF-type FMJ for the 9mm Luger, left, with a No. 377 Saeco cast replica, at about 122 grains weight.

Marvelux casting flux is far and away the best such material I've encountered to the present. A pinch is all it takes, every twenty minutes or so, as noted.

Several years ago, I became solidly hooked on the use of lithium-base bullet lubes. These are made of lithium-base greases plus other ingredients, not without a lot of technical difficulty, due to the inordinately high melting point of the lithium-base grease. That same factor, however, makes it a bullet lube with no peers I've encountered to date. I will merely note that the lithium lubes have enabled me to drive plain base cast bullets to velocities well over 2000 fps with excellent accuracy and no detectable amount of bore fouling.

If you wish to make your own jacketed bullets, it's not as difficult as you might suppose. The man to query about it is Dave Corbin, Box 758, Phoenix, OR 97535. He makes and markets the Corbin Bullet Press and dies for use with it. He can also supply dies for making bullets in conven-

tional reloading presses, but the CBP is the canniest route to follow, I think.

To make swaged bullets, you need the basic press and dies plus some cores and some jackets of appropriate size. You can make the cores by cutting the right size of lead wire into suitable lengths. Corbin can supply the jackets, lead wire and core cutter or, if you prefer, a core-casting setup. Having extensive bullet casting facilities at hand, I prefer to cast some selected bullet design in pure lead and use that as my core because it's economical in terms of time and material cost.

The prescribed regimen for producing swaged bullets is to start by swaging the raw cores down to uniform diameter and weight. For that, you use Corbin's swaging die with three small holes equidistant about the periphery from which the excess lead is bled in short rod-shaped segments.

With all the cores thus swaged into uniformity, you seat them into the jackets by use of the core-seating die, which

Lyman's No. 311227, at about 90 grains, is a fine performer in the various .30 and .32 calibers. Here we see it as cast, left, and after being lube/sized.

Gang moulds can help in quantity production, as discussed here. This is a six-cavity set by Saeco in their No. 448, a 180-grain for use in caliber .44 loads. In their No. 377, they cut the long blocks with 8 cavities.

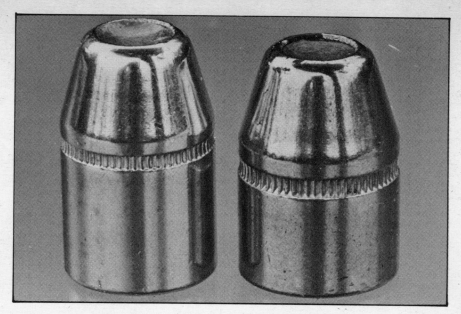

Another interesting approach is to remanufacture existing factory jacketed bullets, such as the 220-grain Silhouette bullet by Sierra, left above. Putting it in the Corbin Bullet Press, reversed, so as to form a new point on the former base, produces intriguing FMJs with semi-pointed noses, as here.

may have a smaller protrusion in its tip to allow for making hollow point bullets.

With the cores seated in the jackets, you install the nose-forming die set and contour the finished bullet to the desired format. At each of the mentioned phases, the processed bullet is expelled from the die under full press leverage, eliminating the need to knock it out with a mallet.

If you're impatient and not terribly critical, you can drop the cast bullet core into the jacket, run it into the point-forming die and have a bullet all ready to load and shoot, lickety-split. I have followed that maverick method on various occasions with sinfully gratifying results.

Having the Corbin Bullet Press and a suitable range of tooling sort of puts you in possession of a skeleton key to Pandora's box, insofar as a variety of jacketed bullets is concerned. With only a modest amount of manual dexterity and innovating ingenuity, you can come up with such a dazzling variety of bullet makes/weights/types that you may find yourself enmeshed in the beguiling delights of producing prototype bullets to the exclusion of loading and/or firing them. You may also find, as I do, that you end up with an untidy large amount of experimental designs cluttering up the top of your loading bench.

Corbin also offers a preparation called Core-Bond; a flux to enable you to solder the inner core quite tenaciously to the walls of the jacket. Thus, you can have a bash at duplicating the justly famed Hot-Cor bullets marketed by Speer. The adhesion between core and jacket on such bullets tends to minimize the loss of starting weight on impact. The core-bonding approach can also be employed to produce ultra-lightweight experimental bullets if you care to explore the upper attainable reaches of velocity with a given cartridge.

Acquiring the ability to make your own bullets can save you usefully impressive hunks of cash, meanwhile providing unexpected aspects of commanding interest.

Try it. I think you'll like it!

CHAPTER 14

COLLECTING TRENDS IN AUTO PISTOLS

Viewed As Eminently Collectible, Certain Autos Command Special Interest And Tips Are Included On Others Destined To Increase In Value Over The Coming Years

(I assigned this chapter to Chuck Karwan because I consider him the most knowledgeable and lucid authority on the subject. — DAG)

LEST SOMEONE think that this chapter is about machine pistols let me assure you that the term *automatic pistol* is being used here interchangeably with the terms semi-automatic pistol or autoloading pistol. In fact in modern usage one must use fully automatic to convey that the weapon in question can fire more than one shot for each pull of the trigger.

As a group, automatic pistols have been around since the 1890s. They did not become widely used until the period just before and during WWI. It was WWI that established without a doubt that the automatic was an efficient and effective handgun, though even to this day there are those that would dispute this fact.

In the collecting world the old argument of which is better, the revolver or the automatic, doesn't really matter. The autoloader offers such a wide variety of mechanical systems that the revolver field cannot even begin to compare to it. Most of your "modern" single-action revolvers differ little mechanically from those of more than one hun-

dred years ago. The world of double-action revolvers is not much better off. That hit home one time when I took the grips off my Model 1892 Colt DA .38 and found that they were a perfect fit on my modern Colt Python. Regardless, there is something special or different about collecting auto pistols.

For starters there is a National Automatic Pistol Collectors Association (NAPCA). I know of no other field of gun collecting that has such an orientation. There isn't a revolver collector's association or a bolt-action rifle collector's association or anything quite like NAPCA. Most specialty gun collecting organizations center around one manufacturer such as Colt, Winchester, etc.

NAPCA, on the other hand, has members who are interested in such a wide variety of auto pistols that it boggles the mind. There is a monthly newsletter which is a gold mine of information as well as an annual gun show sponsored by NAPCA. If you are interested in joining NAPCA they can be reached at Box 15738, Tower Grove Station, St. Louis, MO 63163. Annual membership costs $20. I know of at least four gun dealers who specialize in automatics. A couple of them wouldn't have a revolver in the shop. This kind of loyalty is just an example of that little something special about collecting autos.

Chuck Karwan — shown on the facing page with a Model 1896 Mauser Broomhandle and stock holster — is an enthusiastic firearms collector, highly knowledgeable on the subject and capable of discussing it well.

Probably the first automatic to be produced commercially in any quantity was the awkward and ugly Borchardt. It was a toggle breech pistol that eventually was redesigned by Georg Luger to become the famous Luger pistol. Many of the first-generation automatic pistol designs such as those by Bayard, Mauser, Bergmann, Gabbet-Fairfax, Roth, Schwarzlose, Mannlicher, Browning and company are truly fascinating because the respective inventors were breaking new ground.

The German Pistole '08 aka Luger is a fascinating design, made in a vast number of variations, which also tends to enhance interest among collectors.

Of all these only the Mauser M1896, the Browning Model 1900, and the Luger-redesigned Borchardt were truly successful in the marketplace. The evolution of the auto pistol was fast. Browning, in particular, improved his designs to the point that the Colt M1911 is to this day a design that is hard to beat. The Luger and Mauser survived into WWII virtually unchanged though their respective designs were already obsolete by the time the M1911 Colt emerged.

Much the same can be said of the Mauser Model 1896 Military. If you look closely, you'll note several minor differences between these two, for example.

There are certain automatic pistols that stand out as all-time classics due to their long production, high recognition, and a certain agelessness. Though I'm sure that every auto pistol buff has his own opinion, my pick for the all-time classics are: the Mauser M1896 "Broomhandle," the Luger, the Colt M1911, the Walther PP/PPK, and the Browning Model 1935 Hi-Power. The earliest of these — the Mauser Broomhandle — had one of its first recorded uses in combat in 1898 by none other than Winston Churchill at the battle or Omdurman in the African Sudan. In the recent *Star Wars* movies the hero Luke Skywalker uses a Mauser Broomhandle only his version shoots lasers. From a Nineteenth Century cavalry charge to a galaxy far,

As Karwan notes, design changes by manufacturers tend to add value to the obsolete design, such as the blued .45 Detonics at the top, which is fitted with a quilted maple stock by Bullshooter's Supply. It also "wears" a standard M1911 magazine in photo.

far away — now that's a classic!

The Luger is so famous that even non-gun people recognize it or have at least heard of it. Its wide use by our enemies of two world wars, the Germans, is probably the major factor behind this. The Luger has several things going for it as a collectible. They are invariably beautifully made and finished, there are myriad variations, they have a classic styling, and they have historical significance. I still find them to be somewhat of an enigma in that they were obsolete from the engineering standpoint by 1911.

Mere age does not always equate to value. A few years ago, this Walther, made from 1910 to 1918, commanded an asking price of only $200 at a show.

WALTHER
CAL .32 ACP
MADE. 1910-1918
MDL. 4
200.00

The Colt National Match Gold Cup generally is judged to have a somewhat higher value than your typical Parkerized military model; one of the other considerations affecting present and future values.

The design is unnecessarily complicated, fragile, and sensitive as well as difficult to make. Yet it persists in popularity with many people even today. Amongst collectors there is almost a Luger cult and its popularity has never been higher.

Unlike the Luger, the Colt M1911 pistol became a classic out of the excellence of its design, not in spite of it. It is unique among pistols in that it was born in the early days of automatic pistol development, yet to this day it is one of the best of all designs for its intended purpose as a personal defense weapon. Many newer designs offer more and different features than the M1911 but never without some compromises and disadvantages. Even Browning's own "improvement," the Hi-Power, is inferior to the M1911 in several ways. These include the ability to be detail-stripped without tools, adaptability to a wide range of cartridges, and power, to name a few. Collectors of the M1911 series have dozens, if not hundreds, of variations to pursue.

The military issue Model 1911s have been made by a number of manufacturers including Colt, Remington, Remington Rand, Springfield Arsenal, Ithaca, Singer, Union Switch & Signal as well as foreign licensed manufacture by Norway and Argentina. A major problem in collecting the M1911 series is that the manufacturer's markings are only found on the slide and it is all too easy to change the slides from one pistol to another. This was all too often done by Army repair facilities as well as individual GIs.

There are several serial number lists in circulation that purport to show the manufacturer by the serial number. The problem here is that the lists which come from ord-

Hoffschmidt's book is published by Blacksmith Corp., Harpsichord Tpk, Stamford, CT 06903 and it's a gold mine of good dope on the M1911/A1 service pistols. Above, a Walther PP, from pre-WWII Zella-Mehlis.

nance records, the Colt factory, and similar sources do not agree with each other in all cases.

I've found that the best approach is to learn the characteristic proof marks, inspector's marks, and other clues of each manufacturer which can be found on the frame of the pistol itself. The situation is further complicated by the fact that several manufacturers made slides for government contracts but not complete pistols. Thus, it is possible to find M1911 variations with slides marked by Savage,

The Browning Model 1935 Hi-Power has been used by a number of military forces and made in various modifications, making it eminently collectible.

Drake, and SanColMar. Regardless the M1911 series is highly coveted by collectors and it is a most interesting field.

My fourth choice of all-time classic automatic pistol is the Walther PP and PPK series. Historically they came into the forefront as being the first commercially successful double-action automatic pistol. Like the other classics mentioned the Walther is quite popular with collectors. Of all the pistols mentioned so far some of the best bargains on the collector's market can be found in this field. This was brought about by the recent decision by the German police to switch from the .32 ACP automatics that they have had as standard for most of this century to the much more powerful 9mm Parabellum round.

Since by far the most common pistol in use by the German police was the Walther PP the world market was flooded with PP .32s. When they first hit the U.S. these traded at prices in the $200s, but as the market got saturated it was not uncommon to see them change hands at $150 or even less. Included in this lot of German police pistols were dozens of variations even including Walther PPs made on contract in France. This was a collector's bonanza and it will be many years before all the variations and markings will be sorted out.

What the Luger is to collecting, the Browning Hi-Power is fast becoming. In many ways they share a number of similarities including manufacture by a number of different countries and wide adoption the world over. In many instances the Browning Hi-Power was the very pistol that replaced the Luger. Unlike the very obsolete Luger, the HP is still one of the top service handguns in the world.

The one major drawback in collecting the Browning is

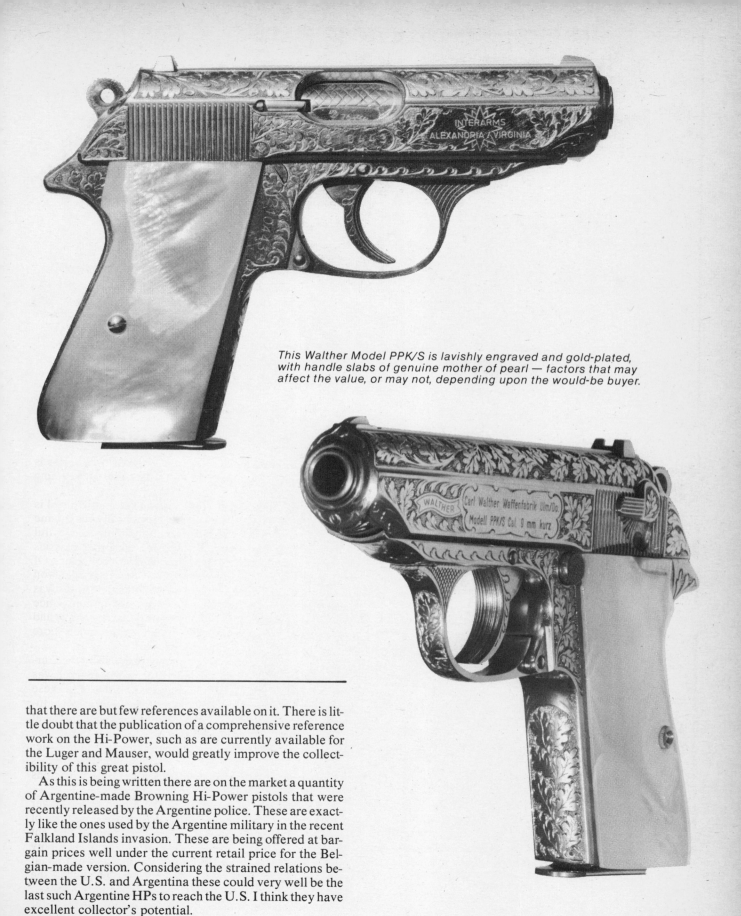

This Walther Model PPK/S is lavishly engraved and gold-plated, with handle slabs of genuine mother of pearl — factors that may affect the value, or may not, depending upon the would-be buyer.

that there are but few references available on it. There is little doubt that the publication of a comprehensive reference work on the Hi-Power, such as are currently available for the Luger and Mauser, would greatly improve the collectibility of this great pistol.

As this is being written there are on the market a quantity of Argentine-made Browning Hi-Power pistols that were recently released by the Argentine police. These are exactly like the ones used by the Argentine military in the recent Falkland Islands invasion. These are being offered at bargain prices well under the current retail price for the Belgian-made version. Considering the strained relations between the U.S. and Argentina these could very well be the last such Argentine HPs to reach the U.S. I think they have excellent collector's potential.

The labels in the exhibit read:

COLT A.M.U.
ONE OF 20 MADE AT COLT
THIS IS NOT A KIT GUN
COMMERCIAL RECEIVER

COLT GOLD CUP
FIRST CHOICE OF
COMPETITIVE SHOOTERS

BALLESTER MOLINA
VERY SIMILAR TO RIGAUD
PATENTED BY "HAFDASA"
MADE 1937

BALLESTER RIGAUD
FIRST ATTEMPT TO AVOID
COLT PATENTS
MADE 1937

PUSAN JIN IRON WORKS
NORTH KOREAN COPY
MARKED FREEDOM PISTOL
Ser. # 45

VIET CONG
HAND MADE COPY PRESENTED
TO G.T. ROYEN COMANDER
62th CONG 1963

ARGENTINE (SNEAK)
MADE ON COLT PATENTS
BUT WITHOUT PERMISSION
OR PAYMENT

COLT ARGENTINE
TAKEN FROM COMMERCIAL
PRODUCTION FOR THE MARKED
ARGENTINE ARMY ONLY

AUGUSTA ARSENAL
REFURBISHED AND RE-
NUMBERED WITH
"A" PREFIX

COLT "CLINT PEOPLES"
TEXAS RANGER C.PEOPLES KILLED
MURDERER PERKINS AFTER JAIL
ESCAPE WACO TX.

ARGENTINE D.G.F.M.
"DOMINGO MATHEAU"
MODEL MADE IN ARGENTINA
GOVERNMENT ARSENAL

ARGENTINE F.M.A.P.
FABRICA MILITAR de ARMAS
PORTATILES MADE IN
ROSARIO ARGENTINA

COLT-SPECIAL
MADE FOR
"Teddy duplay"
DOUGH-NUT KING

COLT B.B.
ONLY 600 MADE WITH
SPECIAL BARREL BUSHING
PRIOR TO GOLD CUP

"PRESIDENTE PERON"
SPECIALY MARKED FOR POLICE
OF UNAUTHORIZED PROVINCE
OF JUAN PERON

ARG. BALLESTER MOLINA
MADE FOR ENGLAND
BRITISH PROOFED AND
2 SETS OF Ser. #'s

COLT-ORIGINAL
COMANDANTE ESPECIAL

COLT
FACTORY NICKLE

LLAMA
SPANISH COPY

STAR
SPANISH COPY

I (D.A.G.) snapped this photo and the one on the facing page at 1979 NRA convention in San Antonio, Texas. The exhibit was by collector Gus Cargile, of Corpus Christi, Texas and it gives some idea as to the possibilities for collecting offered by this country's increasingly venerable Government Model auto. Gun at upper left is tagged as a Colt A.M.U., one of twenty made up by Colt; not a kit gun on a commercial receiver.

The guns shown here are the formal Cargile collection. He has many others, including a pretty hilarious sample of a "Singer" .45 (with sewing machine tag on the handle) and an authentic .45 once owned by a New Orleans pimp. Curiously enough, that one has ivory stocks, not pearl, as Gen. Patton used to deride.

The problem with collecting the classic automatics is that they are usually quite expensive. There are a number of extremely interesting areas of collecting that have many reasonably priced guns as the general rule. One of these

In the text below, Karwan comments upon the lure of collecting Spanish autos, broad in their variety and fairly modest as to price tag. Here are two samples.

areas is Spanish handguns. The automatic pistols of Spain have suffered an entirely undeserved reputation for shoddy workmanship and materials. During WWI France ordered huge quantities of .32 automatics from various makers in Spain. These orders so overwhelmed the Spanish gun industry that practically everyone in the city of Eibar got into the act subcontracting the manufacture of pistol parts and whole guns.

When the war ended and these contracts ceased, literally everybody in Eibar, Spain, was in the gun business. The world market was flooded with cheap autos from Eibar.

Unfortunately many of these cheap pistols were of marginal quality at best and it is these that gave the Spanish firearms industry a black eye. Interestingly though, many of these Spanish autos are of good quality and often show a good bit of innovation. Some of these that I have observed include .32s the size of the typical .25, .25s that are exceptionally small, autos with a feature that allows cycling the slide with the firing hand, .32s with huge magazine capacities and so on.

Because of their bad reputation, most of these Spanish autos can be had at surprisingly reasonable prices, almost always under $100 and often as low as $50. They are a most interesting collecting field and one could spend several lifetimes trying to find one of each variation. There are presently just three manufacturers of handguns in Spain, with their output sold under the trade names Astra, Llama, and Star. Qualitywise, I have never seen a bad Astra or Star and the Llamas are usually quite satisfactory, also.

The word is starting to get around on the Astra and Star automatics that they are of high quality but they can still be had at reasonable prices in most cases. Both makers have produced a wide range of autos ranging from .22 sporting autos, through pocket .25s, .32s, .380s, and locked-breech 9mms. Astra produced a Mauser Broomhandle lookalike at one time and Star has made many .45s.

One specimen that I own is a Star target pistol of such high quality that it takes a back seat to nobody's products. This specimen is in 9mm Largo and appears to be a common Star Model A at first glance. The only external giveaway is that the front of the grip frame has extra material at the bottom to aid in recovery when shooting rapid-fire and it has a low-matted rib with sights adjustable for windage. Where the quality of this pistol comes out is when one inspects the fit of the slide to the frame. The fit is so tight and smooth as to compare favorably to a Swiss SIG P210. The trigger pull is remarkably crisp and consistent 1½ pounds that is totally reliable with no doubling or hammer

Here are some more Spanish autos, as represented by the Astra, made in several model variations.

As Karwan notes, the Star autos, such as this one in 9mmP, often turn out to be excellent in every respect.

The Tokarev is the official USSR sidearm and minor variations are used by many other Iron Curtain forces.

following problems. Believe me, anyone who thinks all Spanish handguns are of low quality, should see this one.

Another area that has a lot of bargains is the field of Tokarev pistols. The Tokarev was adopted by Russia in 1930 beginning with the TT30 and followed soon after by the slightly simplified TT33. They chamber the Russian 7.62mm pistol cartridge that is virtually identical with the Mauser 7.63mm round. Probably because the ammunition is not readily available, these excellent pistols often can be had in the $150 range.

The Tokarev has several excellent design features such as a hammer system that can be removed in one piece. Many Chinese copies of the Tokarev were brought into the

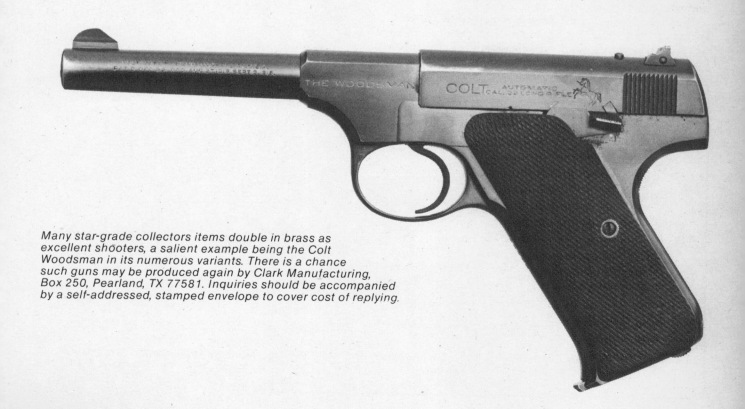

Many star-grade collectors items double in brass as excellent shooters, a salient example being the Colt Woodsman in its numerous variants. There is a chance such guns may be produced again by Clark Manufacturing, Box 250, Pearland, TX 77581. Inquiries should be accompanied by a self-addressed, stamped envelope to cover cost of replying.

This almost ended up as our Government Model auto. These two experimental prototypes, in .45 ACP, were made up for the 1911 acceptance tests by Savage Arms; they're from the Gus Cargile collection, noted earlier.

Post-WWII Colt Match Target pistol did not carry
The Woodsman designation; was made in this and
six-inch barrel lengths before final discontinuation.

Smith & Wesson's Model 52 target auto in .38 Special
(lower) and Model 41 in .22 LR are further examples
of superb choices for long-term appreciation in value,
meanwhile offering some really top-drawer shooting.

Many variants of the High Standard .22 auto pistols were made over the years. The upper one here is a
Model H-D Military, the lower a Model HB. Like the Woodsman, they're highly collectible and fine shooters.

U.S. by returning Vietnam vets as war trophies. They are virtually identical to the Russian version except for the markings. A handful of Polish- and Hungarian-made Tokarev pistols also came via Vietnam. These are particularly rare but when found can be often purchased for the same or only slightly more than the Russian model. There are even a few Hungarian-made models in 9mm Parabellum around that were originally made for Egypt. This variation is called the Tokagypt.

Don't get the idea that only center-fire automatics are collectible because there are many .22 rimfire models that are equally collectible. Since Colt discontinued the manufacture of all its .22 autos except the Service Ace, all of the Colt Woodsman series of .22s are now in the realm of collector's items. This holds particularly true for the pre-WWII versions. While many collect the Colt .22s because of the Colt name, many highly collectible .22s by other makers are overlooked.

One of the best of these is the High Standard line of .22 pistols, particularly those prior to 1950 or so. These include the models B, HB, HD, U.S.A., HD Military, A, C, and others. Generally they can all be had for prices well under the corresponding Colt models. These earlier High Standards are intresting guns and are of high quality manufacture.

I have an old HD Military that can shoot right along with the best modern competition models. Many model Bs and HD U.S.A.s were bought by the U.S. government for training troops. Occasionally specimens will show up with U.S. Property markings. These usually command a premium price.

Another pair of excellent designs from Spain, by Star, in .45 ACP and 9mmP, as discussed here.

A latterday Luger, here in the aluminum-alloy framed version of Stoeger's .22 LR autoloader.

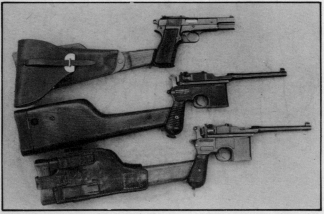
Military pistols with detachable stock/holsters, such as this Browning and a pair of Mausers, are a fine addition to a collection, if you can manage to take care of the necessary red tape and paper work.

Don't get the idea that an auto pistol has to be old to be collectible. Recently S&W announced that the models 559 and 539 blued steel 9mm autos would be discontinued in favor of the 659 and 639 stainless steel models. Roy Jinks, S&W's historian, told me recently that total production for all 559s and 539s combined amounted to only about 18,000. Folks, in the world of handguns that's a drop in the bucket. There are many so-called limited editions and commemoratives that have a larger production than that. Best of all, as this is written, it may be possible to buy either model quite easily through the normal outlets for retail price or less. Though interest is moderate at present, my crystal ball says that S&W automatic pistols will become a remarkably hot item among collectors.

A whole new area of automatic pistol collecting opened up a couple of years ago when the Bureau of Alcohol,

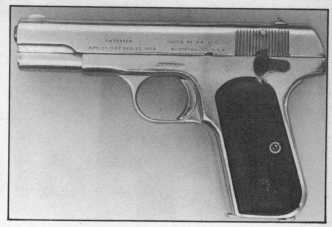

I rounded up this quartet of photos to illustrate the myriad variations that can be found, even within a single make and model — the Colt Pocket Model Hammerless, in this instance. Finishes can be blued, nickel or gold plated, with factory engraving and monogrammed ivory stocks, down to battered plain-Jane specimens.

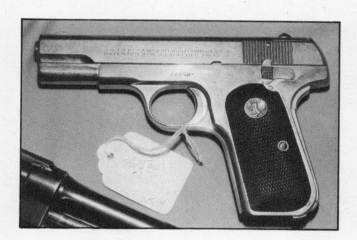

Tobacco and Firearms (BATF) declared that many collectible pistols with their original shoulder stock were curios and no longer under the restrictions previously in effect for pistols with shoulder stocks. Prior to this ruling, all pistols with shoulder stocks came into the category of short-barreled rifles and thus had to be treated with the same restrictions as a machine gun including registration and the payment of a $200 tax. With this ruling in effect many of the most desirable shoulder-stocked pistols could be collected complete with their stock. Models included in this ruling are all the Mauser Broomhandles; all the Navy, artillery, and long-barreled Lugers; the Pre-WWII Browning Hi-Power as well as the Canadian-made version; most Astra and Star shoulder stocked pistols; the stocked Nambus; and a number of others. To make sure that you don't inadvertently run afoul of the law you should obtain a copy of the BATF published listing.

Be apprised of the fact that the fakers and con artists are operating in the field of automatic pistols, too. A favorite approach is to add marking to otherwise run-of-the-mill specimens to make them appear to be more desirable. The most common of these is to add Nazi markings to Star Model B, French M1935A and S, Astra Model 600, and Steyr M1912 pistols. In all of the mentioned cases a genuine Nazi-marked specimen is worth a substantial premium over the common item. As always, let the buyer beware.

Don't let the above discourage you though. In general, gun people are very honest. Automatic pistol collecting can be highly rewarding. Like all gun collecting, there is the thrill of the chase and a lot of satisfaction when a specimen is added to your collection. There is the extremely enjoyable treasure-hunt aspect as you look for the sleeper or under-priced example. You will also come into contact with some of the finest people in the world.

CHAPTER 15

CAVEAT EMPTOR, and all that...

If Prime Collector Items Are In Expensively Short Supply, Someone Will Try To Generate A Supply To Meet The Demand — Clandestinely!

THE TWO words of Latin in the title translate to "Let the buyer beware," certainly a basic maxim for collectors of exotic firearms to note and remember. If a particular variant is of great rarity and immense value, what's to stop some clever if unscrupulous artisan from modifying a mill-run example of the same gun into specifications identical to the rarity and, having done so, what's to stop the blackguard from fobbing it off and absorbing the difference? As it all turns out, nothing much stands in the way and it seems to happen, every now and again.

The Model 1896 Mauser pistol has become a gun of great interest to collectors and, as a predictably direct result, it has brightened the eye and quickened the pulse of those gentry who have more manual skill than moral integrity. In fact, it seems the practice has become so common that a term has been coined for such tawdry treasures. They are known among the Mauserphiles as "Witch's Brooms." John Breathed, from down Houston way — to whose vaster expertise on such topics, I bow respectfully — is about to give us some thoughts he has on the matter.
— DAG

THE MUCH MALIGNED and seldom praised Broomhandle Mauser pistol has now become a respectable member of the fraternity and holds its head up almost as high as the mighty Luger. Collectors are legion and they wave the Mauser banner proudly.

In the early Sixties an outfit in California, called Golden State Arms, had several barrels full of Broomhandles in their store and you could buy as many as you wanted for $39.95 each. Now, at that price, only the more stupid of the gun fakers, engravers and lathe jockeys had time to lavish any creativity on a Mauser, plus there was little information available as to what rare variation to re-create.

All that changed in 1968 with the publication of a Wish Book called *System Mauser* which included pictures and data on over a hundred variations, some just rare, others priceless.

One steel artist down in Kentucky galvanized into action when the price of a Persian Contract Broomhandle hit $600. He put a new edge on his engraving tools and carved

"Funny" Persian Contract Mauser has a wide milled border around the lion, but no "sunburst" at left side rear of the ejection port. Nonetheless, it nervously wears a born-again serial number in the 154### range.

A factory photo of a very early Cone Hammer with "System Mauser" engraving over chamber. This was inspiration for Semi-Fake #10X.

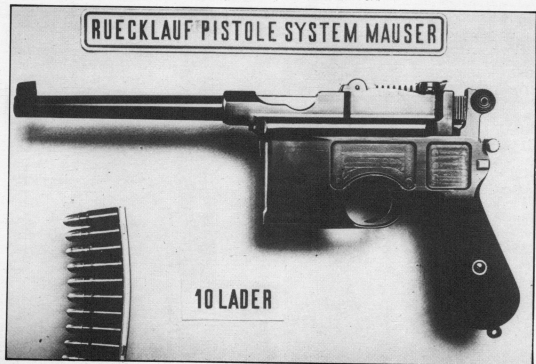

RUECKLAUF PISTOLE SYSTEM MAUSER

10 LADER

Stripped frame #10X, as found in parts box at Deep River Armory down in Houston, Texas.

out some Royal Sun Lions that would have earned high praise from the Shah himself. He forgot one detail; the milled border around the panel on the pistol frame, where the factory had impressed the Sun Lion with dies, was comparatively narrow compared with contemporary pistols which were not made for the Persian Contract. Even though he had advertised his fakes with the hard-to-alter, wide-milled border, our hammer and chisel man did a brisk business in "funny Persians" until arthritis cut him down in his prime years. Oh, yes, he also forgot to add the small sunburst on the left rear of the ejection port, a feature of the original contract guns.

Close on the heels of this Persian Plagiarist, a clever chap from central California, who owned the barrel and

Stoeger used to advertise a full-auto Model 711, along with a twenty-shot, clip-fed semi-auto Model 712 — that was in Stoeger's #18 catalog — but the Funny Broomenwerke launched their Model 713 quietly. There's nothing even faintly unostentatious about their asking price, however: Caveat emptor, remember?

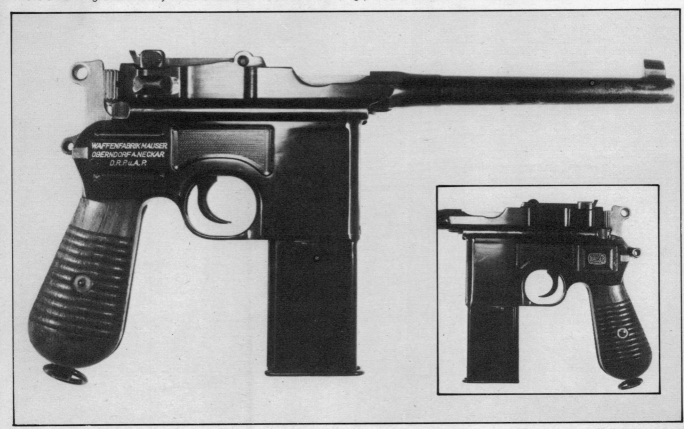

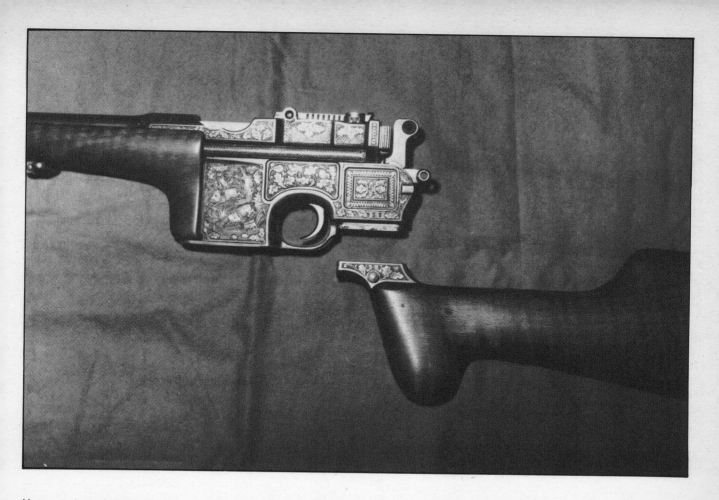

Here are two views of a genuine Mauser pistol carbine, #959, with 17½-inch barrel and covered with traditional German engraving. Note details of the shoulder stock attachment and mating areas.

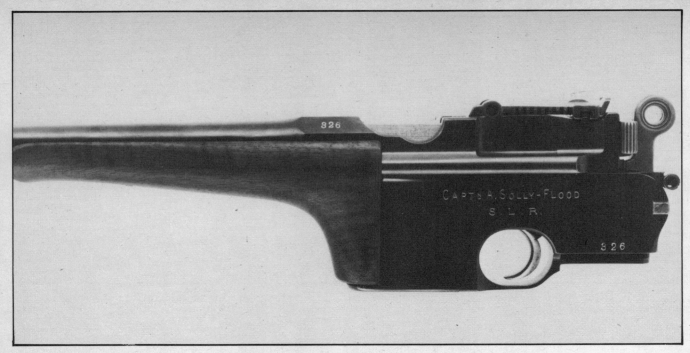

Pistol carbine with an authentic pedigree proves that a face lift and a butt tuck is a restoration, not a Witch's Broom although, as Breathed notes, some might term it a "pushed broom."

receiver only of a System Mauser-engraved, three-digit serial number, cone hammer gun, had the chance to purchase the stripped frame of the same pistol, complete with the same three digit number. He tore down one of his old scurvy cone hammer pistols, did a little heliarc welding, restamping of numbers, filled in a superfluous locking notch in the bolt, and before you could say, "Matching System Mauser Cone Hammer with full checkered grips," he had one! The gun still lives out on the West Coast and was displayed at the Houston Gun Show a while back for

about the same price as a Corvette. We call that a "semi-fake" when two parts are original and matching, the rest born again.

On the same table at that show was another rare Broom-handle variation, the semi-auto Model 1930 Commercial with removable twenty-round clip — or so it seemed. Close examination showed it to be a Schnellfeuer machine pistol with the switch removed, the hole heliarc welded closed and the frame reblued. That's a bummer, for as the man said, "Once a machine pistol, always a machine pis-

Here are details of the forestock attachment fitting on all authentic carbines. Remove the floor plate of the magazine and if it does not look like this, you'll do well not to part with copious bales of green for it.

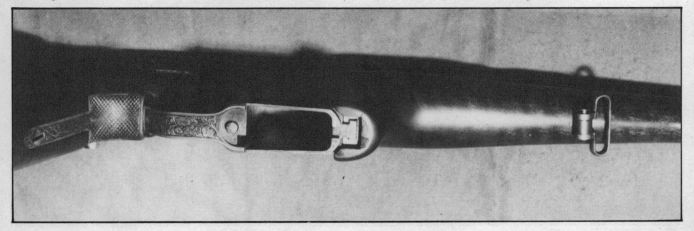

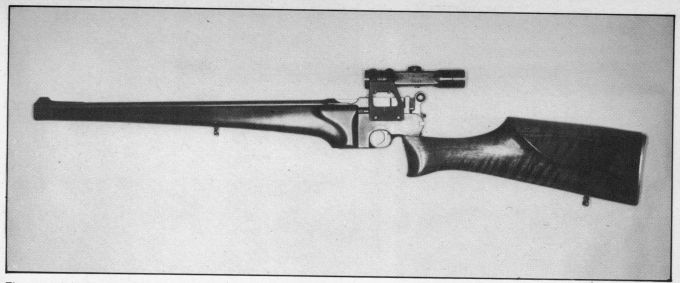

The complete Big Fake: Slabside pistol manicured into a carbine, with Steyr-inspired forestock, Buck Rogers-inspired shoulder stock and a ZF4 scope saddle mounted to the frame. Hang onto your wallet!

tol," and the jolt in a Federal Sneezer that awaits the unauthorized owner of such a manicured Schnell is not worth the price.

Another approach to that variation is a complete, matching 1930 Commercial with the front half of the frame milled off and the magazine well portion of a Schnell frame heliarc welded on.

If you run into one of these ultra-rare variations and its price is in the same bracket as a 1941 Lincoln Continental, politely ask the owner to field strip the pistol so you can examine the interior of the frame. If it is a Witch's Broom you should be able to pick up the locale of the heliarc welding on the non-blued inside surface. If you can spot it — or if the nervous owner refuses to field strip — as they say in Texas, "Move on out and don't look back."

If that twenty-shot broom look turns you on, keep your money in your pants pocket if you run into the handiwork of a West Coast chap with a penchant for turning ten into twenty with his silver solder talent. No illegal Schnell frame is required; just a clean 1930 Commercial pistol, the

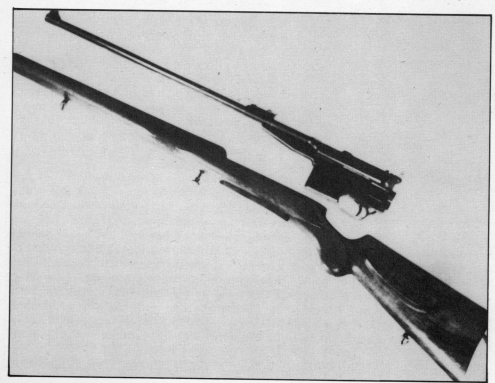

European-styled re-creation complete with butt trap, as made by loving hands at the Austrian Fakenfabrik by Der Gebruders Foneymachen in the Nineteen-Thirties.

Two views of a Schnellfeuer — German for speed-fire/full-auto — manufactured by Mauser for Asian consumption. The laundry-marks on the magazine housing say "Made in Germany." Note the switch hole in the lower photo. Even if these are filled in by heli-arc welding, the BATF still says it's a full-auto gun.

bottom half of a Schnell magazine, a jeweler's saw and some low-temperature brazing equipment and, voila, a plain vanilla collectors item has its selling price hiked up by a factor of five.

This Funny Gun Fabriken Und Waffenfake Gesellschaft really got busy when it came to the highly desirable and always expensive Mauser pistol carbine, a variation

that the factory produced in a quantity of about a thousand. The originals came in all conceivable variations: cone hammer, large or small ring hammer, barrels from 11½ to about 18 inches and in at least two calibers, 7.63 Mauser and 9mm Mauser Export. The fakes nearly all have barrels in the sixteen- to eighteen-inch range and the small forestock is attached with a machine screw threaded into a steel frame extension, silver-soldered to the front of the magazine housing. (The original dovetails on to a male T-sectioned rib machined into the front of the magazine housing).

The "funny" carbines either have a shoulder stock permanently attached to the frame or it is attachable with a crude dovetailed fitting, the male portion of which is silver-soldered to the frame where the pistol grip frame has been removed. Believe it or don't, but a wealthy Texas Mauser carbine collector sold off the best four of five of his factory original carbines and kept the "most valuable one," a carbine obviously gunsmithed from a pistol on special order from GECO, the old German gun distributor who proudly marked the stock pad with their logo. If you are offered a bargain Mauser pistol carbine and suspect it might have a dubious ancestry, look for a telltale difference in the color

Non-genuine "rare semi-auto version of the Schnell," with a new trigger, welded-up switch holes and lettering, with twenty-shot hopper. Computes to "Gotcha" by BATF if not suitably registered...

Cone Hammer pistol with twenty-shot "removable" clip; a "variation" staunchly disclaimed by Mauser.

of the rust blue steel where artisans at Das Fakenfabriken D.R.U.P. have joined the new, long barrel to the bobtailed stub of the old tube. Sometimes that area is lightly knurled to cover the welding of the old with the new. Mauser did make a few experimental pieces with barrels screwed into the receiver, but they were not carbines.

Ever had the experience of welcoming back your ugly secretary from vacation to find she has returned with her nose bobbed, chest lifted, fanny tucked and hair platinumed? I'm too old to notice what the secretaries look like, but an old friend, a slab-side carbine, with the name *Capt. A. Solly-Flood,* engraved on the left side showed up not long ago and if it was not for the distinctive engraving I would have failed to recognize the rather moldy carbine run in *System Mauser* on page 169. The half-missing butt plate had been replaced with a new one, freshly cast from Space

A handmade Broomhandle produced by a picturesque Old World (Asian) craftsman who barely got a quick and none-too-close look at the real von McCoy. His tools are believed to have consisted of a file and pipe wrench, as Breathed theorizes.

Age plastics, the deep pits were gone and were replaced with a coat of deep cold rust blue that would have pulled a long, low whistle from old Paul Mauser. The finishing touch was the engraved name; it had been expertly "chased" and looked as crisp and new as the day Capt. Solly-Flood picked it up at Westley-Richards before he went off to the Boer War. Now that's not a fake; it's what they call a "restoration," or — in some circles — a "pushed broom."

A new pair of grips seems to be one of the favorite means of increasing the value of an otherwise merely expensive Broomhandle. There is a System Mauser-marked cone hammer with serial number under 100 which used to have a pair of filed-down, funny-looking, plain grips in a picture published in Dunlap & Belford's Mauser book just before 1970. The same pistol, still living on the West Coast, now flaunts a pair of beautiful, matching, fully-checkered, walnut grips like it had when it left Oberndorf. Push your money clip a bit deeper in your pocket when you encounter matching grips that appear to have come from the wood of a walnut tree that was only a seedling when the pistol was produced.

Lest you scoff at my warnings, hark to the tale of the experience I shared with a fellow broom fan in Los Angeles, as we photographed a few new variations we had both come up with. An acknowledged local Luger aficionado had bored us to tears with his self-acclaimed prowess as a worldwide, bullet-proof, and invincible Mauser '96 consultant expert and all-around smart fellah. We had three or four '96s torn down to photograph details, so we

put together a composite pistol made up from components that were decades apart in the chronological development of the Mauser '96. It had a cone hammer, twenty-shot mag-type frame and grips from a large ring shallow panel gun; in short, a variation that never saw the inside of the Pistole Haus on the Neckar River.

We chickened out and never sent the resulting print to the expert, but somehow copies got out and I was deluged with sincere requests to name my price for the wild and wonderful cone hammer with the twenty-shot removable clip. My protestations that the pistol simply did not exist seemed to add fuel to the fire we had unwittingly kindled. It really got out of hand when we got a heart tugging note from Germany begging us to, "Please sell me great-grandfather's very own personal pistol," and signed F. Feederle III.

You think that's funny? Well, I can probably convince the grandson of the reported inventor of the Mauser '96 pistol that the "Cone Hammer That Does Not Exist" is not old Grandpa Feederle's, but what about the clone of that very pistol? Somewhere, in this troubled world, a very close copy of the famous spur-hammered prototype patent pistol, with the *15. MARZ 1895* engraving on the left side, lays smugly in some collection, knowing, perhaps nervously, that it started its existence in Oberndorf as a lowly standard cone hammer pistol.

Suppose Captain George Mauser, U.S. Army, old Paul's grandson and a '96 fan in his own right, tracks down this spurious spur hammer; I wonder if I have the intestinal fortitude to tell him it is just another Witch's Broom.

The Grandpappy of them all: the patent model with the spur hammer. An almost exact copy exists with no serial number, but it has pure producton Cone Hammer frame parts, bolt and firing pin. Field strip if in doubt!

CHAPTER 16

THE CELLINI M.B.R.R.

"For every action, there is an equal and opposite reaction."
— Sir Isaac Newton

"...it ain't necessarily so."
—George Gershwin, *Porgy and Bess*

Ferguson tries out one of Cellini's Browning Model 1935 Hi-Power 9mms fitted with the Cellini MBRR device.

As Ferguson notes, the Browning Automatic Rifle or BAR was hard to control in full-auto fire, chambered in .30/06 Springfield. The BAR above, from the J. Curtis Earl collection, carries the Cutts compensator.

(I hope Gershwin fans will forgive the minor para-phrasing of his quote? Tom Ferguson is about to offer you an account of a novel and remarkably effective solution to that plaguing problem of a firearm's recoil. As I've pointed out elsewhere, it's a great rarity to encounter modern and basic improvements in the performance of a handgun, but it sounds as if the M.B.R.R. will qualify for that status. — DAG)

HARNESSING the expanding gas of muzzle blast and using it to reduce recoil or perform other tasks is an old idea. In the past, it has been applied with varying degrees of success to both smallarms and artillery, with the latter getting most of the attention. One of the earlier examples is found on a British artillery piece dating from 1816, and consists of several round holes bored in the upper half of the muzzle, slanted to direct the blast rearward. The theory was that this provided a jet effect and would carry the gun forward against its own recoil, thus minimizing aiming and handling problems for the crew. In fact, it did work to some extent, but was dropped from consideration when it was discovered that the modification impaired both range and accuracy. Apparently the benefits didn't outweigh those disadvantages and experiments with braking devices lay dormant for nearly a century.

World War I provided the incentive to resume investigation of the muzzle brake, especially on smallarms of new types just coming into use. Thousands of Lewis guns mounted in aircraft had muzzle brakes as standard equipment, marking the first adoption of the device by the military. On the ground, U.S. troops were fond of the newly introduced Browning Automatic Rifle, or BAR, but found this eighteen-pound .30/06 hard to control in fully automatic fire.

Before the war ended, some unknown but resourceful doughboy had invented a cure by filing the upper front edge of the flash hider at an angle to deflect some of the gas upward. Naturally, this had the desired effect of pushing the barrel downward, reducing or even eliminating muzzle climb. While this isn't a true muzzle brake and does little to control rearward impulse, it nevertheless improved the handling of the BAR and increased the accuracy of fully automatic fire.

One of the best known of all muzzle brakes is the Cutts Compensator which appeared shortly after the end of the Great War. Designed and patented by Colonel Richard M. Cutts of the U.S. Marine Corps, this device was a hollow tube attached to the muzzle. Slots cut in the tube at right angles to the bore reduced recoil and prevented muzzle climb. It worked well with low pressure cartridges of pistol type, and was made standard equipment on the Thompson Submachine gun in .45 ACP caliber. This cartridge operates at 16,000 pounds per square inch (psi) and doesn't have a high level of muzzle pressure.

When attached to the Springfield service rifle using the .30/06 cartridge at 50,000 psi or so, the Cutts Compensator was less satisfactory due to bothersome blast directed backward at the shooter, as well as to the side. This is a common problem with any brake used with high intensity

An earlier version of the BAR, carrying a rudimentary flash-hider. As Ferguson notes, an enterprising WWI doughboy managed to modify the flash-hider with a file so as to achieve some degree of control over recoil.

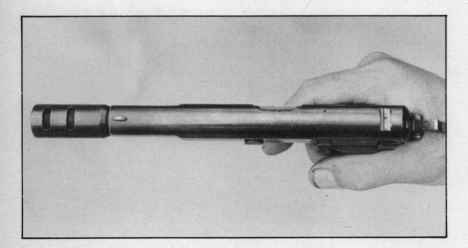

Top view of a Browning Hi-Power fitted with the Cellini MBRR brake.

cartridges. Later, the Cutts Compensator was introduced to the civilian market and enjoyed great commercial success installed on shotguns. For many years, it was a rare thing to see a pump or autoloading shotgun that wasn't equipped with a Cutts. Shotguns operate at pressures similar to most pistol cartridges, or lower, in the 11,000 to 12,-000 psi range, and are well suited to braking devices. The Cutts reduces recoil up to thirty percent without undue backblast or shooter discomfort.

During the two decades of relative peace following WWI, the muzzle brake continued to develop, and appeared in various forms on sporting guns. During that era, this meant rifles and shotguns almost exclusively. Some heavy caliber rifles renowned for vicious recoil were equipped with muzzle brakes. These were largely custom bolt-action guns intended for African use, such as the .375 H&H, .416 Rigby and the .505 Gibbs. Built on the big, expensive Mauser action, they were seldom seen or used in the States. The muzzle brakes used on these rifles still provided plenty of backblast and increased report for the hunter, but in contrast to the soldier, he fired few rounds. The effect was easily ignored. While they never really fell out of favor, the use of these rifles was restricted mainly to those able to afford a safari for the Big Five, and is now further limited by the difficulties of hunting the African Continent.

War has a way of putting the spur to weapons research and development, and WWII was no exception. Many of the belligerents entered the war with outdated equipment but, by 1945, the contrast was remarkable. Almost all mobile artillery such as tank cannons were equipped with effective muzzle brakes, as well as many machine guns and

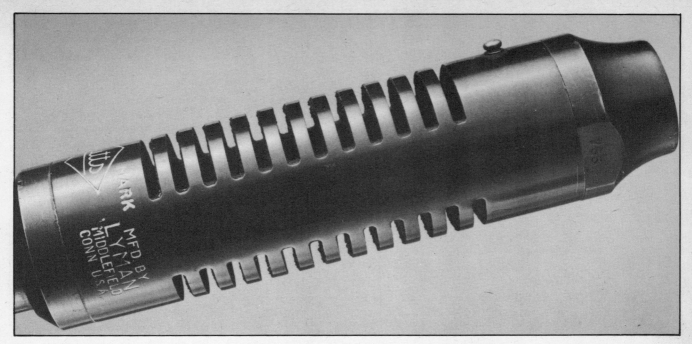

The Cutts compensator has long been manufactured by Lyman for installation on shotguns and they offer a variety of screw-in tubes that are installed at the muzzle to provide chokes of various suitable degrees.

smallbore rapid-firing cannon. The trend extended to individual weapons such as the Russian Tokarev infantry rifle in 7.62mm, a full-power semi-auto with a muzzle brake. This rifle was later withdrawn from use due to functional problems and replaced with the old reliable Moisin-Nagant bolt-action, but was the first military rifle issued with a brake. American GIs fought that war, and one after with the M-1 Garand. It was an excellent rifle, but didn't have a muzzle brake.

Vito Cellini is an American-born inventor who grew up with the sounds of WWII dinning in his ears. Taken back to Italy as a child by his Italian-born parents, Cellini was still there at the outbreak of war, and was caught in Il Duce's draft. Conscripted into the Italian Army, he obeyed orders faithfully until the chance came to desert, then he promptly did so. Joining a group of Yugoslav partisans, he fought the remainder of the war on the side of the Allies, and had plenty of opportunities to study weapons used by both sides. Impressed by the increased accuracy and firepower of braked weapons, especially those which were fully automatic, he never forgot the lessons they taught. This is apparent today in his designs for lightweight, improved submachine guns on which he holds several patents. Following the war, Cellini gained additional weapons experience serving in various capacities in various countries, right up until the recent past. He is understandably vague about these shadowy doings and one gets the impression that he really doesn't care who is fighting who, as long as he gets to do some of it. Whether or not this is a fair appraisal, the important thing is that Cellini knows a lot about combat weapons and how to use them, and a lot about muzzle brakes.

Hoping to increase the combat efficiency of the pistol, Cellini developed a muzzle brake which fits popular combat handguns such as the Colt .45 M1911A1 and the

Without the Cutts compensator, the Thompson SMG tends to climb almost uncontrollably from recoil. This one, in 9mmP from the J. Curtis Earl shop, probably has considerably less of a problem.

Browning 9mm M1935. Fairly conventional in appearance, the brake is a length of carefully machined steel attached to the end of the barrel by one of several means, provided with several slots or vents. These direct the muzzle blast in the optimum direction to reduce recoil, just as in other brakes. The Cellini MBRR, or muzzle brake recoil reducer, incorporates several design features which give it more functions than other muzzle brakes. For example, it acts as a flash suppressor and has internal features built in which enhance accuracy. The patents are still pending on some of these designs, and Cellini prefers to remain silent until they are granted, so they won't be detailed.

It may be enough to say that I tested four different autoloaders equipped with the Cellini MBRR, and found that it was indeed an effective device in reducing recoil and

Inventor/designer Vito Cellini demonstrates his MBRR on a Browning Model 1935 9mm Hi-Power.

Inquiries on the MBRR should be directed to: Cellini Muzzle-Brake Stabilizer, P.O. Box 17792, San Antonio, TX 78217, accompanied by an SASE.

minimizing muzzle whip, the twin foes of fast combat shooting.

Until they gain a certain familiarity with it, most shooters complain that the .45 auto has excessive recoil. Even after much practice and training, many shooters find it hard to control in rapid fire due to the weight of the slide running back over the hand in recoil. Because I have this trouble myself with the gun, I asked Vito for several .45 s to test. He obliged with two steel-framed guns and also provided a Colt LW Commander model with an aluminum alloy frame. This latter gun is a hard kicker, weighing only twenty-six ounces, and puts the MBRR to a severe test. From long experience, I realized if it could tame this featherweight, it would probably be effective on the others as well. However, I first chose a standard model as these are the ones in common use in IPSC and other types of combat shooting.

The first gun was an Auto-Ordnance copy of the 1911A1 Colt, equipped with rubber Pachmayr grips and Bo-Mar sights. The front sight is attached to the slide, not on the

brake itself like the other design. This particular model is attached to the gun in what Cellini refers to as the "bayonet" method. Made in one piece, it replaces the standard bushing, slipping over the barrel and locking into place using the bushing cutout inside the slide. The fit is precise, and the brake requires some effort to twist into place. No tools are necessary, however. The tube measures one inch in diameter, and is 2⅜ inches long, slotted with five fairly broad vents cut at right angles to the bore. Weighing but 2½ ounces, it has little or no effect on balance or handling qualities.

After familiarizing myself with the crisp four-pound trigger, I loaded the magazine with Federal 230-grain ball ammo and began to shoot. In order to give the .45 full opportunity to make a run at me, I used a one-handed target stance, gripping the gun just tightly enough to control the sight picture. Not surprisingly, the big gun did make a run at me with this weak, limp-wristed grip. Cellini explained that the MBRR requires a solid, secure hold for best results. I found no problem with this, as most combat shooting is done with a grip that would crush granite or throttle a weasel as some like to say. For the balance of the magazine I used such a grip and found the results gratifying to say the least. Held tightly, but still in one hand, the gun remained steady and level as the slide cycled. There was no muzzle whip, and little rearward thrust. The best part was that I never lost the sight picture and had the target in sight at all times.

The Cellini MBRR on this Browning has been threaded to the muzzle of the barrel. The device does not in any way reduce the sound of the pistol report and thus cannot be regarded as a silencer or sound suppressor.

Pleased at this good performance, I switched over to the lightweight Colt Commander. This gun is equipped with Herrett stocks of checkered walnut and an MMC rear sight. Like the other gun, the front ramp is on the slide, maintaining sight integrity. In the case of the Commander, the MBRR is quite different. It is smaller and lighter than the first brake and is slightly less than an inch in diameter at 15/16-inch. It attaches by screwing on to a threaded portion of the muzzle and does not replace the bushing in this instance. Instead of being machined flat at the rear, the MBRR is tapered or radiused to ensure a tight and precise

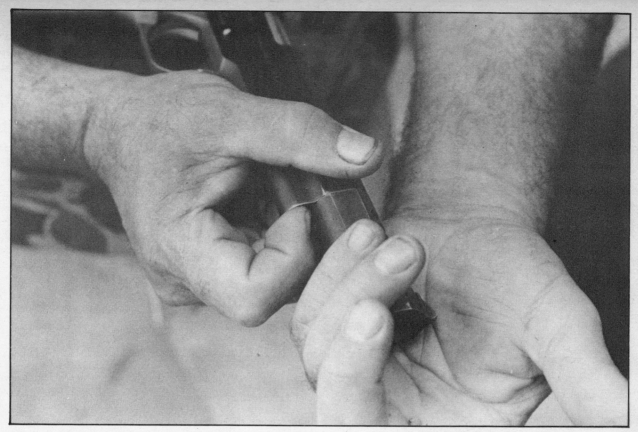

The Cellini MBRR as fitted to this M1911 Colt replaces the regular barrel bushing and is installed in the same manner of the original-equipment bushing, making a most convenient technique for mounting.

fit as the slide and bushing telescopes over it. As we later proved, this simple method increases accuracy by repositioning the barrel to the same spot after each shot.

Using the same box of Federal 230-grain .45 round nose ammo, I loaded the Commander and resumed shooting. This time I used the strong combat grip, but held the gun in my right hand only. Once again, there was no muzzle whip or heavy recoil and I was able to keep the target in full view. The rearward motion, or "kick" felt about like that of a .38 Special wadcutter target load, not at all objectionable. The MBRR actually made the little gun pleasant to shoot, and I ran several magazines through it. Using the two-hand Weaver stance reduced recoil even further, making bursts of several shots possible.

At this point it might be a good idea to remark on the functioning aspect of the .45s equipped with the MBRR. Although standard recoil springs are used, just as they come from the factory, Cellini states that the guns cycle faster with the MBRR. In spite of this there is no frame battering or other damage to the gun due to the cushioning effect of trapped gases. During rapid fire tests, I had no trouble keeping four or even five ejected cases in the air at one time, and there were no malfunctions. Cellini makes the claim that reliability is improved, and based on what I saw, I agree.

Although fully satisfied with the results obtained with the Auto-Ordnance .45 and the Commander, I went on to try the third .45 auto. It was the Standard Colt Mk IV '70 Series with standard factory stocks and MMC rear sight,

but in this case the front sight was milled as an integral part of the MBRR. An early design, this model locked into place "bayonet" style, and had five vents. Heaviest of all at four ounces, it measured one inch in diameter and 2⅜ inches long. The bottom portion of the tube was fitted with a contoured, full-length muzzle weight which attached with two screws.

The addition of the weight made it more pleasing to the eye than the other models, at least in my opinion. The additional heft served to dampen any tendency to climb in recoil as well. During the test firing, I attempted to tie this gun up by jerking the trigger rapidly, but didn't succeed. The gun just kept spitting out those chunky 230-grain slugs, without a hitch or bobble. At one point the gun was cycling so rapidly I began getting unburned powder particles in the face, and had better than half a magazine full of empty cases in the air. This sort of speed is approaching the upper limits of the mechanism. Anything faster would have to be full-auto.

At this particular session, Cellini had brought along a Browning 9mm Parabellum, M1935, and this gun provided us with a peculiar experience in accuracy, all inadvertently. The MBRR on this weapon was a screw-on type resembling the one used on the Colt Commander, but had three slots or vents. Absentmindedly, while diddling around and meddling with the guns, I unscrewed the MBRR about 2½ turns and forgot to tighten it prior to shooting. Cellini must have thought I was a lousy shot when the firing began, and I scattered the 115-grain Federal FMJs over five inches at

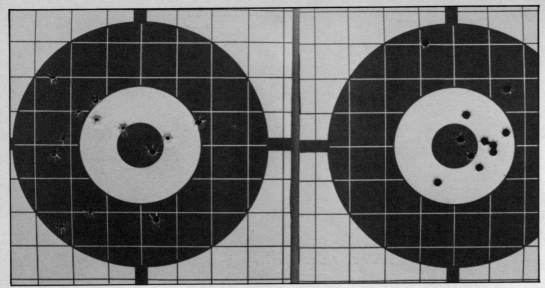

The effect of a slightly loose MBRR is remarkable. Ferguson fired the target at left with the device not quite turned to solid engagement with muzzle, tightened it and got the group in the target at right: quite a difference!

The MBRR, here on a .45 ACP Government Model, can be carried in a conventional holster if it's open at the bottom. Otherwise, a special holster's needed.

Gun at left has just run dry and locked its slide back. Note the barrel remains almost perfectly horizontal. Not only is the up-flip greatly reduced but so is kick.

twenty-five yards. Since this was an accuracy test, I was firing from a sandbag rest, forearms braced. Taking the gun back, Cellini twiddled the MBRR and found it loose. No wonder, he said. After tightening it to a fully-seated position, he handed the gun back with a loaded magazine. This time the hot Federal loads cut into the ten-ring in a tight 2½-inch group. It illustrated clearly the accurizing effect of the tapered MBRR.

Recoil from the Browning was virtually nil, even after switching over to some hot Federal JHP ammo.

During this session, I didn't press the accuracy bit too much. The guns were all from Cellini's personal battery and had been used as demonstrators for the MBRR. In short they had a lot of miles on them, having digested thousands of full-power, jacketed factory loads. Probably some of the barrels were beginning to wash out, but even so, the combat accuracy was quite acceptable. The .45s would go into 2½ inches easily, sometimes two inches at twenty-five yards, and the 9mm did the same, even though

handicapped by tiny factory sights of the fixed variety. As everyone knows, the man behind the gun is an important factor too, and I'm sure a better shooter would get improved results. I make no claim to IPSC proficiency, having been out of the game for nearly a decade.

Cellini has hours of video tapes which show the MBRR in action on a wide variety of weapons. These range from high-powered rifles in .30/06 and 7mm magnum, to the M16 in .223 and the Ruger carbine in .44 mag. In the handgun category, the guns scatter from the Thompson Contender in .44 mag to the .45 auto, 9mm Browning, an Astra M600 in the same caliber, and numerous .38 and .357 revolvers. Watching the M29 S&W .44 in various barrel lengths is interesting; even this hard kicker doesn't move much. Occasionally the tape will show a bright flash issuing from the top of the MBRR. Cellini explains this is the device cleaning itself of unburned powder granules and metal deposits, and occurs about every twenty-five shots. The flash isn't visible to the person firing the gun, and can only be seen from the side. Although Vito uses mostly factory jacketed ammo for demonstration purposes, preferably in the heaviest bullet weights, many handloads with lead bullets have gone through the guns with no problems. The lead will sometimes build up, but always blows out when the unit cleans itself. The use of lead bullets will not solder the MBRR to the gun.

Every MBRR is carefully machined by Cellini himself from 4140 ordnance steel for added strength. Many compensators and flash suppressors now being marketed are made of sintered metal, which won't take the strain of muzzle pressure, and may crack sooner or later.

The value of the MBRR in competition was made clear to me at the 1983 Bianchi Cup Match in Columbia, Missouri. At the nearby practice range, well-known writer and author Massad Ayoob and I tested the device on the falling metal plates. In this event, the eight-inch steel plates are fired on at 10, 15, 20 and 25 yards. Allowed only one second for each of the six plates, the competitor must be fast and accurate. Beginning at the ten-yard distance, I first fired a standard Mk IV .45 auto which had been set up as a pin gun for use in the Second Chance match. Instead of a muzzle brake or compensator, it had been fitted with a twin spring system resembling the one used in the Detonics pistol. This gave a recoil spring tension of twenty-seven pounds. Firing rapidly in an effort to meet the time, the first three shots downed three plates, but I could feel myself "losing" the gun due to heavy recoil. My last three shots went over the plates completely. Switching to an Auto-Ordnance .45 equipped with the MBRR, the six plates fell easily with no misses.

Virtually everyone who has seen and used the brake, or MBRR, is pleased and enthusiastic. Cellini has traveled widely promoting the device and has many supporters in various parts of the country. These include John L. (Jack) Schatzel, firearms instructor for the Kingston, New York, police department, and officer Jeff Jacobson of the Odessa, Texas, police department. Both men used the Cellini MBRR in the 1983 Bianchi Cup.

At the time of this writing, the cost of the MBRR for .45 and 9mm autos is around $150. Cellini prefers to have the gun shipped to him so that precise fitting is possible, citing numerous instances of excessive play or tolerance in slides, even commercial Colts. Copies such as the Auto-Ordnance or AMT Hardballer are apt to be worse, however, the custom fitting removes any objection.

Over the past year I've tested and fired most of Cellini's guns fitted with the MBRR. He has one .357 revolver which always hurts my ears when I fire it, perhaps due to a combination of incorrectly cut vents and the high chamber pressure of the .357 magnum cartridge. The others don't have this fault, and neither does the 9mm Browning, operating at about the same pressures.

The MBRR does not, as a rule, have any unpleasant blast effects on the shooter, even on rifles. In December of 1982, I made a one-shot kill on a Texas whitetail using the 7mm magnum, and found recoil about like a .30 carbine. Although it resembles a silencer from the days of Al Capone, the MBRR does nothing to muffle report. Silencers have been illegal in the U.S. for many years, and Cellini isn't anxious to have the MBRR mistaken for one.

Although I have small experience with muzzle brakes

Above, four different installations of the MBRR show the variety of approaches available. Below, preparing to install the threaded type on Browning.

now on the market, I found the MBRR tames even the hardest kickers admirably, and don't see how it could be any better. For the hunter using a rifle, it allows him to keep the game in sight after the shot instead of bouncing away from recoil. For silhouette shooters using heavy cartridges in handguns, it would be ideal. Most of all, for the combat shooter it offers quick recovery and accurate follow-up shots.

CHAPTER 17

SMALL AUTOS VS. SNUBNOSE REVOLVERS

In Which Claud Hamilton Essays A Comparative Evaluation Of The Two Basic Designs And Makes His Final Choice

Semi-wadcutter bullets from the .38 Special do not upset at short-barreled velocities for that cartridge. This one penetrated one foot of clay and on into the backstop filled with pillow stuffing.

(A really tireless, not to say intrepid researcher, friend Hamilton has sometimes ventured far into the outer boondocks of left field in quest of a suitable and valid analog for use in testing handgun loads. I recall a truly wondrous affair he assembled once, consisting of frozen frankfurters, sections of lath, balloons filled with water, slabs of modeling clay, polyester pillow filling — and might have included the kitchen sink except he couldn't get it loose. I

don't recall exactly what he proved that time, beyond the undeniable fact that, when struck by speeding bullets, it created one goshawful mess in his basement.

(I mention that as a probable explanation as to why he contented himself with oil-base clay as his impact medium for the session at hand. — DAG)

HOW MANY times have you heard it said that "American generals always fight the next war using the weapons and tactics of the last..."? I'm sure we have been guilty of this more than once, but soldiers are not the only mental malingerers. I guess it can happen to most any of us. Take, for example, those who have a legitimate need to carry a gun concealed.

Lawmen in plain clothes, other security personnel, guards, homeowners and business people in certain high-risk occupations make up the majority of such people. Lawmen and security personnel have a real need to conceal their business as well as the fact that they are armed. Jewelers, diamond salesmen, bodyguards and currency brokers also need to be armed, but find it embarrassing to deal with their legitimate customers and associates while openly wearing a gun.

I think it is safe to say that most of the Americans who carry concealed guns today do so in pancake, hip-hugger holsters worn behind the hip, and the guns they carry are 2- or 2½-inch barrel revolvers in caliber .38 Special or, occasionally, .357 magnum. Is this the best solution, or are we perhaps giving away to an opponent the advantage of more thoughtful weapons selection? Is this the old story all over again: Cavalrymen armed with "trap door" Springfields facing Indians carrying Winchester repeaters?

Ten years ago if that thought had occurred to me I wouldn't have wasted two minutes of it. The answer was just too obvious. We all knew that a "quality American revolver is a more reliable and much safer arm than any auto pistol..." Recently, though, three things have happened that have made me reconsider.

To begin with, there has been a real revolution in handgun ammunition during the last fifteen years or so. New jacketed soft and hollow point bullets are now available that have greatly improved the effectiveness at least of some pistol calibers, such as the 9mm Parabellum and .38

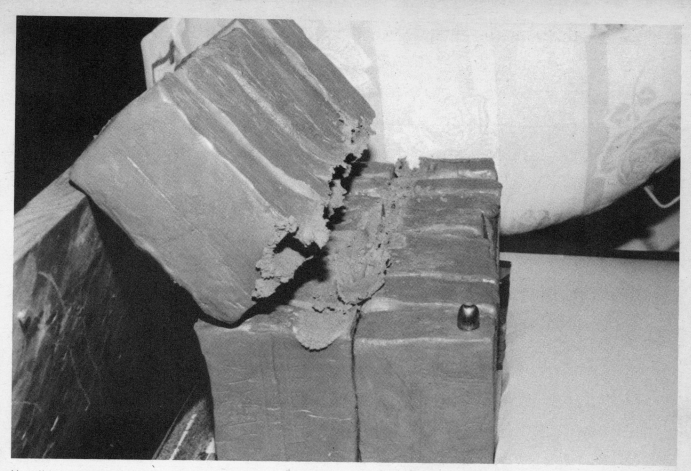

Nor did the jacketed hollow point bullet for the .380 ACP perform any better than the one on opposite page. It appears rather unlikely that these will upset at typical .380 velocities. The recovered bullet, after going through eight clay blocks, appeared so undamaged it probably could have been reloaded and fired again.

Super. Their shapes have been perfected to the point where they feed as reliably as the full metal jacketed bullets for which the pistols were originally made.

A second, but less noted change has been a continued improvement in the quality of American ammunition. This has improved pistol performance also.

Finally, there seems to have been real improvement in the quality and design of the small pistols now being offered. I am much impressed with this after having spent several days visiting the better local gun shops, examining guns and talking to knowledgeable proprietors such as Steve Richards, of Hunters' Haven in Alexandria, Virginia. They deal with these new guns every day and have shot most of them. And they seem to think highly of them, too. Can it be that these little guns, in their best available caliber .380 Auto, may outperform the revolvers?

What does "outperform" mean? What is "better"? Most serious shooters I have known have been intensely attached to their favorite guns, sometimes to the point of defying reason, or so it seemed. The relationship between a man and the gun he depends upon for his life can become a pret-ty intimate thing. I guess what I am trying to put into words is that the answers I came up with may very well not be the same as yours; features and qualities I liked may be repugnant to you.

There are some preliminary points we can agree on, I think: the gun must be safe to carry loaded and must be accurate enough to assure consistent hits on a man-sized target at twelve yards. If these are satisfied, I'd want answers to four questions:

— Which gun is most easily concealed and most comfortably carried?
— Which gun can I draw most rapidly and fire most effectively?
— Which gives me best accuracy and best ability to handle multiple targets?
— Are the cartridges concerned effective for defense at twelve yards?

The guns I selected to look at seemed to me to be the best in their classes:

SNUBBIES	POCKET PISTOLS
Colt, Detective Special, two-inch, Caliber .38 Special	Beretta, Model 84, Caliber .380 Auto
S&W, Model 36 Chiefs Special, two-inch, Caliber .38 Special	Walther, Model PPK/S, Caliber .380 Auto

Holster	Comfort	Concealability	Score
Shoulder	9	1	10
Ankle	5	10	15
Hip Hugger, outside	5	5	10
Hip Hugger in waistband	6	7	13
Crossdraw, outside	8	5	13
Crossdraw in waistband	7	9	16

I sometimes think we give too much importance to how easy a gun is to carry, and comfortable it is when carried concealed. I guess, though, that we all feel as I do...if it ever comes to shooting, it'll be someone else...not me! So the hedonist in us all takes over.

I've carried sidearms for forty years-plus, but rarely concealed, so I wasn't overly familiar with the new holsters popular these days. I managed to persuade a friend, Martha Penso, to join me in trying most of the more common carries and, after a day with each, we rated them for comfort and concealability (ten is best):

We pretty much agreed that a well-fitted shoulder holster is tops for comfort with today's lifestyle which involves so much sitting. It needs a good tie-down to the belt, however. Ankle holsters maximize concealment, but are hot and uncomfortable and, for me at least, always slipping down. We hate the hip huggers. They grind on chair backs slowly chewing up gun, holster, chair and us.

The crossdraw is a tad better and, for me, makes the gun a lot more controllable. For those of us on the heavy side, concealability is really a joke with today's lifestyle. Only bankers and just a few others wear coats indoors. Double-knit, lightweight close-fitted clothes are bad enough, but when your size is "portly, bordering on elephan-tine"...forget it! Martha, however, is quite slender and had no trouble at all effectively concealing guns by either the hip hugger or the crossdraw carry.

The guns themselves make surprisingly little difference, and they are quite close in physical characteristics, also:

Winchester's Silvertip hollow point expanded nicely and penetration was through five clay blocks. The Silvertip has a lubricated jacket of aluminum.

Gun	SPECIFICATIONS			Weight Loaded (oz.)
	Length (in.)	Height (in.)	Thickness (in.)	
Colt Detective Special	6.75	4.44	1.39	24
S&W Chiefs Special	6.5	4.0	1.31	21
Beretta Model 84	6.55	4.8	1.39	27
Walther Model PPK/S	6.0	4.7	1.14	24

All of which does not prove too much. Both revolvers come in airweight versions which shave several ounces from their weight.

Going beyond the pure figures, these are the things that stick in my memory: The thickness of the Colt detracts from comfort I suppose because it is all at the cylinder area. The Beretta distributes the same thickness throughout the whole grip area. The shape of the revolver grips causes them to give awkward jabs at various parts of the anatomy from time to time...but it also facilitates a smooth and quick draw.

To check out drawing and shooting qualities, we adjourned to the pistol range out at Fairfax Rod & Gun Club. Martha and I alternated. First I took five practice shots, then five more against time while she held the stop watch. Then we reversed roles and I took over the watch. We used the holster we each preferred, for Martha the outside hip hugger and for me the crossdraw inside the waistband. We

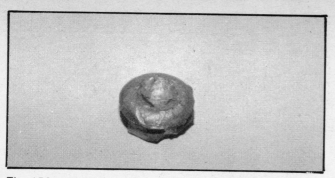

The 158-grain lead hollow point bullet in the +P .38 Special load upset to the classic mushroom shape.

In the beginning both of the little revolvers proved easier for me, except for one thing. Every now and then the hammer spur would catch on my shirt or trousers. With time I learned to grasp the gun extending my thumb up to the hammer to protect it against snagging. This works but it does not speed up or help my performance. Some shooters "de-horn" their small revolvers to get around this; both Smith & Wesson and Colt offer versions of their guns that have shrouded hammers, but these are rare for some reason. Bianchi offers a fine soft grip for the Chiefs Special that performs this function well.

The small pistols gave me quite a different problem. They were unfamiliar to me and it took me time to learn how to grasp and handle them well. The Walther grip is full. Short, too, unless the finger support is used on the magazine. The hammers of the pistols never seem to catch in the draw, and their double-action function is quite good, though not quite so smooth as that of the revolvers.

The next stage, handling multiple targets, was duck soup for the Beretta. I was beginning to get used to it by then, and I had no trouble at all getting two hits, each, on five paper targets at twelve yards. The best any of the other guns could do was three targets. I made the arbitrary rule that we'd take two shots per target because of the uncertainty of fast shooting under these circumstances. Of course, at this point there arises the perfectly legitimate question: Just how many assailants do you expect to have to face? This has to be your own judgment call.

averaged our results and the only shots that counted were those that scored hits on a man-size target at twelve yards. Here's how we came out:

Gun	Average Time To First Hit (seconds)	Gun	Average Time To First Hit (seconds)
S&W Chiefs Special	3.0	Beretta M-84	3.3
Colt Detective Special	3.0	Walther PPK/S	3.5

From left, .38 Special hollow point lead semi-wadcutter, .38 Special Silvertip and .380 Silvertip.

The .380 Walther PPK/S,
with its magazine removed.

For me, the hardest part of the drill was the last: Are the cartridges concerned effective for defense at twelve yards?

I doubt that any two American handgun shooters today would agree all the way on what is or is not an adequate cartridge for defense. I know a trim, young grandmother who has unshakeable faith in her little old Woodsman pistol and its .22 long rifle hollow points — and she's deadly accurate with it! On the other hand, I know two street-wise law officers both of whom consider the .357 magnum marginal. For them the .41 is just about right!

Experienced law officers used to assign the .38 Special a manstopper rating of about fifty percent. This, of course, was with the old loadings, and it meant that only about half your solid body hits could be expected to put your man down. By contrast, the .45 ACP or Colt were rated at about eighty to ninety percent.

In summary form, here's generally what we have available in factory loads for both these cartridges:

Cartridge	Bullet		Muzzle Velocity (.38 Spl - two-inch .380 Auto 3¼-inch) (fps)	Muzzle Energy (fpe)
	Weight (gr)	Type		
.38 Special	158	LRN	700	185
	158	LSWC	700	185
	200	LRN	590	161
	148	LWC	660	110
.38 Special +P	110	JHP	940	234
	125	JHP	865	227
	95	STHP	1020	236
	150	LRN	820	248
	158	LHP	825	265
	158	LSWC	825	265
.380 Auto	90	JHP	1000	200
	95	FMC	955	190
	88	JHP	990	191
	85	STHP	1000	189

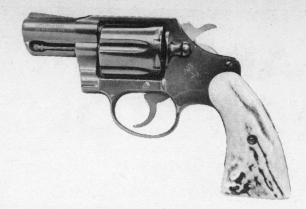

The two-inch Colt Detective Special in .38 Special.

rely upon handloads for defense. We may be good, but we cannot match the factories for reliability, and that is the bottom line when your life depends upon it.

I have recently tested most of the new hollow point loads from the factories in an oil-base clay. For me, the +P .38 Special with the 95-grain Silvertip hollow point and the 158-grain lead hollow point expand reliably and well and deliver their energy in a short distance, say four or five inches. In the .380 Auto, only the 85-grain Silvertip hollow point will do the same thing. I make no pretense that my clay test medium predicts what the same bullet will do in human tissue, but it does serve to compare the performance of different bullets.

The first thing to note is that in two-inch revolvers, the .38 Special is more than equaled in terms of muzzle energy by the .380 Auto...unless you resort to the +P ammunition not recommended for use in these light-frame revolvers. The plain fact is that neither of these cartridges is quite up to the velocities needed to give good expansion performance with the new jacketed hollow point bullets. They tend to over-penetrate and pass through human targets. Such hits don't stop well...even though they may eventually be fatal.

What about handloads? Sure: I have made excellent lead hollow point bullets in the 110- to 130-grain range that, for me, fed well through the pistols as well as in the revolvers. But, I cannot seriously recommend that anyone

The S&W Model 36 Chiefs Special in .38 Special.

The Beretta Model 84, with staggered column magazine holding twelve rounds of .380 ACP.

As far as the cartridges are concerned, I find them too similar. There is just no basis for choice. I believe that with the new bullets such as the Silvertip hollow points they might achieve a sixty percent stopper rating.

All things considered, I would select the Beretta M-84 as my defense concealment gun. In the beginning I gave the nod to the revolvers because they felt so much more natural in my hand, and I could get at them and draw them more easily. However, once I became accustomed to the pistols and discovered how reliable they were, they began to grow on me. In the final analysis, it is that thirteen-shot magazine capacity that makes the choice for me.

CHAPTER 18

ACCURACY CAPABILITIES OF THE AUTO PISTOL

Autos Can Group Suprisingly Well — Providing You Can Control The Human Factor!

The Smith & Wesson Model 539, as it came from the factory. Even with its original factory barrel, it grouped well.

ACCURIZING is a word you won't find in most dictionaries, despite the fact it finds a considerable amount of current use among members of the handgunning fraternity/sorority. The somewhat maverick term refers to the practice of improving the accuracy potential of a given firearm. Customizing is a similar term, likewise little sanctioned by lexicographers.

The words are not necessarily synonymous. Accurizing concerns itself, as you'd assume, with improving and enhancing the gun's accuracy to as great an extent as may be possible and practical. Customizing is the departure from strictly factory specifications, with attention devoted to cosmetic considerations as well as improving the actual operating efficiency.

One of the earliest subjects of the accurizer's deft ministrations was the venerably legendary Model 1911 Colt auto and its modern counterpart, the Model 1911A1. Few would argue that it stood in hard need of such services; certainly none who ever tried to cope with the old thumbbuster in its goose-loose military status.

It helps to lend perspective to learn the ten-ring of the military slow-fire target — for use at a distance of twenty-five yards, — was six inches in diameter. For the timed-fire and rapid-fire courses, you moved in to fifteen yards and used the same target. The first time I ever fired the qualification course with the Government auto, my score was a shameful and ignominious thirty-three percent!

It was also the first time I'd fired the old brute and no one had prepared me for the way it bucked and twisted when fired, nor for the goshawful noise it made. Each report was like a high-pressure jet of ice water blasted into both ears. The time was the summer of 1943, long before anyone had seen reason to fashion the modern earmuff-type hearing protectors. Heck, they didn't even so much as offer you a couple tufts of cotton, even though cotton is hardly better than no protection at all.

Likewise, for some reason I never fathomed, the military at that time decreed the pistol must be fired in the classic offhand target stance. If any shooter had been so rashly innovative as to try steadying the aiming hand with

Present owner of the Bar-Sto-barreled Model 539 is — as his expression suggests — ecstatically delighted with it. As no more than a small number of M539s were made, it should become even more of a collector item than it now is.

The .38 Colt Super barrel for the Colt Government Model has a small relief cut on the lower rear surface of the barrel shroud (arrow) to clear the shallow rim of the case. This does not provide adequate chambering support in firing, however.

the free hand, the instructor would have flayed the hapless wight verbally and pegged the hide out to cure in the sun.

The typical as-issued military M1911 varied in innate wretchedness across a fairly broad gamut. That's to say some were less atrocious than the mill run. A few years after my ranklesome first encounter with the .45 auto, the Fates maneuvered me into a position where I was one of the instructors on a .45 pistol range. Still smarting at the odious memory, I buckled down and essayed to master the blasted blaster, come H or high W.

Even today, I feel I owe apologies to the taxpayers of this country. I'm not certain how much our participation in WWII cost the country, but a fair chunk of it went for .45 ACP ammo I burned up on the pistol range when no students were about. I poured loads through those things until you could almost strike a kitchen match on the muscle that separates the thumb and palm. The range had a working inventory of perhaps sixty pistols, kept securely locked in the range house during off-duty hours. At one time or another, I believe I tried out each and every one of them, experimenting with shifting magazines in effort to perfect the feeding reliability and making thoughtful note of the serial numbers of any that demonstrated uncommon grouping ability.

Toward the end of the project, I even tried swapping parts to eliminate some of the ridiculous amount of play between barrel, slide and receiver. I also did some patient smoothing of mating parts on the sear and hammer with a small half-round India stone that is still in my gunsmithing kit, some forty years later.

I managed to round up an empty case measuring .898 inch and it dropped well below the rear face of the barrel shroud, as can be seen here and below.

The project paid off. Even with the dubious performance of the GI hardball ammo — we were well into the steel case stuff by that time — I managed to coax a score of something like 390 x 400 possible out of my primitive accurizing job. Being a natural northpaw I did that with the right hand, but went on to get within a few points of the same score a week or ten days later firing southpaw. I'll always contend shooting is done more with the eye and brain than the hand alone.

Ah, but that was long ago and a vast amount of progress has been hacked through the jungle since those days. Quite a lot of the improvement has taken the form of removing the slap/lurch/wobble in the fit of the barrel, barrel bushing, slide, recoil link, slide stop and receiver so all are solidly immovable when the action is locked in battery.

Armand Swenson used to employ a simple tool for checking the amount of play in a pistol. It was just a piece of brass rod turned down so it was a snug fit in the bore of a .45 auto, with a flat area on one end. Swenson would fasten the flat end in his bench vise, sliding the muzzle over the round end of the rod until it was solidly held. Then, with the rapt expression of a Jimmy Valentine attacking a high-class combination lock, he would move — or attempt to move — the pistol with its barrel held immovably. A few microns

here, a couple of Angstrom units there — all were entered in that formidable computer behind the genial blue eyes, earmarking special attention to this or that part before the gun came up for its next wiggle-test.

Swenson — who gets his mail at Box 606, Fallbrook, CA 92028 — has a legendary reputation in the field of accurizing the Model 1911 pistol. The owner of such a gun, wishing to have it improved by Swenson's gifted ministrations, needs a generous amount of patience for waiting out its eventual return. Like any gunsmith worth his bluing salts, Swenson has a waiting list bordering upon the astronomical. I've not visited Swenson's shop in many years but I well recall his system of organization when he worked out of Gardena. Each incoming gun was tagged and put into a cigar box where it remained during the course of its treatment and modification.

Bar-Sto Precision Machine, formerly of Burbank, California and currently headquartered at 73377 Sullivan Road, Twentynine Palms, CA 92277, is owned and operated by Irving O. Stone, Jr., and his wife Barbara. The firm name is a contraction of Barbara and Stoney, as the proprietor is known amoung his friends.

Bar-Sto makes stainless steel barrels for certain auto pistols, including the Colt Government Model and Commander, the Model 1935 Browning Hi-Power and, in more recent times, the S&W Model 39 and Model 59 in their sundry prefixed and suffixed variations such as the 439, the 39-2, the 559, 639 and so on. Actually, the barrel is identical and interchangeable between the 39 and 59.

Barrels for the Browning or S&W guns are produced solely in the customary 9mm Luger/Parabellum cartridge. For the Colts, Bar-Sto offers a choice of .45 ACP, .38-45 Clerke, .38 Colt Super and 9mm Luger. The barrels can be sent through the mail, without red tape, fuss or folderol, but I would recommend that arrangements be made to send the gun to Bar-Sto for handfitting by Stoney's skilled hands.

With that done, the odds are highly favorable the re-barreled pistol will group far better than with its original barrel. The exact degree of improvement will vary in accord with several factors, but I can offer a few illustrations.

Stone fitted one of his .38 Colt Super (CS) barrels in a

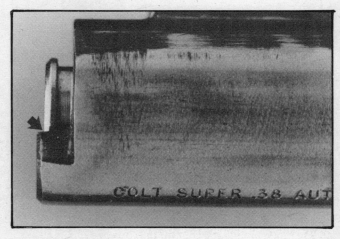

Arrow indicates discrepancy of something like .065 inch between head of chambered .898-inch case and rear face of barrel shroud. In actuality, extractor would support it against firing pin blow, as noted.

The same case in the Bar-Sto chamber rests solidly with its head about .005 inch below shroud shoulder.

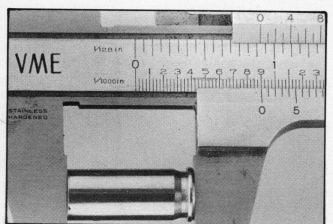

It's rare to find a straight-sided pistol case that's up to the specific length — .900 inch for the .38 CS — but this one came within about .002 inch of making it.

What's the secret? Well, at least one of them — for there must be several — is Stone's attention to letting the cartridge headspace its case mouth against the ledge at the front of the chamber. The .38 Colt Super has a semi-rimmed case, its head is .406-inch in diameter against .380-inch for the body diameter. The nominal length for the case is .900-inch from head to mouth.

Now straight-sided pistol cases show an amazing variation in length, which would be simple to correct by trimming, except they're all considerably shorter than they're supposed to be in the first place. I've just returned from a safari to the shop to verify that. Typical .38 CS cases, fired several times, ran from .008-inch to as much as .016-inch scant of the prescribed .900-inch length. I did, however,

Government Model .38 Super I'd purchased in 1969. He, Johnny Adams and I took it out to the desert to a shooting site that accommodated Adams' Ransom Rest and we put the gun in that with the Bar-Sto barrel and fed it some of the Shelbyville Super Vel loads with the 112-grain jacketed soft point (JSP) bullets. It proceeded to slam five of those into a center-to-center spread of 1 5/16 inches, at a distance of fifty yards.

Curious as to the extent of improvement, indeed if any, we pulled the gun out of the rest and reinstalled the original factory barrel. Put back into the rest, firing the identical load, with all other conditions equal, the five-shot group spanned a trifle over eighteen inches; nearly fourteen times as sprawly as the Bar-Sto's tight cluster.

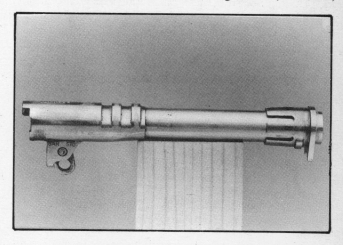

My .38 Super Bar-Sto barrel dates from the days when Stoney used to employ the collet-type bushing. The current pattern of National Match bushings will group as well, he says, meanwhile with fewer dings.

manage to isolate one lone Super Vel case that mikes .898-inch, pretty close.

Probing with the depth gauge end of the vernier calipers turned up some curious information. The ledge at the front of the chamber of the original Colt barrel has a considerable amount of taper, making it nearly impossible to verify its location. The ledge of the Bar-Sto chamber is neatly square, readily measured at perzackly .900-inch ahead of the rear face of the barrel shroud; the point that is theoretically flush with the head of the chambered case.

It is a singular feature of M1911 barrels for the .38 CS cartridge that they have a tiny ledge about .050-inch ahead of the rear face of the barrel shroud to accommodate that vestigial rim of the cartridge. Being truly rimless, neither the .45 ACP nor 9mm Luger barrels have that feature. The rim of the .38 CS case is .050-inch thick, according to the dimensional drawings.

Exploratory checks with the case that is only .002-inch under specified length turned up some intriguing data. Hook it on the shroud ledge of the Bar-Sto barrel, push gently to let it slide off and it would stop with the case mouth against the chamber ledge up front, after all but undetectable movement. Try the same experiment on the Colt barrel and, after sliding off the shroud ledge, it wouldn't come to rest again until the head was about .065-inch ahead of the rear face of the barrel shroud.

True, the chambered case in the Colt barrel probably derives its major support from the extractor as do most, if not all cartridges, in the .45 ACP and 9mm Luger.

Not all the barrels that start down the production line at Bar-Sto meet the final spec's with impeccable credentials, which is to say they have some amount of rejects. At one time, Stone used to contour such rejects and offer them as chambering gauges. I have one example of those, in .45 ACP, and would not consider any sensible offer to part

with it, since I find it addictively convenient when setting my seating die for turning out a run of .45 ACP.

Along the way, Stone has stopped offering the chambering gauges, which I regard as a great pity. Initially, the Bar-Sto barrels were produced with a collet-type barrel bushing more or less similar to the one Colt introduced in their Mk IV '70 Series. Bar-Sto could, would and did furnish barrels for the Colt Commander with collet-type bushings, unmindful of the fact that Colt had said such things were impossible.

Once fitted, a collet-type bushing is not designed to come off the end of its barrel, nor is it supposed to be thus removed. If you manage to muster sufficient savage effort to wrench them free of the muzzle, it's quite likely you'll

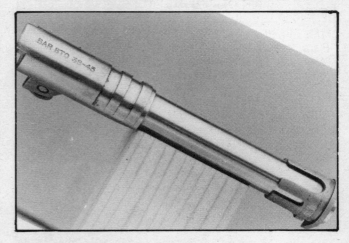

Bar-Sto barrel for the .38/45 Clerke wildcat round — the .45 ACP case necked to take .355-inch bullets — still has the older collet-type bushing.

Current Bar-Sto markings, as on this Government Model 9mm, are visible in the ejection port when installed. You'll perhaps note it says Bar-Sto here and Bar Sto (no hyphen) on the one on the facing page.

break off one of the exquisitely dimensioned fingers in so doing. Customers kept sending back bushings with busted collet fingers and finally, some little while ago, they ruptured Stoney's sunny patience to the point where he decreed Bar-Sto barrels would be furnished with the earlier National Match-type barrel bushings henceforth and hereafter.

Now the NM bushing is no pathetic slouch, performancewise and the latterday Bar-Sto barrels aren't all that seriously hamstrung, as we'll see in just a bit. I can't help contemplating all this, however, in terms of friend Kar-

wan's comments on collectibles, back in Chapter 14. If you happen to own a Bar-Sto barrel with a collet-type bushing up front, you possess an indubitable collector item that will never be made again. Cherish it, use it with due awareness of its unique value and barter it not lightly!

Smith & Wesson made quite a goodly slew of the Model 39 and the later Model 59, with its staggered-column magazine, with a few numerically-suffixed updates. Then they brought forth their 439 and 459, still with frames of aluminum alloy, but with adjustable rear sights and assorted other good stuff. Then they came up with the Models 539 and 559, with all the prior goodies, plus a receiver of handsomely blued steel. The final variation — to date, at least — is the 600 series: Models 639 and 659, made of stainless steel. There are changes over and beyond the metal used in the frame. Internal parts are redesigned and modified to some extent, as well. Thus, a 559 is not simply a steel-framed Model 59.

I managed to get hands upon a Model 539 in the summer of 1982, along with a Model 39-2. It was about the time Stone had commenced to produce Bar-Sto barrels for the S&W autos and I got the 539 out to him to be fitted with one.

Prior to that, I ran a test session to compare the 539 and 39-2 in their original states. The 39-2 was well broken in and enjoying the prime of its career while the 539 still had its fresh-from-the-box stiffness. I have fired other Model 39s, but none that grouped as well or cycled with the smooth reliability this one displayed. Even so, it was a standoff between them.

When the 539 made its way back from the Bar-Sto shop, bearing its handfitted stainless barrel, I removed the stock

The so-called "Robot Pistolero," a movable, scope-aimed base for the Ransom Rest, atop the portable shooting bench, M539 mounted.

Another view of the Robot Pistolero, providing further construction details. A Weaver mount rail is held to upper edge of vertical plank with sheet metal screws and Weaver rings hold the 4X Lyman scope. Up front, two short pieces of one-inch hardwood dowel serve as feet and, centered at the rear is a length of ⅜-16 threaded rod, topped by a hex nut and wing nut, jam-tightened to serve as elevation adjustment knob.

slabs and installed it in the Ransom Rest. The details of that setup are illustrated nearby. It's on a small portable base that has a four-power rifle scope attached to the upper edge of the vertical member. The Ransom Rest has their accessory windage base so as to permit the installed gun to be harmonized with the scope. Once you get aim and impact fairly close, the fine tuning is completed by means of the internal adjustments in the scope turret.

I call that the Robot Pistolero, for want of a better term. As inventions go, it is strictly a child of necessity. There is no provision for a proper concrete anchoring base to hold the Ransom Rest where I do most of my shooting. I lifted a leaf from the late Bill Corson's notebook and built myself a Ransom Rest base that can be anchored quite convincingly by running one of the front wheels of my old Buick onto its horizontal base plank. That works fairly well but (1) it takes up a gross amount of space in the car to haul it and (2) when in use, the sound waves reflecting off the fender leave you in a state of third-degree shell shock after just a few rounds, even if you're wearing the earmuffs. For those reasons, I do not use the big base all that frequently.

The RP base, on the other hand, is a joy and a delight. A heavy-frame .357 magnum revolver is about the limit of its capacity, however. Anything larger than that causes severe movement of the whole assembly, reducing any pretense of accuracy to stark hilarity.

The Bar-Sto-barreled Model 539 took to the Robot Pistolero like a happy baby duckling to a placid pond. After a few shots and minor adjustments at twenty-five yards, I walked the target on out to a generous fifty yards and a bit on beyond that, determined to put the new rig to the acid test.

The load that performed the best was 6.7 grains of Hercules Herco powder behind the 88-grain Speer JHP bullet — Speer's catalog number 4000 — which printed five into just 1.694 inches between centers, extreme spread, at the distance of fifty-plus yards.

True, that's not apt to trigger an imsomnia epidemic among the benchrest rifle shooters, but it's respectable by common handgun standards and it's the tightest group I've gotten out of the 9mm Luger cartridge to the present.

My trusty chronograph happened to be down with the

Here's Stoney at his bench in the old shop at Burbank, daintily stoning away a bit of metal here, another wisp there in the handfitting operation he does so well. If you do something thousands and thousands of times, it gets easy, he says.

feebles at the time of that session so I was unable to clock the quoted load and Speer does not list Herco in their current 9mm tables. Extrapolating with crossed fingers, I'd say it was in the low 1400 fps brackets, at which pace the 88-grain JHP gets notably boisterous upon impact.

Given a load obviously capable of impressive performance, the next logical step was to take it out of the rest, reinstall the stocks and see how it performed in the hand, off the sandbag rest. Candidly, it was somewhat disappointing. With the target brought back in to the twenty-five yard distance, I wasn't able to duplicate the Ransom's fifty-yard groups with that load or several others. It gave good average performance or a bit better, but nothing all that supernatural.

I no longer have that particular pistol. It was, as noted, in the summer of 1982; a bleak time for California handgunners. A proposed initiative called Propostion 15 was up for the November ballot and anything beyond a single handgun purchased in that calendar year was scheduled to be confiscated without reimbursement, provided Prop-15 went through. The prospects of defeating it didn't look all that bright as the summer went along and I couldn't bear to contemplate the prospect of such a nice pistol being recycled into beer bottle caps or suchlike.

I had a friend and shooting buddy who didn't own gun number one at the time, so I let him pay the asking tab and take over its ownership on his guarantee to give it a good home. As it all turned out, Proposition 15 was rejected by a thumping margin and I stopped sweating out two or three other guns I'd bought earlier that year before the initiative reared its scaly head at us. In the meantime, the notable pistol's new owner is happier than a pup with a bedroom slipper flavored to taste like postman's ankle and I wish him much joy with it.

Any auto pistol capable of holding within less than two

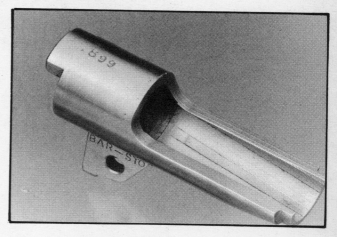

No longer available, these super-handy little gauges were made from rejected Bar-Sto barrels at one time.

inches of spread at fifty yards can be justifiably termed uhh "tackurate" — words coined and juleps minted while you wait — even if it requires the assistance of the nerveless Ransom Rest to bring it off. Those are produced and sold by C'Arco, Box 308, Highland, CA 92346, under the guidance of Chuck and Joan Ransom. The basic rest with one standard insert lists at $245; another $105 for the windage base and standard inserts are $32.50 for all the popular autos and revolvers. Special-order inserts for the T/C Contender, High Standard Crusader and Dan Wesson Revolvers are $40 per set. Prices subject to change, F.O.B. the factory, and California residents add six percent sales tax.

The Robot Pistolero base is a simple project, given moderate skill and a few tools. The base and upright are of

A typical, underlength .45 ACP case in the Bar-Sto chamber gauge doesn't quite come flush with the barrel shroud.

Chamber gauge is cut for perfect fit with .899-inch cases and rifling leade will indicate if bullet seating depth is correct.

nominal two-inch plank, butt-glued and carrying a removable diagonal brace at the rear. Up front, on the lower surface of the base, there are two short pieces of one-inch hardwood dowel to serve as feet and minimize rocking about. Centered between them, at the lower rear, a length of ⅜-16 threaded rod can be turned up or down to provide fine adjustment of the elevation. It passes through a little hardware fitting called a Tee-Nut, installed on the lower surface to put steel threads in the wood of the plank.

In use, the RP base is placed on the portable shooting bench — a remarkably steady platform — and shifted right/left by hand until the vertical crosshair of the scope reticle aligns with the intended aiming point. At that point, the knob atop the elevation screw is turned to line it up the other way and when all is dead-on, as viewed through the scope, the trigger-tripper on the Ransom Rest is pressed gently until the shot is fired. Magazines of auto pistols can be used in the usual manner and that approach seems to give tighter groups than chambering each round singly, by hand.

A long Weaver scope base is secured to the upper edge of the side piece by means of four fairly long sheet metal screws, about size 8x1½, as I recall, with the scope — an old Lyman Perma-Center, vintage about 1958 — held in place by Weaver rings.

Some time soon, I plan to make up and install a footpiece at the lower end of the elevation screw to spread the slam over a broader area. I'm also trying to figure out how to rig an accessory trigger release that will operate by pressure on a standard cable release for cameras as an alternative to the trigger lever supplied.

By taking most of the human factor out of the equation, such a setup enables the performance of some fairly impressive shooting at distances usually considered far beyond effective handgun range. Once the scope is all lined up and ready, you could shift your eye to a separate spotting scope, press the cable release and watch the bullet strike. All the sampling to date indicates it's a most intriguing pursuit. I only wish I had more time away from the typewriter to explore it further.

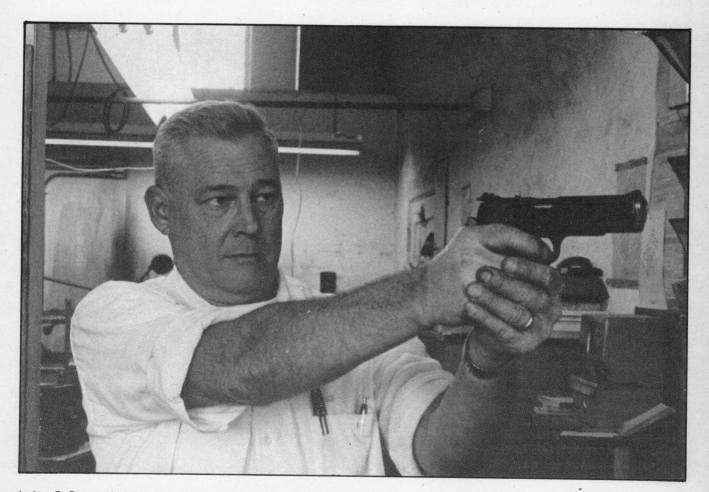

Irving O. Stone, Jr., checking the trigger pull of one of the guns going through his shop in the Burbank days. As noted, Bar-Sto barrels can now be had for the M1911 Colts, Browning Hi-Powers or S&W 9mm autos. It is, in my humble opinion, one of the most effective steps in upgrading performance, especially if handfitted.

CHAPTER 19

ROUTINE CARE AND MAINTENANCE OF AUTO PISTOLS

Proper Procedure Commences Before You Fire The First Shot From A New Gun!

Cleaning rods, bronze brushes, cleaning solvents, lubricants and similar supplies are among the things you need to perform the basic maintenance as discussed here. Hoppe's #9 Powder Solvent is just that: a solvent, and it can attack nickel plating, if employed incautiously. It is neither a rust preventive, nor a lubricant.

As discussed below and elsewhere, take great caution when removing the recoil spring plug of the M1911 to prevent losing the plug and, perhaps even worse, to avoid having to get loose and pot you in the eye.

Note: Claud S. Hamilton gives us his thoughts and comments on this timely topic and, in editing it for use here, I found myself in close general agreement with nearly all his modus operandi. He does not mention one step in prefiring inspection I've long come to regard as utterly mandatory, particularly before firing a new gun for the first time. That consists of first making certain there is no loaded ammunition in the magazine or chamber, removing the magazine — if any — and then taking a thoughtful look down the bore to check for any impediment to the bullet's flight that may be present.

That simple but vital routine has enabled me to spot one instance where a bullet was lodged in the bore, an inch or so up from the chamber. By skirting around the potential disaster on that single instance, I figure the small amount of time it takes is amply compensated.

As a usual rule, I do not remove the stocks from a Model 1911 when cleaning it. The stock screws on those are rather fragile and, unless you take really exquisite care, it is awfully easy for the screwdriver blade to get off-center so as to make unsightly gouges in the nearby stock material. More, frequent removal and reinstallation of the stock screws is prone to burr the screw slots in a manner painful to contemplate.

Hamilton's warning on the hazard posed by a runaway recoil spring plug when taking the M1911 apart is quite valid and I commend it to your thoughtful attention. I tend to think of that as "pulling an Eadie." In one of Leonard Hastings Nason's books, Sgt. Eadie, a WW1 artilleryman, had to take his issue pistol apart in the uneasy darkness of No Man's Land. As he rotated the barrel bushing, the plug went sproing and hurtled away, never to be found again. Eadie was left with a useless pistol in a time and place where a reliably functioning pistol was a truly priceless asset. I think of the hapless Eadie, every time I take one of the old boomers apart. In point of fact, most of the plugs have a small lip inside to engage the end of the spring, usually restraining the plug if it should slip loose. The end of the spring is locked to the plug by turning in a clockwise direction, but don't pin total faith on even that. — DAG

AS WITH any new gun, the first thing which should be done as it comes from the factory box is to give it a good visual inspection. Look for defects or factory errors. I once saw a .41 magnum revolver that came from the factory with a .44 magnum cylinder installed. These things are rare, but they can happen.

Don't look just for mechanical things, consider also the condition of your gun. Look particularly for foreign matter, dirt, and the like, which may have gotten into the action. I bought a new Series '70/Mk IV Colt Government Model .45 some years ago and the first time I fired it at the range it "doubled" on me! That is a very unsettling experience *and* a dangerous one; you cannot control the shots after the first one and the recoil is enough to nearly tear the gun from your hand. I disassembled the pistol afterward and discovered a blob of nearly-solidified gun grease engulfing the sear. I washed that out and never had another problem with the gun.

Over the years I have made a set of informal rules to guide me in my dealings with pistols; they are:

1. Treat every pistol like a piece of fine, precision machinery.

2. Never, never force things. If the mechanical function is not as you think it ought to be, stop and see if you can discover why.

3. Do not overdo cleaning and disassembly. Do not snap a pistol on an empty chamber, and do not open and close the slide excessively. When dry firing and opening the action, insert a fired case in the chamber to take up part of the shock.

4. Never leave pistol magazines loaded unless a gun is needed for security purposes over an extended period. When that happens, arrange to rotate magazines so that no one magazine remains loaded for more than a week without being allowed to rest.

I am sorry if this comes as a surprise, but routine care and maintenance of pistols begins before they are fired, not after! Before taking a pistol to the range, or otherwise getting one ready for possible use, there are certain minimum things I do. First, I give the gun a visual inspection, wipe off excess lubricant inside and out, and run a patch through the bore lightly saturated with Break Free CLP. This excellent cleaner contains Teflon, and I like to let some dry on the feed ramp of the barrel where it seems to aid smooth feeding. Check to be sure the bore is clear and insure that

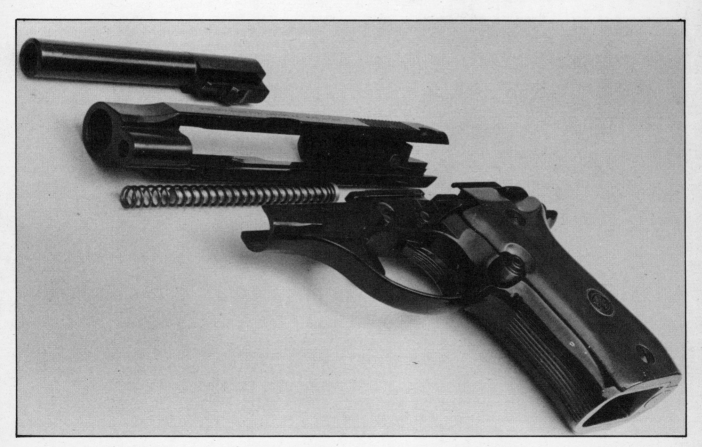

Here are the parts after field-stripping for cleaning and maintenance for the Colt Gov't. Model (top, opposite), the Walther Model PPK/S (bottom, opposite) and the Beretta Model 84, above. Take care to avoid mislaying small but vital parts and, for example, avoid stripping them over tall grass or even in a thick shag carpet!

magazines which have been successfully used in this particular pistol are on hand.

The first consideration in the care of semi-automatic pistols is their disassembly; all must be dissassembled, at least to some degree, to be properly cleaned and maintained.

All pistols of which I am aware have three main parts:

— A receiver, which contains the grips, the lock work for firing, and receives the magazine which supplies the ammunition.

— A barrel which contains the cartridge and directs the fired bullet toward the point of aim.

— A slide, which provides a breech to secure the loaded cartridge in the chamber of the barrel at the moment of firing, a firing pin to ignite the primer and an extractor to remove the spent case from the chamber after firing.

I once made up this matched set of K-Spinners with mahogany holding rack and bestowed it upon friend Hamilton, who finds it handy for case polishing and similar chores. The Happich's Simichrome polish works extremely well for polishing brass or nickel.

These three main parts vary widely in size among different types of pistols. At one extreme you have the Luger in which the slide consists of no more than a small breech block moving back and forth in a channel cut in the upper receiver/barrel combination. In the medium range are found pistols like the Walther P-38 and Berettas in which the slide attaches to rails on the upper part of the receiver, but provides little or no contact with the barrel forward of the breech. Finally, there are the heavy Browning designs such as the 1911 Colt, the Model of 1935 and the modern S&W 9mms in which the slide is longer than the receiver and supports the barrel at the muzzle as well as at the breech.

The best way to go about pistol disassembly is to carefully follow the instruction booklet usually provided by the maker. If the arm comes to you second-hand, the maker will usually be glad to supply a copy of the manual in response to a mail request. Other useful books to have are *Firearms Assembly II — The NRA Guidebook to Hand-*

guns which shows exploded views of many arms and *The Gun Digest Book of Firearms Assembly/Disassembly, Part I, Automatic Pistols,* which details in photos how to take-down and reassemble forty-one of the most popular autoloaders.

COLT GOVERNMENT MODEL .45 ACP (Factory Model 0-45) (Model 1911A1)

Depress magazine release catch and withdraw magazine.

Draw back slide and verify that the chamber is empty (these two steps apply to the disassembly of *any* and *all* pistols).

Cock the pistol and lock the safety catch. This locks the slide, barrel and receiver together as a unit and makes the next step easier and safer.

Depress the recoil spring plug beneath the barrel enough to permit the barrel bushing to be rotated to the right (clockwise) enough to clear the plug. *(Be extremely careful. The plug is under considerable pressure and can be quite dangerous if shot out into one's eye!)* Remove the plug releasing pressure on the recoil spring.

Release the thumb safety and draw the slide slowly rearward until the relief cut lines up with the rear of the slide latch. The latch pin can then be pushed through from the right side of the pistol and removed. Slide and barrel can then be moved forward and off the receiver rails easily.

Remove the recoil spring and guide from the rear. Turn barrel bushing to the left (counterclockwise) until its lug clears and it can be drawn forward out of the slide. Pivot the recoil link forward before removing the barrel. The

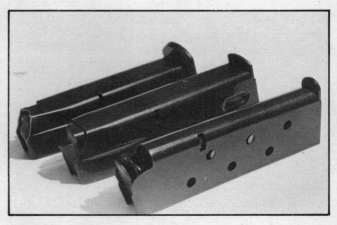

Magazines for the various makes and models of auto pistols require their share of maintenance, also.

barrel can then be tilted free of the locking lug grooves and withdrawn through the front of the slide. As a final step, remove stock screws and stocks. This is as far as the owner should disassemble the gun for care and cleaning. Have a gunsmith do anything more. Assembly is essentially a reverse of these steps.

The Walther P'38, field-stripped for maintenance.

WALTHER PP, PPK and PPK/S PISTOLS, CALIBER .32 ACP AND .380 ACP

Once again, the first step is to depress the magazine release and remove the magazine. Open the action and verify that no cartridge is in the chamber.

Reinsert the empty magazine. Pull the trigger guard downward and push to the left. Draw the slide back with a lifting motion until the rear end clears the rails on the receiver. Ease the slide forward over the barrel mounting and off the receiver. Loosen stock screws and remove stocks. Do not attempt to remove barrel as that is a factory operation. To reassemble, reverse these steps.

BERETTA MODEL 84, .380 AUTO PISTOL

Remove magazine by depressing release button; check to be sure the chamber is empty.

Holding pistol in left hand, depress dissassembly latch release button with left forefinger. (The button is located just above the trigger on left side of the frame.)

With the right thumb, rotate the dissassembly latch counterclockwise until it stops. (Latch is located on right side of frame just above the trigger guard.)

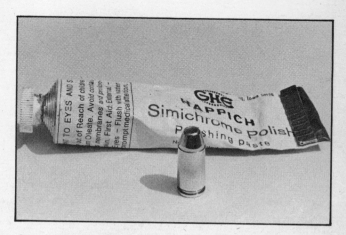

Simichrome polish is sold by Brownell's and can be found in most motorcycle shops. Lacking it, the chrome cleaners sold for automobiles work well.

From the makers of RIG 3 degreaser comes a new product, +P Stainless Steel Lube, the best stuff yet to prevent galling on surfaces of that material. Below, the Pin Pal is a handy little device for disassembling the M1911 autos. You can get one from: Pin Pal, 1626 Wilcox, Suite 636, Hollywood, CA 90028. It's in use on opposite page.

Pull slide and barrel forward off the receiver rails.

Using care, depress the recoil spring slightly under barrel then lift it free and carefully allow it to lengthen and relax. The barrel can now be removed from the slide. No further disassembly should be undertaken except by a capable gunsmith. Do no attempt to remove the stocks from these pistols unless you have the exceptionally fine-bladed screwdriver required.

WALTHER P'38 9mm PISTOL

Pull slide back to the fully open position. If the magazine is empty the slide will be latched open. Remove the empty magazine and turn safety catch to safe.

Turn down the slide lock lever at the front of the receiver on the left side just above the trigger guard.

Keeping slide and receiver under control in both hands, turn down the slide catch allowing slide and barrel to move forward. Depress trigger and slide, barrel may be removed from the receiver rails.

Invert the barrel and slide and push the bright metal locking plunger to disengage the barrel lock. Barrel may then be separated from the slide. Remove grip screw so cleaning may be accomplished. Reverse the process for reassembly.

Now, a few words about routine cleaning after firing. I will admit that I do not normally disassemble a pistol after firing these days. Rather, I remove the grips and magazine, open the slide and clean the barrel carefully using Hoppe's

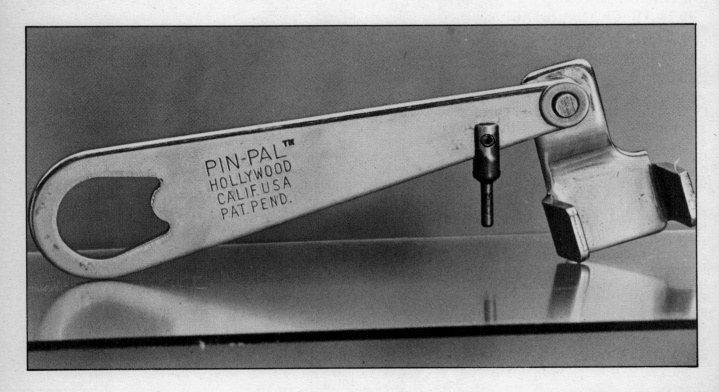

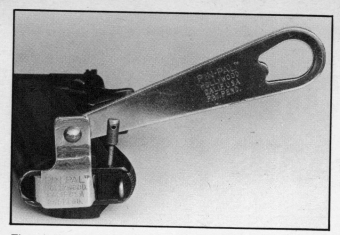

The two lugs are inserted into the magazine well to position the tip of the punch over the mainspring housing pin and a simple push drives that loose.

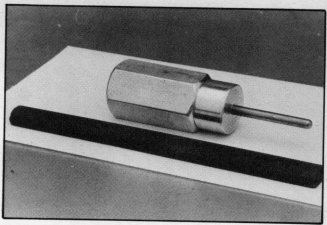

Here's the half-round India stone that's seen over four decades of grateful use; above it, a homemade tool consisting of an alumnum handle with a piece of brass rod for driving out the housing pin and a number of similar chores like removing firing pin.

No. 9 solvent. I don't use the brass brush unless I detect residue in the tube after a good wipe dry. If there appears to be combustion products in the breech area, I usually wash out the whole gun liberally using Gun Scrubber. As the excess drains off, the remainder quickly evaporates, and it is then important to saturate the arm thoroughly with an aerosol oil, such as Sheath.

If by some chance you happen to have fired corrosive primed ammunition, then it becomes necessary to go a step farther and clean the slide and receiver with Hoppe's No. 9, wherever combustion products are found. Don't forget, however, to remove all the Hoppe's No. 9 from all nickel or other plated surfaces. Hoppe's will attack the plating in time and ruin it.

Gun storage is a problem that sooner or later faces us all. Before I put a gun in storage where I am reasonably sure that I will not be able to get at it for maintenance in a year or so, I like to give it a more thorough cleaning than usual. I finish up not with Sheath but with a good grade gun grease. Then I wrap the gun, grips removed, in two plastic "baggie" food storage bags and place this in a fleece-lined "gun rug". I find that the "baggies" slow the evaporation of the rust preventive grease, and protect against the tendency of the gun rug to hold moisture.

Though I did not list them among the three main parts of pistols, there are two other elements which are essential, and which require special care: the magazine and the ammunition.

Pistol magazines come in as many shapes and sizes as there are pistols; I know of none that are interchangeable between different guns. Magazines are perhaps the most delicate parts of pistols. They consist of a tube of stamped metal shaped to control the movement of cartridges upward and present them one after the other in correct attitude for loading. Magazines must be kept clean inside and out. I wash them out thoroughly, when empty, using

Gun Scrubber and follow that with a coat of Sheath as a lube and rust preventive. Magazines vary a great deal in quality, and some can be disassembled for cleaning. Since all tend to be delicate and easily bent and damaged, I don't go the disassembly route. Watch out for dents to the magazine tube. These can hamper the upward flow of the cartridges or the follower and cause feeding failures. Take special precautions to protect the lips of your magazines. These control the way the cartridge is presented for loading, and they have to be just right or jams will result. Finally, I recommend that magazines not be left loaded for extended periods of time. The quality of the spring steels used varies greatly. I have heard of magazines left loaded for years that worked well, but my own experience has been just the opposite. I have pulled many a .45 M1911 magazine out of a guard room drawer and found it still loaded but with a dead spring, and wondered what the sergeant of the guard would have done had he ever had to draw his pistol on duty!

Some may find it strange that I speak of care and maintenance for ammunition, but it is certainly needed. Ammunition should be kept under lock in a cool, dry place where there is little seasonal change in temperature. Water is still ammunition's greatest enemy. I like to take a good grade of metal polish, such as Happich Simichrome available at motorcycle shops, and polish pistol cartridges to a high shine. Next, I use a small piece of crocus cloth to clean the case mouth, on which most pistol cartridges headspace, and the extractor groove. If I find a gouge or a rough place that the cloth cannot smooth out, I reject the round or empty case.

Before beginning firing at the range, I will often spray a light coat of Break Free CLP over the ammunition then wipe off all excess on a soft cloth. The remainder dries quickly and leaves a thin deposit of Teflon which seems to make feeding easier and more reliable.

FACTS, FIGURES AND ASSORTED HANDY DOPE

Being A Raft Of Incantations You Can Punch Into Your Pocket Calculator To Find Out Things You May Not Have Been Aware You Wanted To Know In The First Place*

Some gun writers of my acquaintance have $3000 to $5000 or more invested in computers, word processors and other sophisticated gadgetry. For my needs (and talents), the Sharp Model EL-5100 scientific calculator is entirely adequate. It can be programmed with up to five equations and will give the answers to bullet energy problems, for example, with only a few touches of the keys. It's compact, the original set of batteries are holding up well after two years of hard use and it only cost about $64! It is by no means necessary to go that far: A simple $10 calculator will handle everything covered here.

INCOMING MAIL brings questions from readers of the magazine that employs me, as well as from readers of the various books I've written. I try to reply to such inquiries, provided I can find the answer and also provided I can steal time at the typewriter before the letter gets lost in the churning ferment of paperwork. Quite a number of such inquiries concern loading data or fairly elementary ballistics. By way of enlightened self-interest, I like to include a chapter providing basic information to enable the reader to work out the answers to at least some of those questions, thereby bilking the postal service of small amounts of revenue.

*Such things run fourteen to the raft, fifty-three to the slew and 157 to the scad.

KINETIC ENERGY/MOMENTUM

It's customary to quote bullet velocity in feet per second (fps), or meters per second (mps) in the metric system. The customary unit of weight is the grain or its metric counterpart, the gram. Here are the conversion factors for changing the units back and forth:

$$\text{fps} \times .3048007 = \text{mps}$$
$$\text{mps} \times 3.2808321 = \text{fps}$$
$$\text{fps} \times .68181818(...) = \text{miles per hour (mph)}$$
$$\text{mph} \times 1.4666(...) = \text{fps}$$
$$\text{mph} \times 1.6093419 = \text{kilometers per hour (kph)}$$
$$\text{kph} \times .6213327 = \text{mph}$$

Before discussing units of weight, let's specify we're dealing with the avoirdupois system, not the troy system nor the apothecary system. Avoirdupois is the familiar scale by which one buys a pound of butter, sugar or shingle nails.

The grain is the customary weight unit used in reloading or discussing bullets. There are seven thousand grains in one avoirdupois pound and 437.5 grains in one avoirdupois ounce. Curiously enough, the grain seems to be a constant weight that carries over unchanged into both the troy and apothecary systems.

The grain relates to the gram as follows and I'll include the other weight conversions, as well:

grains x .0647989 = grams
grams x 15.43236 = grains
pounds x .4535924 = kilograms
kilograms x 2.2046224 = pounds
grams x .0352739 = ounces
ounces x 28.349527 = grams

The customary units of kinetic energy is the foot-pounds of energy (fpe) and the kilogram-meter (kgm). Here's how they compare:

fpe x .1383 = kgm
kgm x 7.233 = fpe

Given the velocity of a moving body — projectile, in the current instance — in feet per second and its weight in grains, momentum is calculated by multiplying the velocity times the weight and dividing the product by 225,200. Thus, as an example, a 230-grain bullet at 850 fps has a momentum of:

230 x 850 = 195,5000 ÷ 225,200 = .868117229

or .87, rounded off.

The primary emphasis upon momentum is among silhouette shooters intent on toppling the massive steel rams at the two-hundred-meter distance. Most other discussions focus upon the kinetic energy as given in fpe.

For convenience and clarity, let's use the following abbreviations or symbols in discussing the equations:

V = velocity in fps
W = projectile weight in grains
E = kinetic energy in fpe

G = constant for gravity, in feet per second per second (fpsps)

The basic equation for calculating E, with V and W given, is velocity squared, divided by 7000 (the number of grains in one pound), divided by $2G$, times W, equals E.

We have come up to to a minor problem and there is no easy way around it. I refer to the value for G. Traditionally, 32.16 fpsps is the figure given in physics texts and similar sources. Gravity is not a uniform force across the entire planetary surface. It varies with altitude and latitude as well as with composition of the planetary crust underfoot, although the last factor has the least effect. Starting from

the north pole and moving south — or vice versa — it's obvious that, as you approach the equator, the effect of centrifugal force from the rotation of the planet will have a slight counteracting effect upon gravitic attraction. Increase the distance above sea level and you increase the centrifugal force slightly, meanwhile getting farther from the center of the planetary mass.

International standards currently assign a value for G of 32.1740 fpsps, based upon sea level standard at forty-five degrees latitude.

At present, two other values are in use as components of what is termed the *ballistic atmosphere*. They are known as Standard Meteorological Conditions — Standard Metro for short — and the International Civil Aviation Organization standard, or ICAO.

Standard Metro assumes G to be 32.1522, while the ICAO value for G is 32.1741 fpsps.

I will note that, throughout this book and others, I've used 32.16 as the value of G. I have reasons I consider valid. If you multiply 32.16 times two, you get 64.32 as the value for $2G$ and that times 7000 gives you a nice even number: 450,240. Let us assign a handy symbolic abbreviation to that and henceforth term it F; short for foom-factor.

The compelling charm of using F is that you merely need to go velocity-times-velocity, dividing that by F and going on to multiply the quotient by W to arrive at the value for E, saving a useful amount of scratch-paper or key-punching in the process.

The corresponding value for F, in the other three systems mentioned, is:

International standard — 450,436
Standard metro — 450,130.8
ICAO — 450,437.4

So okay-already: With all that finespun nitpickery duly noted let us work an example and find out just how much difference it makes which one is used. Let's hark back to our 230-grain bullet traveling at 850 fps. Rounded to the nearest whole number, the value for E is:

Physics textbook standard — 369
International standard — 369
Standard Metro — 369
ICAO — 369

I trust you see what I mean? It doesn't make all that frothy-much difference unless you're hellbent on establishing the foot-poundage to a number of decimals, which is a bit silly, when you're familiar with the fairly coarse variation from shot to shot.

If you happen to be engaged in working out E for a uniform W at several different values for V, it is also a helpful simplification to make use of a further shortcut. Just divide F by W. In the example cited, we can divide 450,-240 by 230 to come up with the custom-tailored foom-factor for 230-grain bullets: 1957.565217 in the long version. Let's see how that works out.

Square the velocity:

850 x 850 = 722,500

722,500 ÷ 1957.565217 = 369.0809346

Yes, we're still awfully close to the same answer obtained via all the tortuous roundaboutery discussed earlier; close enough for government work, you might say.

There may be times when you wish to determine the bullet weight to deliver a desired amount of fpe, with the velocity known. Conversely, you may want to know the velocity required to obtain — for example — 480 fpe with a 230-grain bullet.

For the example just given, divide 480 (E) by 230 (W), to obtain the quotient of 2.086956522; multiply that by 450,240 (F) to obtain the product of 939,631.3043; take the square root of that, which comes out to 969.3458126 (fps/V) or so.

Let's check that: Squaring the final answer, quite naturally, gives us the same 939,631.3043 we had a moment ago and that divided by 450,240 gives us 2.086956522 which, multiplied by 230 (grains/B) gives us a nice, precise 480.00; our specified kinetic energy.

If you work that on a pocket calculator, it is necessary to enclose the calculations in parentheses or brackets in the following manner:

$$\sqrt{[(E \div W) \times 450,240]} = V$$

You also need parentheses or brackets to get the right answer out of most pocket calculators for the other example: Figure the value for W, given V and E:

$$E \div (V^2 \div 450,240) = W$$

As an illustration, what bullet weight is required to deliver 327 fpe at a velocity of 1228 fps?

Square the velocity: 1228 x 1228 = 1,507,984;

1,507,984 ÷ 450,240 = 3.349289268

327 (fpe/E) ÷ 3.349289268 = 97.63265393 (grains/W)

Running that rather improbably precise bullet weight back through our original equation gives an answer of 327.0000000 fpe. Closer than that, you can't hardly get and it's my sole excuse for the show-offy prolixity of decimals. They pose no added effort on the pocket calculators, and they make the answers come out even. In normal use, I press the TAB key, then the zero key, which programs the calculator to round-off to the nearest whole number for a useful and realistic saving of time.

VOLUME AND DENSITY FOR SPECIFIC GRAVITY

Recently, as may be discussed and illustrated in Chapter 13, I had occasion to make up some life-size pilot models of bullets on the lathe. A local friend who makes bullets commercially had a supplier who'd undertake to produce custom moulds, given a full-scale model in steel. Creating the prototypes was absorbing fun. I didn't bother even making a rough sketch, let alone a dimensional drawing. I'd just chuck a bar of cold-rolled steel in the headstock, pare it down to the suitable diameter and sculpture it to shape, freehand.

As there was a length delay before the moulds came back — about ninety days — it was desirable to form a close estimate of the weight of the given design when cast in lead or typical bullet alloys. Dividing the specific gravity of lead — about 11.34 — by that of steel — 7.8 — gave a conversion factor of 1.454 for purposes of estimation. Merely weigh the prototype on the reloader's scale, multiply its weight by 1.454 and it gave a plausible prediction for the weight of the resulting cast bullet.

We have the first two moulds back — the two designs in 9mm — and their weights come out quite close to the estimates. In cutting the cherry to make the moulds, the maker took a bit of artistic license with the original designs, so it's hard to say if the factor would have been dead-on, had the moulds fitted the prototype a bit more closely.

Chemistry textbooks and similar sources carry tables termed periodic charts of the elements which list several figures for each of the elements. Although specific gravity is the common term, they usually call the same thing density. Likewise listed is the atomic weight for the element and it should be noted the correlation between atomic weight and density is rather casual, as a few spot checks quickly prove. Density — or specific gravity — is a comparison of the weight of a given volume of the substance with the weight of an equal volume of water. The density of a gas is in comparison with air.

It is moderately difficult to find a precise figure for the density of water. The usual assumption is that a cubic foot of water weighs 62.5 pounds. With a bit of roundabout calculation, it may be possible to shave that a trifle finer.

As it happens, the metric system puts a rock-solid decree on the weight of a specific volume of water. One cubic centimeter (cc) aka milliliter (ml) of pure water, at a temperature of 4°Celsius/Centigrade — 39.2°Fahrenheit — at sea-level altitude weighs exactly one gram, *by definition*. One thousand cc/ml of water is one liter of water and it weighs one kilogram (kg); still assuming the same temperature which, incidentally, is the temperature at which water achieves its greatest density.

The relevant conversion factors are:

cubic centimeters x .0610234 = cubic inches
cubic inches x 16.387156 = cubic centimeters
grams x 15.43236 = grains
grains x .0647989 = grams

Thus it becomes a simple matter to punch the calculator keys and find that one cubic inch of water weighs 16.387156 grams or 252.8924908 grains.

There are 437.5 grains in one ounce, 7000 grains in one pound, so it works out a cubic inch of water weighs .578039978 ounce or .036127498 pound. As there are 1728 cubic inches in one cubic foot, simple multiplication gives us 62.42831773 pounds as the weight of one cubic foot of water — *still at 39.2°F and sea-level altitude*.

According to Homer S. Powley, one cubic inch of lead weighs 2870 grains, or 6.56 ounces, or .41 pound and the last figure, times 1728 gives us 708.48 pounds as the weight of one cubic foot of lead. That, divided in turn by 62.42831773, produces 11.34869601 as a tentative figure for the density/specific gravity of lead, via that slightly maverick system. Usually, it's cited as a slightly larger

PROPERTIES OF THE METALLIC ELEMENTS

Element	Chemical Symbol	Atomic Number	Melting Point °C	Melting Point °F	Density (Specific Gravity)
Aluminum	Al	13	660	1220	2.70
Antimony	Sb	51	630.5	1166.9	6.62
Arsenic	As	33	817	1502.6	5.72
Barium	Ba	56	714	1317.2	3.5
Beryllium	Be	4	1277	2330.6	1.85
Bismuth	Bi	83	271.3	520.3	9.8
Cadmium	Cd	48	320.9	609.6	8.65
Calcium	Ca	20	838	1504.4	1.55
Cerium	Ce	58	795	1463	6.67
Chromium	Cr	24	1875	3407	7.19
Cobalt	Co	27	1495	2723	8.9
Copper	Cu	28	1087	1988.6	8.96
Gallium	Ga	31	29.8	85.6	5.91
Germanium	Ge	32	937.4	1719.3	5.32
Gold	Au	79	1063	1945.4	19.3
Iridium	Ir	77	2454	4449.2	22.5
Iron	Fe	26	1536	2796.8	7.86
Lanthanum	La	57	920	1688	6.17
Lead	Pb	82	327.4	621.3	11.4
Lithium	Li	3	108.5	227.3	.53
Magnesium	Mg	12	650	1202	1.74
Manganese	Mn	25	1345	2453	7.43
Mercury	Hg	80	-38.4	-37.1	13.6
Molybdenum	Mb	42	2610	4730	10.2
Neodymium	Nd	60	1024	1875.2	7.00
Nickel	Ni	28	1453	2647.4	8.9
Niobium	Nb	41	2415	4379	8.4
Osmium	Os	76	2700	4892	22.6
Palladium	Pd	46	1552	2825.6	12.0
Platinum	Pt	78	1769	3216.2	21.4
Potassium	K	19	63.7	146.7	.86
Praesodymium	Pr	59	935	1715	6.77
Rhodium	Rh	45	1966	3570.8	12.4
Rubidium	Rb	37	38.9	102	1.53
Ruthenium	Ru	44	2500	4532	12.2
Samarium	Sm	62	1072	1961.6	7.54
Scandium	Sc	21	1539	2802.2	3.0
Selenium	Se	34	217	422.6	4.79
Silver	Ag	47	960.8	1761.4	10.5
Sodium	Na	11	97.8	208	.97
Strontium	Sr	38	768	1414.4	2.6
Tantalum	Ta	73	2996	5424.8	16.6
Tellurium	Te	52	449.5	841.1	6.24
Thallium	Tl	81	303	577.4	11.85
Thorium	Th	90	1750	3182	11.7
Tin	Sn	50	231.9	449.4	7.3
Titanium	Ti	22	1668	3034.4	4.51
Tungsten (see Wolfram)					
Uranium	U	92	1132	2069.6	19.07
Vanadium	V	23	1900	3452	6.1
Wolfram	W	74	3410	6170	19.3
Ytterbium	Yb	70	824	1515.2	6.98
Yttrium	Y	39	1509	2748.2	4.47
Zinc	Zn	30	419.5	787.1	7.14
Zirconium	Zr	40	1852	3365.6	6.49

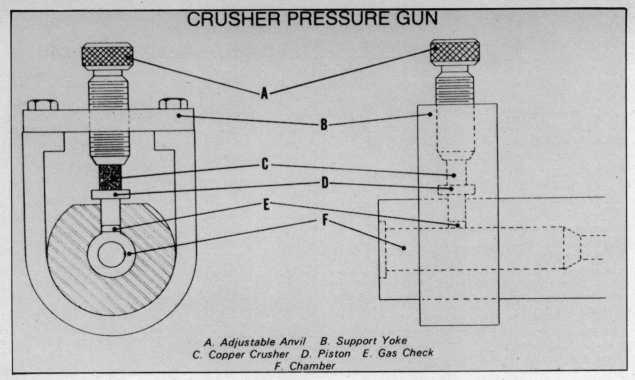

CRUSHER PRESSURE GUN

A. Adjustable Anvil   B. Support Yoke
C. Copper Crusher   D. Piston   E. Gas Check
F. Chamber

This illustration of the layout of a crusher pressure gun, as used for measuring peak pressures in a given load for a given cartridge appeared originally on page 557 of the tenth edition of the Speer Manual and it is reproduced here by the friendly courtesy of Omark/CCI-Speer, et al. C is the copper cylinder that is shortened by pressure.

number, such as 11.37 or sometimes 11.4 and other numbers in the nearby neighborhood. Presumably, they use warmer water as their standard for such things. If we divide 708.48 by 62.5, we get 11.33568 for the density of lead but, as we've just seen, about 62.43 pounds is as heavy as a cubic foot of water can be expected to get.

TEMPERATURE AND MELTING POINTS

To most of us the Fahrenheit scale remains the most familiar of the systems for measuring heat or the shortage of same. What used to be called the Centigrade scale has been rechristened Celsius. The Kelvin scale is encountered much less frequently; usually in a context of the coloration of light and spectral wavelengths.

Theoretically, absolute zero is as cold as anything can get and that frigid limit is pegged at -273.15°C/-459.67°F/0°K. From that starting point, the Kelvin scale operates in standard degrees Celsius:

Celsius + 273.15 = Kelvin
Kelvin - 273.15 = Celsius

If it helps to keep track of that, recall Silent Cal, our thirtieth president and reflect that thirty degrees Kelvin is still awfully...uhh...Koolidge.

Fahrenheit and Celsius/Centigrade correlate in the following manner:

Fahrenheit - 32 x .5555(...) = Celsius
Celsius x 1.8 + 32 = Fahrenheit

In the foregoing, I've used the decimal equivalents of the two fractions often given. The fraction 9/5 works out to 1.8, even-steven, but 5/9 comes out .5555 and five to the outer city limits of the known universe, probably even beyond that; hence, the parenthetical three-dot symbol. Curiously enough, both systems intersect precisely at -40°, diverging again below that point.

It is a bit difficult to pin down melting points of metal with much pretense of precision and perhaps that accounts for modest disparities in the figures given for the melting point of this or that metal in the various reference sources. The greater the degree of purity in a metal, the higher its melting point. The melting point of an alloy cannot be readily inferred from the melting points of its constituent elements. Indeed, there are a few metallurgical anomalies, such as Wood's metal, with melting points substantially lower than *any* of their components.

In his monumental book, *Complete Guide to Handloading,* the late Phil Sharpe included a table giving the melting point of all the elements generally known at the time of its publication, along with the specific gravity of many of them. I wish I had a dime for every time I've looked something up in that table. I'm not inclined to be quite that exhaustive, but I'll include a table covering the elements deemed to be of at least marginal interest to a typical reader of the work at hand. It strikes me as unlikely any reader will attempt to cast bullets of helium, which solidifies at 6.15°K...or perhaps a trifle below that, since the quoted figure is its melting point.

Given suitable cryogenic capabilities, however, it might be possible to cast bullets in mercury, which solidifies at about -40° — F or C, it makes no nevermind. Sharpe cites the specific gravity of mercury as 13.58, at a temperature of 60°F and that's substantially denser than lead. Lead objects float if placed in a small container of mercury, a rather eerie spectacle.

Since the figures in the table may not coincide with those in other sources, I'll note I used the periodic chart appearing in the Random House Dictionary, converting the Celsius melting points to Fahrenheit via the equation given earlier.

PRESSURE

The metric unit for pressure is kilograms per square centimeter (ksc), corresponding to pounds per square inch (psi), the unit by which we inflate our tires and perform similar operations. Standard atmospheric pressure is 14.7 psi and that, times 144, works out to more than one ton per square foot; 2116.8 pounds, to be exact.

In dealing with and referring to the peak pressures developed by the products of burning powder within the chamber of a gun, it was once the custom to use psi as the unit. At some unrecalled exact date in the latter Sixties, arms and ammunition makers substituted copper units of pressure for rifle and handgun cartridges; lead units of pressure for shotgun shells. You may encounter the former abbreviated as CUP, cup, C.U.P., or c.u.p. and a similar assortment for l.u.p. In the present book, I've endeavored to stay with c.u.p. so as to avoid confusion with the useful item of chinaware customarily reposing atop a saucer.

Peak chamber pressures are measured in various ways, but always with complexities, difficulties and no small amount of expense. The usual technique is to use a vented pressure barrel such as the one illustrated on page 557 of the tenth Speer Manual. When a cartridge is chambered and fired, its case ruptures in the portion unsupported by the vent, blowing high-pressure gas up into the opening to move the gas-checked piston. That, in turn, compresses the copper crusher cylinder, reducing its length by an amount that can be measured with a micrometer.

The copper crusher cylinders usually are supplied with a table of tarage that essays reasonable pretense of making it possible to reconcile their performance in comparison to other — not necessarily identical — lots of crushers. Initially, hopeful efforts were made to interpolate and extrapolate the reduction of length in the used crusher so as to equate it to some given number of psi that was developed in firing. The complications attending that should be obvious. Hence, we had the thoroughly logical agreement to employ figures that reflect the compression of the copper cylinder, making no implication it correlates with a like number of pounds per square inch. When testing shotgun loads the pressures are somewhat lower so they use lead crusher cylinders, rather than copper, accounting for the difference in designation.

MISCELLANEOUS ITEMS

The ratio between the diameter of a circle and its circumference is 3.141592654, commonly designated by the lower-case Greek letter pi, which can be described as a pair of vertical lines with a squiggly horizontal line atop them. Diameter times pi gives circumference. Radius squared, times pi, gives the area of a circle in square inches or square centimeters, depending upon the unit used for the radius.

Divide pi by six and you get .523598775 and that, times the cube of a sphere's diameter, gives the volume of the sphere. For example, a .358-inch sphere would have a volume of slightly over .024-cubic-inch and, if composed of pure lead — 2870 grains per cubic inch, remember? — the sphere would weigh about 68.95 grains.

Measurement of time and angles — even in those countries that have embraced the icy logic of the metric system — still seem to be handled in units to the base twelve. The group dispersion of rifles and, less commonly, handguns is sometimes given in terms of the minute of angle (MOA). At a distance of one hundred yards, one MOA is a bit over one inch: 1.047197551 inches, to slice it fairly fine.

With that in hand, the value for one MOA can be given as:

.0147197551 inch for one yard
.004906585 inch for one foot
.016097682 inch for one meter
.408881920mm for one meter
25.90676880 inches for one mile
and so on and so forth.

DISTANCE

As long as we're citing metric coordinates, it would be moldy cheese to omit the basic interrelationship between the foot, the meter and suchlike. That goes:

millimeters x .03937 = inches
centimeters x .3937 = inches
meters x 3.2808321 = feet
meters x 1.0936109 = yards
kilometers x .6213327 = miles
inches x 25.40005 = millimeters
inches x 2.540005 = centimeters
inches x .0254005 = meters
feet x .3048007 = meters
yards x .914402 = meters
miles (statute) x 1.6093419 = kilometers
miles per gallon (mpg) x .4251758 = kilometers per liter (kpl)
kpl x 2.3519678 = mpg

The exact size of the meter, if you'd wondered, derives from one-fourth the vertical circumference of our native planet, Terra/Sol III. From the north pole to the equator, it's exactly ten million meters, by definition; or 10,000 kilometers, comes to that. Please don't ask if it's the same distance on down to the south pole. I've wondered about that, myself.

CHAPTER 21

HANDLING DOUBLE-ACTION AUTOS

How To Make The Most Effective Use Of This Increasingly Popular Feature

(Note: I subcontracted this discussion to my old friend and associate, Tom Ferguson and, having reviewed his thoughts and comments, feel certain I could not have handled it nearly as well. Thus, the first-person-singular for the entire chapter is Ferguson, not Grennell. —DAG)

Opposite page, Ferguson uses the Weaver stance to control recoil. Note the barrel is still level, with an ejected case in midair. Above, Walther Model PP, left, and Mauser Model HSc, both in .380 ACP.

Here and in the two photos on the opposite page, Ferguson demonstrates drawing the small DA auto from the shoulder holster. Had he intended to fire, he would have been wearing shooting glasses and ear protectors. Photographs for this chapter were taken by Tina (Mrs. Tom) Ferguson.

T HE DOUBLE-ACTION (DA), self-loading pistol fought and eventually won a long, hard battle for acceptance in the United States. Although the concept was received with immediate enthusiasm by Europeans, who considered it the last word in handgun design for defense and even military use, American critics viewed it with dark askance for half a century. The first non-experimental, commercially successful self-loader with DA capability was the Walther PP, introduced in Germany in 1929. Despite being chambered for a series of low pressure, blowback-type cartridges such as the .25, .32 and .380 ACP, the gun was adopted without delay by many European police departments. The huge success of the Walther PP spawned a number of worthy competitors, among them the Mauser HSc and Sauer DA autos. In a few short years this popularity led to the development of the world's first DA military auto, the Walther P'38 in 9mm Parabellum. Replacing the sometimes cranky, single-action Luger P'08, it was used throughout WWII by the German military and proved itself an excellent service pistol.

On this side of the Atlantic, circumstances worked against the DA pistol from the very beginning. During the time Europe was thundering toward annihilation, the United States was isolationist in mood and burdened with domestic problems, principally the Great Depression. Military needs were given low priority and, at any rate, the army seemed content with the Colt .45 auto developed much earlier.

By and large, civilian America was revolver country, and the few domestic pocket autos available were single-action (SA) designs. In whatever stage of sophistication, the revolver had tamed the West, armed the police, and was well adapted to target and defense needs. American distrust of autoloaders extended to the now-legendary Colt .45 M1911. True, it had been to war in 1918 and those familiar with it approved, yet even in WWI its fans were relatively few in number. The intrinsic excellence of the .45 auto as a military handgun was yet to be proven and that was finally established during WWII. The America of the Thirties wasn't necessarily backward, it just had no need of better sidearms than those already in use, and remained indifferent to the DA pistols from Europe.

Exposure to captured specimens of German DA autos of various makes was the first large-scale experience Americans had with a weapon of this type. Such pistols generally were well-liked by American troops, and many GIs carried them throughout the war by preference. A well-handled pistol is deadly in close combat of the house-to-house kind, and the DA feature shows up to good advantage. Although the big U.S. .45 auto was reaffirming the functional reliability and manstopping virtues it possessed all

In the photo above, you'll note the trigger finger is just approaching the trigger as the gun clears the leather and the muzzle no longer points at the shooter's hip. With a DA auto, that's important! In the photo below, the free hand moves in to take up the two-handed hold used with the Weaver stance.

In the five-frame sequence above and continuing on the opposite page, Ferguson demonstrates his draw from the hip holster and procedure of taking the Weaver stance for improved control of recoil in DA firing mode.

along, the DA autos were gaining a reputation all their own. Chambered for smaller, less powerful cartridges such as the .32 and .380 ACP or 9mmP, none had the bruising force of the .45, but were superior in both safety in carrying and speed into action. Being a single-action design, the U.S. service pistol required that the hammer be cocked manually to fire the first shot. By contrast any Walther PP, Sauer, Mauser HSc or P'38 could be carried in hand or holster with the safety off and the hammer down on a loaded chamber. To fire the first round, it was only necessary to make a longer pull of the trigger, after which the gun fired in normal semi-automatic SA mode. The recoiling slide cocked the hammer for all subsequent shots. This is the standard method of operation for most DA designs, and while a few pistols of DA-only style have been made, none have become extremely popular to the present.

Although DA autos proved battle-worthy during four long years of war, and showed such pistols could withstand hard combat conditions, post-war criticism wasn't long in coming. By the early 1950s, the new sport of combat shooting was in full swing and as the game progressed, it eliminated competition from frivolous and obsolete weapons and got down to serious business. In a relatively short time the gun which came to reign supreme was the Colt .45 auto, M1911A1. The reasons aren't hard to understand. It was widely available, and .45 parts, ammo and components were cheap and easy to get. Thousands of shooters

were former servicemen who had become familiar with its simple, rugged mechanism during the war. Most important of all perhaps was the fact that the .45 is the most powerful combat auto used by any government, and strikes a telling blow. This latter virtue tends to mute many objections to the M1911 Colt.

Experts who came to the forefront in combat shooting seldom had a good word for the DA auto, and much of their criticism centered around its lack of power. WWII served to dispel the myth that DA autos were fragile, but the fact they were available only in rather impotent calibers remained. For many years, the heaviest chambering was in 9mm Luger or Parabellum, a caliber which some view as only marginally effective at best. Today, that situation has improved greatly by the use of modern expanding bullets for the 9mm which turn it into quite a respectable combat round, as well as a proliferation of new designs built around the .45 ACP cartridge.

Some critics seem to have an aversion to the DA system itself, contending that the "cocked and locked" method of carrying the .45 or similar single-action autos is both safe and practical. This may indeed be true, provided the gun is in their own skilled hands. For those less able and not as well trained, the hammer-down feature of the DA auto seems a wiser choice. It can be argued that these people aren't safe with a handgun of any kind and shouldn't carry one, but the real-life fact is, they do.

The gun used in this series is the Browning Model 1935 Hi-Power in 9mm Luger. You will note in the photo at left above, he has not bothered to cock the hammer and yet the photo at right was taken immediately after firing — forgot your muffs and glasses, didn't you, Ferg? — all without thumb touching the spur of the hammer. Those familiar with the admirable Browning will rightly view this in askance. It's explained on the next page.

Probably the most frequently-heard objection regarding DA autos is the supposed difficulty in switching from a DA first shot to a subsequent SA shot or shots, in midstream as it were. Long held to be difficult, even for experts, this argument appeared to have some validity and deserved investigation, I thought. Though I had owned and often carried a DA auto for more than ten years — principally the Walther PP in .380 ACP — I had never really given the DA system a lot of use nor exploration.

Because I wanted to test the DA system itself — not necessarily a given caliber or even a specific gun — I chose two that were readily available. These were the Walther PP in .380 ACP and the Mauser HSc in the same caliber, both classic examples of the DA auto. Extensively used in WWII, thousands came home with returning GIs and were so well liked that as wartime souvenir specimens began to dwindle through normal attrition, both were marketed with considerable commercial success. Although the two guns differ internally in important ways, they are closely similar externally. Designed before modern shooting techniques, in an era that placed great emphasis on pointability, they point extremely well. Drawing from ei-

ther hip or shoulder holster they line up on target with little effort. Each rides low in the hand to minimize recoil and "lock on" with greater ease.

Most importantly, both guns have a deeply-curved back-strap and trigger. As later test firing showed, this proved to be an asset in controlling the trigger.

Trigger control has always been a stumbling block to proper handling and accurate placement of the first and second shots. Although they are true double-actions — for the first shot at least — no DA auto can match the smooth, light DA pull of a Colt or S&W revolver. Trigger pulls are not only stiffer in typical guns, but longer and sometimes grittier as well. Most seem designed for fast, close-range emergency use only, and the effort required to cycle them through the DA pull has an extremely adverse effect on the next SA shot. To gain enough leverage for the first shot, the shooter must use the first joint of the trigger finger instead of the tip. When the shot goes, the gun reloads itself and leaves the hammer cocked for a SA shot which needs much less pressure to let-off. This can be disconcerting, even in skilled hands. In a defense situation it could be disastrous — the stiff trigger pulls the muzzle out of alignment, caus-

One of but two fully double-action M35 Browning Hi-Powers in existence, here's the mystery pistol being used on the preceding two pages. The only other such pistol reposes in the F.N. museum in Belgium. See further details below.

A closer view offers further details on the L.W. Seecamp DA conversion of the Browning. This one was a military model, modified considerably so as to pose so many complications that Seecamp completed the conversion and never made another on the Browning. Although not discussed in the text, Ferg reports that it was the smoothest performer of all the DA autos he tested before writing this.

ing the first shot to miss. Forgetting that the next shot is SA, the shooter applies the same amount of force and fires the second shot prematurely, also missing. By this time he may be in real trouble if such nonsense continues. Nobody can afford that many strikes against himself in a gunfight, and few opponents will give him the opportunity.

The situation is unique to DA autos and has caused a lot of consternation. In earlier attempts to master the DA trigger, some shooters attempted to switch to fingertip control for the second SA shot. The fingertip is more sensitive than the first joint and can apply pressure delicately, but this sort of thing is groping in the dark. Few persons are cool enough to remember to "switch" in a gun battle.

Some idea of the problem can be gained by measuring both DA and SA trigger pull weights. For example, on my own well-used and thoroughly broken-in Walther PP, the hammer drops from single-action mode at a comfortable four pounds. This is just right for a defense pistol. However, the DA pull requires eleven pounds of pressure —

almost three times as much. On the newer Mauser HSc both pulls are heavier. SA is six pounds, which is tolerable, but the DA pull is an incredible twenty-two pounds. Even before doing any shooting, I despaired of doing well with this gun. As it turned out, this was one of several preconceived notions and second-hand beliefs that had no basis in fact.

I have to admit that, while planning this test, I was prejudiced by things I had read earlier about DA autos. Prepared to accept that the trigger control problem was all but insurmountable, as had been declared many times by various experts, I devised half a dozen schemes and stratagems to illustrate and finally overcome it. These included pitting DA pistols against cocked and locked autos, firing at separate targets in DA/SA mode to show disparity in point of impact, and other involved tests. After a somewhat prolonged dry-firing session and a preliminary shoot using live ammo, I discovered the results were so good and decisive that they needed no embellishment. Patching together modern techniques, some DA revolver methods, and a large dose of common sense, I began getting hits right from the start. Nothing was needed that I didn't know already, and any more sophisticated approaches would be sheer gingerbread.

For the sake of realism, I decided the guns should be drawn from a holster, just as they probably would be drawn in a gunfight. For the sake of better illlustrations, I ommitted the sports coat, which isn't much of a handicap to the draw anyway. For a shoulder rig I had the Bianchi X15-small, designed for the Walther PP and Mauser HSc; an excellent holster. It fits both guns snugly, and proved so satisfactory that I did the biggest part of the work from this rig. Also used was a Safariland paddle holster with thumb-break which fit only the Walther, but proved to be very fast. I had worn both holsters many times before, but had never tried any speed work from them.

Virtually all DA autos have configurations designed to aid shooting double-action, so an obvious first step is to take advantage of the design features of the gun itself. Already mentioned, the deep curve of the backstrap, and to a lesser extent, the trigger, are important assets of the Walther and Mauser. The net effect is to pull the gun snugly into the web of the hand during the triggering cycle, reducing muzzle waver. A proper, firm grip is absolutely essential to good performance, whether point-shooting with one hand or precise work at longer distances, using the Weaver stance.

Ideally the web of the gun hand should be jabbed downward into the deepest portion of the backstrap curve for initial contact. A split second later, the fingers close around the gun and draw it from the holster as the index finger finds its way to the trigger. Using the first joints of the trigger finger, the trigger may be hauled rearward to fire the gun as it lines up on target, or the weapon may be raised into the two-handed Weaver stance. In the latter case, the supporting hand pulls back slightly against the forward tension of the strong hand, making the gun rock-steady.

Oddly enough, the stiff trigger ceases to be a handicap using this method. If anything, it usually helps by pulling the gun more securely into the "vee" of the shooting hand. Throughout my dry-firing and live ammo tests, this effect was so pronounced that the hitherto despised Mauser — with its twenty-two-pound DA pull — actually became my favorite gun. Unfortunately it has rather poor sights and a few other shortcomings which reduce it to a rather general state of wretchedness.

It might be thought that the effort required to pull the heavy trigger to the rear hampers the forward push required by the Weaver position, but in practice it does not. Two separate sets of muscles are involved: The trigger pull is totally controlled by the wrist and forearm muscles, while the large shoulder muscles shove the gun against the supporting palm. It sounds more complicated than it is in reality. Those who are dubious can profit from a simple dry-fire exercise.

Suitably decked out in muffs and glasses, Ferguson demonstrates the shoulder holster draw again, this time using the Mauser Model HSc. I suspect he was pausing for Tina to wind the film here because I've seen him doing this and it all takes place in about the space of three wing-flaps of a hummingbird. Our boy is fast...

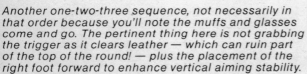

Another one-two-three sequence, not necessarily in that order because you'll note the muffs and glasses come and go. The pertinent thing here is not grabbing the trigger as it clears leather — which can ruin part of the top of the round! — plus the placement of the right foot forward to enhance vertical aiming stability.

First: check the gun to make sure it isn't loaded. Then, *check it two more times*. With that done — leaving the gun uncocked — assume the Weaver stance and align the sights carefully on a small mark. (I use a penny taped to the wall). Keeping the sights as steady as possible, pull the trigger through the DA cycle, taking note of any deviation of sights from the mark. Naturally there will be a slight tremor, but not necessarily more than if the gun were fired in SA mode. The point is immediately clear. The familiar Weaver stance needn't be changed. Persons already skilled in the use of DA revolvers should have no problem triggering the first round from a DA auto and sending it to point of aim. Beginners may have difficulty with the hard pulls found on some pistols but as the strength in their trigger-pulling muscles increases with practice, the problem will disappear. Unfortunately, learning to control the following SA shot requires actual shooting, and no amount of dry-firing is apt to help. Beyond familiarizing yourself with the SA pull, little further can be done. The reason is the recoil and normal cycling of the action, which must leave the weapon in a cocked condition. The object is to avoid using

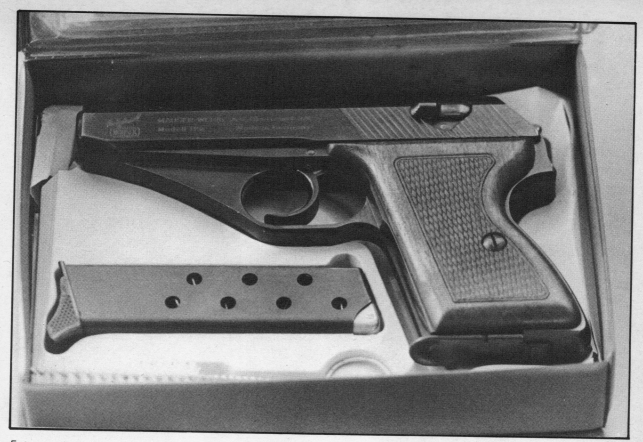

Ferguson's Model HSc Mauser came with a spare magazine.

Here is the Walther Model PPK/S in .380 ACP, as currently made in this country under Walther license.

too much trigger pressure too soon, releasing the shot before the gun is realigned on the target.

Some experienced handgunners — myself included — may run into a bit of trouble here. Thorough familiarity with double-action revolvers is no help. With the revolver, the trigger finger may safely remain on the trigger face after firing the first shot because the trigger is fully returned. In fact it's common to allow the strong trigger return spring to carry the finger forward with the trigger. Nothing of the sort occurs with the DA auto. As the gun recoils, the slide moves back to cock the hammer and eject the empty cartridge case, then forward to chamber the next cartridge. The trigger is caught by the sear far short of the fully-returned DA position and remains locked well to the rear. Lacking full forward thrust by the trigger, the finger has only minimal contact with the trigger face after the DA shot, and sometimes is completely disengaged. A hurried attempt to resume pressure or take up the slack inevitably will result in firing the shot too soon.

Two hits, about two inches apart, from seven yards, firing the first in DA mode and the second as the gun shifts to SA. With practice and proper control, the supposed gear-change problem can be overcome.

In a high-speed draw-and-shoot situation, the muzzle of the gun is stabbed toward the target much as one might point the index finger. The Browning's in use here and note the right foot is slightly forward.

Because these events occur rapidly, it may be difficult to identify the problem. A test using live ammo will tell you if this is happening. Using the pistol SA-only, fire a tight group in the center of the target: I like to use a full-sized silhouette for this exercise. Afterward, reload the gun for a series of two-shot bursts. The firt shot should be fired DA, aimed carefully at the previous group. Rather than rely on a single bullet hole for guidance, repeat the two-shot bursts several times. The errant shooter who is right-handed will find the premature shots clustering above and to the right of the others in about a two o'clock position. The reason is that the gun is torquing up and right in recoil and is being fired before full recovery. The bullet holes tell the tale plainly.

Not being left-handed, I have no idea where the premature shots will strike for a shooter of that preference. However, the drill will show it up quickly, once started. The certainty is that these shots will be some distance away from the central group.

Fortunately, the pistol itself will help correct the problem with a minimum effort at concentration. As already mentioned, the trigger will be caught short of the fully-returned position, leaving the finger in mid-air. Instead of stabbing to re-establish contact, LEAVE IT THERE until recovery from recoil is complete, and the sights are once again aligned on the target. Then, with no attempt to switch to a fingertip position, use the first joint to fire the gun. Through practice, the interval between becomes shorter and shorter until rapid fire is possible, but never so short that the shot goes off prematurely. At the risk of sounding simplistic, you merely have to leave your finger off the trigger until ready to shoot. The solid, two-hand hold aids by suppressing recoil and thus eliminates the chance of the gun bouncing into the trigger finger and firing too soon.

Although the Walther and Mauser are natural pointers, along with some other pistols, I dislike using this method except at the closest ranges. Certainly it should be restricted to a maximum of seven yards, preferably closer. Even if practiced daily, the chance of a complete miss is always present. Whenever time permits, I'm a strong advocate of a solid Weaver grip and aimed fire. However, the characteristics of the DA auto permit some good work to be done at short distances and it probably should be practiced against time of need. In fact, most gunfights occur inside the twenty-one-foot danger zone and the DA pistol comes off looking good in one-hand, instinctive shooting.

It is quite a bit better than any single-action auto drawn in the cocked and locked method. With no desire to be overly critical, the latter gun is not too well suited to a maximum-speed draw, and is badly supported. For safety

Drawing the Browning from the shoulder rig is much the same as with smaller autos, with the weak hand wrapping around the shooting hand at an angle of about forty-five degrees, coming up.

The gun comes to level, Ferguson acquires the sight picture and you'll note the hammer still has not begun to move rearward. He notes the Seecamp conversion compares to a good S&W revolver in DA.

Although the Mauser Model HSc had a somewhat stiffer DA pull than the Walther, Ferguson found he actually could shoot the Mauser better, to his surprise.

Earlier in its colorful career, Ferguson's Browning was accurized by Armand Swenson and the tight rapid-fire cluster shows it retains the Swenson touch.

reasons the finger must remain outside the trigger guard as the weapon is pulled from the holster, and the thumb is held high to perform the separate motion of releasing the manual safety. Until the gun lines up, the thumb can exert no really useful pressure. By simple subtraction, this leaves only three fingers grasping the gun and controlling the movement.

With the DA auto, it is a different story: As the draw begins, the thumb may be used to exert pressure against the frame and assist in alignment. With no sensitive SA trigger to be leery of, the trigger finger may enter the guard a little sooner and begin rearward pressure. In practice, this comes at about the half-way point in the draw. It isn't necessary to wait until the gun is pointed at the target. By the time the gun comes into battery it is supported at three points: at the rear, it is snugged into the web of the hand. At the side, thumb pressure prevents any roll or torque. Finally, rearward pressure on the trigger secures the front. There is no uncontrolled movement, as these points constitute a triangle.

When the range is close and the danger is great, the gun should be jabbed forward at the target in a stabbing motion, as if it had a bayonet on the end of the barrel. This helps align the muzzle and minimizes any wobling. The technique isn't a lot different from that used with a DA revolver. Under no circumstances should the first DA shot be considered a "throw-away" round. There isn't any such thing in a pistol fight, and if you have learned the correct way of shooting it, the DA auto will give you a hit. In speed work from the holster, I found it beneficial to place most of my weight on the right foot, and begin a half-turn to the left as the gun jabbed toward the target. Doing so was especially

important in drawing from the shoulder holster, as there is a tendency to swing wide as the gun crosses the body. It also provides a better index of direction, and the gun clears leather much faster. In a real fight, only a partial profile would be presented, reducing the chances of taking a hit.

It also give the left foot an excellent start in the process of fleeing, should that become necessary.

Summing up: My first experiences with handling DA autos in DA/SA mode demolished many previously held beliefs. Among other things I discovered that heavy, rough trigger pulls were not the handicap they seemed to be, and the well-known Weaver stance need not be modified. Most of the techniques used in shooting DA revolvers can be safely applied, with the important exception of not following the trigger.

After a long period of neglect, modern shooters in the U.S. are accepting the DA auto, and the newest designs incorporate this feature. Some day the single-action auto may be as much a part of the past as the SA revolver of Wild West fame and legend.

Another compact DA auto in 9mm Luger is the Walther Model P5, a design derivative from their wartime P-'38.

Colt Gold Cup

COLT GOLD CUP NATIONAL MATCH MK IV SERIES 70: .45 ACP; 7-shot magazine; 5-in. barrel with new design bushing; 38½ oz.; 8⅜ in. length; checkered walnut stocks, gold plated medallion; ramp-style front sight, Colt-Elliason rear adjustable for windage and elevation, sight radius 6¾ in; arched or flat housing; wide, grooved trigger with adjustable stop; ribbed-top slide; hand fitted, with improved ejection port.

Detonics Scoremaster

DETONICS SCOREMASTER TARGET PISTOL: .45 ACP, .451 Detonics magnum; 7-shot clip; 5-in. heavy match barrel with recessed muzzle, 6-in. barrel optional; 41 oz; 8¾ in. overall length; Pachmayr checkered stocks with matching mainspring housing; blade front sight, Low-Base Bomar rear; stainless steel; self-centering barrel system; patented Detonics recoil system; combat tuned, ambidextrous safety; extended grip safety; National Match tolerances; extended magazine release. Introduced 1983. From Detonics.

High Standard X Series Custom 10-X

HIGH STANDARD X SERIES CUSTOM 10-X: .22 LR; 10-shot magazine; 5½-in. bull barrel; 44½ oz.; 9¾-in. overall length; checkered walnut stocks; undercut ramp front sight, frame mounted fully adjustable rear; completely custom made and fitted for best performance; fully adjustable target trigger; stippled front- and backstraps; slide lock; non-reflective blue finish; comes with two extra magazines; unique service policy; each gun signed by maker.

HIGH STANDARD SUPERMATIC TROPHY MILITARY: .22 LR; 10-shot magazine; 5½-in. bull, 7½-in. fluted barrel; 44½ oz.; 9¾-in. (5½-in. barrel) length; checkered walnut stocks with thumbrest, undercut ramp front sight, frame mounted rear click adjustable; grip duplicates feel of military .45; positive action magazine latch; front and back straps stippled; trigger adjustable for pull, over-travel.

HIGH STANDARD VICTOR: .22 LR; 10-shot magazine; 5½-in. barrel; 47 oz.; 9⅝-in. overall length; checkered walnut stocks with thumbrest; undercut ramp front sight, rib mounted click adjustable rear; ventilated rib, interchangeable barrel; 2-2¼-lb. trigger pull; blue finish; back and front straps stippled.

High Standard Supermatic Citation Military

HIGH STANDARD SUPERMATIC CITATION MILITARY: .22 LR; 10-shot magazine; 5½-in. bull, 7¼-in. fluted barrel; 46 oz.; 9¾-in. (5½-in. barrel) length: checkered walnut stocks with thumbrest; undercut ramp front sight, frame mounted rear, click adjustable; adjustable trigger pull; over-travel trigger adjustment; double acting safety; rebounding firing pin; military style grip; stippled front- and backstraps; positive magazine latch.

M-S Safari Arms Matchmaster Pistol

M-S SAFARI ARMS MATCHMASTER PISTOL: .45 ACP; 7-shot magazine; 5-in. barrel; 45 oz.; 8.7-in. overall length; combat rubber or checkered walnut stocks; combat adjustable sights; beavertail grip safety; ambidextrous extended safety; extended slide release; combat hammer; threaded barrel bushing; throated, ported, tuned; blue, Armaloy, Parkerize, electroless nickel finishes; also available in lightweight version (30 oz.) and stainless steel. Made by M-S Safari Arms.

M-S Safari Arms Model 81 Pistol

M-S SAFARI ARMS MODEL 81 NM PISTOL: similar to the Matchmaster except weighs 28 oz.; is 8.2-in. overall; has Ron Power match sights; meets all requirements for National Match Service Pistols; throated, ported, tuned and has threaded barrel bushing; available in blue, Armaloy, Parkerize, stainless steel and electroless nickel. From M-S Safari Arms.

M-S SAFARI ARMS MODEL 81 BP: similar to the Matchmaster except designed for shooting the bowling pin matches; extended slide gives 6-in. sight radius but also fast slide cycle time; combat adjustable sights; magazine chute; plus same features as Matchmaster.

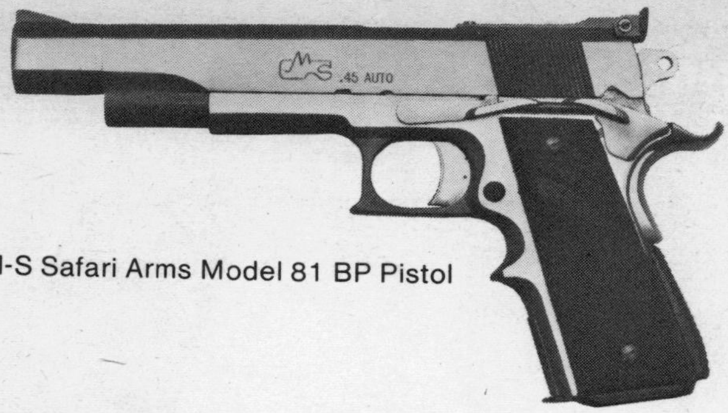

M-S Safari Arms Model 81 BP Pistol

M-S SAFARI ARMS MODEL 81 PISTOL: similar to Matchmaster except chambered for .45 or .38 Special mid-range wadcutter; available with fixed or adjustable walnut target match grips; Aristocrat rib with extended front sight is optional; other features are the same. From M-S Safari Arms.

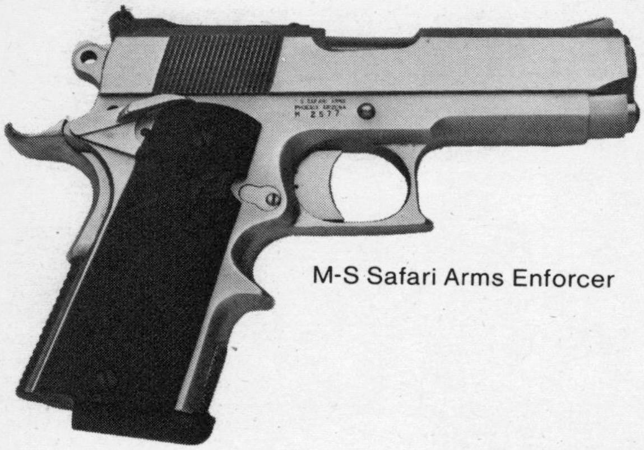

M-S Safari Arms Enforcer

M-S SAFARI ARMS ENFORCER PISTOL: shortened version of the Matchmaster; has 3.8-in. barrel; overall length of 7.7 in.; weighs 40 oz. (standard weight); 27 oz. in lightweight version; other features are the same. From M-S Safari Arms.

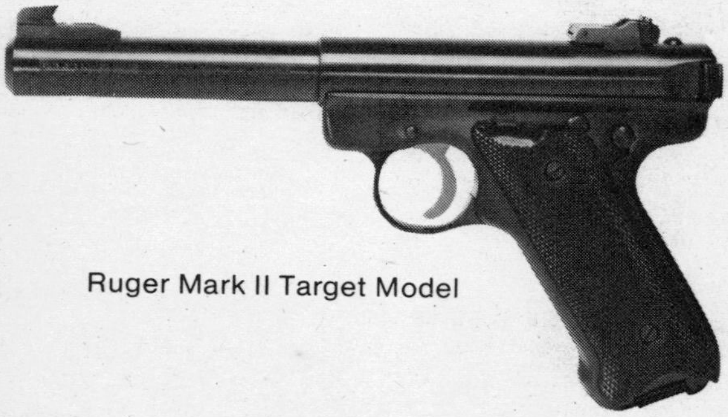

Ruger Mark II Target Model

RUGER MARK II TARGET MODEL AUTO PISTOL: .22 LR only; 10-shot magazine; 6⅞- or 5½-in. bull barrel (6-groove, 14-in. twist); 42 oz. with 6⅞-in. barrel; 10⅞-in. (6⅞-in. barrel) length; checkered hard rubber stocks; ⅛-in. blade front sight, micro click rear, adjustable for windage and elevation, sight radius 9⅜-in. (with 6⅞-in. barrel). Introduced 1982.

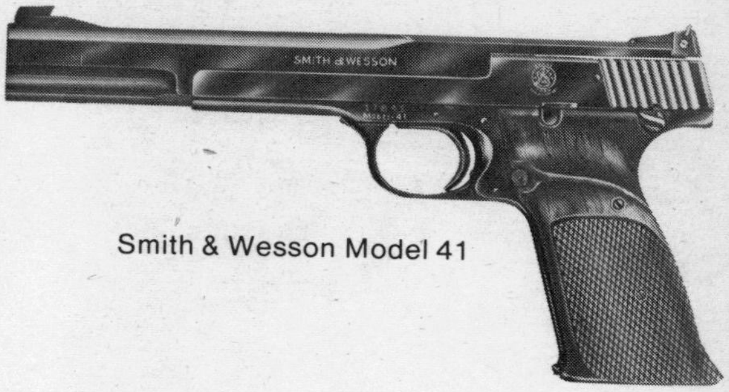

Smith & Wesson Model 41

SMITH & WESSON .22 MATCH HEAVY BARREL M-41: .22 LR; 10-shot clip; 5½-inch heavy barrel, sight radius, 8 in.; 44½ oz.; 9-in. length; checkered walnut stocks with modified thumbrest, usable with either hand; ⅛-in. Patridge sight on ramp base; S&W micro click rear, adjustable for windage and elevation; ⅜-in. wide, grooved trigger; adjustable trigger stop.

SMITH & WESSON .22 AUTO PISTOL MODEL 41: .22 LR; 10-shot clip; 7⅜-in. barrel, sight radius 9-5/16 in.; 43½ oz.; 12-in. overall length; checkered walnut stocks with thumbrest, usable with either hand; front sight, ⅛-in. Patridge undercut, micro click rear adjustable for windage and elevation; ⅜-in. wide grooved trigger with adjustable stop; weights available to make pistol up to 59 oz.

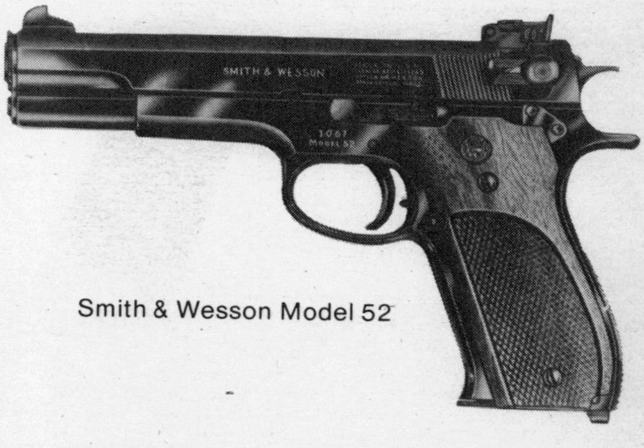

Smith & Wesson Model 52

SMITH & WESSON .38 MASTER MODEL 52 AUTO: .38 Special (for midrange W.C. with flush-seated bullet only); 5-shot magazine; 5-in. barrel; 41 oz. with empty magazine; 8⅝-in. length; checkered walnut stocks; ⅛-in. Patridge front sight, S&W micro click rear adjustable for windage and elevation; top sighting surfaces matte finished; locked breech, moving barrel system; checked for 10-ring groups at 50 yards; coin-adjustable sight screws; dry firing permissible if manual safety on.

FOREIGN-MADE COMPETITION HANDGUNS

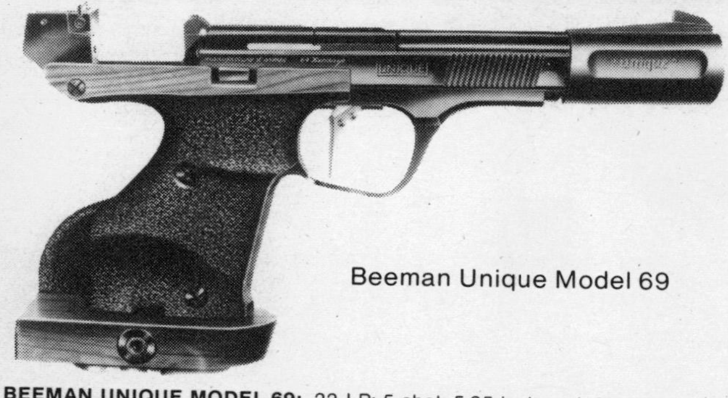

Beeman Unique Model 69

BEEMAN UNIQUE MODEL 69: .22 LR; 5-shot; 5.85-in. barrel; 35.3 oz. empty; French walnut target-style stocks, thumbrest and adjustable palm rest, checkered panels; ramp front, micrometer-adjustable rear sight mounted on frame; 8.66-in. sight radius; fully adjustable, multiple-position trigger; dry-firing safety device; 4 counterweights for adjusting balance; meets UIT standards; special slide action between sights; comes in fitted hard case with spare magazine, cleaning rod, tools, proof certificates, test targets. Imported from France by Beeman, Inc.

BEEMAN/FAS 601 MATCH PISTOL: Similar to SP-602 except has different match stocks with adjustable palm, shelf; .22 short only weighs 40 oz.; 5.6-in. barrel; has gas ports through top of barrel and slide to reduce recoil; slightly different trigger and sear mechanisms.

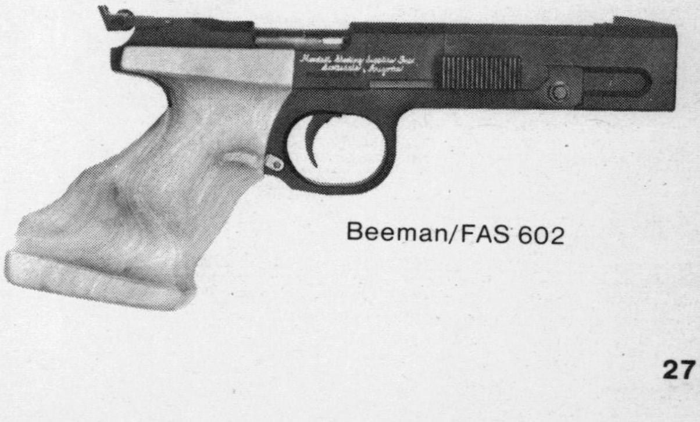

Beeman/FAS 602

BEEMAN/FAS 602 MATCH PISTOL: Caliber .22 LR, 5-shot; 5.5-in. barrel; 41 oz.; 11.02-in. overall length; full target stocks, adjustable, one-piece, left-hand style available; match sights, blade front, open notch rear fully adjustable for windage and elevation; sight radius 8.66 in.; line of sight is only 11/32 in. above centerline of bore; magazine is inserted from top; adjustable and removable trigger mechanism; single-lever take-down; full 5-yr. warranty. Imported from Italy by Beeman Inc.

Hammerli Model 212

Bernardelli Model 100

Hammerli Model 215

BERNARDELLI MODEL 100 PISTOL: .22 LR only; 10-shot magazine; 5.9-in. barrel; 37¾ oz.; 9 in. overall; checkered walnut stocks with thumbrest; fixed front sight, rear adjustable for windage and elevation; target barrel weight included; heavy sighting rib with interchangeable front sight; accessories include cleaning equipment and assembly tools, case. Imported from Italy by Interarms.

Beretta Model 76

HAMMERLI MODEL 215: Essentially a deflossed version of Model 208, omitting 35 out of 665 operations; principally in matter of finish, for a saving in price. Not imported at present.

Hammerli Model 230 Rapid Fire Pistol

BERETTA MODEL 76 PISTOL: .22 LR; 10-shot magazine; 6-in. barrel; 33 oz., empty; 8.8-in. overall length; checkered plastic stocks; interchangeable blade front sight (3 widths), rear is fully adjustable for windage and elevation; built-in, fixed counterweight; raised, matted slide rib; factory adjusted trigger pull from 3 lbs. 5 oz. to 3 lbs. 12 oz.; thumb safety; blue-black finish; wood grips available at extra cost. Introduced 1977. Imported from Italy by Beretta U.S.A.

HAMMERLI MODEL 230 RAPID FIRE PISTOL: .22 short; 6.3-in., 6-groove barrel; 43.8 oz.; 11.6-in. length; walnut stocks; match-type sights, sight radius 9.9 in., Micro rear, click adjustable, interchangeable front sight blade; semi-automatic; recoil-operated, 6-shot clip; gas escape in front of chamber to eliminate muzzle jump; fully adjustable trigger from 5¼ to 10 oz. with three different lengths available; designed for International 25-meter Silhouette Program. Imported from Switzerland by Mandall Shooting Supplies.

Britarms 2000 MK.2

Hammerli Model 232

BRITARMS 2000 MK.2 TARGET PISTOL: .22 LR; 5-shot magazine; 5⅞-in. barrel; 48 oz.; 11-in. overall length; stippled walnut stocks, anatomically designed wrap-around type with adjustable palm shelf; target front and rear sights, interchangeable front blades of 3.2mm, 3.6mm or 4.0mm, fully adjustable rear; offset anatomically correct adjustable trigger, top loading magazine; satin blue-black finish; satin hard chrome frame and trigger. Introduced 1982. Imported from England by Action Arms Ltd.

HAMMERLI MODEL 232: Shorter barreled version of the Model 230; barrel length of 5.12 in. instead of 6.3 in. Not imported at present.

SIG/HAMMERLI MODEL 240: .32 S&W Long wadcutter; 5-shot magazine; 5.91-in. barrel; 10.51-in. overall length; 8.27-in. sight radius; positive safety, hammer intercept notch; variable trigger pull with trigger stop from 35.28 to 49.39 oz.; match-style walnut stocks, adjustable hand rest. Not imported at present.

HAMMERLI MODEL 212: .22 LR; 8-shot magazine; 4.96-in. barrel; 8.4-in. overall length; sight radius 6.73 in.; weight 47.98 oz.; optional safety catch; design derives from Model 208 match pistol as adapted for hunting. Not imported at present.

SIG/Hammerli Model 240

SIG/Hammerli P-240

SIG/HAMMERLI P-240 TARGET PISTOL: .32 S&W Long wadcutter; 6-in. barrel; 34¼ oz.; 10-in. overall length; walnut stocks, target style, unfinished; ⅛-in. undercut front, ⅛-in. notch micro rear click adjustable for windage and elevation; semi-automatic; recoil operated; meets I.S.U. and N.R.A. specs for Center-Fire Pistol competition; double pull trigger adjustable from 2 lbs. 15 oz. to 3 lbs. 9 oz.; trigger stop; comes with extra magazine, special screwdriver, carrying case. Imported from Switzerland by Mandall Shooting Supplies and Waidmanns Guns International.

WALTHER FREE PISTOL: .22 LR; single-shot; 11.7-in. barrel; 48 oz.; 17.2-in. overall length; walnut stocks, special hand-fitting design; fully adjustable match sights; special electronic trigger; matte finish blue. Introduced 1980. Imported from Germany by Interarms.

H&K P9S Competition

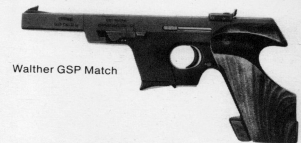

Walther GSP Match

HECKLER & KOCH P9S COMPETITION PISTOL: 9mm Parabellum; 5.5-in. barrel; 32 oz.; 9.1-in. overall length; stippled walnut stocks, target-type; blade front sight, fully adjustable rear; comes with extra standard 4-in. barrel, slide and grips, as well as the target gun parts and tools and is fully convertible. Imported from West Germany by Heckler & Koch.

WALTHER GSP MATCH PISTOL: .22 LR, .32 S&W wadcutter (GSP-C); 5-shot; 5¾-in. barrel; 44.8 oz. (.22 LR), 49.4 oz. (.32); 11.8-in. overall length; walnut stocks, special hand-fitting design; fixed front sight, rear adjustable for windage and elevation; available with either 2.2-lb. (1000 gm.) or 3-lb. (1360 gm.) trigger; spare mag., barrel weight, tool supplied in Match Pistol Kit. Imported from Germany by Interarms.

WALTHER OSP RAPID-FIRE PISTOL: similar to Model GSP except .22 short only; stock has adjustable freestyle hand rest.

U.S. HANDGUNS — AUTOLOADERS, SERVICE & SPORT

American Arms TP-70

AMT .45 ACP HARDBALLER: .45 ACP; 5-in. barrel; 39 oz.; 8½-in. overall length; checkered walnut stocks; adjustable combat-type sights; extended combat safety; serrated matte slide rib; loaded chamber indicator; long grip safety; beveled magazine well; grooved front and back straps; adjustable target trigger; custom-fitted barrel bushing; all stainless steel. From AMT.

American Derringer 25 Auto

AMERICAN ARMS TP-70: .22 LR, .25 ACP; 2.6-in. barrel; 12.6 oz.; 4.72-in. overall length; checkered, composition stocks; open, fixed sights; double-action; stainless steel; exposed hammer; manual and magazine safeties. From M&N Distributors.

AMT "BACKUP" AUTO PISTOL: .22 LR, 8-shot magazine; .380 ACP, 5-shot magazine 2½-in. barrel; 17 oz.; 5-in. overall length; smooth wood stocks; fixed, open, recessed sights; concealed hammer; blowback operation; manual and grip safeties; all stainless steel construction; smallest domestically-produced pistol in .380. From AMT.

AMT .45 ACP HARDBALLER LONG SLIDE: .45 ACP; 7-in. barrel; 10½-in. overall length; checkered walnut stocks; fully adjustable Micro rear sight; slide and barrel are 2 in. longer than the standard .45, giving less recoil, added velocity, longer sight radius; has extended combat safety, serrated matte rib; loaded chamber indicator; wide adjustable trigger; custom fitted barrel bushing. From AMT.

AMERICAN DERRINGER .25 AUTO: .25 ACP or .250 magnum; 7-shot magazine; 2.1-in. barrel; 15½ oz.; 4.4-in. overall length; smooth rosewood stocks; fixed sights; stainless or ordnance steel; magazines have finger extension. Introduced 1980. From American Derringer Corp.

Arminex Trifire Pistol

Browning Challenger III Auto Pistol

ARMINEX TRIFIRE AUTO PISTO: 9mm Parabellum (9-shot), .38 Super (9-shot), .45 ACP (7-shot); 5-in. barrel; 38 oz.; 8-in. overall length; contoured smooth walnut stocks; interchangeable post front sight, rear adjustable for windage and elevation; single-action; slide-mounted firing pin block safety; specially contoured one-piece backstrap; convertible by changing barrel, magazine, recoil spring. Introduced 1982. Made in U.S. by Arminex Ltd.

Browning Challenger III Auto Pistol: similar to the Challenger III except has a 5½-in. heavy bull barrel, new lightweight alloy frame and new sights; overall length is 9½ in.; weight is 35 oz. Introduced 1982.

Bauer Stainless Auto

Bushmaster Auto Pistol

BAUER AUTOMATIC PISTOL: .25 ACP; 6-shot; 2⅛-in. barrel; 10 oz.; 4-in. overall length; plastic pearl or checkered walnut stocks; recessed, fixed sights; stainless steel construction; has positive manual safety as well as magazine safety. From Bauer Firearms.

BREN TEN STANDARD MODEL: 10mm Auto, 11-shot magazine; 5-in. barrel; 38 oz.; 8.75-in. overall length; textured black nylon stocks; adjustable sights, replaceable, 3-dot combat-type; full-size combat pistol, with double- or single-action; has reversible thumb safety and firing pin block; blued slide, stainless frame. Introduced 1983. From Dornaus & Dixon.

Bren Ten Pocket Model: similar to the Standard Bren Ten except smaller; has 3.75-in. barrel giving 6.90-in. overall length; weighs 28 oz.; fires full load 10mm Auto cartridge with 8-rd. capacity; has hard chrome slide, stainless frame.

BUSHMASTER AUTO PISTOL: .223, 30-shot magazine; 11½-in. barrel (1:10-in. twist); 5¼ lbs.; 20½-in. overall length; synthetic rotating grip; post front sight, adjustable open "y" rear; steel alloy upper receiver with welded barrel assembly; AK-47-type gas system; aluminum lower receiver; one-piece welded steel alloy bolt carrier assembly. From Bushmaster Firearms.

Charter Explorer S II Pistol

CHARTER EXPLORER II & SII PISTOL: .22 LR, 8-shot magazine; 8-in. barrel; 28 oz.; 15½-in. overall length; serrated simulated walnut stocks; blade front sight, open rear adjustable for elevation; action adapted from the semi-auto Explorer carbine. Introduced 1980. From Charter Arms.

Browning Challenger III Sporter

Colt Government Model

BROWNING CHALLENGER III SPORTER: .22 LR, 10-shot magazine; 6¾-in. barrel; 29 oz.; 10⅞-in. overall length; smooth impregnated hardwood stocks; ⅛-in. blade front sight on ramp, rear screw adjustable for elevation, drift adjustable for windage; all steel, blue finish; wedge locking system prevents action from loosening; wide gold-plated trigger; action hold-open; standard grade only. Made in U.S. by Browning.

COLT GOV'T MODEL MK IV/SERIES 70: 9mm, .38 Super, .45 ACP, 7-shot; 5-in. barrel; 40 oz.; 8⅜-in. overall length; sandblasted stocks with walnut panels; ramp front sight, fixed square notch rear; grip and thumb safeties; grooved trigger; Accurizor barrel and bushing; blue finish or nickel in .45 only.

Colt Conversion Unit: permits the .45 and .38 Super Automatic pistols to use the economical .22 LR cartridge; no tools needed; adjustable rear sight; 10-shot magazine; designed to give recoil effect of the larger calibers; not adaptable to Commander models; blue finish.

Colt Combat Grade Gov't.

Colt Combat Grade Government Model: same as the standard Government Model except has a higher undercut front sight; white outline rear; Colt/Pachmayr wrap-around grips; flat mainspring housing; longer trigger; beveled magazine well and angled ejection port. Introduced 1983.

Colt Service Model Ace

COLT SERVICE MODEL ACE: .22 LR, 10-shot magazine; 5-in. barrel; 42 oz.; 8⅜-in. overall length; checkered walnut stocks; blade front sight, fully adjustable rear; .22 caliber version of Gov't Model auto; based on the Service Model Ace last produced in 1945; patented floating chamber; original Ace Markings rolled on left side of slide. Introduced 1978.

Colt Combat Commander

COLT COMBAT COMMANDER AUTO PISTOL: .45 ACP, 7-shot; .38 Super Auto, 9-shot; 9mm Luger, 9-shot; 4¼-in. barrel; 36 oz.; 8-in. overall length; sandblasted walnut stocks; fixed sights, blade front, square notch rear; grooved trigger and hammer spur; arched housing; grip and thumb safeties.
Colt Lightweight Commander: same as Commander except high strength aluminum alloy frame, wood panel grips, weight 27 oz., .45 ACP only.

Coonan 357 Auto

COONAN .357 MAGNUM PISTOL: .357 magnum, 7-shot magazine; 5-in. barrel; 42 oz.; 8.3-in. overall length; smooth walnut stocks; open sights, adjustable; unique barrel hood improves accuracy and reliability; many parts interchange with Colt autos; has grip, hammer, half-cock safeties. From Coonan Arms.

Detonics Auto Pistol.

DETONICS .45 PISTOL: .45 ACP, .451 Detonics magnum, 6-shot clip; 9mm Parabellum, .38 Super, 7-shot clip; 3¼-in. barrel; 29 oz. empty; MK VII is 26 oz.; 6¾-in. overall length, 4½ in. high; checkered walnut stocks; combat type sights, fixed, adjustable sights available; has self-adjusting cone barrel centering system; beveled magazine inlet; full-clip indicator in base of magazine; standard 7-shot (or more) clip can be used in the .45; throated barrel and polished feed ramp; Mark V, VI, VII available in 9mm and .38 Super; MC1 available in 9mm Parabellum. Introduced 1977. From Detonics.

Detonics Super Compact

DETONICS SUPER COMPACT DOUBLE ACTION AUTO: 9mm Parabellum, 7-shot clip; 3-in. barrel; 22 oz.; 5.7-in. overall length, 4 in. high; smooth composition stocks; fixed sights; stainless steel construction; ambidextrous firing pin safety; trigger guard hook for two-hand shooting. Available late 1983. From Detonics.

Interdynamic KG-99 Pistol

Jennings J-22 Pistol

JENNINGS J-22 AUTO PISTOL: .22 LR, 6-shot magazine; 2½-in. barrel; 13 oz.; 4-15/16-in. overall length; walnut stocks; fixed sights; satin chrome frinish. Introduced 1981. From Jennings Firearms.

F.I.E./INTERDYNAMIC KG-99 PISTOL: 9mm Parabellum, 36-shot magazine; 5-in. barrel; 46 oz.; 12½-in. overall length; high-impact nylon stocks; blade front sight, fixed, open rear; straight blowback action fires from closed bolt; entire frame is high-impact black nylon. Introduced 1982. From F.I.E. Corp.
    F.I.E./Interdynamic KG-99K Pistol: similar to the KG-99 except has 3-in. barrel, overall length of 10 in. and weighs 44 oz.; standard magazine is 25-shot, with 36-shot optional. Introduced 1983.

F.I.E. "THE BEST" A27B PISTOL: .25 ACP, 6-shot magazine; 2½-in. barrel; 13 oz.; 4⅜-in. overall length; checkered walnut stocks; fixed sights; all steel construction; has thumb and magazine safeties; exposed hammer; blue finish only. Introduced 1978. Made in U.S. by F.I.E. Corp.

F.I.E. "TITAN 25" PISTOL: .25 ACP, 6-shot magazine; 2-7/16-in. barrel; 12 oz.; 4⅜-in. overall length; smooth nylon stocks; fixed sights; external hammer; fast simple take-down. Made in U.S.A. by F.I.E. Corp.

L.A.R. Grizzly Mag

L.A.R. GRIZZLY WIN. MAG PISTOL: .45 Win. magnum, 7-shot magazine; 5-7/16-in. barrel; 51 oz.; 8⅞-in. overall length; checkered rubber stocks, non-slip combat-type; ramped blade front sight, fully adjustable rear; uses basic Browning/Colt 1911-A1 design; interchangeable calibers; beveled magazine well; combat-type flat, checkered rubber mainspring housing; lowered and back-chamfered ejection port; polished feed ramp; throated barrel; solid barrel bushing. Announced 1983. From L.A.R. Mfg. Co.

Guardian-SS Stainless Pistol

Lone Star 380 Auto

LONE STAR .380 AUTOMATIC PISTOL: .380, 6-shot magazine; 3-7/16-in. barrel; 20 oz.; 6-in. overall length; checkered walnut stocks; fixed sights; recreation of the 1910 Browning; has grip, thumb and manual safeties; comes with extra magazine and soft case. Introduced 1983. Made in U.S. by Lone Star Arms.

GUARDIAN-SS AUTO PISTOL: .380 ACP, 6-shot magazine; 3.25-in. barrel; 20 oz.; 6-in. overall length; checkered walnut stocks; ramp front sight, combat-type rear adjustable for windage; double-action; made of stainless steel; custom Guardian has narrow polished trigger; Pachmayr grips; blue slide; hand-fitted barrel; polished feed ramp; funneled magazine well. Introduced 1982. From Michigan Armament, Inc.

HIGH STANDARD SPORT-KING AUTO PISTOL: .22 LR, 10-shot; 4½- or 6¾-in. barrel; 39 oz. with 4½-in. barrel; 9-in. overall length with 4½-in. barrel; checkered walnut stocks; blade front sight, fixed rear; take-down barrel; blue only; military frame.
    High Standard Survival Pack: includes the High Standard Citation pistol (see Competition Handguns) finished in electroless nickel, extra magazine, and a padded canvas carrying case with three interior pockets for carrying the extra magazine, knife, compass, etc. Introduced 1982.

IVER JOHNSON MODEL X300 PONY: .380 ACP, 6-shot magazine; 3-in. barrel; 20 oz.; 6-in. overall length; checkered walnut stocks; blade front sight, rear adjustable for windage; loaded chamber indicator; all steel construction; inertia firing pin; thumb safety locks hammer; no magazine safety; lanyard ring. Made in U.S., available from Iver Johnson's.

IVER JOHNSON TP22B, TP25B AUTO PISTOL: .22 LR, .25 ACP, 7-shot magazine; 2.85-in. barrel; 14½ oz.; 5.39-in. overall length; black checkered plastic stocks; fixed sights; double-action. Introduced 1981. From Iver Johnson's.

IVER JOHNSON PP30 "SUPER ENFORCER" PISTOL: .30 U.S. carbine; 9-in. barrel; 4 lbs.; 17-in. overall length; American walnut stocks; blade front sight, click adjustable peep rear; shortened version of the M1 Carbine; uses 15- or 30-shot magazines. From Iver Johnson's.

O.D.I. VIKING COMBAT D.A. AUTO PISTOL: .45 ACP; 5-in. barrel; 36 oz.; smooth teakwood standard stocks, other materials available; fixed sights, blade front, notched rear; made entirely of stainless steel; brushed satin, natural finish; features the Seecamp double-action system; spur-type hammer; magazine holds 7 rds. in .45 ACP. Made in U.S.A. From O.D.I.

Randall Service Model

Smith & Wesson Model 439

RANDALL SERVICE MODEL AUTO PISTOL: 9mm, .38 Super, .45 ACP; 5-in. barrel; 38 oz.; 8½-in. overall length; checkered walnut stocks; blade front sights, fixed or adjustable rear; all stainless steel construction, including springs and pins; available with round-top slide and fixed sights, or ribbed slide with adjustable sights. Introduced 1983. Made in U.S. by Randall Mfg.

Randall Compact Service Model: similar to the Service Model except has 4½-in. barrel, 7¾-in. overall length; weighs 36 oz; same stainless steel construction, checkered walnut grips. Introduced 1983.

SMITH & WESSON MODEL 439 DOUBLE ACTION: 9mm Luger, 8-shot clip; 4-in. barrel; 27 oz.; 7-7/16-in. overall length; checkered walnut stocks; ⅛-in. square serrated ramp front sight, square notch rear is fully adjustable for windage and elevation; rear sight has protective shields on both sides of the sight blade; frame is alloy; new trigger actuated firing pin lock in addition to the regular rotating safety; magazine disconnector; new extractor design; comes with two magazines. Introduced 1980. Also available in stainless as the Model 639.

Raven P-25 Pistol

Smith & Wesson Model 659

RAVEN P-25 AUTO PISTOL: .25 ACP, 6-shot magazine; 2-7/16-in. barrel; 15 oz.; 4¾-in. overall length; smooth walnut stocks; ramped front sight, fixed rear; available in blue, nickel or chrome finish. Made in U.S., available from EMF Co.

SMITH & WESSON MODEL 459 DOUBLE ACTION: 9mm Luger, 14-shot clip; 4-in. barrel; 28 oz.; 7-7/16-in. overall length; checkered high-impact nylon stocks; ⅛-in. square serrated ramp front, square notch rear is fully adjustable for windage and elevation; alloy frame; rear sight has protective shields on both sides of blade; new trigger actuated firing pin lock in addition to the regular safety; magazine disconnector, new extractor design; comes with two magazines. Introduced 1980. Also available in stainless as the Model 659.

Ruger Mark II Auto

Smith & Wesson Model 469

RUGER MARK II STANDARD AUTO PISTOL: .22 LR, 10-shot magazine; 4¾- or 6-in. barrel; 36 oz. (4¾-in. barrel); 8¾-in. (4¾-in. barrel) length; checkered hard rubber stocks; fixed sights, wide blade front, square notch rear adjustable for windage; updated design of the original Standard Auto; has new bolt hold-open device; magazine catch; safety; trigger and new receiver contours. Introduced 1982.

Smith & Wesson Model 469 Mini-Gun: basically a cut-down version of the Model 459 pistol; gun has a 3½-in. barrel, 12-rd. magazine, overall length of 6⅞ in., and weighs 26 oz.; also accepts the 14-shot Model 459 magazine; cross-hatch knurling on the recurved-front trigger guard and backstrap; magazine has a curved finger extension; bobbed hammer; sandblast blue finish with pebble-grain grips. Introduced 1983.

SILE-SEECAMP II STAINLESS DA AUTO: .25 ACP, 8-shot magazine; 2-in. barrel, integral with frame; about 10 oz.; 4⅛-in. overall length; black plastic stock; smooth, no-snag sights, contoured slide and barrel top; aircraft quality 17-4 PH stainless steel; inertia operated firing pin; hammer fired double-action only, hammer automatically follows slide down to safety rest position after each shot; no manual safety needed; magazine safety disconnector. Introduced 1980. From Sile Distributors.

STERLING MODEL 302: .22 LR, 6-shot; 2½-in. barrel; 13 oz.; 4½-in. overall length; black Cycolac stocks; fixed sights; all streel construction.

Sterling Model 300 Pistol

Taurus PT-22 Pistol

STERLING MODEL 300: .25 ACP, 6-shot; 2½-in. barrel; 13 oz.; 4½-in. overall length; black Cyclolac stocks; fixed sights; all steel construction.

TAURUS PT-22 DOUBLE ACTION PISTOL: .22 LR or .25 ACP; 2.75-in. barrel; 18 oz.; smooth Brazilian walnut stocks; serrated front sight, fixed square notch rear; pop-up barrel; blue finish. Introduced 1983. Made in U.S. by Taurus International Mfg., Inc.

Sterling Model 400 MK. II D.A.

Thompson 1911A1 Auto Pistol

THOMPSON 1911A1 AUTOMATIC PISTOL: 9mm Parabellum, .38 Super, 9-shot; .45 ACP, 7-shot magazine; 5-in. barrel; 39 oz.; 8½-in. overall length; checkered plastic stocks with medallion; blade front sight, rear adjustable for windage; same specs as 1911A1 military guns — parts interchangeable; frame and slide blued; each radius has non-glare finish. Made in U.S. by Auto-Ordnance Corp.

STERLING MODEL 400 MK II DOUBLE ACTION: .32, .380 ACP, 7-shot; 3¾-in. barrel; 18 oz.; 6½-in. overall length; checkered walnut stocks; low profile, adjustable sights; all steel construction; double-action.

Stoeger Luger .22 Auto

Universal Enforcer Model 3000

UNIVERSAL ENFORCER MODEL 3000 AUTO: .30 M1 Carbine, 5-shot magazine; 10¼-in. barrel with 12-groove rifling; 4½ lbs.; 17¾-in. overall length; American walnut stock with handguard; gold bead ramp front sight, peep rear; accepts 15 or 30-shot magazines; 4½- to 6-lb. trigger pull.

WILDEY AUTO PISTOL: .45 Win. magnum, 8-shot; 5-, 6-, 7-, 8-or 10-in. vent rib barrel; weighs about 51 oz. with 6-in. barrel; select hardwood stocks, target-style optional; blade front sight, rear adjustable for windage and elevation; interchangeable barrels; patented gas operation; selective single or autoloading capability; 5-lug rotary bolt; fixed barrel; stainless steel construction; double-action trigger mechanism; has positive hammer block and magazine safety. From Wildey Firearms.

STOEGER LUGER .22 AUTO PISTOL: .22 LR, 10-shot; 4½-in. barrel; 30 oz.; 8⅞-in. overall length; checkered walnut stocks; fixed sights; all-steel construction; action remains open after last shot and as magazine is removed; grip and balance identical to P-08.

WILKINSON "LINDA" PISTOL: 9mm Parabellum, 31-shot magazine; 8-5/16-in. barrel; 4 lbs. 3 oz.; 12¼-in. overall length; checkered black plastic pistol grip stock, maple forend; protected blade front sight, Williams adjustable rear; fires from closed bolt; semi-auto only; straight blowback action; cross-bolt safety; removable barrel. From Wilkinson Arms.

Wilkinson "Linda" Auto Pistol

Walther PPK/S American

Walther American PPK/S Auto Pistol: similar to Walther PP except made entirely in the United States; has 3.27-in. barrel with 6.1-in. length overall. Introduced 1980.

FOREIGN HANDGUNS — AUTOLOADERS, SERVICE & SPORT

Astra A-80 Pistol

BERETTA MODEL 92 SB, 92 SB COMPACT: 9mm Parabellum (15-shot magazine, 14-shot on Compact); 4.92-in. barrel; 33½ oz.; 8.54-in. overall length; smooth black plastic stocks, wood optional at extra cost; blade front sight, rear adjustable for windage; double-action; extractor acts as chamber loaded indicator; inertia firing pin finished in blue-black. Introduced 1977. Imported from Italy by Beretta U.S.A.

BERETTA MODEL 81/84 DA PISTOLS: .32 ACP (12-shot magazine), .380 ACP (13-shot magazine); 3¾-in. barrel; weighs about 23 oz.; 6½-in. overall length; smooth black plastic stocks, wood optional at extra cost; fixed front and rear sights; double-action, quick take-down; convenient magazine release. Introduced 1977. Imported from Italy by Beretta U.S.A.

Beretta Model 70S Pistol

ASTRA A-80 DOUBLE-ACTION AUTO PISTOL: 9mm Parabellum, .38 Super (15-shot), .45 ACP (9-shot); 3.75-in. barrel; 40 oz.; 7-in. overall length; checkered black plastic stocks; square blade front sight, square notch rear drift-adjustable for windage; double- or single-action; loaded chamber indicator; combat-style trigger guard; optional right-side slide release (for left-handed shooters); automatic internal safety; decocking lever. Introduced 1982. Imported from Spain by Interarms.

ASTRA CONSTABLE AUTO PISTOL: .22 LR, 10-shot; .380 ACP, 7-shot; 3½-in. barrel; 26 oz.; moulded plastic stocks; adjustable rear sight; double-action, quick no-tool take-down; non-glare rib on slide; .380 available in blue or chrome finish; engraved guns also available — contact the importer. Imported from Spain by Interarms.

BERETTA MODEL 70S PISTOL: .22 LR, .380 ACP; 3.5-in. barrel; 23 oz. (steel); 6.5-in. overall length; checkered black plastic stocks; fixed front and rear sights; polished blue finish; safety lever blocks hammer; slide lever indicates empty magazine; magazine capacity is 8 rds. for both calibers. Introduced 1977. Imported from Italy by Beretta U.S.A.

Beretta Model 92 SB Compact

Bernardelli Model 80

BERETTA MODEL 950 BS AUTO PISTOL: .22 short, .25 ACP; 2½-in. barrel; 8 oz. (.22 short, 10 oz.); 4½-in. overall length; checkered black plastic stocks; fixed sights; thumb safety and half-cock safety; barrel hinged at front to pop up for single loading or cleaning. From Beretta U.S.A.

BERNARDELLI MODEL 80 AUTO PISTOL: .22 LR (10-shot), .380 ACP (7-shot); 3½-in. barrel; 26½ oz.; 6½-in. overall length; checkered plastic stocks with thumbrest; ramp front sight, white outline rear adjustable for windage and elevation; hammer block slide safety; loaded chamber indicator; dual recoil buffer springs; serrated trigger; inertia type firing pin. Imported from Italy by Interarms.

around soft rubber stocks; blade on ramp front sight, adjustable combat-style rear; rotating six lug bolt; ambidextrous safety; combat-style trigger guard and adjustable trigger; military epoxy finish; contact importer for extra barrel prices. Announced 1982. Imported from Israel by Magnum Research Inc.

Browning BDA-380 Pistol

Erma KGP22 Pistol

BROWNING BDA-380 D/A AUTO PISTOL: .380 ACP, 13-shot magazine; 3-13/16-in. barrel; 23 oz.; 6¾-in. overall length; smooth walnut stocks with inset Browning medallion; blade front sight, rear drift-adjustable for windage; combination safety and decocking lever will automatically lower a cocked hammer to half-cock and can be operated by right- or left-handed shooters; inertia firing pin. Introduced 1978. Imported from Italy by Browning.

ERMA KGP22 AUTO PISTOL: .22 LR, 8-shot magazine; 4-in. barrel; 29 oz.; 7¾-in. overall length; checkered plastic stocks; fixed sights; has toggle action similar to original Luger pistol; slide stays open after last shot. Introduced 1978. Imported from West Germany by Excam.

Browning Hi-Power Auto

ERMA KGP38 AUTO PISTOL: .380 ACP, 5-shot; 4-in. barrel; 22½ oz.; 7⅜-in. overall length; checkered plastic stocks, wood optional; rear sight adjustable for windage; toggle action similar to original Luger pistol; slide stays open after last shot; has magazine and sear disconnect safety systems. Introduced 1978. Imported from West Germany by Excam.

ERMA-EXCAM RX .22 AUTO PISTOL: .22 LR, 8-shot magazine; 3¼-in. barrel; 21 oz.; 5.58-in. overall length; plastic wrap-around stocks; fixed sights; polished blue finish; double-action; patented ignition safety system; thumb safety. Assembled in U.S. Introduced 1980. From Excam.

BROWNING HI-POWER 9mm AUTOMATIC PISTOL: 9mm Parabellum (Luger), 13-shot magazine; 4-21/32-in. barrel; 32 oz.; 7¾-in. overall length; walnut stocks, hand checkered; ⅛-in. blade front sight, rear screw adjustable for windage and elevation, also available with fixed rear (drift-adjustable for windage); external hammer with half-cock and thumb safeties; a blow on the hammer cannot discharge a cartridge; cannot be fired with magazine removed; fixed rear sight model available. Imported from Belgium by Browning.
    Browning Louis XVI Hi-Power 9mm Auto: same as Browning Hi-Power 9mm Auto, except fully engraved, silver-gray frame and slide, gold plated trigger, finely checkered walnut grips, wtih deluxe walnut case.
    Hi-Power 88 Auto Pistol II: similar to the standard Browning Hi-Power except available only with fixed rear sight, military parkerized finish, black checkered polyamid grips; comes with extra magazine. Introduced 1982. Imported from Belgium by Howco Distributors, Inc.

F.I.E. TZ-75 Pistol

Eagle 357 Magnum

EAGLE .357 MAGNUM PISTOL: .357 magnum, 9-shot clip; 6-, 8-, 10-, 14-in. interchangeable barrels; 52 oz.; 10¼-in. overall length with 6-in. barrel; wrap-

F.I.E. TZ-75 DA AUTO PISTOL: 9mm Parabellum, 15-shot magazine; 4.72-in. barrel; 35.33 oz.; 8.25-in. overall length; smooth European walnut stocks; undercut blade front sight, open rear adjustable for windage; double-action trigger system; squared-off trigger guard; rotating slide-mounted safety. Introduced 1983. Imported from Italy by F.I.E.

F.I.E. Super Titan II

Heckler & Koch P7 (PSP) Pistol

F.I.E. "SUPER TITAN II" PISTOLS: .32 ACP, .380 ACP; 3⅞-in. barrel; 28oz.; 6¾-in. overall length; smooth, polished walnut stocks; adjustable sights; blue finish only; 12-shot (.32 ACP), 11-shot (.380 ACP). Introduced 1981. Imported from Italy by F.I.E. Corp.

HECKLER & KOCH P7 (PSP) AUTO PISTOL: 9mm Parabellum, 8-shot magazine; 4.13-in. barrel; 29 oz.; 6.54-in. overall length; stippled black plastic stocks; fixed sights, combat- type; unique "squeeze-cocker" in front strap cocks the action; squared combat-type trigger guard; blue finish; compact size. Imported from West Germany by Heckler & Koch, Inc.

F.I.E. Titan II Pistol

Heckler & Koch HK-4

F.I.E. TITAN II PISTOLS: .32 ACP, .380 ACP, 6-shot magazine; .22 LR, 10-shot magazine; 3⅞-in. barrel; 25¾ oz.; 6¾-in. overall length; checkered nylon stocks, thumbrest-type, checkered walnut optional; adjustable sights; magazine disconnector; firing pin block; standard slide safety; available in blue or chrome. Introduced 1978. Imported from Italy by F.I.E. Corp.

HECKLER & KOCH HK-4 DOUBLE ACTION PISTOL: .22 LR, .25 ACP, .32 ACP, .380 ACP, 8-shot magazine (7 in .380); 3-11/32-in. barrel; 16½ oz.; 6-3/16-in. overall length; black checkered plastic stocks; fixed blade front sight, rear notch drift adjustable for windage; gun comes with all parts to shoot above four calibers; polygonal (hexagon) rifling; matte black finish. Imported from West Germany by Heckler & Koch, Inc.

Heckler & Koch P9S Pistol

F.N. BABY BROWNING: .25 ACP; 6-shot magazine; 2⅛-in. barrel; 4-in. overall length; standard or deluxe finish; 8 oz. empty. Not imported.

HECKLER & KOCH P9S DOUBLE ACTION AUTO: 9mm Parabellum, 9-shot magazine; .45 ACP, 7-shot magazine; 4-in. barrel; 31 oz.; 7.6-in. overall length; checkered black plastic stocks; open combat type sights; double-action; polygonal rifling; delayed roller-locked action with stationary barrel; loaded chamber and cocking indicators; cocking/decocking lever. Imported from West Germany by Heckler & Koch, Inc.

Heckler & Koch VP 70S Pistol

Llama Large Frame Auto

HECKLER & KOCH VP 70Z DOUBLE ACTION AUTO: 9mm Parabellum, 18-shot magazine; 4½-in. barrel; 32½ oz.; 8-in. overall length; black stippled plastic stocks; ramp front sight, open rear; recoil operated; double-action; only 4 moving parts; double column magazine. Imported from West Germany by Heckler & Koch, Inc. Koch, Inc.

LLAMA LARGE FRAME AUTO PISTOLS: 9mm Parabellum, .45 ACP; 5-in. barrel; 40 oz.; 8½-in. overall length; checkered walnut stocks; fixed sights; grip and manual safeties, ventilated rib; engraved, chrome engraved or gold damascened finish available at extra cost. Imported from Spain by Stoeger Industries.

Helwan Auto Pistol

Llama Small Frame Auto

HELWAN 9mm AUTO PISTOL: 9mm Parabellum, 8-shot magazine; 4½-in. barrel; 33 oz.; 8½-in. overall length; grooved black plastic stocks; blade front sight, rear drift-adjustable for windage; updated version of the Beretta Model 951. Made by the Maadi Co. for Engineering Industries of Egypt. Introduced to U.S. market 1982. Imported from Egypt by Steyr Daimler Puch of America.

LLAMA SMALL FRAME AUTO PISTOLS: .22 LR, .32 ACP and .380; 3-11/16-in. barrel; 23 oz.; 6½-in. overall length; checkered plastic stocks, thumbrest; fixed front sight, adjustable notch rear; ventilated rib, manual and grip safeties; Model XV is .22 LR; Model XA is .32 ACP; Model IIIA is .380; Models XA and IIIA have loaded indicator; IIIA is locked breech. Imported from Spain by Stoeger Industries.

Llama Omni D.A. Pistol

MAB Model P-15

LLAMA OMNI DOUBLE-ACTION AUTO: 9mm (13-shot), .45 ACP (7-shot); 4¼-in. barrel; 40 oz.; 9mm, 8-in. overall length; .45, 7¾-in. overall length; checkered plastic stocks; ramped blade front sight, rear adjustable for windage and elevation (.45), drift-adjustable for windage (9mm); new DA pistol has ball-bearing action; double sear bars; articulated firing pin; buttressed locking lug and low-friction rifling. Introduced 1982. Imported from Spain by Stoeger Industries.

MAB MODEL P-15 AUTO PISTOL: 9mm Parabellum, 15-shot magazine; 4½-in. barrel; 41 oz.; 8⅛-in. overall length; checkered black plastic stocks; fixed sights; rotating barrel-type locking system; thumb safety, magazine disconnector; blue finish. Introduced 1982. Imported from France by Howco Distr., Inc.

Manurhin-Walther

MANURHIN: Manufactures pistols of the Walther design under license, including the PP, PPK, PPK/S, Sport-C; first 3 in a choice of .22 LR, .32, .380 ACP.

Turkish MKE Pistol

MKE AUTO PISTOL: .380 ACP, 7-shot magazine; 4-in. barrel; 23 oz.; 6½-in. overall length; hard rubber stocks; fixed front sight, rear adjustable for windage; double-action with exposed hammer; chamber loaded indicator. Imported from Turkey by Mandall Shooting Supplies.

MAUSER HSc SUPER AUTO PISTOL: .32, .380 ACP; 3.56-in. barrel; 29 oz.; 6-in. overall length; checkered walnut stocks; blade front sight, rear drift adjustable for windage; double- or single-action; low profile exposed hammer; combat-style trigger guard; blue finish. Made under license by Renato Gamba. Introduced 1983. Imported from Italy by Interarms.

RG 26 AUTO PISTOL: .25 ACP, 6-shot magazine; 2½-in. barrel; 12 oz.; 4¾-in. overall length; checkered plastic stocks; fixed sights; blue finish; thumb safety. Imported by RG Industries.

SIG P-210-1 Pistol

SIG P-210-1 AUTO PISTOL: 7.65mm, 9mm Parabellum, 8-shot magazine; 4¾-in. barrel; 31¾ oz. in 9mm; 8½-in. overall length; checkered walnut stocks; blade front

sight, rear adjustable for windage; lanyard loop; polished finish; conversion unit for .22 LR available. Imported from Switzerland by Mandall Shooting Supplies.

SIG P-210-6 AUTO PISTOL: 9mm Parabellum, 8-shot magazine; 4¾-in. barrel; 37 oz.; 8½-in. overall length; checkered black plastic stocks; blade front sight, micro adjustable rear for windage and elevation; adjustable trigger stop; ribbed front strap; sandblasted finish; conversion unit for .22 LR consists of barrel, recoil spring, slide and magazine. Imported from Switzerland by Mandall Shooting Supplies.

SIG-Sauer P-220 Pistol

SIG-SAUER P-220 D.A. AUTO PISTOL: 9mm, .38 Super, .45 ACP (9-shot in 9mm and .38 Super, 7 in .45); 4⅜-in. barrel; 28¼ oz. in 9mm; 7¾-in. overall length; checkered walnut stocks; blade front sight, drift adjustable rear for windage; double-action; decocking lever permits lowering hammer onto locked firing pin; squared combat-type trigger guard; slide stays open after last shot. Imported from West Germany by Interarms.

SIG-SAUER P-225 D.A. AUTO PISTOL: 9mm Parabellum, 8-shot magazine; 3.8-in. barrel; 26 oz.; 7-3/32-in. overall length; checkered black plastic stocks; blade front sight, rear adjustable for windage; double-action; decocking lever permits lowering hammer onto locked firing pin. Squared combat-type trigger guard; shortened, lightened version of P-220. Imported from West Germany by Interarms.

SIG-Sauer P-230 D.A. Pistol

SIG-SAUER P-230 D.A. AUTO PISTOL: .380 ACP, 7-shot; 3¾-in. barrel; 16 oz.; 6½-in. overall length; one piece black plastic stocks; blade front sight, rear adjustable for windage; double-action; same basic design as P-220; blowback operation; stationary barrel. Introduced 1977. Imported from West Germany by Interarms.

Sile-Benelli Model B76 Pistol

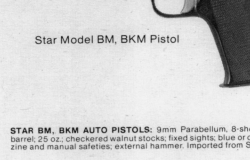

Star Model BM, BKM Pistol

STAR BM, BKM AUTO PISTOLS: 9mm Parabellum, 8-shot magazine; 3.9-in. barrel; 25 oz.; checkered walnut stocks; fixed sights; blue or chrome finish; magazine and manual safeties; external hammer. Imported from Spain by Interarms.

SILE-BENELLI B76 DA AUTO PISTOL: 9mm Parabellum, 8-shot magazine; 4½-in. barrel, 6-groove, chrome-lined bore; 34 oz. empty; 8-1/16-in. overall length; walnut stocks with cut checkering and high-gloss finish; blade front sight with white face, rear adjustable for windage with white bars for increased visibility; fixed barrel, locked breech; exposed hammer can be locked in non-firing mode in either single- or double-action; stainless steel inertia firing pin and loaded chamber indicator; all external parts blued; internal parts hard-chrome plated; all steel construction. Introduced 1979. From Sile Dist.

Star Model 28 DA

Sterling MK7

STERLING MK7: 9mm Parabellum; 4.2, 7.8 in. barrel lengths; 10-, 34-rd. magazine; 15 in. overall length with 4.2-in. barrel; weight empty, 6 lbs. with 34-shot magazine; black plastic stocks; blued finish with black crackle paint; post front, U-notch rear sights, both adjustable by use of tools supplied. Introduced 1983. Imported from England by Lanchester USA, Inc.

STAR MODEL 28 DOUBLE-ACTION PISTOL: 9mm Parabellum, 15-shot magazine; 4.25-in. barrel; 40 oz.; 8-in. overall length; checkered black plastic stocks; square blade front sights, square notch rear click-adjustable for windage and elevation; double- or single-action; grooved front and backstraps and trigger guard face; ambidextrous safety cams firing pin forward; removable backstrap houses the firing mechanism. Introduced 1983. Imported from Spain by Interarms.

Star Model PD Pistol

Steyr GB D.A. Pistol

STAR MODEL PD AUTO PISTOL: .45 ACP, 7-shot magazine; 3.94-in. barrel; 28 oz.; 7-7/16-in. overall length; checkered walnut stocks; ramp front sight, fully adjustable rear; thumn safety; grooved non-slip front strap; nylon recoil buffer; inertia firing pin; no grip or magazine safeties. Imported from Spain by Interarms.

STEYR GB DOUBLE ACTION AUTO PISTOL: 9mm Parabellum, 18-shot magazine; 5.39-in. barrel; 33 oz.; 8.4-in. overall length; checkered walnut stocks; post front sight, fixed rear; gas-operated; delayed blowback action; measures 5.7-in. high, 1.3-in. wide. Introduced 1981. Imported by Steyr Daimler Puch.

TARGA MODEL GT27 AUTO PISTOL: .25 ACP, 6-shot magazine; 2-7/16-in. barrel; 12 oz.; 4⅝-in. overall length; checkered nylon stocks; fixed sights; safety lever take-down; external hammer with half-cock. Assembled in U.S. by Excam, Inc.

TARGA MODELS GT32, GT380 AUTO PISTOLS: .32 ACP or .380 ACP, 6-shot magazine; 4⅞-in. barrel; 26 oz.; 7⅜-in. overall length; checkered nylon stocks with thumbrest, walnut optional; fixed blade front sight, rear drift-adjustable for windage; chrome or blue finish; magazine, thumb, and firing pin safeties; external hammer; safety lever take-down. Imported from Italy by Excam, Inc.

TARGA GT380XE PISTOLS: .32 ACP or .380 ACP, 12-shot magazine; 3.88-in. barrel; 28 oz.; 7.38-in. overall length; smooth hardwood stocks; sights adjustable for windage; blue or satin nickel; ordnance steel; magazine disconnector, firing pin and thumb safeties. Introduced 1980. Imported by Excam.

Walther P-38 Auto Pistol

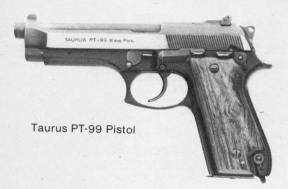

Taurus PT-99 Pistol

WALTHER P-38 AUTO PISTOL: .22 LR, .30 Luger or 9mm Luger, 8-shot; 4-15/16-in. barrel in 9mm and .30; 5-1/16-in. barrel in .22 LR; 28 oz.; 8½-in. overall length; checkered plastic stocks; fixed sights; double-action; safety blocks firing pin and drops hammer, chamber loaded indicator; matte finish standard; polished blue; engraving and/or plating available. Imported from Germany by Interarms.

TAURUS MODEL PT-92 AUTO PISTOL: 9mm Parabellum, 15-shot magazine; 4.92-in. barrel; 34 oz.; 8.54-in. overall length; black plastic stocks; double-action; exposed hammer; chamber loaded indicator; inertia firing pin; blue finish. Imported by Taurus International.
    Taurus PT-99 Auto Pistol: similar to the PT-92 except has fully adjustable rear sight; smooth Brazilian walnut stocks; available in polished or satin blue. Introduced 1983.

Walther P-5 Pistol

Walther PP Auto Pistol

Walther P-5 Auto Pistol: latest Walther design that uses the basic P-38 double-action mechanism; caliber 9mm Luger, barrel length 3½ in.; weight 28 oz.; overall length 7 in.

WALTHER PP AUTO PISTOL: .22 LR, 8-shot; .32 ACP, .380 ACP, 7-shot; 3.86-in. barrel; 23½ oz.; 6.7-in. overall length; checkered plastic stocks; fixed sights, white markings; double-action; manual safety blocks firing pin and drops hammer; chamber loaded indicator on .32 and .380; extra finger rest magazine provided. Imported from Germany by Interarms.

Walther P-38IV Auto Pistol: same as P-38 except has longer barrel (4½ in.); overall length is 8 in.; weight is 29 oz.; sights are non-adjustable. Introduced 1977. Imported by Interarms.

MANUFACTURERS

AMMUNITION (Commercial)

Dynamit Nobel of America, Inc., 105 Stonehurst Court, Northvale, NJ 07647; 201/767-1660 (RWS)
Federal Cartridge Co., 2700 Foshay Tower, Minneapolis, MN 55402; 612/333-8255
Frontier Cartridge Co., Division Hornady Mfg. Co., Box 1848, Grand Island, NE 68801; 308/382-1390
Midway Arms, Inc., RR #5, Box 298, 7450 Old Hwy. 40 West, Columbia, MO 65201; 314/445-3030
Omark Industries, Box 856, Lewiston, ID 83501
Remington Arms Co., 939 Barnum Ave., P.O. Box 1939, Bridgeport, CT 06601
Service Armament, 689 Bergen Blvd., Ridgefield, NJ 07657
Super Vel, Hamilton Rd., Rt. 2, P.O. Box 1398, Fond du Lac, WI 54935; 414/921-2652
Winchester, Shamrock St., East Alton, IL 62024

AMMUNITION COMPONENTS — BULLETS, POWDERS, PRIMERS

The Alberts Corp., P.O. Box 233, Budd Lake, NJ 07828; 201/691-8575 (swaged bullets)
Cabin Enterprises, 3424 4th St., Kenosha, WI 53142; 414/553-9441
DuPont, Explosives Dept., Wilmington, DE 19898
Federal Cartridge Co., 2700 Foshay Tower, Minneapolis, MN 55402; 612/333-8255 (nickel cases)
Godfrey Reloading Supply, Hi-Way 67-111, Brighton, IL 62012 (cast bullets)
Green Bay Bullets, see: Cabin Enterprises
Hercules Powder Co., 910 Market St., Wilmington, DE 19899
Hodgdon Powder Co., Inc., 7710 W. 63rd St., Shawnee Mission, KS 66202; 913/362-5410
Hornady Mfg. Co., Box 1848, Grand Island, NE 68801; 308/382-1390
Lomont Precision Bullets, 4421 S. Wayne Ave., Ft. Wayne, IN 46807; 219/694-6792 (custom cast bullets)
Lyman Products Corp., Rte. 147, Middlefield, CT 06455
Omark Industries, Box 856, Lewiston, ID 83501; 208/746-2351
The Oster Group, 50 Sims Ave., Providence, RI 02909 (alloys f. casting bull.)
Remington-Peters, 939 Barnum Ave., P.O. Box 1939, Bridgeport, CT 06601
S&S Precision Bullets, Box 1133, San Juan Capistrano, CA 92693; 714/643-1401
Sierra Bullets Inc., 10532 S. Painter Ave., Santa Fe Springs, CA 90670
Speer Products, Box 856, Lewiston, ID 83501
Taracorp Industries, 16th & Cleveland Blvd., Granite City, IL 62040; 618/451-4524
Taylor Bullets, P.O. Box 21254, San Antonio, TX 78221 (cast)
Winchester, Shamrock St., East Alton, IL 62024

BULLET & CASE LUBRICANTS

Cabin Enterprises, 3424 4th St., Kenosha, WI 53142; 414/553-9441; (EZE-size case lube)
Corbin Mfg. & Supply Inc., P.O. Box 758, Phoenix, OR 97535; 503/826-5211
Hodgdon Powder Co., Inc., 7710 W. 63rd St., Shawnee Mission, KS 66202; 913/362-5410
Lyman Products Corp., Rte. 147, Middlefield, CT 06455 (Size-Ezy)
Mirror Lube, P.O. Box 693, San Juan Capistrano, CA 92675
Northeast Industrial, Inc., 2516 Wyoming, El Paso, TX 79903; 915/532-8344 (Ten X-Lube; NEI mould prep)
Pacific Tool Co., P.O. Box 2048, Ordnance Plant Rd., Grand Island, NE 68801; 308/384-2308
RCBS, Inc., Box 1919, Oroville, CA 95965
Saeco Reloading, 2207 Border Ave., Torrance, CA 90501; 213/320-6973 (bullet moulds and casting equipment)

BULLET SWAGE DIES AND TOOLS

C-H Tool & Die Corp., 106 N. Harding St., Owen, WI 54461; 715/229-2146
Lester Coats, 416 Simpson St., North Bend, OR 97459; 503/756-6995 (lead wire core cutter)
Corbin Mfg. & Supply Inc., P.O. Box 758, Phoenix, OR 97535; 503/826-5211
Huntington's Die Specialties, P.O. Box 991, Oroville, CA 95965

Independent Machine & Gun Shop, 1416 N. Hayes, Pocatello, ID 83201 (TNT bullet dies)
L.L.F. Die Shop, 1281 Highway 99 North, Eugene, OR 97402; 503/688-5753
Rorschach Precision Products, P.O. Box 1613, Irving, TX 75060; 214/254-2762
Sport Flite Mfg., Inc., 2520 Industrial Row, Troy, MI 48084; 313/280-0648

CHOKE DEVICES, RECOIL ABSORBERS & RECOIL PADS

Cellini Muzzle Brake Stabilizer, Box 17792, San Antonio, TX 78217
Lyman Products Corp., Rte. 147, Middlefield, CT 06455 (Cutts Comp.)
Mag-na-port Arms, Inc., 30016 S. River Rd., Mt. Clemens, MI 48043 (muzzle-brake system)
Mag-na-port of Canada, 1861 Burrows Ave., Winnipeg, Manitoba, Canada R2X 2V6

CHRONOGRAPHS AND PRESSURE TOOLS

B-Square Co., Box 11281, Ft. Worth, TX 76110
Custom Chronograph Co., Box 1061, Brewster, WA 98812; 509/689-2004
Diverter Arms, Inc., P.O. Box 22084, Houston, TX 77027 (press tool)
Oehler Research, P.O. Box 9135, Austin, TX 78756
Telepacific Electronics Co., Inc., P.O. Box 1329, San Marcos, CA 92619; 714/744-4415
Tepeco, Box 919, Silver City, NM 88062; 505/388-2070 (Speed-Meter)
M.York, 5508 Griffith Rd., Gaithersburg, MD 20760; 301/253-4217 (press. tool)

CLEANING & REFINISHING SUPPLIES

Break-Free, a Div. of San/Bar Corp., 9999 Muirlands Blvd., Irvine, CA 92714; 714/855-9911
Browning Arms, Rt. 4, Box 624-B, Arnold, MO 63010
Dri-Slide, Inc., Industrial Park, 1210 Locust St., Fremont, MI 49412
Frank C. Hoppe Div., Penguin Ind., Inc., Airport Industrial Mall, Coatesville, PA 19320; 215/384-6000
Jet-Aer Corp., 100 Sixth Ave., Paterson, NJ 07524 (blues & oils)
Marble Arms Co., 420 Industrial Park, Gladstone, MI 49837; 906/428-3710
Micro Sight Co., 242 Harbor Blvd., Belmont, CA 94002; 415/591-0769 (bedding)
Outers Laboratories, Rte. 2, Onalaska, WI 54650; 608/783-1515 (Gun-slick kits)
Rig Products, P.O. Box 1990, Sparks, NV 89432; 703/331-5666
San/Bar Corp., Break-Free Div., 9999 Muirlands Blvd., Irvine, CA 92714; 714/855-9911
WD-40 Co., 1061 Cudahy Pl., San Diego, CA 92110
Williams Gun Sight, 7389 Lapeer Rd., Davison, MI 48423 (finish kit)

GUN PARTS, U.S. AND FOREIGN

Badger Shooter's Supply, Box 397, Owen, WI 54460
Austin F. Behlert Custom Guns, Inc., Rte. 1 North, Box 227, Monmouth Junction, NJ 08852
Hunter's Haven, Zero Prince St., Alexandria, VA 22314
Numrich Arms Co., West Hurley, NY 12491
Pacific Intl. Merch. Corp., 2215 "J" St., Sacramento, CA 95816; 916/446-2737 (Vega .45 Colt mag)
Triple-K Mfg. Co., 568 6th Ave., San Diego, CA 92101 (magazines, gun parts)

GUNS (Foreign)

Beretta U.S.A., 17601 Indian Head Highway, Accokeek, MD 20607; 301-283-2191
Browning (Gen. Offices), Rte. 1, Morgan, UT 84050; 801/876-2711
E.M.F. Co., Inc. (Early & Modern Firearms), 1900 E. Warner Ave., 1-D, Santa Ana, CA 92705; 714/966-0202
Firearms Center Inc. (FCI), 308 Leisure Lane, Victoria, TX 77901
Firearms Imp. & Exp. Corp. (F.I.E.), P.O. Box 4866, Hialeah Lakes, Hialeah, FL 33014; 305/685-5966
Gil Hebard Guns, Box 1, Knoxville, IL 61448 (Hammerli)
Heckler & Koch Inc., 933 N. Kenmore St., Suite 218, Arlington, VA 22201; 703/243-3700

Interarms Ltd., 10 Prince St., Alexandria, VA 22313 (Mauser, Valmet M-62/S)

Magnum Research, Inc., 2825 Anthony Lane So., Minneapolis, MN 55418; 612/781-3446 (Israeli Galil)

Odin International, Ltd., 818 Slaters Lane, Alexandria, VA 22314; 703/549-2508 (Valmet/military types; Zastava)

Pachmayr Gun Works, 1220 S. Grand Ave., Los Angeles, CA 90015

RG Industries, Inc., 2485 N.W. 20th St., Miami, FL 33142 (Erma)

Sile Distributors, 7 Centre Market Pl., New York, NY 10013; 212/925-4111

Steyr-Daimler-Puch of America, Corp., Gun South, Inc., Box 6607, 7605 Eastwood Mall, Birmingham, AL 35210; 205/592-7932

Stoeger Industries, 55 Ruta Ct., S. Hackensack, NJ 07606; 201/440-2700

GUNS (U.S.-made)

AMT (Arcadia Machine & Tool), 536 N. Vincent Ave., Covina, CA 91722; 213/915-7803

Armament Systems and Procedures, Inc., Box 356, Appleton, WI 54912; 414/731-8893 (ASP pistol)

Auto-Ordnance Corp., Box ZG, West Hurley, NY 12491

Bauer Firearms, 34750 Klein Ave., Fraser, MI 48026

Browning (Gen. Offices), Rte. 1, Morgan, UT 84050; 801/876-2711

Bushmaster Firearms Co., 803 Forest Ave., Portland, ME 04103; 207/775-3324 (police handgun)

Charter Arms Corp., 430 Sniffens Ln., Stratford, CT 06497

Colt Firearms, P.O. Box 1868, Hartford, CT 06102; 203/236-6311

Coonan Arms, Inc., 570 S. Fairview, St. Paul, MN 55116; 612/699-5639 (.357 mag auto)

Crown City Arms, P.O. Box 1126, Cortland, NY 13045; 607/753-8238 (.45 auto handgun)

Day Arms Corp., 2412 S.W. Loop 410, San Antonio, TX 78227

Detonics 45 Associates, 2500 Seattle Tower, Seattle, WA 98101 (auto pistol)

Dornaus & Dixon Enterprises, Inc., 15896 Manufacture Lane, Huntington Beach, CA 92649; 714/891-5090; (Bren-Ten)

Firearms Imp. & Exp. Corp., P.O. Box 4866, Hialeah Lakes, Hialeah, FL 33014; 305/685-5966 (FIE)

High-Standard Sporting Firearms, 31 Prestige Park Circle, East Hartford, CT 06108

Iver Johnson Arms Inc., 2202 Redmond Rd., Jacksonville, AL 72076

M&N Distributors, 23535 Telo St., Torrance, CA 90505; 213/530-9000 (Budischowsky)

MS Safari Arms, P.O. Box 23370, Phoenix, AZ 85062; 602/269-7283

O.F. Mossberg & Sons, Inc., 7 Grasso St., North Haven, CT 06473

Raven Arms, 1300 Bixby Dr., Industry, CA 91745; 213/961-2511 (P-25 pistols)

Remington Arms Co., 939 Barnum Ave., P.O. Box 1939, Bridgeport, CT 06601

Ruger (See Sturm, Ruger & Co.)

Semmerling Corp., P.O. Box 400, Newton, MA 02160

Smith & Wesson, Inc., 2100 Roosevelt Ave., Springfield, MA 01101

SSK Industries, Rte. 1, Della Dr., Bloomingdale, OH 43910; 614/264-0176

Sterling Arms Corp., 211 Grand St., Lockport, NY 14094; 716/434-6631

Sturm, Ruger & Co., Southport, CT 06490

Thompson/Center Arms, Box 2405, Rochester, NH 03867

Wildey Firearms Co., Inc., P.O. Box 4264, New Windsor, NY 12250; 203/272-7215

Wilkinson Arms, Rte. 2, Box 2166, Parma, ID 83660; 208/722-6771

GUNSMITH SUPPLIES, TOOLS, SERVICES

B-Square Co., Box 11281, Ft. Worth, TX 76110

Austin F. Behlert Custom Guns, Rte. 1, Box 227, Monmouth Junction, NJ 08852

Brownells, Inc., Rt. 2, Box 1, Montezuma, IA 50171; 515/623-5401

Dem-Bart Checkering Tools, Inc., 6807 Hiway 2, Snohomish, WA 98290; 206/568-7536

Dremel Mfg. Co., 4915 21st St., Racine, WI 53406 (grinders)

Forster Products, Inc., 82 E. Lanark Ave., Lanark, IL 61046; 815/493-6360

Francis Tool Co., Box 7861, Eugene, OR 97401; 503/746-4831 (reamers, powder measures)

Michaels of Oregon Co., P.O. Box 13010, Portland, OR 97213; 503/255-6890

HANDGUN ACCESSORIES

Bar-Sto Precision Machine, 13377 Sullivan Rd., Twentynine Palms, CA 92277; 619/367-2747

Austin F. Behlert Custom Guns, Rte. 1 North, Box 227, Monmouth Junction, NJ 08852

C'Arco, P.O. Box 308, Highland, CA 92346 (Ransom Rest)

D&E Magazines Mfg., P.O. Box 4876, Sylmar, CA 91342 (clips)

Essex Arms, Box 345, Phaerring St., Island Pond, VT 05846 (.45 auto frames)

Laka Tool Co., 62 Kinkel St., Westbury, L.I., NY 11590; 516/334-4620 (stainless steel .45 auto parts)

Lee Precision, Inc., 4275 Hwy. U, Hartford, WI 53027 (pistol rest holders)

Kent Lomont, 4421 S. Wayne Ave., Ft. Wayne, IN 46807; 219/694-6792 (Auto Mag only)

Pachmayr, 1220 S. Grand Ave., Los Angeles, CA 90015 (cases)

Sile Distributors, 7 Centre Market Pl., New York, NY 10013

HANDGUN GRIPS

Art Jewel Enterprises, Box 819, Berkeley, IL 60163; 312/941-1110

Fitz Pistol Grip Co., P.O. Box 55, Grizzly Gulch, Whiskeytown, CA 96055; 916/778-3136

Herrett's, Box 741, Twin Falls, ID 83301

Millett Industries, 16131 Gothard St., Huntington Beach, CA 92647; 714/842-5575 (custom)

Mustang Custom Pistol Grips, see: Supreme Products

Pachmayr Gun Works, Inc., 1220 S. Grand Ave., Los Angeles, CA 90015; 213/748-7271

Jay Scott, Inc., 81 Sherman Pl., Garfield, NJ 07026; 201/340-0550

Sile Dist., 7 Centre Market Pl., New York, NY 10013; 212/925-4111

Supreme Products, 1830 S. California Ave., Monrovia, CA 91016; 213/357-5395

HEARING PROTECTORS

AO Safety Prods., Div. of American Optical Corp., 14 Mechanic St., Southbridge, MA 01550; 617/765-9711 (ear valves, ear muffs)

Bausch & Lomb, 635 St. Paul St., Rochester, NY 14602

David Clark Co., Inc., 360 Franklin St., Worcester, MA 01604

Norton Co., Safety Products Div., 16624 Edwards Rd., Cerritos, CA 90701; 213/926-0545 (Lee-Sonic ear valve)

Safety Direct, 23 Snider Way, Sparks, NV 89431 (Silencio)

Smith & Wesson, 2100 Roosevelt Ave., Springfield, MA 01101

Willson Safety Prods. Div., P.O. Box 622, Reading, PA 19603 (Ray-O-Vac)

HOLSTERS & LEATHER GOODS

Bianchi Holster Co., 100 Calle Cortez, Temecula, CA 92390

Boyt Co., Div. of Welch Sptg., Box 1108, Iowa Falls, IA 51026

Brauer Bros. Mfg. Co., 2012 Washington Ave., St. Louis, MO 63103; 314/231-2864

Browning, Rte. 4, Box 624-B, Arnold, MO 63010

J.M. Bucheimer Co., P.O. Box 280, Airport Rd., Frederick, MD 21701; 301/662-5101

Colt, P.O. Box 1868, Hartford, CT 06102; 203/236-6311

Hoyt Holster Co., P.O. Box 69, Coupeville, WA 98239; 206/678-6640

Don Hume, Box 351, Miami, OK 74354; 918/542-6604

The Hunter Corp., 3300 W. 71st Ave., Westminster, CO 80030; 303/427-4626

Jackass Leather Co., Galco Intl. Ltd., 7383 N. Rogers Ave., Chicago, IL 60626; 312/338-2800

John's Custom Leather, 525 S. Liberty St., Blairsville, PA 15717; 412/459-6802

Kolpin Mfg. Inc., P.O. Box 231, Berlin, WI 54923; 414/361-0400

George Lawrence Co., 306 S.W. First Ave., Portland, OR 97204

Roy's Custom Leather Goods, Hwy. 1325 & Rawhide Rd., P.O. Box G, Magnolia, AR 71753; 501/234-1566

Safariland Leather Products, 1941 S. Walker Ave., Monrovia, CA 91016; 213/357-7902

Smith & Wesson, 2100 Roosevelt Ave., Springfield, MA 01101

LABELS, BOXES, CARTRIDGE HOLDERS

MTM Molded Prods., Box 1438, Dayton, OH 45414; 513/890-7461

Peterson Label Co., P.O. Box 186, 23 Sullivan Dr., Redding Ridge, CT 06876; 203/938-2349 (cartridge box labels; Targ-Dots)

LOAD TESTING and PRODUCT TESTING (CHRONOGRAPHING, BALLISTIC STUDIES)

Kent Lomont, 4421 S. Wayne Ave., Ft. Wayne, IN 46807; 219/694-6792 (handguns, handgun ammunition)

John M. Tovey, 4710 104th Lane N.E., Circle Pines, MN 55014

H.P. White Laboratory, Inc., 3114 Scarboro Rd., Street, MD 21154; 301/838-6550

PISTOLSMITHS

Allen Assoc., Box 532, Glenside, PA 19038 (speed-cock lever for .45 ACP)

Bar-Sto Precision Machine, 73377 Sullivan Rd., Twentynine Palms, CA 92277; 619/367-2747 (S.S. bbls. f. .45 ACP)

Austin F. Behlert Custom Guns, Rte. 1 North, Box 227, Monmouth Junction, NJ 08852 (short actions)

F. Bob Chow, Gun Shop, Inc., 3185 Mission, San Francisco, CA 94110; 415/282-8358

J.E. Clark, Rte. 2, Box 22A, Keithville, LA 71047

Day Arms Corp., 2412 S.W. Loop 410, San Antonio, TX 78227

Dan Dwyer, 915 W. Washington, San Diego, CA 92103

Giles' 45 Shop, 8614 Tarpon Springs Rd., Odessa, FL 33556; 813/920-5366

Gil Hebard Guns, Box 1, Knoxville, IL 61448

J.D. Jones, Rte. 1, Della Dr., Bloomingdale, OH 43910; 614/264-0176

L.E. Jurras, Box 680, Washington, IN 47501; 812/254-7698

Kart Sptg. Arms Corp., 1190 Old Country Rd., Riverhead, NY 11901; 516/727-2719 (handgun conversions)

Terry K. Kopp, Highway 13, Lexington, MO 64067; 816/259-2636 (rebblg., conversions)

Kent Lomont, 4421 S. Wayne Ave., Ft. Wayne, IN 46807; 219/694-6792 (Auto Mag only)

Mag-na-port Arms, Inc., 30016 S. River Rd., Mt. Clemens, MI 48043; 313/469-6727

Pachmayr Gun Works, 1220 S. Grand Ave., Los Angeles, CA 90015

SSK Industries (see: J.D. Jones)

L.W. Seecamp Co., Inc., Box 255, New Haven, CT 06502; 203/877-3429 (DA Colt auto conversions)

Silver Dollar Guns, P.O. Box 475, 10 Frances St., Franklin, NH 03235; 603/934-3292 (.45 ACP)

Spokhandguns Inc., Vern D. Ewer, East 1911 Sprague Ave., Spokane, WA 99202; 509/534-4112

Irving O. Stone, Jr., 73377 Sullivan Rd., Twentynine Palms, CA 92277; 619/367-2747

A.D. Swenson's 45 Shop, P.O. Box 606, Fallbrook, CA 92028

Chuck Ward Guns, 412 N. Jefferson, Box 610, Raymore, MO 64083; 816/331-3857

RELOADING TOOLS AND ACCESSORIES

C'Arco, P.O. Box 308, Highland, CA 92346; 714/862-8311 (Ransom "Grand Master" progr. loader)

B-Square Eng. Co., Box 11281, Ft. Worth, TX 76110

Bear Machine Co., 2110 1st Natl. Tower, Akron, OH 44308; 216/253-4039

Belding & Mull, P.O. Box 428, 100 N. 4th St., Philipsburg, PA 16866; 814/342-0607

Bonanza Sports, Inc., 412 Western Ave., Faribault, MN 55021; 507/332-7158

C-H Tool & Die Corp., 106 N. Harding St., Owen, WI 54461; 715/229-2146

Camdex Inc., 2228 Fourteen Mile Rd., Warren, MI 48092; 313/977-1620

Carbide Die & Mfg. Co., Box 226, Covina, CA 91724

Corbin Mfg. & Supply Inc., P.O. Box 758, Phoenix, OR 97535; 503/826-5211

Dillon Precision Prods., Inc., 7755 E. Gelding Dr., Suite 106, Scottsdale, AZ 85260; 602/948-8009

Forster Products Inc., 82 E. Lanark Ave., Lanark, IL 61046; 815/493-6360

Gopher Shooter's Supply, Box 278, Faribault, MN 55021

Hensley & Gibbs, Box 10, Murphy, OR 97533

Huntington Die Specialties, Box 991, Oroville, CA 95965; 916/534-1210 (Compact press)

Kexplore, P.O. Box 22084, Houston, TX 77027; 713/789-6943

Lee Precision, Inc., 4275 Hwy. U, Hatford, WI 53027; 414/673-3075

Lyman Products Corp., Rte. 147, Middlefield, CT 06455

MTM Molded Prod., 5680 Webster St., P.O. Box 1438, Dayton, OH 45414; 513/890-7461

Magma Eng. Co., P.O. Box 881, Chandler, AZ 85224

Marmel Prod., P.O. Box 97, Utica, MI 48087; 313/731-8029 (Marvelube, Marvelux)

Marshall Enterprises, P.O. Box 83, Millbrae, CA 94030; 415/365-1230 (Hulme autom. case feeder f. Star rel.)

NorthEast Industrial Inc., 2516 Wyoming, El Paso, TX 79903; 915/532-8344 (bullet mould)

Omark Industries, Box 856, Lewiston, ID 83501; 208/746-2351

Pacific Tool Co., P.O. Box 2048, Ordnance Plant Rd., Grand Island, NE 68801; 308/384-2308

Ponsness-Warren, Inc., P.O. Box 8, Rathdrum, ID 83858; 208/687-1331

Marian Powley, Petra Lane, RR 1, Eldridge, IA 52748; 319/285-9214

Quinetics Corp., P.O. Box 29007, San Antonio, TX 78229; 516/684-8561 (kinetic bullet puller)

RCBS, Inc., Box 1919, Oroville, CA 95965; 916/533-5191

Redding Inc., 114 Starr Rd., Cortland, NY 13045

Saeco Reloading, 2207 Border Ave., Torrance, CA 90501; 213/320-6973 (bullet moulds and casting equipment)

SSK Industries, Rte. 1, Della Dr., Bloomingdale, OH 43910; 614/264-0176 (primer tool)

Star Machine Works, 418 10th Ave., San Diego, CA 92101; 619/232-3216

TEK Ind., Inc., 2320 Robinson St., Colorado Springs, CO 80904; 303/630-1295 (Vibra Tek Brass Polisher & Medium, Vibra Brite Rouge)

Texan Reloaders, Inc., 444 S. Cips St., Watseka, IL 60970; 815/432-5065

Webster Scale Mfg. Co., Box 188, Sebring, FL 33870

L.E. Wilson, Inc., P.O. Box 324, 404 Pioneer Ave., Cashmere, WA 98815

Zenith Enterprises, 361 Flagler Rd., Nordland, WA 98358

RESTS — BENCH, PORTABLE, ETC.

B-Square Co., P.O. Box 11281, Ft. Worth, TX 76109; 817/923-0964 (handgun)

C'Arco, P.O. Box 2043, San Bernardino, CA 92401 (Ransom handgun rest)

SCOPES, MOUNTS, ACCESSORIES, OPTICAL EQUIPMENT

Aimpoint U.S.A., 201 Elden St., Suite 103, Herndon, VA 22070; 703/471-6828 (electronic sight)

B-Square Co., Box 11281, Ft. Worth, TX 76109 (Mini-14 mount)

Beeman Precision Airguns, 47 Paul Dr., San Rafael, CA 94903; 415/472-7121

Maynard P. Buehler, Inc., 17 Orinda Highway, Orinda, CA 94563; 415/254-3201 (mounts)

Burris Co., Inc., 331 E. 8th St., Box 1747, Greeley, CO 80631; 303/356-1670

Bushnell Optical Co., 2828 E. Foothill Blvd., Pasadena, CA 91107

Colt Firearms, P.O. Box 1868, Hartford, CT 06102; 203/236-6311

Conetrol Scope Mounts, Hwy. 123 South, Seguin, TX 78155

Heckler & Koch, Inc., 933 N. Kenmore St., Suite 218, Arlington, VA 22201; 703/243-3700

The Hutson Corp., 105 Century Dr. N., Mansfield, TX 76063; 817/477-3421

Interarms, 10 Prince St., Alexandria, VA 22313

Paul Jaeger, Inc., 211 Leedom St., Jenkintown, PA 19046; 215/884-6920

Leupold & Stevens Inc., P.O. Box 688, Beaverton, OR 97075; 503/646-9171

Lyman Products Corp., Rte. 147, Middlefield, CT 06455

Mandall Shooting Supplies, 7150 E. 4th St., Scottsdale, AZ 85252

Robert Medaris, P.O. Box 309, Mira Loma, CA 91752; 714/685-5666 (side mount f. H&K 91 & 93)

Millet Industries, 16131 Gothard St., Huntington Beach, CA 92647; 714/842-5575 (mounts)

Pachmayr Gun Works, 1220 S. Grand Ave., Los Angeles, CA 90015; 213/748-7271

Redfield Gun Sight Co., 5800 E. Jewell Ave., Denver, CO 80222; 303/757-6411

SSK Industries, Rte. 1, Della Dr., Bloomingdale, OH 43910; 614/264-0176 (bases)

Simmons Corp., 8893 S.W. 129 Terrace, Miami, FL 33176; 305/252-0477 (scopes)

Stoeger Industries, 55 Ruta Ct., S. Hackensack, NJ 07606; 201/440-2700

Tasco, 7600 N.W. 26th St., Miami, FL 33122; 305/591-3670

Thompson/Center Arms, P.O. Box 2405, Rochester, NH 03867 (handgun scope)

W.R. Weaver Co., 7125 Industrial Ave., El Paso, TX 79915

Williams Gun Sight Co., 7389 Lapeer Rd., Davison, MI 48423

Carl Zeiss Inc., Consumer Prods. Div., Box 2010, 1015 Commerce St., Petersburg, VA 23803; 804/861-0033

SIGHTS, METALLIC

Accura-Site Co., Inc., Box 114, Neenah, WI 54956; 414/722-0039

B-Square Eng. Co., Box 11281, Ft. Worth, TX 76110

Beeman Precision Airguns, 47 Paul Dr., San Rafael, CA 94903; 415/472-7121

Austin F. Behlert Custom Guns, Rte. 1 North, Box 227, Monmouth Junction, NJ 08852

Maynard P. Buehler, Inc., 17 Orinda Highway, Orinda, CA 94563; 415/254-3201

Paul Jaeger, Inc., 211 Leedom St., Jenkintown, PA 19046; 215/884-6920

Lyman Products Corp., Rte. 147, Middlefield, CT 06455

Merit Gunsight Co., P.O. Box 995, Sequim, WA 98382

Micro Sight Co., 242 Harbor Blvd., Belmont, CA 94002; 415/591-0769

Millet Industries, 16131 Gothard St., Huntington Beach, CA 92647; 714/842-5575

Miniature Machine Co., 210 E. Poplar, Deming, NM 88030; 505/546-2151

Redfield Gun Sight Co., 5800 E. Jewell St., Denver, CO 80222

Williams Gun Sight Co., 7389 Lapeer Rd., Davison, MI 48423